journey

A NOVEL

Debbye Graafsma

Journey by Debbye Graafsma
Copyright © 2010 by Debbye Graafsma
All Rights Reserved.
ISBN: 1-59755-196-1
ISBN 13: 978-1-59755-196-0

Published by: ADVANTAGE BOOKS™
                www.advbookstore.com

This book and parts thereof may not be reproduced in any form, stored in a retrieval system or transmitted in any form by any means (electronic, mechanical, photocopy, recording or otherwise) without prior written permission of the author, except as provided by United States of America copyright law.

Library of Congress Control Number: 2010930838

Cover design by Pat Theriault

First Printing: July 2010
10 11 12 13 14 15 16   10 9 8 7 6 5 4 3 2 1
Printed in the United States of America

Journey

*For my family –
You have taught me the
meaning of Community*

*For Harold and Pam –
Thank you for our experiences in Israel.
Bill and I love you greatly.*

*For Pastors Jack & Anna –
Thank you for teaching
Bill and me the "how"
of relationship with Jesus.
Your influence has changed my life.*

Journey

Endorsements

"Journey is a good read, with wonderful characterization, and a riveting plot. It makes the times and people come to life. The interesting thing is that the reader finds oneself identifying with the struggles and questions of the people – as though they are us."(Sharon N.)

～

"When I was reading Debbye's book, I felt like I had been picked up and placed into the lives of the people who lived in Bible times. As I read, I realized that a lot of women, who have not been nurtured from an early age, feel the things that Mary Magdalene felt. I identified with her feelings. During one scene in particular, I felt the Presence of God draw close to me, bringing personal healing. It was a personal visitation because of the picture of Jesus' ministry. I remember weeping for a long time, and emerging with a sense of healing. At another point during the book, I experienced being strengthened and empowered by the Lord; to accept the freedom to become the woman I was created to become; not afraid of the culture or of other people's reactions and words." (Dianne T).

～

"I really enjoyed reading this book. It was a good read, with a good story line. I loved the richness of the culture, customs and history. It was all so interesting and informative!" (Jean R.)

～

"This story offers a number of benefits as it weaves history, healing and spiritual truths into its pages. I have gained valuable insight into the way that a life in Jesus brings healing to the soul. I have been blessed and changed from reading it." (Jill B.)

～

"I love reading stories about real people. Journey made Jesus real to me. Reading this book has helped me to understand God better."(Carol J.)

～

"I have had the privilege to read Journey by Debbye Graafsma. I found it to be a compelling read. The following is an attempt to explain why I found this book to be so enjoyable. The first requirement I have when I read fiction, is that I must care about the characters. Debbye achieved this by presenting characters who were believable, who had depth, and to whom the average person can relate.

"She allowed you into their lives, warts and all. By doing so, the reader can identify with the characters and care about what happens to them. Another unique aspect of the book was the fact that the culture and architecture was so accurately and vividly portrayed. The reader could envision walking the streets as they existed in Biblical times.

"The discussion of business transactions was also very interesting. The caravans transporting goods, the purchase of linens and cloth, operation of vineyards, the presence of spas – all provided further insight into how people lived and earned money.

"To me, the most unique aspect of this book was how the common people reacted to Jesus. What they thought of Him; How they reacted to Him. This is evidenced by the description of how Jesus delivered Mary of the demons. This sequence was so vivid and moving that it brought tears to my eyes. Also, Mary's anointing of Jesus' feet with oil and wiping them with her hair was very moving.

"The portrayal of Simon the Pharisee gave me, for the first time, a clear picture of the mindset of the religious leaders at the time of Jesus' ministry. I have a better understanding of why the religious leaders wanted to crucify Jesus.

"I am confident that <u>Journey</u> will minister to its readers. I believe both male and female readers would enjoy this book. It will minister to whoever reads it." (Thomas R.)

Table of Contents

Prologue 1 9
Vineyard Springs 15
Clio 27
Tiberius 39
Abiel 46
Migdal 56

Prologue 2 73
"Semichah" 75
Power-Brokers 91
Righteousness 107
Sychar 118
Panic 133

Prologue 3 165
Images 171
Bethany 198
Fragments 218
Emergence 245
Fresh Bread 276
New Wine 302
Epilogue 330

A Note to the Reader 334
Bibliography 336

Journey

Journey

Prologue 1

Upper Room – Jerusalem
29 CE
Day Forty-Four

It would be sunrise soon.

Mary stood, looking down through the latticework, to the street below. Pulling her overwrap tighter, she shivered in the pre-dawn chill. Had it really been just yesterday? It seemed like a lifetime ago.

Or had it been a dream?

He had told them to wait; here.

Here, in the last place they had eaten together.

That too, seemed like a lifetime ago.

Mary looked around the room. Peter, James and John were over in the corner, still soundly asleep. They had been up late last night in quiet conversation. They wouldn't stir for a while yet. Andrew and Philip were up and out of the house already. They had mentioned going somewhere for bread.

Her first recollection of the morning had been Philip's voice. Always practical, he was counting. "We'll need about fifty loaves," he whispered, not far from where she was sleeping. "Do we have enough money to cover that?" Then had come the tinkling of metal, as they had tallied what was on hand. After hearing the door close, she leaned against the wall.

Why couldn't she ever go back to sleep?

"You're up early." Her friend's gentle voice broke the quiet. The younger woman smiled. "I heard Philip and Andrew close the door when they left to buy bread. Did I wake you?"

"No," the older woman replied, stretching. "I heard them too. I've been awake for a little while now… Just trying to get my mind around the happenings of the last few days…just laying here with my eyes closed."

The two women lapsed into silence, and began folding the coverings used for sleep the night before. It was an action they had repeated many times over; somewhat routine in nature. Mary found her mind being drawn to the tasks needing to be accomplished for the morning.

The older woman spoke. "We should wake the others. We'll need help drawing water this morning."

Mary hadn't considered that; but it made sense. After all, the procedure today would be almost like the one they followed when the seventy were traveling with the Master. She looked around, assessing. Were there really more than hundred of them together in this room?

Come to think of it…hadn't their acquaintance with this room begun with water as well?

She looked upward. King Herod had even made the ceiling of this place something to stare at, Mary considered.

She loved the story of how they had come to use the room. The Master had sent Peter and John to find a place to keep the feast. He had said, "Go into the city. You will see a man walking down the street with a water-pot full of water. Follow him. Tell him the Teacher has need of his Great Upper Room. He will take you to the place, and it will be exactly what we need." Imagine! A man with a water-pot! When or where would anyone see that happening, and in the middle of the day as well?

But it had happened -- just that way. Things always did when Jesus spoke. Everything she had ever heard Him say would happen had happened, just the way He said it would!

It was evident that same experience held true for each person here, she thought.. "Each one of us has come to recognize the Master's voice. We each have come to understand exactly who He is – and in a unique and undeniable manner!"

Every individual could describe an experience they could not deny. Something inside had happened to change the heart – forever … …

So they were here. Waiting… No one knew what for.

But each one would know when it came.

The Jerusalem sun was just peeking through the trees as the two women headed to the well in the center of the Quarter. Several others joined them. Salome, Miriam and Elsbeth were the first ones to come.

"Do we have any fish?" Miriam asked. "How much will it take to feed all of us?"

"We still have a little money left." Salome reached into the purse hanging from her belt. "We could purchase enough to have a good meal. I'll have to take up a collection later, though, if we are to eat tonight."

"Philip and Andrew left the house earlier to buy bread. A little fish would be good." The older woman looked into her own purse. "Here, I have a few coins as well."

Miriam and Salome left to find an early morning fish vendor. The other women began drawing water for cooking and preparations that morning. They would carry the water-pots back to the house with them. This would enable everyone to be ready for the events of the day ahead. Mary listened as the women shared conversations at the well.

"It is good of Ezra to allow us to stay here in this quarter of the City. I love their Great Room. I'm so thankful for their hospitality."

"I know. Could you put up with guests staying open-ended?"

"I wonder how long we will be here. Just waiting like this…Did Jesus tell you – did He tell anyone; how long we would be waiting, or what we would be waiting for?"

"No. But it is good for us to be here. If Caiaphas, or Annas, or the Romans for that matter, knew where we were, they would probably come and haul us off as well."

"Something has to happen soon."

Journey

"I know. I can't sleep sitting up on the stone floor. My back hurts."

"I know what you mean. Did you stretch? That sometimes helps me."

"I had a dream last night. I think I must be afraid. I can't go back where I was before, but I have no idea where my life will lead now."

"I feel the same way. What do I do? How do I know what path to take? I feel so alone."

"Surely Jesus didn't mean to just leave us. Didn't he tell you of His plan?"

"He said we were to wait. Just wait… He was sending us a Promise; a Comforter."

"That's what I need; Do you feel overwhelmed – like we've been forgotten? It's a struggle to keep holding on to what He said."

"Where are we going to go from here? Is there a plan?"

In silence, Mary continued to draw from the well, taking note of the dialogue of those around her. Her older companion, as well, continued to draw, quietly paying attention to the messages of Uncertainty and Fear, voiced in the small community of women.

And, although she personally sensed an inner peace and security; all things were on course and on time; there was nothing she could say to bring resolve and closure for these women.

Each one was on her own journey of discovery with Abba Father.

"Jesus never did anything without a reason. He said we would receive power."

"Yes, but when? And how? I'm not sure the men will lead us. Even Simon Peter ran away in the garden."

"No one could lead us like Jesus did."

"Who can I trust now? This isn't like traveling with Jesus; when will things really settle in for all of us?"

The older woman smiled, remembering a moment in her own life when she had expressed very similar concerns about her own future. Her concerns had been rooted in Fear also. She had voiced them to her husband. They had been on their way to Egypt at the time; fleeing into the unknown because of a night vision her husband had experienced. She chuckled, remembering.

How good God had been to them! Their caravan passage had been paid for by gifts from strangers; rich men, who had appeared out of nowhere to worship a Baby Boy…

What a voyage it had been; learning to trust Father's hand; learning to value relationships more than the tasks; learning to ponder and to wait; learning to pray. In the process, she had discovered her own need. She had allowed inner depth and character to be worked into her life. She had learned to choose; to continue; to complete the journey. Even now, she was still learning… learning to focus on what she had on hand, giving thanks, rather than complaining over what she felt was missing…

It all had worked for good.

But hadn't it felt strange at times, too?

Yes, she had felt alone. Yes, she had been afraid.

It had been a difficult thing to watch someone she loved die.

Journey

The older Mary looked up from the well, to see two of her other sons emerging from the Great Room. James and Joseph were good to her, she thought. "Good morning, mother," they both greeted her. She hugged them both, and discovered they were off for an early morning walk through the streets of Jerusalem.

She looked around, considering.

The Essene Quarter was a perfect place for their group to wait, and to pray. How long ago had it been? As long as she could remember, the city had been this way. Not long before her own birth; an earthquake had destroyed the settlement of the Essene monks at Qumran. The Great Herod, the builder, had constructed them a gated community within the city, here in the upper level.

The king had also provided the city a sewer system, and running water in the form of an aqueduct. She could still remember her grandmother telling stories about the 'old days' when a person had been expected to carry their dirty waters down to the river.

How easy it was to take conveniences for granted, she contemplated.

The Essene Quarter had been the work of a genius, really. First, King Herod had constructed a gate providing the monks and their families with private access to the city. They could come and go from their settlement in the desert at will. They could even set their own guard. The gate had been set into the existing wall, and Herod had decreed a section of the city to be set apart just for them. He had utilized parts of the old walls, from Hezekiah's time.

From that gate, the streets wove up to the elevated portion of Mount Zion, called the "Upper City."

Even now, the entrance was referred to as "The Essene Gate." Herod's construction had helped to revitalize that side of the city wall, as well. Until then, that portion of the city had been known for the dumping of broken pottery shards, and animal dung.

The "kohanim," or Essene,, monks loved it here, the older Mary decided. Their number had grown from the original fifty to several hundred during those years.

They were part of history; included with the people of the Living God.

It was the City of David; the City of Melchizedek; the City of Peace.

"The view from the windows of the Great Room alone would have been enough to keep me here," the older woman thought..

She smiled. Her son had shown her this view, on the afternoon of his last meal.

Now, even though the settlement in Qumran was rebuilt, many Essenes had chosen to stay in the city. It was good, too, she reasoned. Their presence added pungent flavor to the city; a reminder of Abba Father's heart and character, in the midst of a broken world.

Besides, where else in Jerusalem would there have been room for all of them; complete with places for cooking and laundry?

Making their way back from the well, the women approached the main house, still in discussion. The Community house in the Essene Quarter was a large enough accommodation. Today the number was over a hundred. She knew it would continue to grow each day.

Journey

In the outdoor kitchen courtyard, at the foot of a stairway leading up the side of the house to the Great Room, two men were working to spark a cooking fire. They greeted the passing women.

Elsbeth stopped to pour her water into cooking pots to heat.

The rest kept walking toward the house. As they came to the stairway, the women formed a single file, to carry the water up to the room. The older Mary led the way.

She heard Peter's voice as she opened the door. She turned, with her finger to her lips to signal quiet to those behind her.

It appeared a meeting was in process.

"The Holy Spirit spoke through David about Judas. He was numbered with us, wasn't he? And doesn't the Scripture say, 'let his habitation be desolate, and let no one stay in it. Let another take his place of leadership?' There are those in this very room who traveled with us when we were with Jesus. We must choose someone to replace Iscariot. After all, the Master chose twelve."

"Joseph Barsabas was with us during the majority of the ministry." John spoke clearly. "I think he would be a good candidate to take Judas' place."

"What about Matthias?" Philip had returned and was breaking loaves into portions for the meal. "He has a good way with people; and he received the same training from the Master as the rest of us."

After some discussion, those involved in the meeting prayed. "Father, you know all things, and you know the hearts of all men. Show us your choice. Who do you want for this place of serving?"

And then, to be sure, they cast lots, similar to drawing straws.

The lot fell to Matthias.

The women began pouring water into various containers in the room, for morning washing and daily preparations.

"So!" Peter stood, rubbing his hands together. "We are twelve again! Blessed be the name of the Lord!"

"Now what, Peter?" one of the women spoke up. "What do we do now? Is that why we are here? Is that what we've been waiting for?"

"No, but it was a step, I'm sure." Peter rubbed his chin. "No, that's not all of it. Now, we obey. We wait. We pray. We listen." He shrugged and smiled at her. "It's the only step I have."

Just then, the smell of fresh fish roasting in the outdoor kitchen below began to waft up through the latticework. Peter lifted his head in response to the scent, and began to chuckle.

"Mmmm!" he declared. "And we eat!"

A ripple of agreement and anticipation moved like a wave through the room. Everyone was hungry.

It was good to be together in this place.

Mary made her way downstairs, with her friend, the older Mary. They would work in the kitchen to help in serving breakfast. Happily, she considered. She would always remember

Journey

these days. Times of laughter, and joy; close fellowship and oneness with those she held dear. Some of these were dearer to her than her own flesh and blood family!

Well, they <u>were</u> family, now, weren't they? The family of God!!

So much had happened. How had she come to this place? How had her life made it here? So much had happened; and how had it begun?

As she helped to serve the meal, her mind was distracted.

The journey certainly had not been an easy one….

Abba Father had been working in her life all along.

Journey

Vineyard Springs

So far as Mary knew, from what others had told her, Eleazar, her father, had been a good man. A wealthy landowner, he had worked hard to provide for his family. It was said by many, his holdings rivaled those of Boaz of old, great-grandfather to King David himself.

The mountain area of EnKarem was a beautiful place to settle down! Not far from its sister village of Bethlehem, the soil was rich for farming! The area had been chosen by those who settled it for its richness and beauty. In fact, EnKarem had been the first village settled *after* Bethlehem. Salma, Caleb and the sons of Hur had loved the area, and had planted deep roots, rich with understanding the price of freedom; the need for persevering in the fight for deliverance.

Eleazar sat admiring his view from the window. For a tradesman, the village was a perfect location. A little more than a half-day's journey from Jerusalem, his family could attend all three of the required feasts at the temple through the year, yet raise the children a safe distance from the city. Life didn't feel busy or overwhelming at all.

In fact, EnKarem still had the small town feel it had always had. It was an ideal setting for maintaining their Jewish identity, he considered; in a world where no culture was without infiltration from the Greeks and the Romans.

Hadn't the Romans even built a bathhouse in Jerusalem? Hadn't Quinerias petitioned for a gladiator training facility?

No, it was better to live outside the city.

Eleazar and his wife, Rachel, had chosen EnKarem as the location to build their home because it was positioned close to the Hill Road, nestled between Hebron and Jerusalem. The Hill Road was the only trade route leading through the high country. Not only that, but just 7 miles away, goods could be transported on the trade-route caravans from Jerusalem, the capital, to Joppa, one of the main ports on the Great Sea.

From the beginning, the couple had been convinced felt their wool, linen, and wine trades would thrive. Thrive they had. Without realizing it, Eleazar had settled in a perfect spot, even for those caravans coming from as far away as Phoenicia; who traveled by way of the Sea Road, or the "Via Maris," as the Romans now called it. Surprisingly, several times a year, even representatives from merchant caravans based in distant Egypt would show themselves on his doorstep, bargaining in support of the best prices for his goods.

Eleazar clasped his hands together behind his head, and sat back in his chair. For farming, he reflected? The entire region was prolific! "Ephratah" had been the name given to the area from Abraham's time! It meant "fruitful." Many said that when God kissed the earth, He must have breathed on EnKarem.

For crops, vineyards, olives, for herds and flocks; for agreeable weather, where could one find a better spot to settle down?

The merchant looked out over the field where his workers were shearing his sheep, one by one. Already there was enough to pay for the next year's hayseed, and they weren't even half finished with the task! ElJireh was good!! The wool this year was thick and strong too! What a blessing!!

The weavers in his weaving house in the city would be able to make many woolen garments to sell in the marketplace. It had been a good investment to buy the large, foot-pedalled looms two years ago.

Perhaps, he mused with a smile, they should venture into the market of colors as well. He should look for a facility, or even build one, to dye the fabrics his workers were creating… He made a note to himself to discuss this concept with Baruch, his steward, the next time they met together.

From his window view, the thirty-five year old man was able to view a vast sampling of his holdings. He had built the house in the mountainous region surrounding Jerusalem, some seventeen miles southwest of the city, situating it just on the rise of a hill. Always a man to concentrate on details, Eleazar's plan had been to prevent the morning heat and evening sun from warming the house more than necessary. The construction allowed breezes from its higher elevation to move through the windows during the night. It had cost him more than three years' earnings to build the house in the manner he had designed it; and he still fabricated construction projects to make it more livable each year. Positioned between two massive, pre-existing sycamore trees, the house perimeter was full of windows with latticework, and shutters for security against thieves and storms.

Yes, the sycamores provided shade and coolness from the heat of the Judean desert's summer, but what he and Rachel loved most was the benefit of the songbirds in the early morning. Just before sunrise each day, both trees would burgeon with a variety of joyous song, awakening the day.

He smiled as he remembered Rachel's delight in watching baby hatchlings become fledglings and begin to fly. Then there had been the day he had come home to find her standing as still as a statue, until the bravest of the tiny creatures would light upon her hand filled with grain and fragments of dried fruits. She had even created a small haven for the birds near the outdoor sitting area. Daily, she filled flat feeding dishes with a mixture of seed, fruit, nuts and day old bread. It had become one of his wife's joys to care for the little creatures, keeping track of their nesting seasons.

Utilizing his contacts in trade, the entrepreneur had managed to build a home with Roman architecture and design, still maintaining a sense of Hebrew heritage. Even the floor tiles were luxurious, imported from the northern hills of Italy!

He had even added a room with a bath, draining to the outside!

The front of the couple's home faced south, where those arriving from distant places could be impressed with its imposing arrangement. Eleazar had purposely constructed a large patio area with Greek columns, attaching it to the front of his home. Rising from the top of the columns was a tile roof, which glistened in the morning sun. The structure was built in the square design of most Roman inns, complete with an outdoor courtyard and kitchen in its center, for privacy and practicality.

As was the case with most construction of his day, the rock-wall formations were just the skeleton of the structure. Builders had discovered long ago that rock and stone allowed the night's coolness to remain in a home long after the sun rose. For this reason, rock quarried from nearby mountains was customarily used for building.

It was not the ability to cut and mortar the rock that amazed him, Eleazar thought. Rather, it was the artisan's gift of making the rough structure smooth and continuous, covering it both inside and out with plaster. How could something so rough become so smooth, he marveled?

Holding to the modern design of the day, the house in EnKarem was white in color, both inside and out. It glistened like a jewel in the sunlight! So many people had come by, just to admire......

The merchant had hired a Greek man and his sons to do the plastering work; as he hadn't had time to do it himself, unlike his neighbors. The Greek hadn't charged him as much as had been budgeted for the job, so Eleazar had commissioned one of the man's sons to paint designs on the courtyard's inner walls with dyes and pigments. In the midst of the task, the boy had confided his work was a copy of the bath house paintings in the desert palace of King Herod the Great at Masada.

The Greek plasterer and his sons had also helped to line the inside of the vast system of limestone winepresses he and his workers had toiled to carve at the foot of the hill. Yes, it had been a good decision to plaster the bases of his winepresses. The cured plaster kept the dust from gathering into the wine, ensuring a lengthier storage season.

Eleazar had researched the best methods for creating his products.

Why, hadn't he even studied the scrolls of Egyptian winemakers, copying many of the methods they had used for over 3,000 years?

It was remarkable, he thought. In the midst of his research, he had also discovered the winemakers' secrets to producing a barley-based beverage called *beer*. The drink had been introduced in the northern regions of Israel some two hundred years before, when the Egyptians had been defeated by Antiochus Ephiphanes and his armies. Beer didn't spoil in the heat as quickly, keeping much longer than wine, although he had discovered it tasted better when it was kept in a cistern, or in the cave on his property.

So, after the winepresses had been completed, his workers had moved to enlarging the cave. It had become a storage facility.

Eleazar's mind went to the underground spring and its brook flowing from the cave on his grounds. The spring had been his original reason for choosing this location to build his home. Over time, it had proven much easier to irrigate the vineyards, and water his flocks and herds; not to mention provide fresh water for his family. The cave was a wonderfully cool location.

Sometimes, in the heat of the summer, he and Rachel would take a lunch basket and sit in the cave, eating and listening to the flowing water.

God had certainly been good to them.

It was good to have your own water supply.

And vineyard....

In addition, he mused, just those two elements had prospered him! Every traveler and trader in the empire found it helpful to cut their water supply with fermented new wine. So doing protected their water supply from disease.

Everyone needed good water.

Yes, he concluded; his was a business that would never fail!

He looked out the window to the terraced mountainside, assessing his crops. Cutting flat areas into the slopes for fruit trees and crops had been an arduous task. Looking back on it now, it had been a good decision.

Yes, level ground had made all the difference.

He considered his operations. Barley was planted in the fall, strengthened in the ground over the winter. It became ready to harvest in April.

From the barley harvest, grain needed for bread-flour and the next year's crop was set aside. Then, beer production resumed.

Later, in May and June, he would sell any excess barley when chickpeas and wheat were harvested. It was good to have two kinds of bread to choose from, he reasoned.

It was always busy at EnKarem. As soon as the wheat was in, it was time to prepare for the grape harvest, and wine pressing. No sooner were the grapes cut from the vines each year, than he would divide the workers into teams.

The first team would work in the winepresses. The second team would bring in the flax crops.

When the wineskins had been hung for aging, everyone moved together to work for the rest of the year in the weaving house; cleaning, combing, spooling and weaving the wool. When the wool was ready for sale, it was time to follow the same process for turning the flax into linen.

He wondered. Could they possibly compete in trade with the weaving houses on Mount Arbel in the north? He would discuss that with Baruch as well.

Nevertheless the vineyards had proven to be the best moneymaker of all.

He smiled, stroking his beard.

Hadn't he already come to agreements with five families in the area for the rental of his winepresses this season? Since grapes were harvested in June, July, August *and* September each year, his workers would find themselves crushing grapes and making new wine four months out of the year! He had never considered what a profitable market it would be when he and Rachel had begun with one tiny grapevine root! And now, the entire mountainside was covered with vines!

When his employees were not shearing sheep, or pressing wine, or harvesting crops, they were making beer. His staff was never idle. There was always something needing to be done.

From morning until evening Eleazar was working.

Journey

Rachel often had told him, as they sat together, what a beautiful place he had created for living. Her two favorite places were the cave and the courtyard, with its painted geometric designs.

Come to think of it, the courtyard was his favorite place to be as well.

It had been a good decision to build barns, he reviewed. While other families in the community; the poor and middle-income classes; kept their animals in the courtyard areas of their homes, it was better to keep his animals outside. No animals were allowed into the house, or in the courtyard of the home, except for an occasional early-born lamb or goat that had taken the heart of his children.

It was written in the Law. Only animals that chewed the cud and had divided hoofs were clean enough, or healthy enough, to be touched or eaten.

It had been the wisest course, he told himself. The center courtyard was for family meals, gathering with friends, and conducting intimate business meetings. He had even added a fountain near to the family cistern, with a small garden of flowers.

God had given him so much. And he had planned well.

Very well.

Eleazar took pride in his accomplishments.

Each of his children would have their own bedchambers, too, with windows to let in the cool night air. He had planned for seven. The rabbis had told him that seven was the number of perfection!! And didn't he and Rachel have the perfect life?

Rachel is too frail to bear seven children.

As quickly as the thought appeared, it was shut away; extinguished by his image of their future.

He had hired servants to plan and take care of details, so his wife could spend more time with him. She would only have to do what he thought she really needed to do in the household… that was to spend time with him and with the children. She could even help in overseeing the businesses too, if she wished.

It was good to be a rich man.

Eleazar and Rachel had sought God's blessing for their children. Earnestly… They had worked for the first portion of their marriage to build the house and beautify the grounds. They had tried to produce offspring. Sadly, for the first 10 years of their life together, his wife had been barren.

Then, abruptly, one day, she had walked into the scriptorium, where he had been working on a scroll of accounts. He remembered not being able to balance the sheet.

"I will have to hire someone to do this," he said absently.

"Eleazar…." She had come behind him and whispered into his hear. "I'm with child."

He hadn't heard her at first. He had been preoccupied. "What?"

"I'm with child. About eight weeks, I think. Anna says we will have a spring baby."

He had danced around the room with her. They had traveled to go to the city to eat a meal with friends and share the news.…

Journey

How could one describe the depth of joy in his heart? Or the thankfulness welling up within him when he thought of his life's journey; how far he had come, and all he had amassed in his name?

Any day now, his wife, Rachel, would give birth to their own little lamb! A third! The little angels she had already borne to him were the joy of his heart! The first had been little Miriam, with her sparkling brown eyes. She was full of never ending questions, packed with curiosity. And resolve? Such an intelligent child! She had inspired him more than once. Her practicality, even at five, had many times ignited his own imagination. Such a creative thinker!! With a mind to find solutions, too!

"She will give some man a run for his money someday," he thought.

And then there was little three year-old Eleazar, his namesake. He would do very well running the business someday. He was already following his father around with his own tiny tablet and stylus.

"How many, Papa?" If Eleazar had a shekel for every time he had heard that question!! Such a smart boy, a strong boy... always was looking for answers. He would go far with an intelligent brain like that!!

The children were always his sanity check. Whenever there was too much to be done, or he was stressed, he would take a break from his day, just to hold them. They were his link to achievement. They were his legacy; not the business. The town elders had told him that was one reason for his high degree of success. He hadn't lost sight of the deeper purposes of God for his life.

For a moment, the image of his Rachel flashed in front of his eyes. Like Jacob's love of old, she was extravagant in her beauty. Her voice was sweet sounding. Her heart was gentle. Her hair was like black silk, long to her waist. And when she walked ... He loved to watch her just float through a room. It seemed that everyone who met her felt close to her almost immediately. She was always listening to someone's woes, seeking to find an answer to their pain. Every so often she would share her discussions with him, and it seemed as though she had taken the pain to her own heart.

He had to admit she was a good listener. Whenever something disturbed him, or he was submerged in details of trade, she would find him in the courtyard, and rub his shoulders and temples. "You are working too hard again, my love," she would tell him.

Although, if he had to choose, Eleazar would have to say his favorite of his wife's physical traits was her laugh.

When Rachel laughed, it was a soft sound, but it had a distinct effect. It was like sunlight, gently dispelling gloom from a dark room. She literally changed the atmosphere wherever she was. What was it about the light in her eyes that made him smile even now, just thinking about her.... Her laugh was like the soft tinkling of those tiny bells she wore on her ankle bracelets.

Her laugh signified the celebration happening in her heart.

Her skin was soft to his touch. He had told her many times it resembled alabaster in its loveliness.

Journey

They were so content here. Most evenings, he would come in from the fields, or from the warehouse in the city, to find his Rachel with Miriam and little Eleazar. They would greet him in the courtyard garden. The servants would bring water and wash his feet.

Then it would begin; the laughter, the playing with the children, the conversation, and long talks with his wife.

So happy… So complete…

Yes, he smiled to himself.

He had done very well.

~~~~

On the day Rachel went into labor, Eleazar rushed home as soon he had received word. The servant burst into the place where he was meeting with Baruch, his keeper of the accounts. They had been looking for a place to invest the extra earnings from the wine sales. Business had been more than good.

"Master Eleazar," panted the servant, "the midwife says to come now. It's time for the little one."

Eleazar patted the back of his assistant, and ran out of the room without his head covering, or his outer tunic. He was so excited. As he ran, he shouted to the neighbors, "It's time!" "I'm going to be a father again!" "Pray to God for a good birth!" "It's my second son!" "It's time!" "It's time!" "My wife is going to have a baby!"

All the way home, his friends responded with promises to pray, wishes for blessing, and good natured chuckles at his exuberance. His heart was so full!! What joy! What joy! All that mattered was that Rachel be safe, and that the baby be healthy!! Oh, what a day!! What a glorious day!!

As he entered the door of his home, little Miriam greeted her father. Her lower lip was extended in a small pout, and she was pulling on her ear – something she always did when she was upset about something, or couldn't sleep.

"Something's not right, Papa," she told him. Picking the child up, he moved through the silent house, toward the chamber he and Rachel shared. Just to hug her, he thought to himself. To touch her hair, to encourage her graceful heart, to tell her the pain would be over soon; that tomorrow things would be normal again. Just as it had been with Miriam and little Eleazar. The labor pains would end, and their lives would go on. They would have a new little one added to their family. They were almost halfway toward the seven he had planned for!! Seven!! God's number of perfection!! The house wouldn't be silent when there were seven to greet him!!

On his way to the bedchamber, he considered. In his mind's eye, he could envision it. He and Rachel would be the example the rabbis would use when they spoke of a happy home in their teachings. They would be the ones who would exemplify what God gave to those who kept the Law. He would share this with Rachel later. Yes, when she was rested from pushing.

But as he entered the chamber, Eleazar realized those exchanges in conversation would not take place today. Not in that way. One look around the room let him know his little Miriam had been correct in her assessment of the situation.

Something *was* wrong.

Dreadfully wrong. Yes, there were the sounds of childbirth – the moaning, the instructions of the midwife, and the sense of anticipation.

There was a red stain on the birthing chair; larger than usual. What was wrong?

Blood. Was it Rachel's blood?

Lots of blood.

More than he remembered from Miriam or little Eleazar's births. And, this time, the color was a deep red, as though a life force was draining from his Rachel's form. What had happened?

A realization hit him. The room felt unearthly quiet to him. He could almost *feel* something dark and foreboding in the room – but it was the middle of the day!! Perhaps it was because Anna had pulled the shutters together for privacy.

No, it was more than that. There was a presence; a sense of warning. Something in the room felt like a heavy cloud, but the air was clear….. It was as though something, or someone, beyond his comprehension or power to bargain for control, were standing in the corner, waiting for something.

And then, it came to him….

Instinctively, he knew.

Death had come to call.

But why?

Hadn't he kept all of the Law? Where had he failed?

Surely this couldn't happen!! Eleazar had planned so well! Well, he wouldn't give in to this without a fight.

But what do you fight with, when the enemy is unseen, and you are unprepared?

Anna, the midwife, moved to his side, and spoke quietly into his ear.

"The baby is coming out the wrong way, Eleazar. I'm doing all I can to turn it, but Rachel is not built for this large a child. She is a delicate girl."

He patted her arm with more calm than he really felt. "You're the best midwife in the whole town, Anna." At that point, emotion began to rise, and he felt his voice choke. "We will make it through this. You will do a good job. I trust you."

Numbly, he put little Miriam down, entrusting her to one of the two serving girls in the room. He knelt by the birthing chair. With wet cheeks, he gathered the love of his life into his arms.

"Rachel, can you hear me?"

She turned her head to face him. She was weeping also, and fighting for breath. "I'm sorry, Eleazar."

"There. There, now. You have nothing to be sorry for."

"I've been so happy with you. I don't want to leave. Not now."

"You are my joy, my dove. I love you. You're going to be fine. You'll see."

Rachel made no response. Her eyes were glassy, and didn't seem to be focused on him.

Journey

He could feel the icy fingers of alarm gaining a grip within him. "Rachel... Rachel!! No!! Don't leave me." He was sobbing now.

"Eleazar... take care of this little lamb...." Her voice faded into a whisper, and the words were coming haltingly now. "I .....love.. you. You have..... always ......been good to me..." She moved, as though trying to rise.

Anna's voice broke the quiet. "One more push, Rachel. Let's birth this baby, and then we will take care of your bleeding."

Rachel lovingly looked, one last time, at her husband, and then shut her eyes. She slowly raised herself up onto her elbows. And then, as though from an undiscovered well, she summoned strength for one last push. With that push came a loud wail, as if something inside of her had become completely expended.

Her eyes went blank.

"Rachel?" Eleazar tentatively reached for her cheek. She roused, but did not see him.

"ElShaddai," she whispered. "Take... my baby... as your own...Protect..."

Then, she was gone.

The mother's whisper was replaced midstream by a baby's cry; tentative at first, and then loud and strong.

A new life had begun.

Miriam would later tell her she had been born feet first, because God knew she would need to think-on-her-feet without a mother.

And sadly, immersed in his pain and loss, Eleazar had found himself unable, or unwilling, to hold her, or even look at her. Nor could the servants raise a response from him to their words.

In shock, he had clung to Rachel's lifeless form until the sun had sunken below the tree line. By Jewish law, her broken and frail body had to be buried before nightfall, but it didn't seem to matter to him anymore. At last, the housekeeper sent a runner to fetch Baruch, from the warehouse.

Baruch had been the one to convince him of the need to bury her before dark. Eleazar never could remember who had spoken what phrases to him. He had allowed himself to be led like a blind child; feeling nothing, hearing nothing, seeing nothing.

Everything had become empty.

Nothing mattered now.

"We must comply with the law, Eleazar."

"Let the women do what they must do. Come into the courtyard."

"Come and see the children."

"Here is this beautiful little girl. She looks just like Rachel. Do you want to hold her?"

Shaking out of his fogginess, Eleazar set his gaze on the child, speaking abruptly. "You have made this a bitter day," he spoke to the infant." Looking at Anna, he continued. "She is rebellious. She wouldn't come the right way. This is her fault."

"Oh Eleazar, I know you are grieving. But just try. You'll feel differently if you hold her." Anna held the now sleeping infant out for him to see. "Here, just take her."

Journey

"No, get her out of my sight." He brushed the midwife away, walking past her into the courtyard.

"She will need a wet nurse," she called after him. "Do you want me to find one?"

"Oh, do whatever you need to do. Don't bother me right now."

Finding the stone bench he had always shared with his wife, Eleazar sank down, alone. He gathered Miriam and little Eleazar into his arms, and wept.

It was days before he could eat, or even speak.

And then, after friends stopped coming by to comfort him, or to see how the children were doing, he buried himself in his work. For a time, he walked through his weeks, seeking just to survive. He was still the same man to the rest of the world, but to the servants, and the children at home, it seemed like a shell had replaced their once attentive master and father.

Additionally, every time Rachel's name was mentioned, a cloud would pass across his face. At first, he would weep, unable to speak about her memory.

Then, as the days passed, he became like stone.

Young Eleazar had described him more than once as a "walking dead man." He never expressed feeling or care. And most of the time, he wasn't even there….. Where had Papa gone? The boy thought it was like a curse had come over his father. And in Papa's place, a grumpy man had come; a man who they weren't sure of anymore; a man who might be angry one minute, and glad the next.

Additionally, it seemed like something was always wrong. There was always something out of place, or someone out of order.

Over time, the children learned to try to fix it so Papa would be happy again.

It was as though they had different fathers, Mary thought. Miriam and Eleazar could always remember their father…. Before. But this man…. this was the only father Mary remembered,

The only image she had of how men behaved.

～～～

Then had come a day, years later. The elder Eleazar came home from the warehouse with gifts. She remembered sitting in the courtyard, watching him play with Miriam and little Eleazar. It was the first time she could remember hearing her father laugh.

She was three years old.

It was also the first time she remembered being held by her father – or even being touched by him.

"I loved your mother, you know. And I love you." Holding Mary close to his heart, he lifted his head, and prayed his first prayer since Rachel's passing. "Oh God," he said, his voice breaking. He had hugged her tightly. "Oh God," he had repeated, and a few tears had come. Then his hands on her arms had tightened, and his voice became full of hurt and anger.

He had shaken her.

"I don't understand," he cried. "You are supposed to be a merciful God."

Then, Mary remembered, something had shifted in the room. She remembered being very afraid, because it felt like the room became dark around her.

The fleeting light that had been in her father's eyes had gone away, and the mean man she feared had returned.

It was as though Eleazar had sealed a door inside himself.

The lightness that had been part of the earlier reverie with her sister and her brother had shifted. It was almost like a mask had come over their father's face. His entire countenance had changed.

Had it been something she had done or said? It had happened when he had held her.

It had to have been, she had decided.

What had happened? Or had anything happened? No one had spoken. No one else had drawn attention to anything being different in their surroundings. And really, nothing physical had changed. The furniture was in the same place it had always been. The fountain was still working. The sun was still shining. Mary wasn't sure if anyone else would even have noticed it. After all, she wasn't sure she even remembered it clearly. Perhaps it had all been in her own mind, and she hadn't really experienced it.

But no, even after the years had passed, it seemed real enough.

And then, Eleazar had looked at the children, his surface demeanor suddenly transformed again; a false brightness presented itself, but his eyes were hollow and without depth of feeling. He smiled at the three of them.

"Look what I have for you!"

From a travel bag concealed under his outer cloak, Eleazar drew three bottles, somewhat translucent in nature, each wrapped in several layers of linen. Each bottle was about 10 inches in height, and all were a creamy color. Through the thin material of the bottle, it was possible to see that each one was full of a red liquid substance, filled almost to the rim. Each was sealed with the same wax seal Eleazar's trading company used on the wineskins from the family vineyard. It was the seal he and Rachel had designed together with the metal-smith when they had begun the business the first month of their marriage. Topping the beauty of each vial was a thin line of gold overlay, where the top of the bottle had been dipped in gold, to provide protection for the fragility of the stone.

"Shiny!" said the little boy.

"Oooh, Papa! This is a pretty bottle!" said Miriam.

Mary had watched him with deep brown, open, toddler eyes.

"They are gifts in honor of your mother. Today is her birthday. I want to give you each a gift to remember her by." His voice broke, and he paused, as thought trying to get through a difficult speech. "These are very valuable. Please take good care of them. They are full of a very expensive ointment. I used the extra profits from the business to purchase them. If you ever have a need that I cannot meet, sell these."

"Oh, Papa! This is a pretty bottle!" exclaimed Miriam.

"No, Miriam, it's not just a pretty bottle." Eleazar grabbed her arms, just below her shoulders. He shook her a little. "Miriam, listen to me. This is important," their father continued.

Somehow he thought that little girls of eight, and three would understand what he was saying. "I put the nard in alabaster because it reminds me of the texture of your mother's skin; so clear; so beautiful…." His voice broke with emotion. "She was perfect in every way, and we were so happy. I want these bottles to remind you girls of what you can become. Each time you look at them, think of the perfection she was to me.

"If you ever open this bottle, just a tiny drop will fill your entire house with fragrance, just like your mother filled my life. You have a lot to live up to, now. Never forget that. When you see your bottle, I want you to see your mother looking back at you. You have a responsibility to become the woman she would have wanted you to become. There is no better model you could copy.

"She is the image you are to become." He had handed the little girls their gifts, and then reached once again into his satchel. "Here, Eleazar, I also had one made for you. Keep it in a safe place, where nothing can disturb it."

He had then called one of the serving girls, and given firm instructions. Each of the bottles was to be put aside in each of their rooms. They were to be kept safe and protected; and in plain view.

Then he had called Clio, the wet nurse who had been taking care of Mary since her birth. He needed her to stay with them, he said. She would be assuming new duties. She would be taking care of all three children, now, instead of just Mary.

He would not be here as much, he said. He would be running the businesses from town.

The housekeeper would help her with the children. He could not stay.

Considering him, Mary realized. She had never really known him the way Miriam and little Eleazar had. She had no other memories to compare with his present behavior.

Miriam had always said it seemed those little bottles had been goodbye presents. From that point on, their father still officially lived in the house with them in EnKarem, but he was seldom there. He traveled on business, he said. The children didn't know where he was.

He was just absent.

Journey

Clio

Clio, her wet nurse, had been the one to call her "Mary." It fit her, she supposed. It meant, "bitter" in the Greek tongue. The Greeks believed that first impression a parent had when the child was born indicated the plan the gods had for that child's life plan and direction.

Hadn't Eleazar said she had made his life bitter by coming out of the womb the wrong way?

That must have been where the initial imprinting came from in her mind, she thought. She was nothing but trouble.

Clio was Greek, full of new vocabulary and new ideas. While the children's father had only spoken to them in Hebrew, fiercely determined to pass on their Hebrew heritage, Clio spoke to them in two other languages as well. Clio spoke the trade language of Aramaic, as well as her own *koine,* the day-to-day Greek language of the land of her birth. At the time, Aramaic was the most commonly spoken language for the inhabited world. Descended from Aram, the grandson of Noah, it had changed in form several times, taking in more and more territory, until it had finally become the accepted language of the Babylonians, the Persians, and now, every trader from Mesopotamia to China.

Clio's second language, Greek, was the language of culture and education, also spoken in the entire inhabited world.

So, when Eleazar had hired Clio as a wet nurse, he had unknowingly also brought the outside world and its influences into his supposedly perfect and sacred environment.

Clio was not Hebrew, nor did she hold to the teachings of the rabbis.

She had her own belief system.

That isn't to say that Clio was indifferent to the practices of Eleazar's household. As an employee, she held great respect for the beliefs of her employer. However, those beliefs were not her own.

In fact, she had been desperate to find a position. Her husband had worked as a chariot driver in the hippodrome in Jerusalem, and had been killed during the games. With Tychus, her newborn son, and no income, she had discovered she had no choice but to find a serving position for a household.

And to think! It had all begun with a wineskin! She had needed more wine for a dinner she was preparing, and had been directed to Eleazar's warehouse. It had been an act of the gods, she said, that she had happened to be in the warehouse on the day Eleazar had rushed by her, excitedly announcing his wife's going into labor. After he had run out of the door,

Baruch had come to the door where the back room met the sales area, with an outer tunic and a man's head covering in his hand.

"Oh, he's already out the door," he had said.

"Do those things belong to your master?" she had asked. "I'll take them to him for the price of a full wineskin."

"His home is in EnKarem," Baruch had replied. "I'll give you *two* wineskins if you will take this to him."

With the infant Tychus strapped to her, carrying two full wineskins, Clio traveled the miles to EnKarem, walking some, riding some. She arrived at evening, just as the household was returning from burying Rachel's body in the family tomb.

When she had first come to the house, the day of Rachel's death, Clio found herself in the midst of a private and secluded culture, complete with a language she did not know. Seeking to please her employer, and to communicate with his children, she set out to learn the Hebrew tongue.

Then, seeking to prepare her son, as well as Eleazar's children, for the world outside their little compound, she set out to teach each of them to speak in Aramaic and in Greek.

Everyone should be able to read, she reasoned. Clio loved to read. In fact, her mother had named her for a Greek goddess who had brought the alphabet from the unseen realm. Reading was knowledge. Knowledge was power.

Power was important in life. She had learned that much, she told the children. Clio decided, the children should be able to read and write as well.

As the years passed, Eleazar's children learned well Clio's methods of communication; and, they also were deeply influenced by her belief systems. She was well versed in the traditions of Greek mythology.

Mary loved her, calling her "Mama."

In addition to all of this, Clio didn't hold to Hebrew traditions either. When asked if the children would be going to the Storyteller's house to learn the Torah, and History, she would throw her head back and just laugh, saying *she* would tell stories of gods and miracles.

The children loved her stories. As the months turned into years, Tychus and Mary began to grow up together, listening to bedtime accounts of Greek gods and goddesses, who sounded more like people than deities. Clio once told Mary that raising them together had been like nursing twins. And, as the children had grown, Tychus had become like a brother to Mary.

As little Eleazar was to Miriam, so Tychus was to Mary.

Clio tried to be a good mother. She would spend countless hours with the children, listening to their stories, and sharing her own. She taught them to haggle in the marketplace, bargaining for the best deal. She showed them how colors went together. She taught Mary and Tychus to recognize shapes and letters. In the evenings, she would gather them in the courtyard by the fire-pit, to tell stories of mythical creatures and magic, as they sat around the fire.

The best time of the day was when Mama told stories, Mary thought.

Journey

She loved to watch her Mama's face light up as she described the adventures of Greek heroes. She would use her hands. Sometimes she would get up and act out the story, just so the children could understand the passion in her heart about what she was telling them. She told them about the wars of the gods; about Mars, and Zeus, and Poseidon. She told them what she believed about how the things they could see in the sky had come into being.

She told them about the goddess Diana, as the Ephesians called her, who had fallen from heaven like a shooting star, come to rule on the earth. She told them how Diana was worshipped in her country; in a temple with sacred prostitutes. She told them how her people looked forward to sacrificing to their gods at their festivals.

One evening, as they sat around the fire, Mary found hidden courage to ask Clio about a marking on her forearm. "What's that, Mama?" she asked, pointing to a blue design just above her nursemaid's wrist. It was a chariot driver, whose horses were in full gallop. He was surrounded by clouds.

Clio looked at her, and her eyes misted. "My husband was a chariot driver. One day, he was driving in the games. He was so close to winning…. Then the driver in front of him swerved into his lane, and they collided. My husband was thrown from the back and trampled by the horses. He died that night." Her voice broke, and she swallowed hard to be able to continue. "There was a Scythian slave working in the stables, who was a close friend of my husband. The day of my husband's funeral, he cut this picture in my arm with a needle and a small knife. Then, he mixed my husband's ashes with copper dust and rubbed the mixture into the wound. When the cuts healed, I had this design. This way, my husband will always be with me, because I carry his ashes with me; even though he is with the gods now."

The children were silent for a long time, thinking about Clio's tattoo.

"Did it hurt?" Miriam asked, rubbing her arm.

"Oh yes, until it began to heal," Clio answered absently, looking at her tattoo. Then she drew her arms around Mary and Miriam who were sitting next to her, and hugged them close. She smiled brightly at Eleazar who sat at her feet.

"But not nearly as much as being left alone. Isn't it good to have each other?" She paused, and then re-directed the story-time.

"Now," she said brightly, "let me tell you about Sinbad and the Golden Fleece. Have I told you about Cyclops? Or how the gods fight wars in the heavens, and what thunder really means when it rains?"

The children had clapped and jumped up and down. "Oh, yes, Mama! Please, please! More stories! We don't want to go to sleep yet."

Mary was fascinated. Over the years, she became enamored with finding a great temple someday, like the one in Athens that Clio described. It must be something great to see. And maybe, she dreamed, someday she would be special enough to be part of those kinds of adventures.

Maybe she could even learn how to be Beautiful and Sacred to the priests, and to the gods….

Journey

As the years passed, Clio taught Miriam and little Eleazar to read and to write; in Aramaic first, and then in Greek. She taught the girls what it meant to be a woman in the days they were living.

Added to her storytelling abilities, Mary loved Clio's laugh…. and her hugs.

She gave such good hugs.

But she always hugged Tychus harder.

She always loved him best, Mary thought.

It was strange, Mary reflected. During those years, she didn't remember seeing much of her father. Yes, there was always plenty of everything. The servants took care of their needs. They were bathed, and fed, and tucked in at night. There *had* been a short season of years when Anna, the midwife who had delivered her, had come and told her stories about Israel, and the miracles of Israel's God, the Creator called Elohim.

When she was five, Mary had especially loved the stories of the plagues in Egypt, and the Passover. And imagine, she thought! A god who could part the sea!!

But over the years, those historical accounts had become mingled with Clio's stories from Greece. How did they fit together, she wondered?

Oh well, Mary thought, hadn't Mama told her that the gods had wars in unseen realms?

One god was a good as another, she supposed.

When she thought about it, if she put Anna's stories in contrast with Clio's stories, the adventures the midwife had shared with her just didn't seem to have much drawing power to them. Maybe they really were good stories, and Anna just wasn't a good storyteller!!

Anna had told her they were true.

But then, Mama had told her that her stories were real as well…

How could any of those things have actually happened?

Over time, it had all just melded together, and faded into childhood.

―――

One day; Mary couldn't remember exactly how old she was; perhaps around seven or so. Clio had come into the playroom with puffy eyes. Mary had asked her what was wrong, and Clio just shook her head.

"Tychus and I have to go away now. Your father can't pay us anymore. Miriam will have to be the one to take care of you from this point on. After all, she's twelve now. You'll be fine. You'll see."

"Where are you going, Mama? When will you be back?

"I won't be coming back, Mary. I have to find another position somewhere. Little Tychus and I have to eat."

She had left within the week. Eleazar had paid her passage to join one of their caravans headed up the Via Maris, the Sea Road, to the North Country. Looking back, Mary realized that times were hard then, and Clio had headed toward the busiest regions in the country, hoping to find a family needing someone to teach and care for their children. She would have to find a family who would accept her religious views as well. There weren't many Jewish households like this one, with a dead mother and an absent father, Clio considered. .

Journey

Well, perhaps she would find a family from a different culture. Like Persians, or even Greeks the same as she.

Mary could not grasp the reasons behind her choice to go.

Didn't Mama understand that they were orphans? Didn't she care? How could she leave them? …And so quickly too!

Just like that. Why hadn't love been strong enough to keep her Mama there? Why didn't it seem to have a hold? Hadn't Mama given them her heart?

She had always believed that her Mama had loved her….

What would happen to her now?

Couldn't Mama hear the pain, or feel her need for love? – Mary, so small and impressionable, was sure the pain could be heard, even if it were silently screaming from a five-year-old heart.

There must be something wrong with her, she concluded, or she would have a mother….

…and a father….

She had never felt as alone as she did after Clio and Tychus left.

That was the first time she had felt real Fear in her heart. From that time forward it became her constant companion.

She was the only one who didn't belong now.

———

Soon afterwards, her father, Eleazar, began coming home during the day. At first, it was just like old times for Miriam and little Eleazar. They would play and laugh together.

But with Mary he was different somehow.

To be fair, Mary was so desperate for love from an adult, any adult, she saw any time with her father as wonderful. Subconsciously, she realized she had needed to have some kind of connection with him.

When would he play with her like he did with Miriam?

And, where Clio had spoken to them in Greek, and taken them to the market to use their Aramaic, their father always spoke to them in Hebrew. He insisted they stay on the family compound. For Miriam and Eleazar it was a comforting language. It reminded them of the days when their mother had been alive, and they had all been happy together.

But for Mary, having to remember three languages was confusing.

Why didn't their father speak to them in Aramaic, at least?

Mary wondered if he just didn't want them to be part of his life outside of their family estate.

Then, something had happened that had sealed her imagery of her father's character in her mind and perception.

One afternoon, Eleazar was spending time with them in the courtyard. The boy began sharing with his father one of the stories Clio had told them around the nighttime fire in the courtyard. Mary could still remember watching it happen. It was lodged in her memory as if it were yesterday.

Journey

"What? Where did you hear this nonsense?" their father exploded. "Do you believe this is true?"

"C-C-Clio, Papa," the boy faltered. "She told us lots of stories."

"And they were *fun* stories, too!" Miriam added.

Eleazar rubbed his hands over his face. "But they're not true!! Hasn't anyone taken you to the Storyteller's house to learn the Torah?"

"Clio said she knew more and better stories, Papa; stories that had better miracles in them, and magic too! Like the man who was half-goat and half-man, and about Achilles, and Hercules, and Aphrodite!!"

"I liked Aphrodite. She was pretty!" Mary blurted out.

Miriam spoke up, seeking to explain the situation and bring peace. She could sense an emotional upheaval was close to the surface in her father. "Clio said that if you wanted us to go to the Storyteller's house, you should come here yourself and take us. But she wasn't going to take Tychus there," she said, seeking to give explanation and bring harmony. Surely that would explain the situation to him.

"Do you know any stories about the Golden Fleece, Papa?" Eleazar was tugging on his father's robe. "Or about Sinbad?"

"They were better stories than the ones Anna told me." Mary said.

"You mean the midwife? What stories did she tell you?" Her father's voice changed, and looked into her eyes. For a moment, Mary thought it looked like the anger might go away for a moment.

"Oh, just some old stuff about some mountain that made a noise like thunder, and a lot of people in the desert. They were really hungry people, but they were mean and selfish. The part where the stick made water come out of the rock was good, though," she answered.

Eleazar became agitated. His voice began to rise in its intensity. "What have you been doing while I have been working? Learning idolatry? Do you even *know* the commandments? What will the elders say? You didn't *want* to go to the Storyteller's house, did you? *You* should have told one of the servants to take you. Why didn't you think of it?"

Mary hadn't been ready for this tirade. She had never seen anyone act this way before. Her father continued, as he paced back and forth across the courtyard.

"Why didn't you ask the housekeeper to take you? Why didn't you tell *me*? *I* would have come home and taken you.... There's no excuse for this."

He stopped in his walking. "I'll tell you why you didn't care about the Law and the prophets."

He turned and bent over to speak into Mary's face.

"Yes, *Mary*," he spat out her name, "you *are* a rebellious one, *aren't* you? This would never have happened in our home, if *you* hadn't come."

He was shouting now. Miriam and little Eleazar huddled together in the middle of the floor, holding each other. They had never seen their father like this. They were terrified.

Mary just stood, afraid, but unflinching, watching, wide-eyed and innocent; unknowingly allowing this moment to impress her memory with an image of fatherhood. Inside her head,

32

she was making a note that she would never do anything again to trigger this kind of behavior in anyone.

Inwardly, she was unaware of the diminishing of her sense of personal worth and dignity. *All she knew was; the longer her father raged, the sadder and more alone she became.*

Eleazar ran his hands over his head. His raised voice penetrated Mary's mind, labeling her with words about her own value. "I don't know why I let her talk me into having a third child," he yelled. "This isn't what your mother wanted! *I know* what *she* wanted!! But now she'll never have anything she wanted, because of *you*!! *She* wouldn't have wanted things this way!! *She* loved God!! But you obviously *don't*! There's a mark on you, Mary. You're damaged goods. I don't know why we ever had you.... You've brought me nothing but bad luck."

He had come after her in a rage at that point. Mary didn't remember much, except that he smelled like wine; so much wine... The stink seemed to come out of the pores of his skin. She had only once before been that close to her father, sensing his breath on her face. Now, she wished to never be that close again.

He smelled bad. And the smell was mingled with the smell of sweat and something else she didn't recognize.

She remembered being lifted up by her left arm and thrown across the courtyard. After that, all she remembered was watching him continue to pace back and forth, berating his children for mistakes of his own doing.

Looking back now, Mary realized that he *had* to blame *someone*. If he had faced the truth, for all of his supposed success and manhood, her father had been too fragile for the weights of fault. He had to pass them on. If he had looked at it too closely, it would have burned a hole in his heart. It might have even killed him. *Someone else* had to take the pain.

The only ones close at hand were his children.

As the years passed, as Mary grew and developed, these evening tirades became commonplace. Over time, she learned to harden her heart against the things he would say. He was always bitter and angry – and wanting revenge on someone.

Why did the someone always seem to be her?

Maybe, she thought, she *did* deserve this. Perhaps it would have been better if she hadn't been born at all. Maybe the gods *had* put a mark on her; it must have been a target.

In contrast, Miriam, her sister, felt sorry for their father. Something had just happened to him; that was all. Wanting desperately to make him happy, she took upon herself the family duties, seeking to earn his acceptance and approval by the performance of household chores. He would come back to them someday, Miriam told herself, if they worked hard enough to make it happen. She began to run the household, eventually learning to do it very well. If she became the source person for the family to come to, she thought, no one would ever have to bother Papa, or cause him to be upset. They were all just a burden anyway to him, she reasoned.

In contrast, the young Eleazar sought to become invisible. If he stayed out of his father's way, he couldn't get into trouble. He found himself at the homes of his friends, and sought out the company and mentoring of his friends' fathers. Many of them remembered Eleazar in happier days, and were more than glad to be able to help his son.

But Mary felt nothing.

As the appetite for wine and beer grew in their father, the family's holdings began to lessen. The children hadn't noticed it as much when Clio was with them, but over the years, there were fewer workers in the fields; fewer harvesters; fewer friends came to call. The household workers diminished, until it was just the children and the housekeeper.

Then one day, *she* didn't come.

Over time, fewer and fewer merchants came to the door, looking for goods. Miriam assumed it because their father was working in Jerusalem. They were meeting him *there* for business. Then, someone in the market had shared with them rumors they had heard of mismanagement of funds at the warehouse.

When Miriam was fifteen, and Mary was ten, a young Greek man from Cyprus, named Lucius, purchased the weaving house. He had been recently widowed and needed a new beginning in a new place, and culture, he said.

Sometime during that year she realized; there didn't seem to be much left besides the house and the land. If things were that bad, she reasoned, why didn't they just sell the land as well? They couldn't really pay anyone to take care of the vines and terraces; much less buy seed for crops.

Most of the flocks and herds had been sold to pay off her father's gambling losses.

And these days, there were many nights when he didn't come home at all…

After Clio left, Miriam had assumed the leadership role and womanly duties in the home. Although she was only twelve at the time, she learned to survive.

So had her brother and sister.

After all, even while her mother had been alive, she had followed the servants during the day. "What's that?" she would ask. "Why do you do that?" "Can I help?"

She learned early on to stay out of her father's way, making sure not to stir his anger. When Clio left, Miriam made it her business to learn from the workers who remained in the fields during the day. She learned to grind grain; to make bread. She learned to milk the goats and make cheese. By the time she was fourteen, she had a grasp on running the house all by herself. She and her brother gathered sticks for the cooking fire each day, and made sure food was ready and warm when their father arrived in the evenings; although the timing was always unpredictable. The children never knew at what hour their father would storm through the outer doors demanding his appetites be satisfied.

He had been a wealthy landowner, after all.

It was his right to eat a good meal when he was hungry.

Miriam began to feel responsible for everything her father complained about. If the milk was too warm, she felt responsible. If the weather made him sweat, it was because she hadn't laid out the right clothing the night before. Each time he was angry, Miriam would berate herself, and find fault with how she had done things.

If she could just push herself a little harder, everything would be all right, she reasoned.

As the years passed, Miriam found herself very capable, extreme knowledgeable, completely practical -- -- and completely numb inside.

"You can't take *all* the blame, you know," her brother would say.

"I just wish I could help him be the way he was *before*..." she confided. "Maybe if I can do everything like Mama did it, he will be happy, and he'll love us again.

"We must be perfect. I know we can do it. Papa expects it.... remember the alabaster bottles."

She worked hard to make things better for her father.

The more of Eleazar's blame and expectations she picked up, the less of her own identity she was able to hold to.

Mary remembered one day, sitting in the courtyard, when Miriam had spoken her heart to her sister. Miriam had been sixteen at the time, and felt her life had become unbearable. They had been working near the fountain in the center courtyard, folding towels in the middle of the afternoon, when her sister spoke to her. It seemed that sometime earlier that day, perhaps in the early morning; Miriam had come upon a discovery.

She had no dreams.

No plans for her future.

All of the other children she had known were making plans, and getting married, or even talking about traveling to distant places.

But she just wanted to survive.

Or did she, really? She wondered.

Surely somewhere, she thought, life has to be better than it is here.

She voiced her thoughts to Mary.

"Don't you wish you could just run away sometimes, Mary?" she asked.

Mary stopped folding and sighed. "It's not so bad. At least we have a roof over our heads." The younger sister was trying to show Miriam something good to focus on. Mary was trying to play the pretend game they had played in their earlier years.

When they were smaller, playing the game had been a way to keep hope alive.

Sadly, it only worked for a little while; this wishing game they participated in. It seemed they were always dancing around what they really felt, as if it were a thorn bush; speaking in a code; an undercurrent of communication.

Mary thought, somehow their hearts had remained connected under it all; in spite of it all.

Even if Miriam *had* become bossy and controlling....

She did love her sister for helping her to grow in her reading skills. It had been one of their many defense mechanisms, developed to help in dealing with their fears, especially on nights when their father had not come home.

Mary considered. If she would admit it, yes, she had thought of running away; perhaps to find Clio, or just to find a safer place. There had to be one somewhere.

For some time she had been hiding belongings precious to her in a satchel behind her door. Each time she had been paid for any duties at all, or for caring for another family's children, she had tucked the money away, along with the now resented alabaster jar.

It had come to symbolize all that she would never be.

Or even *could* be.

After all, she thought bitterly, how could she be the woman her mother had been – without someone to show her the way? How could she remember and emulate memories she had never had?

How can you become something better, when all you see is what is missing?

How can you ask questions about what you feel, when you believe your experiences are normal and common? What questions do you ask?

~~~~

When Mary thought about her father, there was a hard lump in her chest, and a pain in her stomach. Was what she felt for him love?

Or fear?

Did *he* love *her*? Surely not. Surely, she reasoned, she was trash; lower than the other girls her own age. She must have deserved the treatment she had received.

If her father really did love her, why had he removed himself from her, even when she was an infant? If you really loved someone, how could you place a burden on them like expecting perfection? If she had to become the perfection her mother had been, how would she ever really know her own true identity?

She hated him.

Yes, she thought she really must.

And there was more. The truth was, as she had grown older, she had become more and more afraid of her father; and not just his anger.

It was the way he looked at her when no one else was around.

"Come and sit by me, Mary," he had said one afternoon. He patted the cushion next to him.

"I can't right now," she responded, delaying him. "I have too much laundry to do."

"But you look just like your mother. She was beautiful. You have skin just like hers. And your hair is just the same color. Just come and sit by me for a moment. Let me tell you about her. I won't keep you long."

Mary had silently continued to fold, unwilling to move to the cushion.

"I'm so sorry, Mary," her father blurted out. "I never *mean* to hurt you. I'm a weak man. I need you to take care of me. I'll never hurt you again. Just let me come close to you. I'm so lonely, and I miss your mother so...."

So she had sat by him. At first, nice moments were shared. But Mary was preconditioned. She was fearful of another beating or a verbal onslaught.

She could never let herself enjoy the idea of being close to her father.

"It's *your* fault that I get so angry," he told her that afternoon. "You are just too beautiful. You look too much like your mother. Just looking at you causes me such pain, Mary." He had stroked her hair. "Your beauty is the reason I drink, you know."

Then, one day as they sat together, she had become aware that something was far from right in her father's mind. As she sat by him, he began; innocently enough; touching her hair, muttering to himself about her skin, and her eyes. He began to stroke her cheek. Then he put his arm around her middle, and pulled her closer. He began to speak into her ear, and his hands began to move to places that didn't feel right.

At first, she let herself enjoy the attention, and then….

No, this had to be wrong….

But he was giving her attention…..

Why would he touch her like this?

Why would he touch *there?*

This was not something fathers were supposed to do, *was it?*

Mary still remembered the scent of the flowers in the courtyard.

Until that day, it had been her favorite place. Whenever she needed to escape the tension and conflict from within the house, she would come to the courtyard and hide in the same corner where she had landed the night her father had first abused her.

If she curled herself into a small enough package, she thought, no one would see her. Why couldn't she become invisible, she wondered?

Now the courtyard would never be a safe place again.

Would there ever be a true sanctuary for her, she wondered?

Couldn't life, someplace, be better than this?

It didn't matter, she reasoned. Even if there were, she probably didn't really deserve it.

As the days progressed, she began to avoid that part of the house, especially when her father was there.

Then had come Miriam's wedding day… At seventeen, she met Abiel; a young doctor, who worked in a nearby village on the slope of the Olivet Mountain. He was in his twenties, and he had fallen deeply in love with Miriam. It hadn't mattered to him that Miriam didn't have much of a dowry.

Abiel was a kind man, with gentle eyes. Miriam loved him with such intensity. Although Mary felt drawn to him, and wanted to trust him, she couldn't allow herself to open her heart.

"Miriam just wants to get away from here," Mary thought. It didn't hurt that the man needed someone to help him in his practice as well, Mary thought. But she kept her thoughts to herself. Perhaps she was just being cynical. She really wanted Miriam to be happy.

The wedding had been beautiful. There had been days of celebration.

Mary could still hear Miriam laughing as she rode away from the feast to her new home.

Several weeks later, in the middle of the night, while the rest of the world was fast asleep, Mary awakened suddenly. As she opened her eyes, she sensed someone close to her in her room. There was a shadow. As her eyes focused in the semi-darkness, her father's face filled

Journey

her vision. The sickeningly sweet, familiar stench of alcohol emanated from him. Then she realized, he was pulling off her sleeping blanket!

Not again. Fear began to travel its familiar pathway to her heart. And yet, this time, it was different. What was it she was sensing?

"Rachel, my love, I'm here," he slurred, groping his way towards her in the darkness. "Come a little closer."

Horror and anger began to rise to fill her as she slowly awakened to the realization of what was in her father's satiated mind.

What twisted form of fatherly love was this? Had he completely lost his mind?

He began to reach for her, reaching under her sleeping garment, pulling her to himself.

Something inside of Mary's heart and mind snapped: It is enough!

Her emotions began to scream within her. She could not, would not, continue to go through the torture of being mistaken for her mother in his mind.

She had to get away from him.

Immediately!!

"Make room for me… I have plans for you…" Her father reached for her. "It's been a long time. Have you missed me?" His speech was slurred, as he reached for her, drunkenly assuming the form in the bed before him was his deceased wife.

Mary was never sure whether her actions were spontaneous or had been premeditated over time. From an unknown place inside, she discovered strength to strike back. And as she did, she heard a crackling sound as her fist hit her father's nose. He moaned in agony, crumpling into a drunken stupor on the floor beside her sleeping mat.

She was certain he would remember nothing when the sun rose the next morning.

But it wouldn't matter anymore. She would be gone.

Free, for the first time in her life.

Grabbing her satchel, and stuffing whatever else she could find in the darkness, she ran out of the house. Full of fear, and energized by visions of her raging father coming after her, Mary ran down the road towards Jerusalem; to the trade routes beyond.

She was twelve, and she was alone.

She had never experienced life outside of her household walls.

But…. she was determined. She would follow Miriam's path. She would find her sister.

Maybe Clio, her Mama, was out there somewhere as well.

Come to think of it, this was the same direction Clio had taken.

The only parent whom she felt had ever really loved her.

Journey

Tiberius

The world outside of Eleazar's small compound at EnKarem was very different than the one to which Mary was accustomed. Had one been able at that time in history, to measure Palestine's political climate, the assessment would be made that it had become a ticking time-bomb; with imminent disaster written in the winds.

Situations had become far more than stressed. The entire inhabited world of the day was more dangerous, more corrupt, more sexually permissive, more illicit, and more ethnically diverse than it had ever been at any other time on record to that date.

The Roman presence was felt, if not acknowledged, everywhere. In locations where Rome was not acknowledged, she exerted herself onto the peoples in oppression.

Just as a tyrant seeks to infiltrate a nation and overthrow it, creating havoc and fear, so the Roman emperor, Tiberius, was regarded in the environs of and territories surrounding Israel. In every town and city of the provinces, companies of soldiers were stationed as "peacekeeping forces," seeing Rome's will was accomplished, and her way of life upheld, especially on foreign soil, without concern to the cost in life, limb, or emotion.

Additionally, the toughest duty for a man in the Roman military at the time was considered to be Israel. The roughest of the rank and file were sent for arduous duty in the desert; the hot and arid areas.

Few volunteered for a position so far away from the privileges and luxuries of home. Granted, there were Roman colonies in the Israeli desert with a few luxuries, but the people of the cities is Israel still went to wells to draw their water! It was unsanitary to live without an aqueduct providing running water!!

No, to be stationed in primitive Palestine was compared to being sent into exile! Moreover, Israel had long been labeled a troublesome area. The people reportedly required more discipline than the other conquered provinces around them.

In regard to religious freedom, Rome was, as a conquering nation, reasonably tolerant of other ideas. To be a true Roman was to admire the Greeks, and the Greeks worshipped *everything*. With this in mind, it was Roman practice to allow peoples she had conquered to retain a certain freedom of worship, in order to bring about the illusion that the emperor was benevolent and understanding.

Yet, when it came to Israel, this practice of tolerance had backfired. Israel's religion and its political base were unchangeably intertwined. Every Hebrew man, woman and child in the nation knew it. In the core of the being of every Israelite, breathed a revelatory understanding.

The True and *Living God* had founded *their* nation!

Journey

Originally, Israel was a theocracy; it was God-ruled. Kings and prophets Israel had known throughout the lifetime of the nation had merely been designed to serve as representatives to the people of their actual King.

Some had represented Him well; some had not.

For this reason, whenever conquerors had sought to divide the people from their faith, the end result of the effort had always been failure. In actuality, to seek to separate Israel from her religion was to seek to sever her from her identity and Life-force. This action had incited uprisings, revolt and general mayhem among the population of the tiny nation.

No… conquerors had always helped to *define* and *reinforce* Israel's identity, rather than diminish it.

It was a discovery every one of her conquerors had made shortly after the completion of their conquest. By then it had been too late to go back. By then, the difficulties of managing a people with such strong identity had embroiled each ruler in costly, wearying, time-consuming maintenance, requiring an iron-edged rule, leaving no room for relationship.

But Rome would be different. She had the resources to enforce her desires. There would be no rebellion among the desert nomads… These barbarians would learn to curb their fierceness.

Or so the Roman emperor had *thought*.

The Palestine province had long been a difficult state to govern, especially from a distance. As a result, Rome had allowed the people to retain a sense of having their own king as well; Herod the Great, as he had called himself. Enamored with Greek and Roman design, Herod had rebuilt Zerubbabel's temple in Jerusalem, adding to its design.

He had made it spectacular. The scribes and rabbis in Jerusalem would not concede that the work was as spectacular as the Temple Solomon had built, but by common assessment, it was absolutely beautiful!! Everyone said so; even the Romans. Anyone who visited Jerusalem stopped also at the Temple, to experience its beauty of its porches and portico, even if they weren't Jewish.

Besides, the work was still unfinished, the ruler maintained. It would take many years to complete his design plans for the Temple.

Herod the Great fancied himself as an architect. In addition to the Temple, he had built himself not only one great palace, but three! His summer home was in the middle of the desert, and was a stronghold envied by even the Romans.

Herod called it "Masada."

But the great builder never saw the completion of his Temple project.

Just after Mary ran from her father's home, King Herod the Great died. In the years that followed, his sons took up the kingdom he divided among them. There were three distinctly different territories, each with its own set of politics. Rather than choose one son to become heir to his throne, Herod had chosen to divide his kingdom into three parts; with Roman approval, of course. He had worked long and hard to provide a throne for each of his sons, having ruled from the age of twenty. In reality, he was no more than a puppet king, a remnant of the days when Israel had been conquered by the Idumeans.

Journey

Each son, however, vied to be recognized as "the king of Israel." Herod Archelaus, the evil and plotting son, ruled the southern kingdom on the western side of the Jordan River. His middle brother, Herod Antipas maintained the provinces of Galilee and the southern kingdom on the eastern side of the Jordan. North of the Sea of Galilee, was the region of Trachonitis, which bordered Pheonicia. Herod Philip ruled this area. The politics, customs and tributes due varied from region to region, as did the fear of each lesser king's power. Having a Roman emperor and a Jewish king as well, made matters quite confusing for anyone seeking to live in peace with the authorities.

That wasn't all a citizen had to consider. Not only was there the Roman presence, as well as an unstable Jewish government's presence, but there was the Religious presence to please as well. In Jerusalem, there were high priests; Caiaphas and Annas ruled.

Realizing the political power of the high priest's office, the Romans now chose the man who would rule in this office. In the people's minds, it was a reminder of the days when the Hasmonean Priesthood had ruled over Israel. Joseph Caiaphas and his father-in-law, Annas, served their own purposes in Jerusalem. Caiaphas served as the *nasi,* or "prince" of the Sanhedrin in Jerusalem, the governing body over religious issues. The Jewish populace called him the "high priest," although it had been a long time since the office had been filled by a spiritual man. It had been even a longer time since the office had been filled by a son of Aaron.

Joseph BarKayafa, called simply "Caiaphas," was reputed to be insecure and power-hungry, continually sending messengers to Rome to complain to the Senate about how things were going in Israel, seeking to overturn one decision or another. His usual target was whoever had been stationed in Jerusalem as the Prefect, proconsul, or judicial representative of the Roman Senate.

In most situations where a conquering nation had colonized an area, to go over the Prefect's head with an appeal would have meant the death of the man concerned. In this case, however, the Romans were afraid of Caiaphas. If he were to be removed from his place, the conquerors knew riots and war would erupt once again.

Unhappily, then, each Prefect stationed in Jerusalem had to learn to deal with the Sandredin. For this season of time, it was Pontius Pilate, a somewhat emotionally disturbed and indecisive man. He had ended up in Palestine because Caesar Tiberius had looked his way at the wrong time.

To think of it, Pilate was the actual authority set in place by Roman rule, the conquering nation. Caiaphas was a descendant of a dynasty, and sought inwardly to continue to rule over the affairs of state, as a religious ruler. The Herodian kings were direct descendants of Herod the Great, who had given himself the name. His architecture and building prowess had allowed him to keep his throne, as long as he continued to send taxes and appeasements to Rome.

Within this divided state, each "king" competed for power; Caiaphas, the Herods, and Pilate, each paid their own personal army within his jurisdiction. Each man demanded personal loyalty to the exclusion of all others; and each man was willing to enforce his right to govern all.

For any citizen of the general populace, it was imperative a person watch his step, and stay out of the way.

Yes, it was a very dangerous time to be alive.

In his own mind, incessantly sending messengers to the Roman Senate was Joseph Caiaphas' method of maintaining visibility with what he saw as the present occupational army. It also kept turbulence continually stirred in the Jewish populace, maintaining a strange sort of loyalty in the hearts of the people toward the Jewish Temple.

Caiaphas was not concerned about the present conquerors.

As far as he was concerned, all of this was nothing new.

The Hebrews had been conquered before.

In fact, deliverance from oppression had been built into the fabric of their identity as a people. First had been the Egyptians, then the Assyrians, the Persians, the Greeks, the Ptolemies and the Seleucids. Now it was the Romans. With each conquest, there were those who would allow their beliefs to be seduced by the belief system of a pagan and conquering oppressor.

The evidences were everywhere in the culture.

There were places of worship to Greek gods, Roman gods, and even Egyptian gods. There were brothels, with prostitutes spending time near the soldiers' barracks. There was murder, rape and robbery. There were witches and diviners, who set up tents in the marketplace, barking their promises of partial truth to those who would walk by. There were abandoned children, living in the street. There were bathhouses, complete with lewd exhibitionism. There were nude wrestling events at the city's Greek-styled gymnasium. There were bawdy street dramas. There was gambling; there were drug houses, there were tattoo salons; there were flea markets. There were beggars.

There were theatres and philosophical centers. There were medical centers and hospitals. There were libraries and universities. There were homosexuals. There were gladiators. There were slaves. There were places known for their wine, for their song, for their sensuality, for their tastes of far-away lands.

It was a culture driven by the human desire for comfort and pleasure; ridden by the quest for control.

There were those who had chosen to try to just get by. Some had seemingly joined the Roman cause, but in reality just served themselves. Many of these served as tax collectors, reputed for doubling or even tripling the legal tax, keeping the profit for their own pockets.

When the government received its due, Rome looked the other way.

Even the Jewish Temple had followed suit with Rome.

When the Roman emperor refused to provide monies for the continuation of the temple system, the high priests had construed their own plan for developing self-propelling religion. They began to sell animals to be used for sacrifice, guaranteeing the "purity and validity" of each animal offered for sale, at a much higher than reasonable price. Lest anyone think it was merely a convenience for weary travelers to be allowed to purchase their animal, they then refused to accept any money in payment for these animals except the coin approved by the temple. This meant moneychangers had to be installed in the marketplace, as well as on the temple grounds, in order to supply the would-be faithful with the proper coinage to purchase a sacrificial animal. The moneychangers charged as much as eight, nine or even ten percent for their services.

Sacrifice to the Living God had become very costly – and very profitable; especially for the Temple.

Some citizens, however, had remained strong in their faith throughout the seasons of conquest. But, then, even within those ranks, elements of pride and tradition had mingled with true conviction. Descending from the days of the Maccabees, one of the purest of those separations within the Jewish faith were the Pharisees. These were Jewish priests who still believed in the truth of the old accounts of deliverance and miracles. They believed in the resurrection of the dead, and in the unseen spiritual realm. They believed the soul of man was immortal, and that a judgment for deeds done in the body would take place in the afterlife. Many Pharisees could trace their lineage back to the Hasidim, who believed man had a free will, and God's sovereignty would not over-ride it.

There was a second group of priests who held society with the Pharisees. These were the Sadducees. Since the days of Judas Maccabee, their beliefs had come down from the priests who had ruled Israel as kings, some 150 years before, during the Hasmonean Dynasty. The Sadducees didn't believe in an unseen, or spiritual realm, in the resurrection of the dead, or in an afterlife. They also believed that the written law had to be kept completely; that it was very literal in its communication regarding Levitical purity.

To break one law on earth sealed a man's fate forever.

Representatives from these two sects combined, much like a Parliament, to create a Jewish judiciary party known as the Sanhedrin. The Sanhedrin was responsible for religious decisions. Many of these men too, were power hungry, seeking to rule the people.

Where those in political power sought to oppress the people in matters of outer life, the oppression caused by the religious leadership of the day sought to conform the people in areas of inner life issues. *Their* oppression was based in fear of failing God, in fear of judgment and hell, in religious duty, and in the endless arguments over what sin really consisted of.

It was said that at one time, these two sects had argued for days regarding how many angels could dance on the head of a pin.

Then there were those holy men who were just fed up with the whole plan, who had moved out into the desert. The only way to please God, they reasoned, was to have nothing to do with the world, as they knew it. The only way to please God was to isolate oneself from corruption, and seek to become more and more holy. These men dedicated their lives to the study of the Torah, (the books of Moses), and teaching the people in their localities about what the Word of God really meant. It was also their mission to see that the Word of God was maintained, or not lost. So, they set up a settlement outside Jerusalem, where scrolls could be meticulously copied. These men were the Essenes. Many of them refused to marry, and remained celibate and chose to serve God with all of their lives. Others did marry, making their homes in the Judean desert in a place known as Qumran.

Finally, as it has been in every culture since the first settlements of man, there were those who were convinced the only way to be completely righteous, was to free the people from their oppressors by force. With enough weapons, strategy, violence and military power, it was supposed that the culture would somehow become full of peace, joy, and holiness.

Full of zeal, these parties opposed tax payments to a pagan emperor, saying they should only give their heart's allegiance to God Himself. They refused to speak the Greek language in the marketplace, holding always to the Hebrew tongue. Many of them were fierce in their beliefs, prophesying the coming time of salvation, when the nation would be restored to Israel. These were the Zealots, so named for their righteous zeal and anger toward oppression. They were the vigilantes of the day; seeking to bring about justice wherever they saw injustice.

And injustice was everywhere.

At the age of 56, Tiberius Claudius Nero had become emperor. The adopted son of the former emperor, Augustus, he was no stranger to power. But everyone knew that he was not his adopted father's true son.

Not in blood, nor in character.

Augustus had received the throne from Julius, the first Caesar.

Augustus had been a hard-working ruler for forty-one years, who had restored confidence in the Roman government, replenishing the treasury. He had organized the first known police and fire departments in history, and had appointed a supervisor for the nation's grain supplies. In response for these successes, the Senate had temporarily conferred upon Augustus an *imperium*, or power of an imperial state. This meant he was the first citizen of the land, somewhat of a compromise between the dictatorship of Julius Caesar, and the republic of peoples suggested by Octavian.

The people believed him to be more than human as a ruler, and he was deferred to by everyone, as having wisdom beyond the powers of mortality, mostly due to the immensity of his reforms in the empire.

Towards the end of his reign, Caesar Augustus had been worshipped as "Lord and God," *Dominus et Deus*. Although he didn't personally agree with the flattery of his character, he certainly didn't argue with its intent. His personal assessment of himself was stated in the last speech of his lifetime, "I have found Rome brick, and have made it marble."

"If you want to be named as my successor," he told Tiberius, "you must be willing to marry my daughter, Julia."

This meant Tiberius would have to divorce the wife he loved, and had been married to for several years. "What cost, power?" he told himself. Julia was a woman who lived an openly sexually permissive lifestyle. She did not hold to ladylike behavior befitting a ruler's wife, and she did not love Tiberius at all.

Journey

In fact, she barely tolerated him.

How could a sister marry a brother, even if he *was* adopted, she asked?

But Augustus wanted his bloodline to continue to rule.

Really, Tiberius thought, his life-long dream had been to become an ultimate ruler. So he divorced his wife, and unhappily, took Julia as his own.

In response, the Senate conferred upon him the judgment of *imperium* for life. He became the first ruler who could do no wrong.

No one knew exactly what exchanges took place between them, but as a result of this experience, Tiberius became a different man. It seemed that all the joy had left his life. He became sour, vengeful, and haughty. He was distant, suspicious, and hot-tempered. He did manage to remain impartial in his political approaches, however, and this might have saved his life, many times over.

He was not a strategist, and Rome's losses in Germany had shown that to be true.

There were rumors among the slaves in his Roman palace of conspiracies against him. Even among his own Praetorian guard, discontentment regarding conditions, treatment, wages, and politics were hinted at when he wasn't looking. The longer Tiberius ruled, the less he trusted those around him. Daily, domestic wars with Julia over his performance as a husband crowded in upon his already depressed demeanor. Over a period of time, hardness and indifference developed in his heart, and in his character towards others. By choice, he became intent only upon seeing his own needs satisfied, and his own desires fulfilled.

Tiberius became a cruel man.

It was becoming dangerous to even whisper about the menu of the evening meal in his presence.

As a result, even the Roman Senate was becoming unstable.

Journey

Abiel

Like a child struggling to stay afloat in a deep and unruly ocean, Mary entered tides beyond her ability to manage when she stepped outside Eleazar's vast compound in EnKarem.

She was entering a world where even certainties were earmarked with undefined instability.

The evening of her father's final advances towards her, Mary stumbled out of the house, terrified of being stopped by a neighbor, or worse, one of the family's nighttime shepherds. She was petrified she might be followed; expecting her father to run after her and beat her for resisting him.

Perhaps this would be the last beating, and she really would die.

If she thought about it, though, she didn't really *want* to die.

So, she kept running.

Weeping, she stumbled through the darkness, not knowing where she was going.

Away. Just to get away….

She knew she had to get to Miriam's house.

She would be safe there.

But what could she do right now? Darkness had descended, and the town would have closed its gates at the end of the day. Sunset had been hours ago.

It was becoming cold as well.

No, she couldn't go into town…..

She stopped for a moment to catch her breath. How would she know which dwelling belonged to Abiel and Miriam in the darkness? She had only been to their home one time before, assisting Miriam as she helped the sick one day. Abiel had gone to Jerusalem for supplies.

Miriam's intended husband had seemed kind enough at the time….

But who could tell from one encounter?

The only man Mary had ever observed closely was her father…..

What if Abiel became angry with Mary for intruding upon their new home?

He would probably *make* her go back…

No, he would probably *take* her back to EnKarem himself, in a fit of rage.

It would be her own fault, too, she reasoned.

Mary fiercely rubbed the tears streaming down her face once again.

She couldn't afford to become weak now…..

She wondered if Abiel drank. There had been wine at the wedding….

Didn't all men drink? Maybe Miriam's house wasn't such a good idea after all.

She was too tired to think about that now....

For now, she just had to keep moving.

Exhausted, she came to a halt. There was too much to consider just now....

Sleep.

Sleep would be a really good idea. She looked around.

Realizing she had stopped in a grove of palm trees, the exhausted girl spread out her cloak, and prepared herself a temporary bed. There would be time to look for Miriam in the morning. She was so tired. Just a few hours of rest would be good.

Using her satchel as a pillow, she slept until daybreak; guarded by the stars, in a grove of olive trees and date palms. As the sunlight kindled the life of a new day, Mary stirred. She blinked, taking in her surroundings. It took a few moments to gain her bearings. Then she remembered the events of the night before. Tears welled up in her still-swollen eyes, and overflowed once again onto her cheeks.

She brushed them aside, and shook her head.

She mustn't cry.

She must take some more steps. Distance was the key.

Looking around, it was evident she had stopped near a well.

Were those dates on the ground? These must be date palms!! She wasn't used to eating *fresh* dates. There had always been *dried* dates at home in EnKarem.

These might be good, she decided.

Mary scooped up a few of the brightly colored fruits, and suddenly realized just how hungry she really was. Without thinking about whom the well or the dates might belong to, she ate her fill and drew water, preparing for the day.

As she was washing her face, she had a sudden thought.

This must be someone's private garden!!

The fear of being accused of trespassing, and possibly being forced to return home caused adrenaline to flow once more, speeding her along. Quickly reloading up her meager belongings, she continued the trek towards Miriam's house.

Upon arriving at the village, it wasn't difficult to find the newlyweds' dwelling. After asking someone on the street, she discovered theirs was the house with a full portico of people waiting to see Abiel.

Apparently the doctor was working today.

Mary joined the crowd, and listened to the conversations around her, hoping to learn something about her new brother-in-law. She slid down against the stone wall, which created a fence-like partition from the street. Huddling on the ground, in the corner of the portico, she was hidden from view. She would rest here until Miriam would have time to see her, she concluded. Perhaps Abiel wouldn't be angry if she didn't bother them until they were finished with their day.

The middle son of a wealthy lawyer in Jerusalem, Abiel had chosen to dedicate his life to the sick and needy in this small village. His method and concept of providing care was

Journey

relatively new. After reading accounts from Greece and Egypt, the young man had expressed a desire to create a permanent place for treat those who needed long-term attention.

"Perhaps we should develop a better way to help people," he had told his father.

The older man had smiled. "What would you call it, Abiel?"

"I don't know yet," came the reply. "Perhaps we could use the Greek words for 'physician' and 'sickbed' and put them together: *Klinike* or *Klinikos*. What do you think?"

Over the years, the name had been shortened by the villagers in Bethany to "clinic." Supported and funded by his loving parents, the young doctor had built his home from cut stone, rather than from the poor man's style of mud-based brick, used by the general populace of the area.

Abiel had spent almost two years working on this house, it was told. And after the rock formations had been set in place, he had mixed and spread the plaster with his own hands!!

The gifted physician had begun the project to facilitate a larger need of those in the village who were infirm and diseased. The small, borrowed, mud-brick home, where he had begun his work upon his initial arrival in their midst, had been quickly outgrown.

Then, just as the townspeople thought he was ready to begin finishing the inside of the house; halfway through his project, he had torn off the back of the house to create an inner courtyard with a garden! Mary heard someone in the waiting area say he had built it for his new bride, after he had first seen her, and been to her home. It seemed she had confided to him that a courtyard like this one was her favorite resting place in her father's house. Hadn't he dug a large cistern in the center of the house as well? Imagine! A house with its own water source!!

Abiel must have fallen in love with the girl at first sight, they reasoned. She must be something special, a new patient suggested.

She must be beautiful.

Wasn't she his nurse as well?

Mary dozed off. It was cooler here in the shade.

It would be all right to sleep awhile.

Miriam came out of the door into the portico with a pregnant woman and two toddlers following her.

"Thank you for the fig cakes, Leah," she was laughing. "We are so blessed! Everyone keeps bringing us food!"

"It's the only way I can pay you," the pregnant woman replied quietly, looking down at her children.

"You heard Abiel," Miriam laughed happily, her voice tinkling, as she linked her arm through the woman's as though they were close friends. "You don't have to pay us each time. Just make sure that baby gets all the goat's milk you can drink in daytime. You must walk each morning, and do the exercises I showed you. He or she is ready to come any day now. Send your husband, or a neighbor, and we will both come when the time is here."

She hugged the woman, sending her on her way. Then she looked around the courtyard, greeting those she knew. "Who is next?"

Journey

It was mid-afternoon when the crowd finally dissipated. Abiel came out of the small room attached to their home as an office, and stretched his muscles in the brightness of the portico. Taking notice of a quiet bundle in the corner, he took a step forward. Surprised, he called inside to his wife.

"Miriam, there is a sleeping package out here still."

"What?"

"I said," he raised his voice so she could hear him; "there is someone out here still waiting."

Miriam came out into the portico. "I know that Benjamin's daughter was the last...." Her voice stopped midstream, and a small cry of discovery escaped her. "Oh," she said, with her hand to her throat. "Don't you recognize her? It's Mary." She knelt down next to the newly revealed visitor.

"Your sister? I wonder what happened."

"Look at her. Her face is full of tearstains. And look how dirty she is!"

"It can't have been a good night for her. Why would she run away?"

Miriam looked up at her new husband, her own eyes beginning to fill with tears of empathy for her sister. There was nothing about her past she had not shared with him during the days of their courtship. Miriam had found a safe and loving friend in her husband, and they had shared much already in their short life together.

"He always was harder on her than he was on me. I was *afraid* he would do something if I left. This is my doing. I should have been there for her."

Abiel bent down to her, putting his arms around her middle, and pulling her to her feet. He spoke quietly into her ear. "Miriam, my love, you can't walk that road again. I am your protector now. I will take care of you.... *and* Mary, if the need arises. Let your heart heal. Let's get her to stand. We'll go inside and make a place for her."

So, they gently positioned the deeply sleeping Mary into Abiel's arms. They would allow her to stay in one of the extra rooms Abiel had built for just that purpose. As a man called to a community of the sick, he had designed his home for patients who would need extra care or extended recovery time.

Miriam began gathering items they could place in the room to create a space specifically apportioned for Mary; a little lamp from the front room, a small bowl and towel for washing, a reflection tray, her extra comb.

Abiel had carried her up to the room himself.

Such a small, frail girl, he thought. No matter.

She would live here now.

She would have a new beginning.

They would take care of her now.

It was late in the evening when Mary finally awakened. A small lamp flickered in the room. Was this *her* room? Had her father come and carried her back to EnKarem from Miriam's portico?

Then she realized.

No, these were not her walls.

As her eyes adjusted to the light, she thought she recognized the figure sitting next to her bed. "Is that you Miriam?" she asked.

Miriam looked up, and then turned her head towards the door. "She's awake!" she exclaimed to someone, who was not in the room with her.

Mary sat up in bed. "How did I come here? Am I in your house? Did Father come after me?" The words tumbled out one upon another.

Miriam moved to her side, speaking in a quiet, soothing voice. "It's all right, Mary. You're here, with Abiel and me. And you're safe. No, father didn't come. Don't worry." She smiled. "Come to think of it, I don't think Abiel would let him see you, even if he *did* show up here." She paused. "Are you hungry? Would you like to bathe?"

Mary looked at her with wide-open eyes, still not comprehending her surroundings. "Is he angry?" she whispered.

"Is *who* angry?"

"You know, *him*… Abiel. Is he angry that I'm here?"

"Why would you think that, Mary? He carried you to this room." Her sister was stroking her hair now, and was drawing her little sister's head close to her heart.

"I don't know. I mean, aren't *all* men angry underneath? Father always has been."

"Well, not Abiel. He is kindness itself. You'll see. Let's get you some food, and a bath."

That night, the three of them stayed awake into the early morning hours. Mary told them of her experiences with her father after their departure for their new home.

She told them how he had looked at her during that past year.

She was able to verbalize her worst fears.

Miriam had heard most of her sister's pain voiced at one time or another in the past. Abiel had nurtured his own suspicions of what had happened to her. Neither of them were surprised at several of her fresh revelations. Still, sitting with her, they instinctively knew she needed to unburden herself. So, they simply listened to and comforted her.

As they did, Mary began to relax. Miriam's home really was a safe place, she realized.

Finally, when the moon began to set, Abiel rose from the table. "The sun will be rising soon. I must go to bed, Miriam. There are poor people who will be at our doors again come daybreak. I need to get a little sleep before we open up." Kissing his wife on the top of her head, he lit a lamp and carried it to their bedchamber.

Watching him walk away, Mary spoke quietly.

"I am afraid for our brother, Miriam."

"Why are you afraid, Mary?"

"He has always been so quiet, and well, almost invisible at home. Now that you and I are both out of the house, he will become father's target when the anger rises to the surface."

Miriam patted her sister's hand. Don't worry about Eleazar. Haven't you noticed our brother is almost a man? He is fifteen now. He has friends in EnKarem, and even in Jerusalem, too. He has been finding his way. He has been staying in Jerusalem with friends;

sometimes for a week or two at a time. Do you remember those nights when he didn't come home? I know our father didn't seem to; I don't know that he even cared.

"Eleazar has been working at the weaving house. Remember when Lucius purchased it? No, I don't suppose you were old enough to remember. But when the workload has been heavy, Eleazar has been staying at Lucius' house. They have become good friends. Lucius has been like a second father to him."

She paused and smiled at Mary reassurringly. "Lucius has been paying our brother to work for him. Eleazar has worked his way up in the company since he was twelve. You were very little, and you were with me at home. But, when he was nine, he began going to the weaving house when Clio would let him; even before Lucius purchased it. And now, because Eleazar knows how to do everything in the house; from cleaning and combing, to spinning, to fixing the large looms. He can run the entire operation, and do it all well, now. Lucius told him a while back he is very useful in the trade.

"Lucius trusts him so much now, he has sent him on errands for trading; no caravans yet, but they are working on it. Eleazar says they can make more money if they have their own camels. Of late, Lucius has been allowing him to use the dye vats. And he is patient with the other workers, too. He is much like our mother was in that regard."

"I had no idea," Mary murmured.

Miriam continued. "He has much more experience than the workers Lucius first hired off the street, even though he is much younger. He is very skilled. Lucius told him it looks like they could head towards a partnership someday."

She covered her little sister's hand with her own. "Don't worry, Mary. Besides, Eleazar has also been putting his money away for good use. He and Abiel have had many long talks. He comes here occasionally, on his way to and from Jerusalem on business. He says his goal is to someday he redeem the family name. The last time he was here, he said he was planning to work some of the fields our father let become fallow. The vines have needed tending."

"I thought everything had been sold," Mary said, blankly.

Miriam rose to pour some water into their cups.

"Well, most everything *was* sold. Lucius bought the weaving house. Baruch, father's steward, had said he would continue to run things. Abiel even tried to help at one point. In fact, Baruch told Abiel he would oversee the vineyard and flocks until Eleazar was old enough to step into the position of ownership. I'm not sure how that worked exactly, though. Eleazar feels there is more to the story there, since father had already begun drinking at the time. It seems that one day, there was an iron lock on the door. You know, like the soldiers use. Father had been locked out of the warehouse. He was told that Baruch had been there late into the evening the night before. And, when he finally got into the building, everything was gone. The vats were still there; but the account scrolls, father's records, all the new wineskins they had filled; everything else was just gone."

"Does anyone else know what happened?" Mary was amazed that Baruch would have stolen from them.

Journey

"No, Abiel has even looked into it, and we have spoken with the Prefect. Abiel said he seemed a little evasive, though. There is so much corruption these days, he says there isn't much they can do, except give out Baruch's description, and keep looking for him. Eleazar is convinced he can get to the bottom of it, if he has enough time and resources. I keep hoping that Baruch had spoken with father, making some sort of agreement. Father just can't remember it. Now, a man who lives near the warehouse did tell us that at some point while it was just standing empty, a group of soldiers came and went through the building.

"Whose soldiers?" Mary wanted to know.

Miriam looked at her. "He said they were dressed like King Herod's guards, but I can't imagine why there would be a connection. The man said they were the ones who locked the building." She paused. "Oh well, at least father still has the house, and some land."

Miriam watched Mary for a moment, noticing how pale her sister had become.

Why had she not seen how thin she was until now?

She decided to change the subject.

"We want you to stay here, you know," she said. "Abiel has made plans to help you."

Mary said nothing. She looked down at her hands. "I don't know," was all that would come out. How could she tell Miriam what she was really thinking?

What if their father came looking for her?

She didn't sleep much that night, having slept most of the day. She lay awake, looking at the ceiling. At one point, she moved to the window, and looked out on the village scene around the stone house. Like her father, Abiel had built a house where the breezes would keep the inner portions of the home cool during the day. And, like her father, he had built a courtyard for Miriam, complete with a courtyard and cistern. He seemed so kind. So different from the picture in her mind of what men were like.

But… Was there something hidden in him that she didn't know about?

Was there a hidden darkness in him? Could he possibly be more like her father in those other ways as well?

Mary decided she wasn't sure she could trust him.

On the other hand, it was nice to be with Miriam.

Maybe she would stay a day or two.

～～～

In the end, she stayed more than five years. She learned to communicate well in all three languages, for all three were used at the clinic. Those who didn't speak Hebrew spoke Greek, and if they didn't know either of those languages, she could always use the marketplace language, Aramaic. Everyone spoke Aramaic, or they couldn't buy bread!

She learned to bandage wounds, and to listen to people's fears and concerns about their illnesses.

She and Miriam developed a deeper bond.

She learned to deliver babies! And to cook!

She even began to trust Abiel… a little.

Journey

Then, one day, Mary stood in the clinic, looking out the window into the portico. Suddenly, she saw a man coming down the street from the direction of EnKarem. Who was this? Her attention was drawn to the man, because she had come to know almost everyone in the village, but wasn't sure who the figure in question could be. Slowly, she felt herself come to a conscious awareness. She recognized his walk! Her father!

What was he doing here? Had he come after her after all this time?

What did he want?

Was Abiel tired of having her live there? Had he sent for her father to come and take her away?

The old, sickening, familiar terror rose up almost immediately as if from nowhere, and lodged itself somewhere in her throat. For a few moments she couldn't breathe, or even move. She was frozen in her stance at the window.

Then, willing herself to move, she stepped back from the window into the shadows.

No... he would see her there.

With a muffled moan, she put her hand to her mouth, and turned from the window. She had not been ready for these emotions to surface. Running to her room, she locked the door behind her. Still not sensing relief from the fears arising within, and feeling exposed and vulnerable, she huddled into the corner, pulling a blanket over her head.

Mary began to pray for death to come and take her away.

She would not go back to EnKarem.

She *could* not.

Several hours later, at suppertime, Miriam found her, still in the same position, still trembling, convinced her father was in the house somewhere.

As it turned out, the man had not been her father at all, but instead was a neighbor's grandfather, coming to visit for a birthday on the next street. Nevertheless, the experience had been enough to spur Mary towards a course of action. Over the next few days, she began to speak of making plans. Within two weeks, she had begun to pack all of her things, preparing to leave Miriam's house. After all, she reasoned, she was twenty now, and weren't most of the girls her age in the village married with at least one child?

She was a woman!!

She could take care of herself.

It was clear, she thought, she was not really out of harm's way with Abiel and Miriam anymore.

"Mary," her sister reasoned with her. "You don't have to leave. You're safe here, for as long as you want to stay."

"No." Mary had been firm in her decision. "I have to get away; as far away from him as I can. And I can't keep living on your and Abiel's charity. You have enough to do with the clinic and everything. And you will have children someday. No, if I am going to make a life for myself, I have to be the one to do it. I have to go."

Journey

Abiel had come to her room as she was folding her clothes, putting them into a neat pile. "I want you to be well taken care of, Mary. Miriam and I would take care of you as if you were our own child, even though you are our sister. We love you, you know. You don't have to run again."

Several days later, when her mind had still not changed, he had pressed a bag of coins into her hand. "I want you to take this. Consider it payment for all the days you have worked in the clinic. It will help you to buy food, lodging, or whatever you need. We will always have a place for you here, little sister," he said. "You don't have to be afraid."

On the day she was making ready to leave, her brother, Eleazar, came for what she assumed was a visit on his way to Jerusalem. He was leading a donkey. Surprised, Mary realized that Abiel and Miriam had sent for him.

There appeared to be a plan.

"If you must go," Eleazar said, "I'm taking you there. Father has no idea where you are, and I'm not sure he would remember if I told him. He's in a stupor much of the time these days."

They loaded the donkey with Mary's few belongings, among which were her satchel, her clothing, her blankets, a pillow, some new sandals, a couple of lamps, as well as food and water for her journey. She was amazed at how much Abiel and Miriam had given her.

Miriam was weeping. "Where will you go, Mary?" "When will you be back?"

For a moment, she remembered asking Clio the same questions, and Mama's face flashed in her mind.

"I don't know," she replied. "I just know I have to find a place where I won't look up and expect to see him coming after me. I need to find some peace." Her small frame was dwarfed next to the donkey.

"I'm afraid something will happen to you." Miriam pleaded. "Please stay here with us."

And although they knew, each within themselves, something would definitely happen if they let her go; they also accepted her insistence upon going. They *could* force her to stay, but that she would never really be happy or settled while with them. In fact, Abiel had told Miriam he was sure she would run away in the middle of the night, alone, if they did not help her to do things this way.

And not Abiel, Miriam, nor Eleazar, were willing to become black marks in Mary's memory. So, they had made a pact to seek to protect her in her choices, and to support her without seeking to control her.

"I'm going to introduce you to someone in Jerusalem, Mary," her brother told her. "He used to drive a caravan for our father. He knew our father when our mother was alive. He is much older now, and has changed some since those days, but he is still someone I think we can trust to help both of us; me to begin a new business venture, and you to find a new life. He has his own caravan now, and is willing to take us on as business partners on his trip to the North Country."

Mary couldn't believe it!! She would be cared for, and still be able to fulfill her heart's desire!! She hugged them all. She knew she was unaware of the amount of difficult

Journey

preparations that had been taken on her behalf. She just knew her family had taken steps to to protect her from potential dangers.

"Oh, thank you!! Thank you for everything! Really, don't worry about me."

Then she turned, preparing to walk away from her past, and everything she had ever known. All she wanted was a new beginning; to find a place where she could feel significant. Armed with only what the donkey could carry, Mary and her brother turned to go to Jerusalem.

"Lord God…. *ElRapha*, please protect her. Surround her and heal her." The voice was Abiel's. "Please, Lord,"

For a few moments of silence, the couple watched her go.

"I hope she realizes," Miriam said to her husband.

"Realizes what?" he asked.

"The picture of God you have been in her life."

"What does that mean, wife?"

"Well, neither she nor I have ever had a *real* father, have we? It dawned on me yesterday what your name means in our Hebrew language."

"Just now? I'm glad it means that much to you!" He poked her in her sides.

She giggled, and poked him back.

"Are you ready to go inside?" she asked. "I'll make you some tea."

"I don't want *tea*," he teased. "Are you kidding? We have an empty house!" They moved into the house to talk; to share their first real days alone since Mary's arrival more than eight years before.

And they were happy. The care for Mary had fulfilled something of purpose and design for both of them. Within their hearts, Abiel and Miriam each had an unspoken, and as yet not completely understood, realization of a special role they had played in a much larger story, to be unfolded in the days to come.

As Mary thought back over those days, she smiled at the deep awareness of the plan of Abba Father even then…. Abiel's name meant "God is My Father."

Migdal

The road to Jerusalem was filled with travelers.

Eleazar watched his little sister as they walked. It seemed like only yesterday they had played by the fountain in the house in EnKarem. How had they come to this? She seemed so small and frail to him; much like he remembered his mother. Mary's voice broke into his thought patterns.

"Where did all of these people come from? Where are they going? Is it always like this on the road?"

He smiled as he replied. "They are all going to Jerusalem for one purpose or another. And yes, it is always like this."

He walked observantly beside Mary, helping her to take in all of the new sights and sounds around her. Her fascination with this new phase of her life caught at his sense of adventure as well. So this was the outside world!! Wasn't it wonderful?

For a long while, they tried to watch the other people walking on the road with them, trying to imagine what their lives were like, and where they might be going. Several times, Mary thought she had put together pieces of family life, just from snatches of overheard conversation.

Twice, the two of them had been forced to rush to the side of the road in order to get out of the way of Roman soldiers coming quickly from behind them on horseback. The first time, there had been a warning. "Make way up there!" had been shouted, and then they had heard the galloping hooves coming quickly behind them. Eleazar had scooped her up and pulled their donkey to the side of the road in one quick movement, just as the soldier flew by them. The man did not seem to notice the fact there were travelers in the road. And, although Mary's brother had become used to this kind of thing happening before in his own travels, for her it was terrifying. With a heightened sense of intensity, Eleazar felt the need to protect his sister.

Wide-eyed and astounded, she looked at him.

Around them, others were also reeling, seeking to recover from the close encounter with disaster.

Eleazar began brushing the dust off of her shoulders, and then his own. "This is a good time to learn the most important lesson of all, if you are going to live in what is now a Roman world, Mary. That is, you must always give the Romans the right-of-way. We are considered the conquered race. Therefore, in their minds, we are second-class citizens. The only people who truly have rights in the empire are those who are Roman citizens. We have no value to them, compared to their duties or their enjoyment. That solider, for instance, was probably delivering a message for his superiors. If we get in his way, we are committing a crime."

"Oh," she said. Well, that was a feeling she was already used to nurturing. She could deal with that. She would just have to look at all Romans the same way she had seen her father, she decided.

The second highway encounter, there had been no warning shouted beforehand, at all! The only notice the travelers received were quickly approaching hoof-beats. Suddenly, horse and rider were almost upon them before they realized what was happening. In the rapid commotion, a rear hoof of the soldier's horse caught upon Mary's outer wrap and veil, tearing it as it yanked from her, just as Eleazar once again scooped her out of the way.

"Mary!" His reprimand was more to cover his own fear than to really scold her. "You must be careful to stay out of the way!!"

As the surprise of the event wore away, Mary began to weep. For the first time in her life, she understood the power of the Roman Empire to take life without regard.

Eleazar brushed off her shoulders, one again, to remove the dust. "There. Now, dry your eyes. We aren't the only ones who have met with disaster here." Indicating with his nod, he continued. "We need to help that old couple over there."

Mary moved dully with Eleazar. They approached an elderly, silver-haired man and his wife who were working to set their cart back upright. The man had a cut in his arm that was bleeding, which Mary began to tend to. Observing, she realized his wife looked somewhat shaken. As they told their story, she felt her heart go out to them. They were potters, and had been on their way to Jerusalem with a cart full of water-pots for sale. Just after passing Mary and Eleazar, the soldier's horse had overturned their small, hand-pulled wagon in the road, breaking most of the couple's wares. To make matters worse, the wagon had now lost a wheel.

Thankfully, no one had been killed, Mary thought.

The wife began weeping as she bent to pick up the shards of fired pots from the ground. Two other travelers stopped to join in the sad task. "Three weeks of work, and now there will be no income to show for it….," she paused. How will we pay the tax? How will we buy bread?"

No one said much in response. These were common happenings. Most of the population had discovered it was useless to protest. Those who did seek to demand justice in the courts of Rome were either ignored, or found "guilty" of a charge trumped up as a reaction by their opponent. Many times, even if a Jewish citizen were to find a fair-minded Prefect, the man would usually shrug, throw up his hands, and say something along the lines of "You can't expect anything else from the soldiers. They have a job to do. Stay out of their way."

That afternoon, many travelers who *weren't* Roman in the crowd, began to stop, give a word or two of comfort, and pick up the pieces of pots; they also worked to reload those wares that could still bring a price. A couple of the men, who had been privy to what had happened, began to work with Eleazar to fix the wagon wheel. It was obvious the couple was terribly poor, and that this had been a great loss for them.

Journey

How did things like this happen to people, Mary wondered?

Sometime in the mid-afternoon, Eleazar and his sister arrived in Jerusalem. Seeing a shady spot near a well, Mary suggested they sit and refresh themselves and talk and little while. Eleazar agreed, having anticipated she would have questions to ask him about this new adventure they had begun together. After drawing water, and serving Mary with a ladle, Eleazar sat down, and began pouring water over his own feet, seeking to bring coolness to the rest of his physical being.

"So, where are we going, brother?" she asked.

"To meet Ebenezer. He's a friend of mine who is here in Jerusalem on business at the moment," Eleazar was scrubbing away at the sand between his toes. "He is a caravan driver, and has offered to help me to rebuild our family's name. He is a good man, and I trust him. I think he will help us. He says he has a family home where you can stay in Migdal, until we have earned enough to buy you a house there."

As the afternoon progressed, Mary learned much about her brother and how he viewed the world. Eleazar seemed to have a plan for everything, and know just how things should turn out. They talked of Miriam and Abiel, both expressing how happy they were that the two had found each other. They talked about the years Mary had spent with them, acquiring the skills of the healing arts. Mary shared funny stories with him, and made him laugh. Then, she told him about the day she had thought she had seen their father coming down the road.

As Eleazar listened to her, his face went from relaxed and laughing, to a non-expressive mask without emotion at all. He asked her questions about what had happened in her relationship with their father, to bring things to the point where she had had to leave. Mary found herself sharing all of it with him, just as she had done with Miriam and Abiel.

When she was finished, there was a long silence.

Finally, Eleazar spoke.

"Father would never have taken a drink if our mother hadn't died, Mary. You have to believe that. It's the wine that made him this way. I remember when he used to play with us, without the anger. He was gentle, too. He would carry me on his shoulders, and take me to work with him. The man who came after you isn't our father. It's as though he has become someone else."

"But Eleazar, maybe that's so, but I don't ever remember him being any other way with me. *This* is the man I know. And what do I do with the *fear*? I lay awake at night sometimes, after a bad dream. I see things coming after me."

"What do you mean? Does he chase you in your dreams as well?"

"Not exactly. Sometimes it begins like that. Sometimes I might see myself folding the laundry in the courtyard, similar to how I did before I left home; then the scene changes. The dream begins with him coming after me. I see him rising from his seat, and moving in my direction. Then, when I look at him again, the face has changed. It first begins like his face, and then it changes to something else...." Her voice trailed off.

"Something else?"

Journey

"It's hard to describe, but it's like one of those creatures Clio used to tell us about when we were children. You know the one; half lizard, with wings, with dark skin. Its eyes have an angry light behind them. There are times when I see the teeth dripping blood, and it is coming after me like it wants to eat me alive. The claws are awful. Sometimes there are more than one of them, and they speak like a man, but the voices are muddled, and deep. What's more is that when it overtakes me, I feel like I did when I hid in the corner all day when I was little. No one came.

"Afterward, I lie in the bed in the darkness, and can't move. It's like a dark cloud fills my room. Sometimes I think I'm going to choke, and I can't speak or breathe. In the one last night, my feet were stuck. I couldn't even run away."

Eleazar was silent for a few moments, contemplating her confession. Mary watched him.

"I've never told this to anyone else," she said.

The boy ran his hand over his sister's back and drew her close in a comforting embrace. "You have to forgive him," he said, in a matter-of-fact voice.

Mary pushed her hand against his chest, drawing back. "Excuse me?"

"This is all happening because you have hatred in your heart. You have to move on with your life. Listen to me. These things are coming to you because you have beckoned them with your behaviors. I have gone to the synagogue. I know what the rabbis say about this kind of thing.

"You have to stop holding on to this idea that our father has so wronged you. You know he would never have tried to touch you if he hadn't been drunk with grief. He loved our mother, and he got you confused with her in his mind. That's all. It's not that large of an issue. The wine did that. He didn't know what he was doing. Just let it go."

Mary was silent, listening to Eleazar talk about their father in these terms. The son couldn't seem to remember the ugly things. Was her brother really telling her that her fears, her confusion, and her pain were her own fault? She considered. Hadn't their father told her that she was the reason her mother died? Those were the only things Mary remembered knowing.

It was almost like she was listening to Miriam, Mary thought, although Miriam had never blamed her father's drinking. Miriam had just questioned Mary's memory of the events. After all, Miriam reasoned, Mary had never known their mother, or seen her effect upon their father. So, Miriam had tried to fill in the gaps in Mary's memory by providing the younger sister a picture of their father, built to suit Miriam's own memory, creating an alternate father image; one who didn't live the way the elder Eleazar was living now. Miriam had always seen their father as a victim; losing the wife he loved the most.

Miriam had been caring of Mary, but hadn't fully understood or even allowed herself to believe Mary's pain.

"He wouldn't ever do anything like that in his right mind, Mary," she had said one afternoon in the clinic. "Are you sure? Didn't you misunderstand his intentions? Isn't it all something you contrived because of a misunderstanding?" she remembered Miriam stroking her arm when she had spoken.

Journey

Was this what serving their God demanded? Blame and denial? Did He really expect them to lie to themselves and others, about things that really happened?

What about reality? What then was she supposed to do with the Pain? Her innocence was gone. It had fled long ago. Were they telling her it didn't matter now?

Eleazar was speaking to her. "Mary?"

"I'm sorry, I was thinking about something else. What did you say?"

"I said, 'Move on, Mary. Life is too short for you to be so bitter at such a young age. This couldn't have been as bad as you think it was. Just forgive him and live your life. Go on with things. You don't have to move away, you know. It's not really as bad as all that."

As Mary listened to her brother that afternoon, her decision to leave became even more cemented in her mind. Yes, Eleazar and Miriam were kind to her, but how could they say they really loved her if they didn't really *believe* her? Didn't they know their refusal to see her pain stopped her from being able to get free from it all? She was so weary. How *could* she just "let it go?"

What would she put in its place?

It wasn't like she had some "perfect picture" to remember, like they apparently did. Didn't they realize what her father had done to her?

She shuddered. Why was it that every time she closed her eyes, she could still smell his putrid breath, and see his yellow teeth and bloodshot eyes? Would those images ever go away?

Perhaps, she reasoned, her brother and sister just had to shut away their own pain, to create their own places to feel safe. Maybe their own grief was so great; they couldn't take on hers as well.

Her final thoughts were not that far from the truth.

If Mary had been able to see into her brother's heart that afternoon, she would have seen a young man seeking to make his way without the leadership or closeness of any father at all; numb, and without direction, realizing that the example he had seen in the older Eleazar was simply an inverted model for manhood;

What *not* to do, who *not* to be, how *not* to behave…

The problem remained: What example does a young man follow if the only lessons he has learned are the lessons of what *not* to do?

Eleazar's self-substituted father, Lucius, who now owned the family's weaving house, was more ideal, and the boy had built him up in his mind to be a man who could do no wrong. Lucius had told him he was to be a man soon; but the younger Eleazar felt lost. How could he be a man, when the closest picture of manhood in his life had failed so miserably?

Mary would have been surprised to see the young boy-child inside the shell of her brother's frame; waiting for recognition, searching for significance; in a world that moved on around him, ignoring his needs, communicating expectations, preoccupied with its own pursuits.

Journey

No, Eleazar did not possess the skills to even come close to empathizing with his little sister that day. He was still searching for his own identity, thinking if he just made the right plans; if he just kept moving toward his own goals; he would succeed.

Without emotional tools, he kept saying, "I will prove myself."

Mary was numb, struggling with her own inner issues; seeking comfort, and finding none. She felt her life would be different if she could just escape all of the memories; the fears and inner threatening terrorizing her mind and heart at night; the expectations of the people she loved.

There had to be a safer place.

Anywhere.

What she needed was a new beginning.

Somewhere; where people didn't look at her and see the mother she had never known. Somewhere; where the look in their eyes didn't change to pity when they recognized her. Somewhere; where she could allow her heart to open up and relax, without constantly looking over her shoulder. Somewhere; where the next man coming down the road would see her for her own self, and not as the cause of their world's ills.

A place without the knot in her stomach – fearing – *him;*

A place where her soul could stretch and breathe;

A place without nightmares….

Sitting by the well with Eleazar that day, Mary had solidified her choices. She would never allow her heart to be wounded again. She would take the reins. She would make things happen. She would take care of herself; without a need for anyone.

Ever.

After all, hadn't Abiel told her she carried strength beyond her years? She would show them. They would see. She would be so successful; they would never question her memory again.

This was the moment to take control of her life.

In the end, Eleazar *had* proven to have a plan; a really promising plan, full of potential to seal their expectations.

By the time they had purchased their lunch from a vendor, sitting in a courtyard outside, Mary became amazed at her brother's ability to see into the future. He had planned for every detail, she thought to herself. As she listened, it became evident he had outlined ambitious preparations for business; having received advice and counsel from those he respected. Eleazar had been working on setting up a trading network for months.

Today it would all begin.

Excitedly, he explained. They were traveling to Migdal in Galilee, and would be living there for a short time, just to get on their feet. Migdal was a village on the shores of the Sea of Galilee, or Lake Tiberias as the Romans called it. The city was named for the tower in the center of town. Literally meaning, "the place where the fish is salted," the more modern Migdal had become the central location for trading. Caravans from the trade routes stopped there for the uniquely preserved fish from the Sea of Galilee.

Journey

The plan was to set up a system of trade, utilizing the network Eleazar had developed; hopefully to earn enough silver to fund the refurbishing and re-establishing of their family properties.

Over the past year, his employer had also sought to help him. Rather than pay him just in coin for his work in the weaving house, Lucius had divided payment. Woven linen and wool had been laid aside as payment for the young man's work alongside him, put into storage until he was ready.

It was a simple plan, really; to trade dyed linen and woolen goods for salted fish; bringing the meat from the north country in Galilee, to the more developed areas in the south. Eleazar would travel with Ebenezer's caravan, conducting trade with other merchants as they moved along.

As for their personal needs, the fabrics from the weaving house would provide clothing for them, he said, and the fish would provide food. They could purchase bread. The only element the plan lacked was shelter; and Ebenezer had already promised they could stay in his family's home in Migdal. The house he offered them even had its own spring-fed well and courtyard!

After all, widowed long ago, the old man told him, he was never there; always on the road. Someone really should live in the house.

The plan was perfect. Eleazar had worked out every detail. Mary began to see her brother with new eyes. This could work! This could really work *well*!

On the way, they would stop at the fishing villages on the shores of the Sea of Galilee, reminding the fishermen and tradesmen of their plans, inviting business partnerships. Ebenezer had already agreed to take their wares onto his caravan, in exchange for a small commission.

When Mary met Ebenezer, the deeply etched, wizened face of the old man had broken into a broad smile. "Oh my," he chuckled, "if I didn't know better, I would think your name was Rachel; you look so much like your mother!" His rough hands had grabbed hers. "You will be a sweet presence in my home in Migdal. It will keep the thieves away. We will help each other." He hugged her. "Agreed?"

It was Ebenezer who had described to her the day her father had left the family warehouse in town to run through the streets, hurrying home on the day of her birth. His caravan had been in Jerusalem, settling accounts with her father and Baruch that day. Ebenezer had even watched her father run out the door, without even a head-dress to protect his head in the hot sun.

From the moment he greeted her, Mary decided she liked him.

And so they began, this unlikely pair; seeking to make a way for themselves in a world they didn't know or understand. Armed only with their mutual desire to have a better life, and with the optimistic oblivion of youth, they started their endeavor.

Traveling from Jerusalem to the north, there were three roads a trader could follow. The "Via Maris," as the Romans called it, connected Egypt to Jerusalem, and led down to the coast of the Mediterranean Sea. This road was used by those travelers and traders coming from nations across the sea. In ancient days of Israel, when God's Judges had governed the land, the road had been referred to as the "Way of the Philistines," because the road had been used as a means of conquest, controlling Israel's accesses to the sea, and to the food the waters provided.

Should traders desire to stay inland, they could take the "Hill Road," which moved along the ridges of the surrounding mountains, and went by EnKarem, and through Bethlehem. The Hill Road connected the northern and southern areas of the country, and was well used.

Leaving Jerusalem, the road descended quickly into the valley, and could be extremely dangerous. The short distance between Jerusalem and Jericho was especially treacherous, having been named "The Valley of the Shadow of Death." It was an area where thieves and brigands lay in wait for those who travelled alone. As a result, just outside the city, a loosely-knit group of retired soldiers and mercenaries waited for those who were taking the road alone, needing protection. Hiring themselves out as guides, these men made quite a living keeping the short patch of road free of unpleasant surprises. It was a well publicized fact that the safest journey from Jerusalem to Jericho was one made in a group, in the protection of daylight.

The third road outlined the border of the nation between Jordan and Israel. Called the "King's Highway," it was a well developed inland trade route, and had been used by various rulers for centuries. Traders carrying silk and spices came from lands as far away as distant Persia, and India, vying their expensive wares with the most prosperous of the citizenry.

The King's Highway was Israel's connection with other cultures outside of her own.

Working their way up the Via Maris, or, as Ebenezer referred to it, "The Coastal Road," Mary and Eleazar were reminded once again of the multiplicity of languages being spoken in their day. Unwilling to make changes to adapt to yet another conqueror, many of the Jewish travelers still referred to the Via Maris as "Derech El Yam," while some of the villages they traveled through simply referred to it as "The Way of the Sea."

As she walked with Eleazar, Mary soon learned not to assume she knew where those who traveled with them had originated from. Since the road connected the trade routes from the Fertile Crescent, Arabia, Mesopotamia, Phoenicia, and even Africa with this new part of the Roman Empire, people from all regions of the known world came to enjoy the landscape, sample the culture, and satisfy their curiosity.

Anyone who wanted to go anywhere traveled on the Coastal Road. It was considered the "road to everywhere."

The first step in setting up the business had been hard work. First, they had visited each of the fishing villages on the shores of the Sea of Galilee, renewing Eleazar's connections with fishermen and tradesmen in the North Country. They had also made a few new friends. Inviting those they met into trade agreements, settling upon a price, and making arrangements for trade; all had taken time.

In the end, the journey to Migdal had taken almost two months.

Journey

When they finally arrived at Ebenezer's home, Mary found she was thankful for the chance to stay in one place for more than two days at a time; and in a house too!! No more sleeping outdoors in a tent! She had walls surrounding her!

The rooftop of the house could be accessed at night by the outside stairs leading upward. Ebenezer quickly set up his sleeping mat in the vine covered arbor area on the roof. He wanted to be able to see the stars, he said. This was where he desired to sleep.

"Besides," he explained, "the house reminds me too much of my late wife. Sometimes, just being in those rooms hurts my heart."

It was sad, Mary considered. The couple had never been able to conceive children.

In the back of the house, Eleazar found a field and a storage area. This was where Ebenezer kept his camels.

And, after two months of journeying with the wretched animals, Mary had developed her own opinion about them. They were such dirty creatures; smelly and mean!! Ebenezer called them a necessary inconvenience, and had even developed relationships with them. Perhaps, she thought, men were more suited to working with the enormous beasts. If she was truly honest about it, they scared her; especially knowing they could kill a man with one bite when they had a mind to.

As the days passed, Mary busied herself setting up housekeeping; cleaning, organizing, arranging. In the end, the largest room in the house was apportioned for storage and selling of fabrics. While Ebenezer had chosen the arbor on the roof as his hide-away, her brother, Eleazar decided to sleep close to the front door, in order to maintain security. The central bedchamber was given to Mary. It was much more than she had ever expected to receive for her usage. She quickly set up her belongings.

"You really do need the largest sleeping room, Mary. You will be the one staying here in the long run," Eleazar had told her.

As she unpacked, she came upon the small and fragile stone bottle of spikenard her father had given to her. It was her only possession of value. She placed it in the center of the table in her room. "It really is beautiful," she reasoned. "And it is the only item of value I own. It doesn't have to remind me of my mother. I can decide. I will let it remind me of the money Eleazar and I want to earn. It will remind me who I can become in business. I will make something of myself."

She had resolved to shut her past behind her, beginning her life in earnest from that point forward. But, without realizing it, she had repeated her father's words from years before. The imprinting and patterns of her past were continuing to dictate her belief system and her goals.

Mary was unaware. Her past was a part of her being.

She had brought it with her.

~~~

Not long after their arrival, Ebenezer went with Eleazar on a trip to an out-lying village to purchase a donkey and a wagon. The best wagon wheels in the region were said to be crafted by a craftsman just a day's journey away. Eleazar was convinced a wagon was the next item needed for their trade business. So, making sure details were covered, hiring one of the neighbors to care for the camels; the two men left early one morning.

On her first night alone in her new life, Mary was visited by yet another nightmare. This time, the images came in color, with colors so vivid; she could not shake them in her waking hours. As before, the images began in the old home in EnKarem, with her father pursuing her. But, this night, the events took a darker turn. For the first time in this recurring nightmare, Mary looked down. As she tried to pull away, retreating from her blood-thirsty attacker, she saw behind her heels the edge of a deep pit, black and empty. Sounds of weeping and screams of torment surrounded her. This time, as the open-mouthed image of the reptile-like creature descended upon her, she instinctively stepped back, and began to fall. She grabbed the edge of the cliff surrounding her abyss, and struggled to pull herself back up to the surface. As she did, large, black snakes began to coil themselves around her feet, pulling her downward.

Trying to scream, she found herself unable to breathe; choking. Terrified, Mary awoke, gagging and coughing, sweat drenching her bed-dress and night covering. Captivated by the pounding silence; unsure of her safety in the darkness; alone, she clutched her bedclothes to her, watching desperately for the first streaks of light to appear with the breaking of the dawn.

That morning when the sun arose, Mary leapt from her bed, and began inventing chores to keep herself busy. She didn't sleep again until after her brother arrived home.

Two days later, Eleazar found her in the garden upon his arrival, still working.

"Mary, where are you?" he called as he and Ebenezer entered the house.

"I'm in the back," she called, "just planting some vegetables."

Eleazar stopped at the back door, watching her. Ebenezer stood behind him with his hands on his hips. As soon as they saw her, they began laughing. "Look at you! You have dirt all over you! For that tiny little patch of ground? How does anyone *get* so dirty!"

Mary paused and looked up at them. Brushing her hair away from her face with the back of her hand, she giggled. She looked down. Her feet were almost black. She felt like a child. "It's fun!" was all she said good naturedly.

Convinced he would not understand; afraid he would blame her for her pain; Mary determined to lock away and ignore her weaknesses. She watched her brother as he joked with their friend.

Yes, it was better to just leave it all alone, she reasoned. Making a silent decision, she resolved to try to bury her fears, and never again to mention to Eleazar her nighttime torment.

Migdal was unlike the other fishing villages nestled near the mountains on the shores of the Sea of Galilee. Located in the Valley of the Doves, the city was a center for commercial trade; sprawling under the cooling shadows of Mount Arbel, which carried a brutal and colorful history. The town was remembered as the site of violent executions in times long past. The mountain's peak was visible from every town, village and settlement, on the shores of the small sea. The shoreline was so densely populated; it was difficult to find a free patch of sand at all! Even on the Roman side of the Lake, where the Gadara wilderness met patchy pasture, farmers and herdsmen worked as closely as was physically possible to the freshwater source.

Because the Sea of Galilee was fed not only by the Jordan river, but also by mineral hot springs, it was rumored that the Ten Cities on the western side of the Sea were as much like modern Rome as possible, complete with bath-houses needing no water drawn to them, and Greek temples with fountains filled automatically by water bubbling up from under the earth..

Mary had never seen such wonders; but she wanted to. Someday, she thought, she would venture north, to see the temples and shrines built to the gods at Panias. The temple to Pan must really be something to see!!

Mount Arbel was the landmark for traders and merchants seeking fine linen goods. Pastures of flax, grown in the valleys around Migdal, were harvested and brought by slaves to the processing houses on the mountain, called *Arbela*. It was said the finest linen in the land was woven at Arbela. Only the best was good enough for the temple priests in Jerusalem.

Years prior, the caravan driver, Ebenezer, had decided to locate his home in this town for good reason. Firstly, the village served as the juncture for two of the trade routes; the Via Maris and the Hill Road. Secondly, it was a convenient place to stop in the midst of his caravan travels, since he would never need to leave the main roads.

Migdal was the agricultural, trading and fishing center of the area.

Long ago, when it had gone by another name, a forgotten conqueror had built himself a tower in the center of town. It was remembered as a landmark for the area's dominated fishermen to bring fish they had netted as tax payment. It was during those years of antiquity, salting and preserving the fish for trade and travel had begun.

Now, in Mary's day, the conqueror and his taxes were a memory, but the practices attached to the tower remained. Migdal had taken the tower's identity as its own. These days, the town's tower was used not only to mark the fish salting and storage facility, but also to provide a lookout for the security of the town. A group of area fishermen, working in cooperation with each other, manned the tower as a watchman's post. They gave pre-warning to the townspeople should there be impending danger. Working three or six hour shifts, these men were well-known and respected for miles around.

As she grew familiar with her new surroundings, Mary made observations.

Migdal had a completely different feel from her EnKarem home, Mary reasoned. The town was much more... what was it? Busy? Yes. Modern? Yes. But there was something else too. Something in the air she couldn't put her finger on.

The town had its own atmosphere; what was the reason for the difference, she wondered? Was it just the nearness to water? No, she didn't think so. Was it cultural? Perhaps; but it was indefinable to her.

What would it be like to live here, now, she wondered?

Journey

It seemed from the day Eleazar acquired the wagon, he set himself into a pattern of continual hard labor. In fact, if Mary remembered correctly, their relationship changed from that point forward.

Most days before dawn, the young man would load his wagon to leave for the fishing villages on the shores of the Sea of Galilee. He would travel from Migdal with woolen goods as his main fare, along with inexpensive pots, lamps and baskets, for which he had traded in the more developed town's marketplace. Arriving at the smaller settlements along the southern border of the Sea of Galilee, he would begin trading for freshly caught fish, or selling his wares for coin. As Eleazar made his way back, the wagon would fill with fish, and empty of his other wares. Every three or four days or so, he would deliver the fish to the tower, where they were salted, preserved and prepared for a journey with Ebenezer's caravan.

Once a month or so, Ebenezer would load his caravan, and work his way to the southern country close to Jerusalem, his camels loaded with preserved fish and other articles he had gathered in his trade route travels. He would sell the fish, and then trade with Lucius for more linen and wool.

Sometimes, he was able to trade wool for the more expensive, finer linen at Mount Arbel, taking those goods back to the temple in Jerusalem. Every third month or so, upon his return, Ebenezer would bring Lucius' goods from the weaving house, along with the monies from selling goods back to the center of their operations in Migdal.

Occasionally, the caravan would bring her gifts from Lucius and Abiel.

One of Mary's favorite items, Ebenezer brought her, was a smooth and sleek tunic, dyed purple, with stitching and beadwork on its hem. It had come all the way from Persia; a delicate new fabric, called "silk." Mary loved to run it over her hands, enjoying the way it felt on her skin when she wore it.

"Ebenezer, we could sell this as raw goods to the women in Migdal, and even in Jerusalem," she told him. "Lucius could dye it. It could be sold for a high price. It might even interest Roman and Phoenician women as well."

"I'll see what I can do," he replied, smiling, watching Mary as she turned one way and then another, watching the light change in warmth and hue, causing the tunic shimmer.

True to his word, on the next journey, Ebenezer brought two camels laden with raw woven silk.

Even Lucius was pleased.

"You're quite a business woman, Mary." He told her on his next visit to the North Country, settling accounts with Eleazar. He had begun a "silk fund" just for her.

For a season, Eleazar lived in Ebenezer's house with Mary, helping her get on her feet, and into the routine of running a business. Mary was glad to have something to do. It kept her mind off of her nightmares, and helped her to maintain a resolve to look forward.

Surprisingly, over time, the three realized just how great the demand for the fresh-water fish from Galilee actually was. Unexpectedly, the fish were considered somewhat of a delicacy! Little by little the business grew, taking in greater and greater stretches of territory.

Journey

The daily trade journeys to the villages on the shores of the Sea of Galilee began to demand more days on the road for Eleazar. He began to be away for longer and longer stretches of time. Eventually, their small company was able to hire a man to meet Eleazar on the road, taking back more goods from the villages to Migdal.

Then, the owners of the Migdal tower had learned of Eleazar's connections with the villages and tradesmen in the south. They had approached him with an offer of a trading contract. As the trade business grew, they were able to add a room or two to Ebenezer's house, expanding their storage areas even more.

In due course, the threesome was able to take on a steward to replace Eleazar in his trade tasks each day. The provision came in the form of a man named Joseph; a middle-aged, married man with a wife and two small daughters. Having been the victim of thieves between Jerusalem and Jericho, Joseph had survived the wounds from his attackers, and felt the need to move his family out of Jerusalem for safety. Still owing Eleazar a large sum, the two men agreed that Joseph would move to Migdal, moving into one of the older, empty homes from the town's southern side.

Eleazar would purchase the home for him. According to the ancient custom, Joseph agreed to serve as an indentured servant without pay, working off his debt for seven years. Eleazar and Mary would supply his clothing, food, and shelter.

The night they had struck the bargain, Eleazar had come home with gifts for celebration. "I will be able to take some of the load from you now, Mary. God is blessing us! I can handle this end of things, and you will be able to not work so hard."

"I *like* working, Eleazar," she protested. "It makes me feel useful. It gives me a purpose."

But then, just as the young entrepreneur thought he would be able to take his ease for a time, his partner, Ebenezer began to experience a failing in his health. The old man found his limbs weak and aching after a cough settled into his chest. His strength began ebbing away earlier and earlier each day.

No longer able to make the long journeys alone, the aged trader began to ask Eleazar to travel with him, learning to take the helm; as Ebenezer gradually went on the road less and less.

Mary and Eleazar slowly became aware their old friend was requiring more rest to strengthen and heal from the pains in his body these days. His body must be wearing out, Mary reasoned.

For his part, Eleazar found himself on a new learning curve, acquiring new skills to take lead in the caravan. He even learned to water and groom the camels!

Then, had come the heartrending day Ebenezer died.

Mary had been making bread in the outside kitchen, and realized that it was midday. She had not seen or heard their comrade stir. Checking on him, she found him in a sleeping position. He was sleeping so much these days, she thought.

She walked away again, continuing to be hushed in consideration.

It had not become evident to her the man had died in his sleep until the next day.

The neighbors had come to bury him.

Journey

She had not wept at his death. She wondered why she felt nothing. He had been such a kind man; so sweet to her and her brother. What was wrong with her, she wondered? Everyone *else* at the burial had wept…

Ebenezer had told them everything he left behind was theirs. He had no heirs; no debt. He had planned to do this, Mary realized. Over time, he had melded all of his accounts in with Eleazar's and Mary's.

He had held no secrets from them.

Mary was grateful, and realized she now had a home of her own.

He had even given them the camels.

Why did the inheritance have to include those horrible creatures, she thought? What was wrong with donkeys?

And what was wrong with her she couldn't seem to appreciate what they provided through trade?

The night of Ebenezer's burial, she saw him in her sleep. A twisted version of the man's face appeared in the pit below her feet. "You caused me to die," it said. "You left me, just like you caused your family to fall apart. You are rebellious. You deserve to die." And this time in the nightmare, when the snakes coiled around her feet, she saw and felt Ebenezer's hands with them, pulling her into the murky darkness. "Come, Mary. You can't escape. You belong to us now. No one else wants you."

She awoke with a start, and stumbled into the living area. With moonlight as a guide, she made her way outside to the woodpile. Using a stick, she lit a lamp and brought it back to her bedchamber. She vowed to never sleep in the dark again.

Two days after Ebenezer's death, a man named Alia came to the door. A trader from the south, he was an attractive man. He stayed in the house for hours, just talking to her. Mary loved watching his eyes dance. She was fascinated by the way he looked at her. There had been something charming about his smile, she thought. At some point during the conversation, it occurred to Mary that if she kept him there, she wouldn't be alone.

So, she invited him to stay to share a meal with her. After dinner, he told her he had missed the opportunity to acquire a room at the inn in town.

Without thinking, Mary invited him to stay in Eleazar's room.

Alia had stayed for several days. Mary felt comforted to have someone in the house during her brother's absence. It had never occurred to her the man might have ideas about her intentions outside of friendship.

Then, the second night during his stay, she had another nightmare. Once again, she awoke in a full sweat, screaming for someone to rescue her. The poor man had come to her door out of concern, and had received more than he bargained for. Like a frightened child, Mary begged him to just hold her, to comfort her, to keep her safe.

Nothing more, in particular, happened that night. As the days wore on, and Alia continued to stay, Mary found herself drawn to him. After all, she reasoned, she didn't have nightmares when he was lying next to her. And didn't he deserve something for comforting her and protecting her?

She began to give herself to him.

From the first, the two of them went everywhere together. How she loved sitting by the sea with him, looking for the glimmers of light shining through the open windows of homes on the shore across the water.

Mary once again felt safe and protected.

It was long before Alia told her he wouldn't be able to stay. It had surprised and hurt Mary when he told her he had a family.

Why had he slept with her and spoken words of love, when already *had* a wife, she asked herself?

Then, he told her he would have to leave soon.

Several weeks later, when Eleazar came home, Alia paid for his wares, and left to return to his home.

She never saw him again.

Although she was alone, it was strange, she thought, shouldn't she feel something? Shouldn't she be sad he was gone? Perhaps she was numb, but she had made a discovery.

For the time being, at least, it was true; no nightmares came when she had someone sleeping in her bed. She felt comforted, and no longer alone.

Hadn't Clio told her that the sexual act was an expression of the gods? Perhaps this was a sign. Yes, that was it. It was the way of the gods to give her freedom from her torment.

Thinking about it, Mary couldn't remember how many men had followed Alia in her life, or how she ended up becoming paid for sexual favors. All she knew was that when she had someone with her, she was comforted. When she was alone, the night visions became darker and increasingly terrifying.

Eleazar was now living closer to Jerusalem, spending half of his time in the family home, and the rest with Miriam and Abiel in their village. It was good for him to rest from journeying. His choice did make, Mary reasoned. After all, all the trade routes to the distant regions crossed in Jerusalem.

Why would Eleazar come all the way to Migdal if he didn't need to?

As a result, Mary became resolved to live alone. She would take care of herself.

Perhaps her father had been right, after all. Perhaps she really *was* destined to be rejected; a woman who should never have been born at all.

Gradually, she began to realize her lifestyle had counted her out of being considered eligible to marry a responsible man, or even the chance to be accepted in neighborhood relationships, especially with women of her own age.

She began referring to herself as "damaged goods."

From time to time, she thought about her relationship with her father.

"If I hadn't sat by him when he called me, all of this wouldn't have happened," she told herself.

"If only I didn't look like my mother;"

"I should have fixed my hair differently."

"My nightmares must be the judgment of the gods on my life."

Journey

"All of this pain is my own fault."
"Perhaps there *is* a mark on me."
"I have no value."
"I'm not worth someone choosing and taking time to know me."
"I wish I could change things, but it's hopeless."
"Perhaps Eleazar was right. I caused it all. I should have just forgiven him."
"But it's too late now. This is all I deserve."
Such were the thoughts in Mary's mind; the words she spoke to herself.

Over time, she became known in the community as a woman who would do anything to please a man's appetite; as though a bonus came with the wool, silk, and fish trade.

Women avoided her; men sought and craved her; religious people judged and ostracized her; only the Greeks and Romans in the area accepted her.

She became known simply as Mary, the Mistress at Migdal, or Magdala, as it was referred to in regions beyond Galilee.

A little more than a hundred miles away to the south, in a little village on the slope of a hill close to Jerusalem, Miriam and Abiel continued to provide medical care for anyone and everyone who came to their clinic. Known simply as "Bethany," or "House of the Poor and Afflicted," the town was a final dwelling place for the infirm, outcasts and misfits from the general populace in the entire region of Judea.

As ones who were poor, sick, and many times unable to pay for medical care, those who lived in the village knew it as a place of resignation; a place where people were who were waiting to die sat in vigil.

Some fortunate few were blessed to have the company of their family, or friends who had been willing to move to the village with them, many times to provide full-time tending. Some had been born in the village, to ill family members, had grown into adulthood and chosen to stay. For this reason, Abiel and Miriam's patients varied in degrees of sickness, and a full spectrum of conditions was certainly on hand to keep the couple busy.

Although there were several others in and near the village of Bethany who offered help in the healing arts, Abiel and Miriam were the only ones who didn't ply the usage of incantations, potions or fortunetelling. For most medics of the day, those spiritual practices were combined with drug usage.

Drug usage for pain management was common. One such practice, common throughout all of the empire, was the placing of a plant known as "cannabis" into a water-filled, lidded clay pot. Heating the pot over a fire, the *pharmakia*, apothecary, or medic, would wait until the smoke and steam from the plant and water filled the pot. Clients would then insert a hollow reed through holes punched in the pot, inhaling until a sense of well-being was induced. In the midst of the cannabis-induced high, the medic would introduce a spell, incantation, or potion, which did little more than create more fear and despair in those who came for care.

In fact, many of those who suffered with great pain, would spend day after day, seeking more and more of the euphoric effect brought by the cannabis plant. A similar practice was followed with elements of the poppy flowers, although they were difficult to grow in the region, making the drug accessible only to the very rich.

So common was the practice of "drinking smoke;" in many cities in the region, merchants had made a business of utilizing everything from rosemary to tobacco, even adding infused oils to the water for flavor. Patrons would pay to sample the newest flavor of smoke available.

Abiel and Miriam's medical practice was far more practical, however. Abiel's family had seen to it that their son was well educated in the beliefs and studies of Hippocrates. They had paid for his education in regard to the structure of the human body, and its systems. He had a far-reaching knowledge of the use of plants, teas, herbs and salves. He understood which medicines encouraged healing in the specific ailments of his patients.

Though it saddened him, Abiel realized for some of his patients, there could be no cure. Some diseases were not understood well enough yet for a cure to be known. As a result, some things had to be trusted into the hands of God, he told those in his care.

And many times, he prayed for his patients, asking the Creator of all for a miracle.

Over time, Abiel became known as a man who cared as much for the emotional condition of his patients as he did for their physical needs. Always practical, Miriam's ability to teach those in her care was sought out and quoted far and wide.

Although the couple tried for years, they were never able to have a child. Twice, in their early years together, Miriam had broken the news to her husband she was with child. Abiel had rejoiced and celebrated with her.

But both times, just as the baby was beginning to change the shape of Miriam's body, early labor pains had come. After two miscarriages, the couple had become reconciled in their inability to bear children.

It had been a good day when Eleazar decided to make their home in Bethany his base of operation, Miriam reasoned. It was good to have her brother with her again. When he was in the house, Abiel laughed more.

In fact, they *all* laughed more.

What was it about having Eleazar around the house that made the atmosphere come alive? What helped her to feel more connected and at peace with the world?

Journey

Prologue 2

Upper Room – Jerusalem
29 CE
Day Forty-Six

In the corner of the Essene Great Room, Simon was waking up a few feet from Zebedee. He and Abigail had placed their sleeping pallets close to their old friends. The four of them had lain awake, speaking softly into the wee hours of the morning. As he awakened, Simon realized the two men's wives had heard kitchen noises downstairs, and had gone outside to help prepare the morning meal. Opening his eyes, he noticed Zebedee stirring as well.

"Good morning, my brother," Simon patted the older man's arm. "Did you sleep well?"

"It's like sleeping on a ship," the older man good-naturedly commented. "I should have packed the cushions for these old hips and knees."

Simon smiled. He agreed with his friend. In fact, his own back was somewhat stiff this morning as well. Slowly moving to stand, the younger man stretched. "I'm going to go for a walk to work out some of my stiffness. Would you like to join me?"

Rising to a sitting position, Zebedee shook his head. "Perhaps I will do that later. For now, I want to find my sons. We haven't been able to speak alone since the Master sent us back here." He grunted and groaned; his knees crackling loudly as he made the effort to stand as well. "Salome and I just need to regroup with our boys. Thank you for the invitation, though. I appreciate it. How about we walk after breakfast?"

Simon was standing, putting on his outer wrap and sandals.

"That's fine. I'll see you."

"Don't miss the fish. Food is always better when it's hot."

"I know, I know. I just need a quiet corner, and I thought a walk would do the trick."

Simon stepped carefully through the crowded room. As he did so, his eyes caught Mary's. She and her sister were deep in discussion. "Good morning, ladies," he whispered as he tiptoed past them toward the single door marking the exit from the Great Room. Beginning his descent of the steps into the courtyard below, he caught sight of his wife, Abigail. He stopped to look at her face. She was so pretty when she smiled, even now in their days of age and change.

Behind him, Zebedee was scanning the room to look for James and John, his sons. There they were, in the corner, with Peter and Andrew. That was good, he thought. Those boys had always been his extended sons as well. He would join them. He moved to the corner, trying not to disturb those who were still trying to sleep in the early morning hours.

On his way across the room, another voice greeted him. "Zebedee, did you happen to notice where see where my little sister went?" Looking down, the old fisherman recognized one of the young Roman women from Capernaum. Her father had been unable to wait with

Journey

them, due to his centurion duties at the garrison. "Little Helena is somewhere with Mistress Abigail," he told her.

"Thank you. I just woke up and she wasn't here. I think I'll go and look for her."

"If you feel you need to; but I'm sure she'll be back soon," Zebedee reassured her. Helena's mother, Julia, had asked Zebedee and Salome to watch over her children during their time in Jerusalem. What good friends Justus and Julia had proven to be, the old man considered. Roman by birth, Justus was a rich man, and had been responsible for almost single-handedly funding the building of the synagogue in Capernaum.

The old fisherman smiled.

Justus had been one of the first among them to recognize the Master for who He really was.

How strange, Zebedee thought; Elohim had shown Himself time and again to choose, speak, and draw to Himself those who saw themselves as outsiders. It seemed to be His plan to ignore the predictable. Well, He was the Author of creativity.

Besides, when had God's ways ever been easy to predict?

"Good morning, father," John greeted his father. "Come join us. We were just sharing memories of the Master."

"Good. That's good," the older man whispered, as he sat down with them. Looking at James and John, he smiled. "Your mother and I were speaking last night. We need to have some time together with you boys during the day today."

The brothers looked at their father. How much he had changed in the past two years! "Let's plan on it, father," James replied. "We want to speak with you as well. Peter was just bringing us up to date on a couple of things."

The five men continued in conversation, as they continued to wait for the Master's Promise.

Simon had paused at the foot of the outside stairs. What was that music? His Abigail was singing! How he loved the sound of her voice. What was the song? He didn't recognize it.

Her voice had such a beautiful, comforting effect.

For a few moments, he forgot he had been headed to take a walk.

Sensing his eyes upon her, Abigail turned. She saw him and smiled. "Good morning, sweetheart," she said. "Did I wake you?"

"No," he said. It was difficult for him to put all of his feelings into words. He was still just discovering that part of himself. How could he tell her all he had been thinking the past few days? When would there be time? What words could he use to express the long- stored-away emotions he had never allowed himself to admit feeling?

All he said was, "I awoke on my own. I think I need to go for a walk this morning." He kissed her cheek. "Thank you for all you do, Abby... all the time."

"It's my joy, my love. Have a good walk."

As Simon moved away from the outdoor kitchen area, his heart and mind were suddenly flooded with a host of memories. The last time she sang was... yes, that was it....

Oh it was good to be free! So good! How had they come to this place?

So much had happened in the last three years. As he walked, Simon remembered.

In the room above him, Zebedee and his sons were also remembering.....

Journey

"Semichah"

Simon loved living in Capernaum. It was so different from his father's home in Jerusalem. The view of the Sea each morning was spectacular. It was amazing, he thought to himself. From any vantage point on the Sea of Galilee shore where one chose to stand, you could see most of the other villages situated by the Sea. It was said that more than 200,000 people had positioned their lives close to the lake.

Most mornings, as he waited for the fishermen to arrive with their nightly catch, he could watch the homes on the shore, even as far as the city of Tiberias to the south and the village of Bethsaida to the east; as the servants and women of the villages rose to light their window lamps. One at a time, each tiny dot of light would emerge before the sun rose, converging to twinkle like the stars; then, slowly fading as the great orb of light in the sky rose higher and higher to rule the day. The power of light to travel across the darkness was still something that amazed him. Where did the darkness really go, he wondered?

Simon loved spending time in the pre-dawn quiet. It provided a good moment to muse upon the thoughts of God, or to work out a particularly puzzling portion of the Torah or the prophets. It was a good time to pray, as he waited to fulfill his rabbinical duties. Each day, except for the Sabbath, of course, Simon waited for the boats to return to the shore. Every morning, he would pray a blessing over each boat's daily catch before it was traded or sold. A prayer, he believed, would continue the generosity of God. So, Simon saw himself as a vital link in the chain of God's provision. Without his blessing and prayer, the prosperity of his village would fail.

Simon loved his God. From the time he was a small boy, he knew he was destined to lead. His father served on the Great Sanhedrin, as one of the Great Sages of Jerusalem, meeting daily in the Court of the Hewn Stones on the Temple Mount in Jerusalem.

When Simon had seen the Inner Chamber and touched the great stones for the first time as a boy, he had stood in wide-eyed wonder at their size. One stone was a large as his entire house! His father's mentor, the great Hillel, had taken him aside to explain the reason for the room's choice as the Council's meeting room.

"Those Hewn Stones are foundation stones that have remained, my boy; placed by Solomon himself. We may come and go, but they remain." It was said, and Simon agreed, the foundation stones spoke of the power of God in continuing to rule and to judge His people. What a great joy, Simon reasoned, to be chosen to share in understanding the judgments of God! Hadn't his father told him the family could link their origins as far back as before the Babylonian captivity? What a blessing to be so honored; a reputation no one could dispute, even his wife told him so!

Simon loved his wife. Born to one of the priestly families in Jerusalem, Abigail could also trace her family's heritage. Didn't her father have a scroll, linking her bloodline back to that of Aaron himself? Imagine! Surely the blessing of God was on his marriage, and would rest even more strongly upon his children!

She was a good wife, he considered, always working about the house diligently; always cleaning; always teaching the children. It would be a fine day when their young sons would begin studies in the town's synagogue school, and then later at the Great Temple with their grandfather.

Simon smiled as he thought about his daughters. Abigail was already teaching each of them the basics of how to care for a home. Even Deborah, the littlest one, could knead the bread, at five! Not given to dilly-dallying, as she put it, his wife took no time for foolish talk or silly games. No, she was given to soberness and careful notice of the laws of Moses, as she should be. Doubly veiling each of their girls before they ventured to the marketplace, the woman was formidable when striking a bargain. There was no need to hire a household steward! Abigail had things well in hand.

Simon loved being a man. What a high privilege he had been afforded because of his gender. Daily, he reminded himself of the Law's provision, just because he had been born a *man* of Israel. A *man* could understand the Law, and could be taught to read and write. A *man* could enter into discussions in the marketplace. A *man* could go anywhere, anytime he chose. A *man* was the true, first created image of God; therefore his thoughts were more like those of God.

A *man* was given to rule. To be a *man* elevated him to status above every woman he saw; at least under Jewish Law. It was forbidden to speak to a woman other than his wife. Who would want to, anyway, he reasoned; especially considering the nature of the more "enlightened" women who were showing up in the empire these days….. They were so deceived!

Simon stopped.

Come to think of it, what about the men who *allowed* their women to conduct themselves in such ways? Didn't they realize that the way a man's property behaved was a reflection upon the man himself? Didn't they realize the protection and blessing of the Law; of his God?

Yes, he thought. It was good that the Oral Torah had decreed that he should not even allow his robes to touch such people.

Justice would show itself, he was sure.

Yes, he considered, that was pleasing to God.

God was just; *truly* just.

God was holy; *most* holy.

Only holiness could help a man attain to the resurrection of the dead.

And Simon wanted to live forever.

Journey

Most of all, *Simon loved being a Pharisee*. What better lifestyle could a man ask for? Why, the very name "Pharisee" meant "separated one." Just to be accepted as part of the sect placed him in a long line of holy men and powerful figures!

To rule a synagogue had always been his dream! Even from the time he was a boy, playing in the streets of Jerusalem, Simon had wanted to be a part of this group; the men set apart as pious keepers and interpreters of God's Laws.

Earnestly, he had listened in his younger years, along with the neighborhood children, to the stories of the kings and prophets when his mother had taught as the Storyteller in his neighborhood. He could still remember her telling of the miracles of Elijah and Elisha. He still was awed by her accounting of the day when Balaam's donkey spoke. His mother was a remarkable woman......

Yes, his home had been his place of learning until his thirteenth birthday. On that day, the celebration of his entrance into manhood had been celebrated in a huge way. Surrounded by his family and friends; there had been so much festivity....

Even now, he could remember the smile on his father's face as he placed the *tallit*, or fringed prayer shawl, over his son's head.

"From now on, you will come to the synagogue and temple with me, my son," his father had told him. Simon loved the years of schooling that followed with his father, observing the good-natured arguments between the Pharisees and the Sadducees; sitting quietly in the corners with other sons and rabbinical students, as the Sages contemplated the meaning of the Torah, translating its implications for daily living.

It amazed him how the tradition of seventy-one men meeting together as a governing body had been able to continue since the captivity. Based on the number of elders chosen by Moses, the group consisted of both Sadducees and Pharisees, who came to seventy in number. The assembly was officiated over by the High Priest, bringing the number to seventy-one. Originally, the high priests had been descendants of Aaron. But sadly, the Levite priests had ceased to seek God. Simon remembered the history from his classes in rabbinical school. Under the Seleucid conqueror, Antiochus Ephiphanes, the high priest had been appointed as a political office. Then, the office had become a ruling, royal office under Judas Maccabee, whose descendents were known as the Hasmoneans.

It was an enigma, Simon considered.

How could a spiritual office, ordained by God, become a political one?

As long as Simon could remember, the high priest had been appointed by the Roman Prefect. And, even though many of the men on the council tried to maintain a spiritual demeanor, the shadow of Rome was always in the Court.

Still, the traditions had continued. He smiled; so did the arguments.

Simon remembered observing a conflict between the two great sages, Hillel and Shammai, during his first week at the Temple with his father. A man who was not Jewish, a gentile, came before Shammai, requesting to convert to Judaism.

"I will even stand on one foot while you convert me, master," the man said. In a sudden flash of anger Simon had not understood at the time, Shammai picked up a long measuring stick and chased the would-be convert from the Judgment Hall. On retreating hastily from the room, the disappointed and rejected man ran into Hillel, who asked what the matter was. "I wanted to convert to your religion, but Master Shammai does not think I am worthy, master," the man told him.

Hillel converted the man on the spot.

When the inevitable resulting conflict erupted in the Sanhedrin that afternoon, Shammai was insulted Hillel had granted the gentile's request, telling the older man he felt upstaged. Hillel just smiled at him.

"Do not do to a fellow man the thing that would be hateful to you." He had looked at the students in the corners of the room. "Is that not what the Torah teaches us?" He looked down at his angry counterpart. "Go and learn." He motioned as if to shoo Shammai out of his way, and moved into the center of the room. He had then delivered a discourse on forbearance and its place in the Torah.

Even the Sadducees had been impressed.

Simon was proud of the fact that Hillel was his distant cousin. From that day forward, the students had coined a phrase: "It is better to be patient and humble like Hillel than to be passionate and rude like Shammai." Yet, in his heart of hearts, Simon had agreed with Shammai that day. As he contemplated what he had witnessed, he discovered his deepest feelings. Shammai's approach had actually been better when he weighed the matter.

Yes, it was better to keep the religion pure.

"Greet everyone with a cheerful countenance, but always maintain clear boundaries," His father told him. Didn't that mean in religious matters as well, Simon thought? Yes, some things were better kept to oneself.

He remembered the day when he completed his rabbinical training. His ceremony was one to remember forever, so sealed was its picture in his mind. The men he had admired for so long had laid their hands upon him, separating him into their number. It had been his day of ordination. He still could hear their blessings and intonations over his choice as a life pursuit. He was now *semichah,* meaning "offered to and supported by God." It meant he was now ordained to serve as one of them; a judge and leader in Israel. Such work had gone into his position; such diligent labor!

Hadn't Shammai even congratulated him that day?

They placed the robes of his office upon him, and strapped the specially crafted phylacteries to his forehead and arm. The small boxes contained tiny parchments with the Laws of Moses written upon them. With these strapped to his body, it was said he would never forget the keep the Law.

What joy had filled his heart!!

Had that really been more than twenty years ago?

Surely time had not moved so quickly!

Simon loved being a Pharisee. He loved wearing the robes and tassels. He prized expressing his knowledge in the synagogue. He treasured helping the people understand the nature of God – he prized the teachings; the Oral traditions were just as important as the

Journey

written Torah of Moses. And there were so many laws; so many things people just didn't understand.

How privileged he was to be one of the few who really understood……

How could he describe the feelings of importance he sensed within himself when he walked through the marketplace? What words could be used to express his gratitude for the respect and awe with which he was viewed in the community?

It was good to be valuable; more valuable than the untouchables in the marketplace; Valuable to God …….And powerful …

When would the common people realize the rules really mattered to God?

Simon felt he had earned his place by his deeds. It was good to be respected, perhaps even feared a little. Well, isn't that what the fathers taught kept the balance of the universe?

Surely he had a special place in the heart of God; so sincere he was in his efforts.

Yes, *Simon loved living in Capernaum*. Even though it was considerably smaller than Jerusalem, the former capital, Capernaum had many modern conveniences. He loved the sense of importance his heritage provided him in this smaller community. As was the case with each synagogue, even in occupied Israel, a twenty-three-man lesser Sanhedrin served to keep the law. This lesser Sanhedrin was a smaller version of the seventy-one member Great Sanhedrin in Jerusalem's Temple. It was Simon's office to rule the lesser Sanhedrin in Capernaum. And he had students of his own now…… This group of dedicated men met each day in the synagogue, to discuss the Torah, and to pass judgment on civil and criminal cases in regard to religious matters.

It had only been a year since the Roman emperor had revoked any Sanhedrin's authority, Lesser or Greater, to try, sentence, and execute criminals. Up until that time, Simon had been allowed to follow the laws of stoning and judgment without seeking prior approval.

It had only been fifteen years since the death of Hillel. That had been the same year the Roman Prefect, Valerius Gratus, had appointed Joseph Caiaphas as high priest over the Great Sanhedrin in Jerusalem. The swiftness of the appointment had taken the breath of the Great Sages away. How did such a man gain the role of ruler in their religious order? Amazed, the body of the Sanhedrin began to pull apart a little, segregating into several splinters of belief and discussion. Was there anywhere truly safe, some of the older scribes had whispered?

It appeared Caiaphas had powerful and influential friends in Rome.

Simon smiled. He and Joseph had known each other a long time. And yes, it was true. Joseph could be something of an unfeeling man; making sure his plans were accomplished. But hadn't the man given God credit for raising him to power and position?

Simon's father told him it was rumored that Caiaphas regularly sent emissaries to Rome, just to keep tabs on the new prefect now ruling Palestine, a man named Pontius Pilate.

Although he tried hard not to let it show, it secretly bothered Simon, as it did most Jewish leaders in his rank and station, to be stripped of the ability to take action against those who were destroying the morals and fiber of his nation. Surely, he thought, the people were better off when the religious leaders were in control; less rabble in the streets; less perversion; less influence of the pagan gods and goddesses of the Greeks and Romans.

Journey

As most Pharisees, Simon avoided being touched by those placed in his care. It was his belief he existed to be an example of God to the people; to make the laws; to pass judgment upon the guilty; to carry out executions. As such, he was called to a higher place of living; he was to be observed and admired, but kept out of reach; a symbol of the unattainable qualities of holiness and purity demanded by God.

"Who can ascend to the hill of the Lord," he quoted King David's psalm to himself, "he who has clean hands and a pure heart." Surely, Simon thought, his hands and heart were purer than anyone else he knew.

Simon raised his hand to shield his eyes from the brightness of the rising sun. Why did the sunlight seem to hurt his eyes these days? Perhaps it was the strong reflection on the water, he reasoned. Were the fishermen coming in late this morning? He had not noticed the time, so caught up had he been in his reverie.

Ah, there was the first of Zebedee's boats. He greeted his friend.

"Good morning, old friend," he called across the water. Zebedee stood in the midst of his craft, bringing in the sail. He waved back at Simon.

"Good morning, Rabbi. It's always good to see you. It lets me know we are in for the blessing of the Lord, blessed be His name."

"Blessed be His name." Simon habitually kissed his fingertips, and then touched the phylactery on his forehead. "How did you fare last evening?"

"We did well, even if my sons were not with me. We caught enough to pay the bills."

"God is good."

"Yes," the older man sighed wearily, "God is good."

Simon looked sideways at his friend. Zebedee's face was deeply lined, as were most of those who fished the Lake; weathered by wind and rain, heat and cold. A wave of admiration swept over him. "You have worked hard to build your business."

"It's true. It's true. I never thought we would be able to build the home we have built, or be able to trade the way we have. I just…" the old man's voice trailed off as he stepped into the water to pull his boat ashore.

"You don't seem yourself this morning," Simon spoke, quietly wishing he could walk away and not have to listen to the man's woes and concerns first thing in the morning. When could he find a place of peace that would last longer than the few moments he had experienced on the shore?

"I miss my wife and sons. I thought they would have been home by now."

"The races again?" Simon referred to the Hippodrome in Caesarea Philippi, where the weekly chariot races were held. Coastal site of the famous aqueduct and Greek theater, it was a well known gambling spot for young men in the empire who had been influenced by the Roman culture. Zebedee's sons, James and John, had earned a reputation for living their lives on the wilder side.

"No, not this time; they went to a wedding with their mother. I don't know, actually. I had *thought* they were settling down a little. I had thought we were going to begin building the business. What if I am left to work alone; once more?" Zebedee sighed, tying the boat to an iron stake driven into the ground. He began to help his employees pull wet fishing nets from the boat; loading the night's harvest of fish into baskets, sorting out the saleable fish from the unusable. The blemished fish would be given to the poor or ground up to be sold as fertilizer to nearby farmers.

"It looks like to you did well." Simon was trying to redirect the conversation. Perhaps he could help Zebedee to give thanks and not complain so much. "You certainly must be blessed by the Lord."

The old man muttered to himself. "Blessed... yes, I suppose I am." He looked up at the rabbi. "Tell me, master, in your trade as a godly man; what will you do if your sons don't want to become religious men? What do you do when your sons walk away from everything you have tried to give them?"

Simon was a little taken back by the question. He hadn't ever considered the possibility. And why would he tell his deep concerns to this laborer? He spoke quickly, without thinking.

"That won't be an option for *my* sons. It is their plan, and their destiny. It is *God's* plan."

"You see, that's what I thought as well. But it seems they have their *own* ideas of what life should look life."

"What do you mean, Zebedee?"

"Lately, they have been talking to some of their fishermen friends from Bethsaida. Several weeks ago, when it was our town's turn to take the watch shifts at the Migdal tower, they shared a few days with their boyhood friends, Simon and Andrew, the sons of Jonas. They have this idea that they want to see what is happening with a prophet in the south, near Jericho."

"Nothing bad could come from a true prophet, Zebedee."

"So you say."

Simon had not heard of the prophet. "Tell me," he said. "What prophet?" Surely if the man was a viable prophet, Simon thought, his father would have sent him word.

A prophet in these days? That would be something to investigate.

"His name is 'John.' He is baptizing in the Jordan River. Apparently, many are being reminded to return to the ways of our fathers. He has garnered quite a following."

"What do you know?"

"From what I hear, the man wears camel hair. He eats locusts and wild honey. He has come out of the desert areas, probably from Qumran. He has the spirit of Elijah, they say."

"Any miracles?" Simon knew from his classes the test of a true prophet was the supernatural; a miracle.

"I don't know."

"Well, Zebedee, I wouldn't worry. From what you say, they don't appear to be gambling anymore, or frequenting the marketplace with the tax collectors and gentile unbelievers. They will come around. You must purpose to take hope, and keep praying,"

Zebedee could tell he was being put off. Perhaps it was as his wife, Salome, had expressed. It was better to only talk about the surface things of life with this religious man.

"Yes, yes. Did you come to bless our catch?"

Journey

Relieved to be coming to the end of a difficult subject, Simon nodded. Raising his hands over the boats, he shouted for everyone to hear, "Blessed are You, God of the Universe, who brings forth fish from the sea! We offer our labors to you as our worship! Hear, O Israel, the Lord our God, the Lord is One!"

In monotone unison, the fishermen responded, "The Lord is One!"

Simon turned to walk away. How could he infuse more enthusiasm into the fishermen, he wondered? Perhaps if he used the names of God, and reminded them of His qualities, the men would become more devout. Perhaps his practices had become too predictable.

He decided he would begin using the names of God in his prayers from that point onward: *ElShaddai*, the God who covers; *Elohim*, the Great and Only God; *ElJireh*, the God who provides; *Adonai*, the Master who is a Friend; *ElRapha*, the Healing God. He made a mental note to research those names. That would do the trick, he was sure.

Walking by the Roman garrison, he pondered his words with Zebedee; poor man. Well, it was a mark of the days they were living in, he reasoned. The fisherman had worked hard his entire life, only to see his sons leave him alone in the midst of the family business. Simon knew the man's sons. Hadn't he even warned his own boys to be careful around them? They were known for their boisterous and angry manners, their base language, and their free thinking. They must have been overly influenced by their mother, he reasoned. Where else could the seeds of deception have come from within them? No, James and John hadn't earned the name 'Sons of Thunder' for nothing.

That evening, the Pharisee made sure to pull his sons aside and warn them once again against keeping company with Zebedee's sons. He would have to work harder to protect them; to insure their future. What was the answer, he wondered? How could a man gain the meat and bread he needed for his household in this world, without sullying his soul with the likes of the common folk?

Making sure to observe Zebedee's home, Simon found the next few days eventful.

Just before Sabbath, the he observed James and John coming into town in with a group who appeared to be travelling together.

"It's just like those boys to bring friends into town, on the Sabbath evening," the rabbi told his wife in somber confidence. "Where will their mother find food for all of those people at this late hour?" Then he had praised his Abigail for being such a good planner, like the wife of King David of old.

How good it was to be of those whose family kept the whole Law.

~~~

The mood was more jovial at Zebedee's house. It was a time of celebration. Not only had Salome, James and John returned home, but they had brought with them sons of some old friends, who were on their way to the village of Bethsaida. Well, there was plenty of time before sundown to put a meal together. Let them come. Let them all come! He wanted to hear what path his sons were taking in their lives.

Salome told him the wedding had been beautiful. It was a pity he hadn't felt he could leave the business to the workers for a few days. The countryside had been striking this time

Journey

of year. The rains had caused so many colors to bloom. There had been so much to see. There was so much to share.

Could they find a quiet moment alone together later?

Who were all these people, Zebedee wanted to know? He knew Simon and Andrew, and Joanna, their mother.

Who were these other people? Why had they been so delayed?

Didn't Salome realize he would be concerned about them? Hadn't the boys thought about his concerns in the midst of their activities? It seemed they had made a stop at one of the homes of those travelling with them on the way. Sorry to worry you, father; again. They had lost track of the time; again.

Well, he thought, the zeal of youth; again.

It was due to the excitement of the happenings around them. They didn't *mean* to be irresponsible, Zebedee reasoned. They were just impulsive and young.

But now they had their mother involved in their behaviors...

What would the rabbis say? What would the Pharisee say?

He would discuss it with them later; the fruit of their actions....

As the evening progressed, Zebedee's heart began to relax a little. There was something about having people in the house that softened his hard exterior. For some unexplainable reason, he felt none of the inner conflict he had anticipated in seeing them all arrive home. He even thought he might be at peace about their lack of participation in the fishing business. Why? He couldn't tell. Although no one brought the subject up in conversation, as the hours passed, so did his fears. It had been a long time since Zebedee had seen the boys laugh so hard, as they told stories of their exploits and episodes of the past few weeks.

They were returning from the same wedding in Cana, and had come, bringing their friends with them. One of the boys, Philip, was a new acquaintance. Apparently, he was also from Bethsaida, and had travelled to the wedding with Simon and Andrew. Zebedee assumed the rest of the group would complete their journeys after the Sabbath tomorrow. In order to keep the Law, Salome had invited them to rest overnight. Always willing to have his home filled with family and friends, Zebedee had given his boys his permission to invite their friends for the evening meal.

Yes, he thought, it was good to have them home again.

It was also good to see Jonas and Joanna's boys again. How long had it been since Simon's wedding? That had been the last time his old friend and partner had come to Capernaum; to gather Simon's bride. Simon had married a local girl, whose family lived just across town. Zebedee couldn't remember.... No matter....

Sitting in the kitchen courtyard, the weary fisherman observed.

Salome was working with Joanna to prepare the meal for all of them, but there was a third woman also. She had offered to help almost immediately upon walking in the door. That was good, too, he felt. Salome didn't need to prepare a meal for the entire group by herself, even though she would have done it willingly. The servants were all in their own

Journey

homes for the Sabbath. Both of his daughters were married, living elsewhere, preparing meals for their own families.

Who was this woman? Zebedee hadn't learned her name yet. It seemed she was the mother of the three other young men also stopping in their home for the night. James had told him this group had also been at the wedding. They had all left Cana at the same time; the women had begun talking during the journey. On the way they all had been invited to stop at home of this group in Nazareth.

What were their names again? Justus, James, Joseph?... And her name was... He would ask Salome when they were alone again.

The woman's oldest son was getting ready to leave home. It seemed that in talking together in the midst of the journey, the boy had communicated he was planning to set up his trade in the Galilee area. So, he, his mother, and his brothers had continued travelling, to help him in the process. It was a sign of a healthy family, Zebedee supposed; everyone wanting to be a part of the decision.

What about Bethsaida? Simon and Andrew had suggested.

What about Migdal? It was a central location for trade.

What about Capernaum? That had been James and John's invitation.

Well, no matter the outcome, all of these people were here for the night, Zebedee thought. Perhaps I can convince Simon and Andrew to go to the in-laws house later, when it comes time to roll out the pallets for sleeping.

But the night became late before Zebedee could speak to Jonas' boys. Sitting on the cushions by the table, he rubbed his eyes. Not long after supper, the woman and her sons had excused themselves, going to retire on the roof. Peter and Andrew had stayed to renew their old acquaintances.

Salome had thanked him for allowing all of them to stay. It was comforting to have young people in the house once again, she said. Zebedee agreed, and found himself listening to their discussion.

"So, Simon," James was saying, "How do you think it happened?"

Simon chuckled. "I'm not exactly sure. All I know is that he told the steward to fill all six of the purification water-pots with water. When they drew the water out of the pots, it had turned into wine. How does that happen?"

"*Which* pots?" Salome asked.

James looked at his mother. "Oh, those 35 gallon things that we use when someone has to take a ritual cleansing bath."

"All *six* of them? I saw them lined up against the wall outside. You mean they drew water to fill them *all*?" Salome asked.

"All of them. It took the servants a couple of hours to do the task." John added. "I watched. After they were filled, no one did anything to them, or even touched them but the servants. And all that went into the pots was the water. It seems they had run out of wine pretty early on in the wedding celebration."

Journey

"That would be a catastrophe," Zebedee put in, having provided weddings for his two daughters.

"It was, and they weren't sure what they were going to do," Simon continued with the story. "Mary, his mother, said, 'Do whatever he tells you to do.' And when they asked *him*, he looked at her and said, 'It isn't time yet. What are you doing?' Then he told the servants to draw the water."

"What did he mean by that, Simon? Time for what?"

Zebedee found himself suddenly alert in the midst of his weariness. "Who is this man, John? Why would they do what he told them to?" He asked his son.

"Is he a rabbi?" his mother asked, with a probing look.

"Simon and Andrew know more than we do, mother," John answered.

"Boys?" Changing her focus, she looked at them.

Salome really wanted an answer, Simon realized. He had seen that look many times when she had caught him and Andrew throwing rocks into their well as children.

Simon took a breath before answering. He was still putting pieces together in his own mind, so he spoke slowly. "Close to three months ago, Andrew and I were in Jerusalem, making some trade arrangements, and we met with a friend who sells olive oil from his grove close to the Mount of Olives. He was late harvesting, because he had been spending so much time out in the desert listening to the prophet John, the Baptizer. He took us to hear him. What a fire must burn in the bones of that man!"

"You do you remember us telling you about John, the desert prophet?" Andrew asked them, taking a breath. "He is the one who has been calling people to change their ways; to come back to the understanding that there is only one God. Almost all of Jerusalem has gone out to see him at one time or another. He also had been telling the crowds that his job is not to be *the* prophet, but to prepare the way of the Lord. He said, 'I baptize you with water, but the one who is coming after me will baptize with fire. I am not worthy to even touch his sandals, he is so great.'

"There came a moment in the middle of his message when he just stopped speaking. A man, *this* man, came and stood on the banks of the river, asking to be baptized. At first John said 'no,' telling him that *he* wanted to be baptized *himself* by this man."

Simon interrupted. "But then, he stepped into the water, and told John that if John would baptize him, it would fulfill righteousness."

"What did he mean by that?" Zebedee asked.

"I'm not sure," Andrew continued. "It's almost as though what he was doing was deliberate, like he was following instructions or something. Anyway, when he came up out of the water, the sky opened up. This bright light shone down on him."

"And out of nowhere, a white dove emerged from the middle of the light and descended on him," Peter interjected. "It hovered over his head, and then just disappeared."

Zebedee and Salome exchanged glances. Was it possible? Could this be the beginning of the fulfillment of Promises?

Journey

"And there's something else," Simon stopped, looking at Andrew. "You tell them. You were close enough to hear it. I wasn't."

Andrew smiled and nodded.

Zebedee probed him. "What did you hear, boy?"

Andrew paused. "I heard a voice, a man's voice, coming out of the middle of the bright light. He said, 'this is my beloved Son, and I am greatly pleased with him."

An electrifying sense of awe sent a rush of awareness through each of them. This had been no ordinary moment.

"What is this man's name, John?" Salome asked her son.

"Jesus," her son answered. "Jesus of Nazareth. Andrew spoke with him after he left the water."

"You did?"

Andrew smiled. "I just asked him where he was staying. He invited us to come and see. So we visited his room at the inn in Jerusalem. The next day he was gone. We ran into him again at the wedding."

"And he is the one who turned the water into wine." Zebedee's words were more of a statement than a question.

"Yes, sir," his boys answered in chorus.

In the early morning hours, Zebedee rose. He never had been able to sleep past the dawn. Perhaps it was because his body had become accustomed to rising in the middle of the night to fish; perhaps it was because he had felt a stirring within himself during the evening's conversation; perhaps it was due to the snoring of the family's visitors – whatever the cause, he found himself sitting at the water's edge, thinking about the events of the day before.

He didn't remember how long he had been sitting there, watching the water lap against the boats; listening to the soft sounds of the insects. It had been a gradual awareness that came upon him.

Someone had joined him, and was sitting next to him. How had he not heard their approach?

Looking to his right, Zebedee recognized the young man who had come with his sons; the one whom they had credited with turning water into wine; the one whom Andrew had told him had known his brother's name without even being introduced; the one the bright light had shined upon in the Jordan River.

"Jesus isn't it?" the old man spoke quietly.

"Yes, that's my name." The voice was deep and strong, but without any edge to it. "And your name is Zebedee?"

The old man nodded. "You didn't say much at dinner."

"It was so good just to listen to the conversation," the young man responded. "I've always loved to hear people laugh."

"We do a lot of it in my house, Jesus. Some things you just *have* to laugh at, because it takes too much energy to worry or to cry. It's best just to keep moving; keep working. You

Journey

know what I mean?" The older man spoke; more to feel out the younger man's values, than to make conversation.

For a long time they had talked together.

Zebedee wondered how such a young man could have so much wisdom and understanding. Surely he was a prophet, or at the least had been to rabbinical school. But no, Jesus said, he had lived in Nazareth and had learned the trade of a carpenter from his mother's husband, Joseph, before he died.

Apparently, the boy had experienced grief and sorrow, even in his few years.

Zebedee decided he liked this man; this Jesus. For a quick moment he wondered what purpose God Almighty might have in placing a carpenter in the paths of his sons' lives at this time. How would their relationship with this man affect their future?

They sat together silently for a few moments, taking in the starlit view. Finally, the older man spoke. "Is it true that you turned water into wine?"

Jesus laughed. "Well, I've always thought that a wedding should be a celebration. It is the beginning of something new." He paused, looking out over the water. "Besides, it has always been Father's plan that Life have a little flavor."

Zebedee smiled in response, and the two of them waited to watch the sunrise.

On the first day of the week, Philip, Andrew and Simon left for Bethsaida. Considering Zebedee's concern over his family's lateness in arriving home, Simon realized a need to be more communicative with his own father. Besides, he explained, his wife and children would be missing him as well. He was heading home, and would be working diligently to make up the income lost in his absence. Philip and Andrew, on the other hand, had discussed another option. They would be returning the next day with supplies for a longer period spent on the road. They had asked permission to travel with Jesus and his brothers to Nazareth, and then join the family in Jerusalem for the feast next month. They would then travel back home together.

The old fisherman smiled. He remembered days when his own energy levels were high; and the craving for adventures would emerge in the spring. The fervor of youth was wonderful....

Philip would make arrangements for his wife and six daughters. Always having been one to plan ahead, their family had put savings aside for just such a season.

Andrew had expressed feeling compelled to discover what would happen next.

As he listened to the growing passion in the younger men around him, Zebedee took note. What was happening? He felt an unexplainable sense of deep anticipation. Surely this was the mark of a new season in the timings of God.

Surprisingly, Zebedee thought, it was his own son John who had asked to go with them as well, and not James. James, being older, had decided he had already left his father to work alone too much of the time. It was a noble choice, Zebedee considered; one that Simon the Pharisee would applaud. Still, the old man thought, if this Jesus *was* sent from God, wouldn't it have been a better choice for both of his sons to garner understanding of things that were truly spiritual, and not just full of tradition?

He did to admit, however, he did appreciate the help; and it was a wonderful surprise and blessing to see his oldest son willing to step up and become responsible. How long would it last?

Perhaps it was time to release more responsibility to the family steward. He would have to give this more thought.

Was this inner nudge a sign of something he needed to prepare for, he wondered?

For the next couple of days, Jesus' family stayed at Zebedee's invitation, waiting for Philip and Andrew to return. During this time, the young man and his brothers scouted the area for a house that could be fixed up, and repaired well enough to facilitate setting up his trade in Capernaum. Simon visited his wife's parents across town.

Zebedee once again took the boats to fish.

During their stay, Mary and Salome became good friends, as women who share common years of living do; discovering many areas of comparison simply because they were both the mothers of sons. In the few days they spent together, Salome found herself confiding and sharing her heart with Mary. For some unknown reason, she felt a sense of safety with this soft-spoken, gentle woman.

Rather than speaking her mind in order to gain the upper hand, as was usually her custom, Salome found herself easily trusting and looking forward to building a friendship. It was funny how some people could evoke a different response, she considered, simply because of their demeanor......

From his perch a few houses away, Simon the Pharisee sat on the roof of his own home, watching with interest. As ruling priest of the town's lesser Sanhedrin, he took careful notice of the comings and goings at Zebedee's home. He was certain the boys were up to no good. Zebedee and Salome could be deeply wounded. What if those frequenting their home were criminals, or worse, he thought?

Subtly, he also questioned the fishermen who worked for the family. Who were these people? What was going on? It was his job to keep track of the happenings of those under his charge.

Maintaining the purity of his people's faith was his passion.

Just before evening on the next Sabbath, Philip and Andrew returned to Capernaum with a third man. Had Jonas's Simon changed his mind? No, as they came closer into view, the Pharisee saw it was someone he didn't recognize. Sending his servant to discover the answer, the priest learned the man's name was Nathaniel.

Simon's servant was amazed by what he had overheard.

Hopeful, but not sure whether he would be invited to travel with the group, Nathaniel had positioned himself under a fig tree behind Zebedee's home. Philip and Andrew had greeted everyone, and then apparently realized Nathaniel had stayed outside. Simon's servant saw Philip gather Nathaniel into the group, and heard Jesus greet the young man.

"Nathaniel, there is nothing devious or cunning about *you!*" Jesus said, upon meeting him.

"How do you know me?" Nathaniel asked.

Jesus looked into his eyes. "Before Philip called you, when you were under the fig tree, I saw you," was the answer.

"I didn't tell him anything," Philip said to Nathaniel.

"Teacher, you must be the Son of God!" Nathaniel said to Jesus.

Jesus laughed. "*That's* all it takes to help you to believe; just because I told you that I saw you under the fig tree?" he asked. "Listen, you're about to see much greater things than *that* happen. You will see angels, ascending and descending on the Son of Man."

When the servant returned, Simon listened intently. The Son of Man, the Pharisee questioned. What did that mean? Was this man calling himself a prophet? Or worse, was this another hoax, a patriot pretending to be the Promised Deliverer? Would there be another uprising?

As soon as Jesus and his party left town, Simon began investigating for himself.

Over the next few days, he retraced each step Jesus and his brothers had taken during their visit, asking direct questions, and making discoveries.

Who did this young upstart think he was? Was he just a rebel trying to stir up trouble?

Or was there something more?

When told of the miracle of the wedding wine, and of John the Baptist, Simon the Pharisee snorted and snapped into action. Quickly, he prepared to make a journey to Jerusalem. He had to discuss these happenings with his father. This would be something of interest. If another rebellion against Roman authority was in the offing, perhaps he would discover an opportunity to further his reputation, and increase his influence and authority.

Didn't the Oral Torah speak of diligence and careful discernment in these matters?

Yes, he had to weigh these things carefully. People needed to be protected; they could be so easily deceived.

Simon expelled a disgusted grunted as he packed his things. It was unfathomable. How could people *be* so duped? What true Israelite would believe that this man was a prophet; or anything else to be esteemed?

Since when would a *true* prophet arrive in this way?

Come to think of it, had there been a true prophet since Malachi? Why would God send one now, after five hundred years? Besides, how could a man be a prophet of Israel and not have gone through the proper channels? Was it true this Jesus had not been schooled in the Law and Traditions of the elders? It was inconceivable he thought to become a true leader in Israel these days, without working to receive his "Semichah!"

No, this could not possibly be a good thing.

Surely, a prophet sent from God would have come to *his* house, *not* Zebedee's; to Simon's own house first; to a righteous house; to a man who was reputable and could help him take the kind of steps that would persuade people to righteousness!

That would have made a *real* difference.

How could this be of God, when the man had not gone through the proper channels of development? This would take some looking into by those with more political power and information.

Telling his Abigail not to worry, he decided. While he was in the area, he might just make a trip into the Judean wilderness to see if he could find a wild-haired locust-eater, dressed in camels' hair.

Power-Brokers

"He who refuses to learn deserves extinction."

"Do not say 'when I have leisure, I will study,' because you may never have leisure."

These were the quotes of Hillel finding their way into the mind of Judah, father of Simon the Pharisee. The words had been an earmark of the great Pharisee's life-approach motivation. A true scholar knew there was always something unknown. A good leader knew they had more to discover. "What is the undiscovered?" his students had been taught ask themselves. "What is the unrealized purpose?"

As *"nasi,"* or prince, over the Great Sanhedrin in Jerusalem, Hillel had been a man who was always encouraging leaders, whether Pharisee or Sadducee, to make it their quest to seek out Truth in any given situation. Remembered as a wise and tolerant man, he had been known for handling particularly difficult issues surrounding the Jewish people and the Roman invasion with great finesse. He was sorely missed, even now, some fifteen years later.

Hillel's son, Simon, still served on the Great Council, along with the dead sage's newly ordained grandson, Gamaliel. It was murmured among the Pharisees, and Judah still firmly believed it to be true, Gamaliel should have been chosen become the successor to his grandfather, instead of Joseph Caiaphas.

Granted, the two priests who had filled the post in the years immediately after Hillel's death had made more sense to the more seasoned members of the Council. They had been righteous men.

Judah still could recall the tremors that moved through his inner being when Gratus, as new Prefect, had announced his choice of Joseph Caiaphas as high priest. In fact, the appointment made by the Roman proconsul had taken them all by surprise.

He sighed. In times past, a time of fasting and prayer preceded the choice of the next high priest and "prince," among them. Lots were cast, and votes were taken. It was a method and tradition traced back through the centuries. But now?

Why had God allowed the process to become one decided by an oppressor?

How had they become a political body, rather than a spiritual one?

Perhaps with the Maccabees, but even more so now...

The tone of the Council had been negative enough under the influence of Annas, but it had taken an ominous turn when Joseph Caiaphas, the son-in-law, took hold.

The change hadn't happened all at once; but now, as he looked back and made comparisons...

In hindsight, he realized, the judgments given by the court most recently had taken a turn; a new flavor. Was there one thing causing it to happen? No, he considered. There was no *one thing* he could put his finger on. More, it had been a gradual overtaking; as if by a cloud; a sense of callous cynicism; an erosion.

How had they arrived at this place?

It was as though heartlessness and brutality had come to rule, inch by inch over the past fifteen years, like the outward creeping of a spider building his web. It was black and full of poison; enveloping into silent and unfeeling tombs, the souls of men who were called touch the heart of God for His people.

Yes, there had been days under Hillel, when the pageantry involved with his position had caused Judah to question his own motives for becoming a Pharisee. Yes, there had been times, even under the old guard, when the oral traditions and interpretations had seemed more religious than effectual; when he found himself commiserating with his mentors over his own personal pride; beating his own chest in prostrate prayers of repentance.

Still, he thought, it had never been anything like this. There had always been concern for the welfare of the people under the fluff. Thinking back, he realized. Even though it felt as though the Oral Torah had taken over at times, he still had found joy in the fact that the symbols of his office still drew the common man to God.

But that sense of God's blessing was gone now.

Yes, that was it.

Now, he realized, the very Court designed to represent the Council of God, was lacking the substance of true spirituality.

What *was* that substance, he asked himself?

Again his mind was drawn to the words of his mentor: "an awareness of failing humanity, and humility before God."

It was a terrifying thing to be unable to trust and be vulnerable with one's peers, Judah reasoned. What should be done?

Granted, there *were* those among the Pharisees in Jerusalem, who were unaware of the schisms taking place in the Court of the Hewn Stones. Thinking of those lesser scribes and Pharisees, Judah felt a twinge of envy.

It was better not to know.

Oh, to be once again blissfully ignorant of the cruelties taking place around him!

Would he ever be able to go back to the days when he could just love God and want to serve Him? And if he could, how would it happen?

No, the wave he was sensing would build into a tide, unless something happened to stop it.

As he waited in the courtyard of his home for his friends to join him, Judah went back over the happenings of that morning. Surely Caiaphas had gone too far this time. Surely Annas would pull him back into line. Surely the Romans …..

Well, did they really *want* Roman intervention on the matter?

… Perhaps not.

Two mornings ago, a temple guard had confided to Judah about changes taking place within the designs of the palace of the high priest. The man had come to Judah, wondering why the Sanhedrin had given Joseph Caiaphas permission to change such an historic structure. Judah had been completely surprised, and asked the man what changes were being made.

The old sage was well acquainted with the high priest's palace, having visited his mentor and dear friend, Hillel, during times when particularly difficult judgments needed extra thought and consideration. The home of the high priest was located in the Essene Quarter of the city, in the Upper Level. It was maintained by the Temple Guard and the high priest's private servants. From his palace, the high priest; any high priest; enjoyed the full rights of a ruler, similar to Herod, as long as conflict with any Roman authority or design was avoided.

According to what Judah had been told, Joseph Caiaphas had taken his privileges to a new level, without making his plans known. It bothered Judah to think that Caiaphas had walked away from what had always been form and practice in the Council. According to the example and pattern set by Moses, they were to stand together as one, representing the judgments and mind of God, with no one man standing up to speak for himself.

Apparently, Caiaphas had forgotten the traditions. He had taken matters into his own hands; working for some time, without the knowledge of those whom he considered "against God's purposes" within the Council members. From what the temple guard had confided in Judah, the below ground-level areas of Caiaphas' palace, utilized for food storage and cooler living during the hot months under Hillel, were now being restructured for torture and imprisonment.

So, this very morning, Judah had found an excuse to visit the high priest's home. Requesting a scroll he which he did not personally own, he expressed his desire to once again borrow it from the Library of the High Priest, located on the middle level of Joseph's palace. While in the library, he had been able to observe what was happening around him.

Yes, it was true. Caiaphas had slaves working to redesign the lower level.

Why now? When their right to execute or punish had been revoked?

Could not those violating the law be simply handed over to the Roman soldiers in the fortress of Antonia close by? Why couldn't the Council remain solely a religious body of leaders, concerned with the benefit and blessing of the people?

Yes, Judah was aware the smaller rooms in the basement of the house had been utilized as cells for prisoners during Hillel's reign; but only once or twice; and certainly not recently.

.... And, certainly not with a "circle for hanging" cut into the ceiling of one room… Certainly not with a room prepared just for flogging!

What need did a Pharisee have for the option of torture?

The thought sent his mind reeling.

The man had too much power.

What would happen if one of those who were not within his "Circle of the Friends of God" should fall out of favor with his whims?

And who in the Roman government would care, as long as Caiaphas gave apparently good reasons for his actions?

His smile got him anything he wanted.

Journey

As his thoughts followed the path of Fear, he shakily sat down, wiping his head of the beads of perspiration that had manifested on his bald head.

Nicodemus, his closest friend on the Council, was ushered into the courtyard as Judah was working through these thoughts.

"Greetings, Judah." Nicodemus was removing his head-dress as he spoke. "I thought the session went well this morning, didn't you?"

"Yes, well enough," Judah replied. "Would you like something to eat? Or drink? I can have the servants bring you something… I want to wait until Joseph gets here before we talk, if you don't mind." Judah's voice trailed off.

Judah referred to their mutual friend Joseph, who also served with them as a Pharisee in the Court. Also appointed to the Sanhedrin during the years of Hillel, Joseph was from a village with its roots in antiquity. Almost seven miles to the north of Jerusalem, the ancient village of Ramah had been the birthplace of Rachel, Mother of the nation. The modern name had developed over the centuries, but had not changed the original flavoring of the town. Like EnKarem to the south, Ramah, now labeled Arimathea, was known for its flocks and farming. Joseph and his wife had hosted various families of the Sanhedrin in their family home for dinner and fellowship, including Judah and Nicodemus.

Joseph was a brilliant man, Judah considered. He marveled at the quiet method Joseph had for remembering and connecting details. And, although Joseph had not shared in their boyhood relationship, both Judah and Nicodemus had confidence they could rely on him. Hadn't he agreed with both of them in countless fierce disputes over the Law? Yes, they were truly brothers; if not in blood, then in belief. Joseph would not misunderstand, nor wrongly interpret their words or intentions.

Across the courtyard, Nicodemus waited in silence, watching his friend. He had known Judah since they were young men together in rabbinical school. They had received "Semichah" together, so close had they been in their studies. Now, even their sons were friends. This was how it should be, he thought.

Judah must be tired; he was so quiet today.

After a few minutes, he caught sight of the water-pot on the table. Perhaps he would drink some water… Standing to reach his goal, Nicodemus looked toward the door, and saw Joseph entering.

In response to Nicodemus' wave, Joseph greeted him with a smile.

"I didn't realize this was another gathering of the minds and hearts," Joseph chuckled. "How shall we open the session with prayer, oh Great Sages of the Law?" Nicodemus grinned in response. Looking Joseph in the eye, he nodded his head towards Judah.

Following Nicodemus' sign, Joseph noticed their friend's distress. "Judah, what is troubling you? Is the family in good health? Did you receive news from Simon? Is your Hadassah well?" Joseph referred to Judah's wife, named for the Hebrew queen of old.

"No, no, we are fine. Everything is fine," Judah answered. "Well, no, that's not exactly what I mean." He flustered. "Do you want something to eat? Drink? I can have the servants bring you something."

"Not yet," Joseph patted his friend's arm, and began removing his headdress. "What is troubling you, Judah?"

"I have learned some news, and I need to trust my brothers. I need your wisdom." Judah looked into the eyes of his friends, and found the encouragement he needed to continue.

"Whatever it is, old friend, you can tell us," Nicodemus spoke. "Let's sit on your benches over there. You look a little weary."

So, Judah shared his experiences of the past few days with them, and unburdened the fears of his soul. What were their observances? Did they share his concerns? Had they sensed the changes happening around them, and within the Council? What hope and counsel could they give him?

As they talked and shared together, Judah found a sense of community and support from Joseph and Nicodemus. This was true partnership; being able to truly know and be known without fear of reprisal.

He knew they would tell him if he had come to wrong conclusions.

Not only did Judah's friends understand his concerns, but they shared them as well. Speaking together that afternoon, the three men discovered they each were losing ground in their ability to find hope for change within their calling. They realized, for reasons unknown and without comprehension, their nation was at the mercy of evil men. They expressed their fears and disappointments. They prayed together; and, as they joined hearts and hands in unity, Judah, Nicodemus and Joseph each found a spark of hope kindling their forgotten dreams of a healthy nation and people.

God was on their side. He had not forgotten them.

He had not left them alone.

Separately, and then in unison, each man expressed the leading of his soul.

They would continue to serve with open hearts; worshipping; praying for the best; waiting for the restoration of their nation's solid footing in the Word and Ways of God.

Before parting ways that afternoon, Joseph suggested they meet the next day at the same time, to pray together for God's purposes to be made known to them. Judah suggested they fast the noonday meal each day as well, in preparation for receiving what God was about to show them.

It was Nicodemus who came up with the idea they should just continue to meet each day for the same purposes; just to pray.

Over the next few weeks, their numbers grew. It seemed the three men weren't the only ones concerned about the alteration in the atmosphere of the Sanhedrin. As they prayed, Judah made certain to always speak carefully and in positive terms regarding Caiaphas, unless he was alone with his trusted friends. It was in the middle of one such afternoon gathering that Judah's son, Simon, arrived from Capernaum.

Surprised to find the courtyard of his father's home filled with members of the High Council, he searched out his mother. He found her in the room where she did her sewing and weaving.

Journey

"Simon!" she had hugged him tightly. "It's so good to see you. How did you make the journey?"

"I was given a ride by a farmer bringing food to the marketplace," Simon answered, dropping his satchel on the floor. "It was a much easier journey than walking. I told him that if he would give me a ride, I would pray a blessing over his crops and sales."

"Did you pay him too?" Hadassah asked.

"No; no need to," Simon answered absently, taking off his outer cloak and headdress. As the sound of prayers rose in the courtyard, he looked once more through the doorway.

Sitting down, Hadassah once more began working on her needlework.

"What is going on here, mother?" he asked, full of curiosity.

"Your father has been called by the Spirit of God to pray and fast for the direction of the Council. These men have been meeting together for the past thirty-eight days. They fast the noonday meal, and spend these hours praying together for the healing of our nation, and for the purposes of God." Hadassah kept her eyes on her needlework, and did not look at her son. She knew that if he saw her eyes, he would know she was keeping something from him.

She had promised Judah she would say nothing of her husband's concerns, or the changes taking place in the high priest's palace. They were a private matter; a matter which had to remain entrusted into the hands of God.

What Judah wanted Simon to know, Judah would tell.

The "Spirit of God;" Simon caught the phrase. It had been a long time since he had heard those words. Which prophet had it been? Zechariah, he thought. "When will he conclude?" Simon wanted to know.

Still working, his mother answered. "They usually end after a couple of hours or so, and then head back to the Temple, to join the rest of the Council for the late day session."

"Not seeing him that much these days, I take it."

"Not much, but we still take time to talk in the evenings."

"So, he will be here for supper?"

"Of course, Simon; we do still eat."

"I need to speak with him. I think it is a matter he will want to take action over."

"Is it urgent? Do you want me to send someone to fetch him? Or can it wait until supper time?" Hadassah smiled, finally looking up. She noticed the tiredness around his eyes. "Why don't you go and refresh yourself from your journey, and take a short nap? That way you will be rested and have your thoughts clear when you and your father speak."

She was so observant and wise, Simon thought. She was right, too. He shouldn't interrupt his father's prayers. It would be embarrassing to both of them. So he agreed. His mother called a servant to help him wash and change out of his robes, into more comfortable apparel. He laid down to rest.

It was dark outside when Simon awoke.

How long had he been asleep? Where was everyone? What was the hour?

Sitting up on his pallet, Judah's son noticed that someone had lit a small oil lamp and left it on the table for him. He squinted in the dimly lit room, looking for an indication of the time

Journey

of day. Moving outdoors to the facilities, he relieved himself. Looking back toward his father's house, he saw light and movement in the upper windows.

He made his way back indoors to find his father, sitting in his scriptorium, concentrating on a scroll. At the entrance to the room, Simon leaned on the doorpost, watching his father. With a twinge, he realized he had not been to see him since the last feast day. How many months ago had that been?

Silently observing, Simon noticed changes in the older priest. He looked a little older, he decided. Had he lost more hair? The old man's head was not quite completely bald yet, and the curls in his beard were smoothed under Judah's thoughtful stroking. His father had always been a studious man, Simon considered. How much time had they spent in this room; reading, discussing, learning? Hadn't this been his favorite room in the house?

"What are you reading, father?" he asked.

Judah looked up; a wide, joyous smile breaking across his countenance. "Simon!" The father rose quickly, suddenly unaware of anything other than his son. As he did so, the cuff of his sleep-robe caught the top edge of his water cup, and sent it flying backwards, where it shattered against the wall.

Nonplussed, Judah continued. "Your mother said you had arrived! What an unexpected gift it is to see you!" He paused. "She also said something was troubling you. Is everyone at home in good health?"

Simon laughed out loud as he hugged his father. "Who needs a water cup, anyway? How many has mother purchased at the market *this* week?"

Judah chuckled, as they bent down to pick up the pieces together. "I don't know; three or four? We don't go through as many of them as we used to, now that you boys have left home."

"I'm sure that's true," Simon replied, blinking his eyes. Suddenly, they felt quite dry. It must have been all the dust from travel, he thought. Smiling at his father, he said, "Although it looks like you have many more guests these days than ever before." What was the gathering this afternoon? Are you moving into politics?"

"No, no, Simon, nothing like that," his father patted him, and took him by both shoulders, to make eye contact. "Now, tell me, how is your family? How are the children? What pranks have the boys played on their sisters? I miss my grand-children. When you return for the feast in a couple of weeks, you must all stay with us. I have been saving up gifts, you know."

For the next hour or more, Simon sat with his father, sharing stories of his wife and family. There were so many things that Judah wanted to know. They laughed together, each finding a comfort in the ability to temporarily compartmentalize their concerns about the world-at-large. Finally, when both men began to yawn in midst of conversation, losing their thoughts due to weariness, Judah called it a day.

"Well, son, let's continue our discussions in the morning. These old bones need a little rest before the sun rises." Judah patted his son's arm, and rose, his knees creaking loudly. Judah rubbed them, sighed, and then arched his back to stretch. "Hadassah is right. I really should walk more," he muttered to himself. Looking at his son, he said, "Your father is getting too old, Simon." He paused. "Would you like to go to the Court with me tomorrow? It would be good for you to stay in touch with things. Then we can talk about the matters you brought with you."

Simon was thrilled. Imagine, he thought. *I* am invited to attend the Great Sanhedrin. I am *related* to the high court; an important man to be invited by one of the Sages! I am part of a righteous heritage! What an *honor*! Outwardly, he shrugged. "I always have a lot to learn, father," he said. "I would hope to be worthy of such a gathering."

"Good boy, good boy," Judah touched his son's shoulders. "I will have the servants wake you for breakfast."

~~~~

The Temple in Jerusalem was a magnificent structure, Simon thought, as he walked with Judah in the early morning sunlight. From any location in the city, a person could see the sun's reflection on the roof of its central chamber, the Most Holy Place. That was the room central to all of Jewish life; where the Ark of the God's Covenant had been kept. Inside the Ark was a jar of manna, the two stone tablets with the Ten Laws given to Moses, and Aaron's rod that had budded with ripe almonds. Each item had survived from the days of The Wilderness Wanderings, and served to remind the people of God's goodness and provision.

Although the Ark had not been housed in the Temple since the days of Babylonian captivity, just the reminder of its presence was enough to draw reverence from every Jewish heart in Israel.

Yes, Simon considered, the Temple was a reminder for the righteous to keep God's Law as the central focus of living.

At least, that was what occurred to him now.

As long as he could remember, there had been divisions in the design of the Temple Courts. He remembered his confusion as a boy over the sectors of the structure.

"Why are there so many courts, father?" he had asked.

"In the days of Moses' tabernacle, there were only three courts," Judah explained to his son. "The Most Holy Place, where the Mercy Seat shows us the Presence of God; the Inner Court of the Priests, where the Light of God, the Bread of Heaven, and the Table of Worship show us how we relate to God; and the Outer Court, where sacrifice is made to prepare us to become priests and kings before God."

"Then why do we have other courts?" the boy had asked.

"I do not know for certain, my son. For myself, I believe it is because it is the sinful nature of man to always add to what God has spoken. We must be careful to stay close to the heart of God, so we can hear when He whispers to our hearts."

Simon thought about those words now as they walked together.

He understood why there was a Court for the Gentiles; they lacked the holiness to draw near to God.

The Court of the Women had been provided because those who had descended from Eve had a tendency toward Deception; the High Court had decreed centuries before that women

Journey

were to be segregated from the men; and although the men of Israel had greater privileges than the women, the women of Israel still had greater privileges than the Gentiles. After his years of schooling, the reasoning made sense to him.

So, the Court of the Men had been simply a re-assigning of the Outer Court in Moses' Wilderness Tabernacle. The divisions had come later, as the nation had developed in form and tradition; the women and the gentiles had been moved a little further from the Presence of God.

It was good though, he considered; Herod the Great had built balconies for the women who wished to observe to be able to do so. How else could they see what was happening in the worship inside the men's court?

He knew his Abigail had grieved many times over not being allowed further than the layered curtain; and although they prayed together at home, she had confided to him it was difficult to deal with being able to trace her lineage back to the days of Aaron, and not be allowed to draw nearer to the Mercy Seat of God.

What had she done wrong? Was there something wrong with her that made her less valuable than the men of Israel? Did God like men better than women?

Was there something out of sync in their understanding of God's purposes?

To think about such things made Simon uncomfortable.

Oh well, some things were the plan of God and should not be questioned.

As they passed through the marketplace, the younger Pharisee looked for his friend, Isaac. Since he had been a small boy, he had visited Isaac's booth on his way to the Temple. His was the booth where doves could be purchased for sacrifice. In seasons just prior to the feasts, the man also sold sheep yearlings.

Simon couldn't find him.

"What do you want to buy?" Judah asked his son.

"I was looking for Isaac, the sacrifice broker," Simon answered. "He must be ill today. I don't see him."

"Oh, that's right. You haven't heard about the changes Caiaphas has been making. Isaac is no longer in the marketplace. He now has his pens set up in the court of the Gentiles."

"What? Why?" Simon couldn't believe what he was hearing.

"Caiaphas convinced a majority of the Council several months ago, just after the last feast. He has this way of persuading people," Judah moved closer to his son's ear in order to be heard above the din of the sellers and bargainers around them.

"But not you," Simon observed.

"Well, they have begun selling oxen, sheep and doves in the Court of the Gentiles, just as one is entering the sacrificial area. You'll see what I mean when we get there. It was difficult enough when we had to begin trading for Temple coins in order to buy sacrifices. But now, we can't enter the Temple sanctuaries without being reminded we are expected to purchase something. It's really become quite a business."

"What has happened to the singers and the musicians with all those animal pens being there now?" Simon wanted to know.

Journey

They were through the marketplace now, and almost to the Temple Gate called "Beautiful." Several beggars, each with a visible physical ailment preventing them from working for a living, had noticed the priests. Hearing the voices calling out for alms, Judah reached into his bag. Simon watched, inwardly breathing a sigh of relief.

He would not *need* to give alms if his father did so.

No need to overdo things.

A stray dog ran between the two men. Simon recoiled. Why didn't someone remove such unclean animals from the traffic ways; especially so close to the Temple entrance!? It was disgusting!

Why were pigs and dogs allowed in the city anyway?

Noticing his son's discomfort, Judah answered the question. "There aren't as many singers in the Temple now as their used to be, or musicians either. The leaders in the high priest's circle have decided dances should be done only by the men when corporate worship occurs, so we have no more of that either. Now, the only worship taking place during sacrifices happens with one or two at specific times, or not at all."

Simon wondered at what he was hearing. One of his favorite aspects of coming to the Temple had always been the continuous music and worship played at all hours of the day. The practice of worship around the clock was one instituted by King David.

Why was it being done away with?

He would miss it. But it was understandable; times change.

He shrugged. Leadership couldn't expect to maintain that kind of energy forever, he reasoned.

Entering the Temple Mount with his father, Simon was amazed at how crowded the Court of the Gentiles now seemed. On his prior visits there had been contemplative silence, broken by musical praise to God filling the entire Temple Mount. Now, the entire area had the same atmosphere as the marketplace outside.

Something inside of him felt a twinge.

Was it fear?

What did God think of these changes, he wondered?

And here was a new development.... walking through the court was difficult. It seemed to Simon every path he sought to walk was blocked by an animal pen or a moneychanger's table. The closer they came to the door into the Inner Courtyard areas, the more increased the clamor and tension became.

"Is it like this all the time?" Simon shouted over the din to his father.

"Yes. It is now," Judah turned his head to look at his son, and put his finger to his lips. Simon silently understood. They would not speak more of this as long as they were on Temple grounds.

Entering the Court of Hewn Stones, Simon found himself greeting old friends, being introduced to new members of the Court. Things had not changed much in this regard since his old days, he reasoned. Perhaps the Roman presence had been a reason for the changes Caiaphas was making...... there had to be a good reason.

Journey

In the midst of his mental deliberations, Joseph Caiaphas and Annas entered the room. Simon noticed the extra tassels and gold filigree that Joseph had added to his robes. How important he looked! Simon had not seen Joseph since the day he had been commissioned to serve in Capernaum. He hoped that Caiaphas would remember him, and count him as a friend.

He was not disappointed.

"Simon!" Joseph Caiaphas moved quickly through the group of men assembled to come to his old friend's side. "Did you come early to the feast? How good it is to see you! Is Abigail well?"

Briefly, Simon remembered that Joseph Caiaphas had thought to marry his wife when they were younger. "Yes, we are all doing well, Joseph. And you?"

"Can't complain, can't complain," the high priest flashed his famous, enigmatic smile. "But look at you! Life in the country has agreed with you! Do you have any sons?"

"Yes; and three daughters." Simon found himself drawn in by the charm of his old friend. No wonder he had been promoted to high priest! What a winsome and charismatic man he had become!

"How wonderful to be so blessed by the Lord!" Joseph moved on toward the front of the room. Simon watched him as he moved through the Council. He seemed to know the right word to say to each one; how to evoke a laugh from this one, and a nod from that one. What would it be like to have that kind of draw and power with people?

The Sages of the Law met for most of the morning. Functioning as the Supreme Court of the nation in regard to religious matters, it was the task of these Pharisees and Sadducees to make judgments in regard to the most difficult decisions; those judgments too difficult for the lesser Sanhedrin Courts throughout the nation, such as the one in Capernaum, where Simon served as ruler.

The word of the Great Sanhedrin was the final word in all matters.

There was no appeal for a righteous man. The unified voice of the Sanhedrin was the representation of God.

Throughout the morning, Simon sat with the rabbinical students, watching and listening as difficult matters were discussed, debated and decided. All the while, he marveled at Joseph Caiaphas' ability to gain control, persuading even his staunchest opponents in regard to the smallest issues. Where had Joseph learned to utilize that kind of control? Inwardly, Simon decided he wanted it. He wanted to learn how to influence men in the same way.

Who had been Joseph's mentor, he wondered?

He would have to seek out his old friend later, and ask him for career strategies.

Toward the end of the morning session, the noise from the outer court filtered into the room; along with the sounds of animals and birds. For a few moments, the Court acted as though they would ignore the interruption. Then, a lamb ran through the open door into the room, accompanied by a small flock of flying doves.

Caiaphas' face darkened. He looked at Malchus, his servant, who was standing close by. "Go and see what is going on out there!" He snapped.

Journey

Malchus ran out of the room, and quickly returned. Breathless and without regard to protocol, he shouted, "Master, you must come. There is a man out there; with a whip. He has opened all the animal cages."

Caiaphas angrily rose from his chair. Thumping his fist on the table in front of him, he yelled, "We will have order!! I will have order!" Looking at Malchus, he stormed, "What man?"

"You have to see this, Master," the servant stammered. "They have stopped everything. There is even silence in the Court of the Gentiles."

With a pompous flourish, Joseph Caiaphas descended from his throne and floated out the door of the Court of the Hewn Stones; in tow was every court member of the Court, as well as the year's rabbinical students.

As Simon came upon the scene, he stopped in his tracks, stunned by what he saw transpiring before his eyes. The rows of animal pens full of "unblemished" animals to be sold for sacrifices, had been emptied; all of them! Animals were running around loose on the Temple Mount; bleating, baaing, mooing and moving, even into the Court of the Women!

The unclean evidences of their presence were being left behind! It was being tracked into the stepping stones, by the shoes of those who stepped in it.

Who was responsible for this sacrilege?

Hearing the sound of coins hitting the ground behind him, Simon turned, coming face to face with the same young man who had been staying at Zebedee's house in Capernaum!

For a split second, their eyes met.

Simon felt as if a lightning bolt had gone through his being.

Where had he seen those eyes before? Then he remembered.

There had been a time during his rabbinical training, when a young boy had been stranded in the city for almost a week. Concerned for his safety, and sure his parents would come to retrieve him, Judah and Hadassah and taken him to their home in the evenings.

Simon remembered those eyes from years ago. He remembered the boy intruding on their family meals, taking his father's attention away. Judah had taken time to discuss the Law with the boy, and discussions had involved other men whom Simon admired at the Temple the next day.

Although the boy had been likeable enough, Simon remembered feeling it wasn't right for the poor son of a tradesman to have the depth of understanding of the Law he held. One evening they sat together in the scriptorium, Simon had listened to the twelve year-old ask questions, conversing about the Law with his father.

He had been jealous of the boy's wisdom; especially when he realized how impressed his father had been by the boy.

Then, the young man's parents had come to fetch him. They had been so worried.

"Why were you afraid? Didn't you know I would be doing business in my Father's House?" Simon still puzzled over the words.

It had been a silly thing to say at the time. Who would dare to call God, "Father?" And wasn't the boy's father standing there beside his mother? Unless…… And who had taught him the Law; his mother? Surely a local priest wouldn't take that much time with someone so low-born.... Simon suddenly realized that there had to be much, much more to learn about this man.

Perhaps there was something gone wrong in his brain... Or was he just *different*?

At the very least he had passion. But that kind of zealous passion could get him into deep trouble, these days.

He was no longer a twelve year-old.

Astonished, Simon felt as if his feet were stuck in their place. The young man was shouting over the noise to the crowd.

"Get these things out of here!" he shouted, picking up an animal crate and tossing it away from the entrance to the Court of the Men. My Father's house is never to be a place for merchandising!! This is not the marketplace!!"

Fearing they might be hit by the small whip, or scourge, in his hand, moneychangers and animal brokers alike were fleeing from the site as quickly as they could.

"Who does this man think he is?" Someone in the crowd asked their neighbor.

Simon was asking himself the same question. Surely this was not a good sign. Coming to his senses, he looked for his father in the crowd. There he was, standing with Nicodemus. Where was Caiaphas?

His eyes moved over the crowd, and stopped on the High Priest, surrounded by several of the High Council. What did his friend think of what was happening?

Enraged, Caiaphas moved to the center of the fray. As he did so, the noise level diminished as those in the Court paused to observe what was about to happen. Joseph shouted at the man who had disrupted his meeting. "What is your name?" he furiously demanded.

"Jesus." The name was said matter-of-factly. The young man continued to work on clearing what appeared to be some sort of pathway. Now, empty animal cages continue to fly, some breaking apart as they hit the ground some ten or twelve feet away. One crate came very close to hitting Joseph Caiaphas in the head.

Aware of the crowd watching him, the high priest ducked out of the way, as the pens went whizzing. "If you are a prophet, show us a sign, so that we can believe what you do is from God," he commanded.

"Destroy this temple, and in three days I will raise it up," came the reply.

Simon's eyebrows went up. Who could dispute such a statement? Who would be willing to follow through on such a claim?

Joseph Caiaphas sneered. "It took forty-six years to build this building, and you will raise it up in three days?" Looking around to his supporters, a raucous laughter rippled through the onlookers.

In the midst of the chaos, Jesus stopped, brushing his palms against each other to remove the dust of his task. He looked at Caiaphas.

Simon noticed the entrance into the Inner Sanctuary of the Temple was now clear of any blockade. A person could venture into the more intimate place of worship without having to think about the condition of his personal moneybag. All of the animal pens, brokers, moneychangers and tables were gone. Nothing barred the way.

Was *that* what he had been trying to do?

A thought flashed across Simon's mind. *Should* money be a person's first concern when approaching God? As though to remove the idea from his mind, Simon shook his head, and once again brought his focus to the fray before his eyes.

Hands on his hips, the young carpenter looked at the high priest and smiled.

"This is a house of *prayer*," he said, "for *all* nations."

Standing in the midst of the Court of the Gentiles, aware of a thousand foreign eyes, the high priest was caught between embarrassment and rage. There was no sentence or one-line witticism available to would put this young upstart in his place. Flustered, furious, and uncharacteristically not having an answer, Joseph Caiaphas stormed from the Temple Mount, retreating to his palace. His followers went with him.

He was livid.

That's odd, Simon thought. Joseph had made no answer. Without thinking, and curious to see what would happen, the Pharisee from Capernaum moved to pursue the "Circle of the Friends of God," otherwise known as Caiaphas' inner circle.

Unknowingly, he had just stepped into the middle of a war; …. a war for his very soul.

The High Council never did reconvene that morning; or the afternoon for that matter; nor did the Court of the Gentiles return to its atmosphere of the early morning. Shaken and confused, the majority of sacrifice brokers and moneychangers spent most of the afternoon trying to round up still-sellable animals running loose in the Courts of the Temple. After spending time corralling the doves now loose in the rafters, pigeon traders returned to their homes, to inventory breeding pens for the next round of "unblemished" birds.

On his way out of the Temple, Isaac, a sacrifice broker spoke to Judah. "I'm done with this, Judah. I'm going back to the marketplace. I didn't feel right about being on the Temple Mount anyway." For some reason, many of the other brokers and moneychangers had made the same decision.

At least for the time being, they said.

Judah and Nicodemus watched with quiet interest. Was this a direct result of their prayers? Everything has a meaning and a purpose, Hillel had said. What does *this* mean, Judah considered?

Just after Caiaphas made his exit, Nicodemus moved to the side of one of those who appeared to be in Jesus' following. He spoke quietly into his ear. "Are you with this man? Where are you staying?" he had asked.

The rough-cut young man, looked to be from the Galilee region, and his accent confirmed his appearance. "We are staying at a friend's home here in Jerusalem," he answered.

"What is your name?" the priest asked.

"John," was the answer.

Nicodemus asked for directions. He had questions.

Journey

Standing beside his friend, Judah had his own thought processes. The priest noticed his son's momentary recognition of Jesus, and also realized the connection. Saddened, he also noticed Simon's apparent allegiance to Joseph Caiaphas, in leaving to follow the man's entourage into the palace.

"Oh God," he whispered with desperation. "Please do not let my son fall as prey before wicked men. Save him from himself. Cover all failings of mine, Lord. Do whatever you must to gain his soul. Show him. Oh, please, show him."

Simon followed Joseph that morning, to see what judgments would be brought against Jesus; to learn how Caiaphas handled opposition to his rule. He found himself talking to his friend.

"They were from Galilee, Simon," Joseph observed. "Do you know them?"

"Not directly, no." Simon discovered he was weighing his words for some unknown reason.

"Are they from Capernaum?"

"Not all of them," Simon answered truthfully. "One of the men is from my town; a son to a friend of mine."

That disclosure opened doors in his relationship with Joseph. Suddenly, inexplicably no longer angry, Joseph placed his arm around Simon's shoulders, and spoke conspiratorially to him in the middle of the crowd. "We leaders have to stick together, Simon," he said. "I know you know what I mean. What would happen if we allowed just any young rebel who called himself a rabbi to come to the temple and take things into his own hands? What would that make us as leaders? Where would our authority go? You understand what I mean, don't you?"

Simon nodded. "Yes, I do. I have noticed things happening even in my own town."

Joseph had smiled his brightest smile, his eyes sparkling; "Things that would interest the court?"

"Perhaps," Simon answered. "I don't know enough to give you a full report, yet, but I will if you like."

A murmur of approval moved through the room. Simon's heart jumped a little. Was this to be a stepping stone into a higher place of influence? Yes, he could be a submitted man.

Caiaphas was speaking again. "Knowledge is power." He moved away from Simon, and began addressing the entire room. He raised his voice. "It is what we know that allows us to maintain our place." He turned his head and spat. "It is not passivity. We must be men of action, unlike those who have broken away from us; those relics of the past. They think we don't know they meet together. They meet together to mourn and pray." This last statement was made with a sneer. He waved his hand as if you brush away unseen debris. "No, they have no power. They can do nothing."

He looked penetratingly at Simon. "But this man…. *this* man can help us. He can be our eyes and ears in Galilee." He then had the servants prepare a feast for the noonday meal. Then, over the meal, the group worked together on a plan to help Simon in sending and receiving messages from Galilee.

Journey

Simon the Pharisee had never felt so exhilarated; not since his ordination! How had this happened? It was too good to be true! In one jump his ambitions were realized.

This was turning out to be a great day; a wonderful day; a life-changing day.

It wasn't until he left Joseph's palace he realized a tingling in his left hand. What caused its numbness? Shrugging it off, he sighed;

Perhaps it was caused by all the copying of the Torah he had been doing of late....

Journey

Righteousness

Word about Jesus, the Healer, had travelled quickly in Jerusalem. By the end of the week, sick people were streaming to Jerusalem's inn to find anyone who could tell them how to find the man. In morning conversations at the well, housewives shared news about the latest miracles: the blind father who no longer would need to beg for a living; the crippled wife who had been able to take a walk to the marketplace after years of back pain! There were even stories about him turning water into wine!!

Who was this man? Where had he come from? Was he a prophet? It was said that he had been baptized by John, and now was baptizing others just outside the city. Had anyone heard what he had done at the Temple? He had been teaching and telling about a new Kingdom… did anyone know what he meant when he said "Kingdom of God?" What marvelous things he was saying!!

It was Hadassah who shared what she had heard with Judah first.

"They say he was baptized by John, Judah." Hadassah's voice carried anticipation. "You remember John, don't you? He's the baby my father's cousin, Elizabeth, had in her old age."

"The Baptist?" Judah looked at his wife. "That's right, I remember now."

"He joined the settlement of the Essenes when Zachariah died," she continued. "But now, they are talking about this man from Nazareth. They are saying that he works miracles, Judah. Do you know who he is?"

"I was there the day he sent the moneychangers from the Temple," her husband answered. "There *is* something about him that I can't seem to put my finger on; I haven't seen enough definitively. I know that I *do* sense the Spirit of God. Only time will tell."

Simon's Abigail and the children joined them in the middle of the week, making the journey with neighbors to Jerusalem for the feast days. How Judah and Hadassah loved spending time with their grandchildren! The house was filled with laughter again; as though the years rolled back before their eyes, renewing younger days!

Time passed too quickly.

Abigail's two middle children even managed to bring a street beggar home during the week. They had not let Hadassah rest until she gave him a place to stay with the animals.

"He doesn't really want to beg," her grand-daughter said.

"He's hungry. Can we feed him?" her grandson asked.

So, Judah's household had taken on a project. The man seemed nice enough, but Hadassah was concerned he might die before the feast week was over. For the sake of the children, she gave the household steward strict instructions to ensure the man's health and welfare.

"Feed him well, and make sure he gets a bath," she said.

"Oh, yes, my lady," the steward answered. "If we go by the smell; do you mind if we do those things in the opposite order?"

"That's fine. That's fine. Oh, and go through some of the old clothes in the storage room. He looks like he might be a little smaller than Judah's frame. Then burn those rags he is wearing."

Hadassah made a mental note to find out who the man was, and whether he had family close by. Surely someone somewhere was worried about him.

Three days later, Simon and his family left Judah and Hadassah's home for Galilee. As they were loading the wagon, Simon pulled his father aside.

"Father, I have been debating whether to tell you," he began.

"You can tell me anything, son," his father assured him. "What's on your mind?"

"Be careful about this Jesus," the younger man warned. "I think he is on his way to making an enemy of the high priest."

"I thought something was troubling you, Simon. What is your concern?"

"He speaks with some undefined type of authority. He works miracles, but has never been to rabbinical school. He...." Simon's voice trailed off, as he drifted into his own thoughts.

"Yes? Simon? Continue," Judah prodded. "What is it?"

"And I think I remember him. Isn't he the boy who stayed with us years ago when he was lost in the city? He would have been close to twelve then."

"I wondered about that too. It was something about his eyes that reminded me," Judah responded.

"Yes, me too.... Father, I don't see how he could be a true prophet."

"Why?" Judah asked. "Weren't each of the prophets, children at one time or another? Shouldn't he have grown up like anyone else?"

"That isn't the thing. It's something else that troubles me. How can a man be truly blessed and called by God, when he has never received his *semichah*? Shouldn't he better at keeping the Law if he were a true prophet? He doesn't even wash his hands before he eats! I have a hard time believing this practice of baptism can actually do anything but cause trouble for our people." Simon was shaking his left hand intermittently as they spoke.

"Why?" Judah asked.

"Well, one of the fishermen in my village, named Zebedee, has two sons. Neither one of them has a good reputation. They are just low-class fishermen. I've been watching them for a long time. Now, one son has left his father's business and is traveling with this Jesus. The man has his followers baptizing people in the waters outside the city. Even the "camel's hair prophet," John, is endorsing him as some kind of promised Deliverer.... I just don't know...."

"What's your difficulty?"

"I always thought that a man should *prove* his place of being right with God by doing all the right things; by keeping the Law... So do most of my friends. Anyway, Caiaphas....

Journey

Joseph.... asked me to keep him informed of where Jesus goes, and what he does. He seems to think he has intentions of beginning a rebellion against Rome."

Judah's eyebrows went up; "By *healing* people?"

"Perhaps," Simon looked down at the ground. "I think it would be more like gaining their trust quickly; by deceiving them through miracles, and then leading them away from the Law. I mean, it's not possible that Jesus could be a really *righteous* man, and have friends and followers with the lack of piety they all seem to have, is it? He's staying at the inn, where the unsavory people are. Why isn't he in the home of a *godly* man? Why doesn't he choose a better place of influence?" Simon paused. "Why didn't he stay *here*, for example?"

"Perhaps because we didn't invite him," the older man countered. "Where in the Law does it say that a priest, or a prophet for that matter, is without sin or weakness? I know I can't live up to that standard; can you? Besides, does ElShaddai care for *all* people? Think about it. If our God wanted to reach the unsavory people, as you call them, wouldn't he have to send his prophet to speak to them? Remember Jonah and Nineveh? Why not here? And what human being can control that kind of spiritual power? Think completely about what you are saying, my son."

"Father, you and I both know that as priests; as the chosen of God, we are not allowed to *touch* such people. Are you trying to tell me that a prophet, a real and true prophet of God, would do something we priests are not allowed to do?"

"Perhaps," Judah replied. "All I know is that as a priest, I am not called to be God *Himself*. The best I can do is offer the sacrifices and be obedient." He paused. "Simon, have you ever wondered about the Oral Torah? Think about something with me." He looked his son in the eyes. "What if, in our seeking to please God, we have added too much to the Law and *we*, the leaders of Israel, have made it too hard to *reach* God?"

Simon frowned. "That's a surprising position, for a Member of the Great Council," he challenged. "So you endorse this man?"

"I don't know enough about him to endorse him, Simon," his father answered. "All I know is there are many conflicting under-currents in our day. It would be dangerous to become swept away by one of them. While we're on the subject, I have concerns for *you*, as my son. Caiaphas is a powerful man. He *could* be a dangerous man, if someone found themselves on the wrong side of his temper."

After that, Simon had purposely re-directed the conversation, bringing things back to the surface. Their talk centered on the grandchildren, and their antics of the morning. As they shared, Simon's arm began to bother him again. Quietly, he realized that his chest felt tight. He drew in a ragged breath.

"Why have you been shaking your arm, Simon?" Judah had asked.

"I think I must have pulled something in my elbow. The joint hurts, and it makes my hand numb sometimes," Simon replied. "Perhaps it's a sign I'm getting older."

"Perhaps," his father replied, thoughtfully. "Maybe you're working too hard."

Journey

Almost a week after the feast celebrations ended, the city of Jerusalem began returning to its habitual rhythms. Afternoon prayers once again resumed in Judah's courtyard. The Council once again deliberated in the Court of Hewn Stones. Children once again played in the streets. Caravan drivers once again gathered in the Plaza, trading stories of faraway places. Housewives once again worked to master their daily chores before sundown; the marketplace once again filled with merchants, tradesmen, and shoppers.

There was one discernable difference in the city, however; one change remaining after the feast. For some unexplainable reason, not one representative of the Temple's sacrifice brokers; nor of its moneychangers had chosen to return to the Temple Mount. Choosing to set up their stations in the marketplace once again, most were discovering it was more profitable to conduct their business away from the Court of the Gentiles.

For each of the Sages who gathered at Judah and Hadassah's home for prayer, the Temple incident invoked considerable thought and discussion. Had the change happened as a direct result of their prayers? Or, had Jesus been prepared and sent by God for such a time as this for an even greater purpose? Was this a sign from God that he was a true prophet? What was this "Kingdom of God" he spoke of? After fasting and prayer, the spiritually perceptive remnant of the Great Sanhedrin drew lots, or straws, and the lot fell to Nicodemus.

After discussion, it was decided. He would wait for a cloudy night, when there was no moon, to seek out the Healer for a secret meeting. There were so many unanswered questions…..

It was close to midnight. The streets were empty and dark; the moon was hidden by clouds rolling in from the Great Sea. Nicodemus could feel the moisture in the air as he pulled his outer cloak around him. When had the wind picked up? He would have to hurry to avoid being caught in the rain.

Approaching the inn, the priest noticed there were people sleeping outside. Was it that full, he thought? Hadn't people gone home after the feast? Being careful to step around the forms and shadows, Nicodemus moved toward the courtyard. How would he find Jesus, he wondered?

Moving into the building, a lamplight came into view. How considerate of the owner to light a lamp for his guests to see their way in the darkness, he thought.

"Hello," a voice spoke. "How can I help you?"

Nicodemus startled. Looking up, he whispered. "I came to see Jesus."

The rough-cut young man in front of him smiled. "I remember you. You were at the Temple. We spoke. My name is John, son of Zebedee."

"I was hoping I would be able to find you; that you were still in town," the sage answered.

"Yes," John laughed. "We are still here. Did you want to see him?"

"Is he awake?"

"Yes, we were just talking together in the courtyard, here. Come join us. There's a nice fire."

Journey

Gratefully, Nicodemus followed John, in silent wonder. How had this happened so easily? Someone "just happened" to be waiting for him? God must be paving the way. Perhaps it was the result of prayers…..

"Who is it, John?" another man's voice quietly inquired from the courtyard.

John looked at the priest. "Nicodemus, isn't it?"

"Yes, I know it's late. I won't keep you long. I just came to find some answers."

John chuckled. "Didn't we all….. " He patted the older man's arm. "Sometimes I don't even know the right questions to ask so I can find the answers…."

The sage pondered the depth of the young fisherman's statement as he moved to sit down. He hadn't needed to wear his priest's robes, he realized. Suddenly, Nicodemus became aware of an attitude within himself. Was his position as a member of the Council something he used for recognition and significance? Was it possible he might be able to relate to these men -- *as men*, without using his place of power and position to distance himself?

Why was he so abruptly aware of own personal humanity? Unexpectedly, the priest found his heart full of questions regarding his own life and purpose; about his family and his future. Most of all, Nicodemus was aware of his need; the need to understand and grasp the meaning of all he saw taking place around him.

He looked into the fire, and rubbed his hands together.

Jesus spoke, also looking into the fire. "Are you married, Nicodemus?"

"Widowed." Just the word caused his eyes to mist. "She died several years ago in the winter."

"Was it a happy marriage?" Jesus asked.

"I could never find anyone to replace her." Nicodemus' throat tightened with unexpected emotion. "The children have lives of their own now. I am never home anyway, with my duties at the Temple." Why, he wondered, did it feel so comfortable to speak about such personal matters to a man he didn't know? He decided to re-direct the conversation.

"Jesus, you are a rabbi. That much is obvious to those of us on the Council. You teach such things; things I don't entirely understand. My friends…. I…. You do such miracles. I have never seen this kind of thing before. I have read about these kinds of happenings in the books of the Kings, and in during the times of the Maccabees; but I have never seen a real miracle until now." He paused.

Looking up, he saw Jesus was looking at him and smiling. "All of life is a miracle, Nicodemus. It is the breath of God."

"That's true," Nicodemus answered, "but I don't think anyone could do the miracles you do unless he was sent from God."

"The healings are just an evidence of something deeper," Jesus said. "It is what is inside a person that determines their life."

"What do you mean?" the priest asked.

"Well, healing the body is a temporary thing. It will fade when the person's life fades. Now, bringing life to the spirit and soul? That is another matter."

Journey

"Life to the spirit and soul?"

"Yes. God gave the Law so man would recognize the depths of his tendencies to exist without experiencing Life; to show people their need for Spiritual Life. But now, the Law has been so added to, all that remains for people to live according to is an outward appearance, with no Inner Life flow of the Spirit of God. The understanding of relationship with God has been lost."

"What is an Inner Life flow? What do you mean?"

"Nicodemus, unless a man is born again, he cannot see the Kingdom of God. He cannot understand it or grasp it," Jesus moved to sit closer to him.

"Born again? How could that even be possible?" Was this man actually saying that a person could enter back into his mother's womb and be born a second time? For a split second, the sage wondered if Jesus might be crazy.

"A person must be born of the Spirit, in order to enter a spiritual Kingdom." Jesus spoke patiently, waiting for the sage to grasp the meaning of his words. "It's not a physical birth, but a spiritual one. Don't mix your kingdoms."

"Mix my kingdoms?"

"Yes. The things that are physical are born by physical means. They are present in this realm. That is the physical kingdom. But, the Kingdom of God is spiritual, and unseen. It is eternal, and exists in God's realm of existence. What is born of the Spirit is spiritual," he paused, "and eternal."

How did such a simple, uneducated man come to such a deep understanding of such matters, Nicodemus marveled?

"Aren't we spiritual beings?" he asked. "That has been the discussion and debate in the Court for years. When we sacrifice, we cover the sin of Adam and Eve in the Beginning, don't we? Doesn't that make us spiritual beings?"

"It is the beginning place. Sacrifice only opens the *door* for the birth to happen. It makes it possible. A person must choose then, to walk through the open door provided."

"I see." Nicodemus nodded.

Jesus continued. "Don't be amazed that I said a person must be born again of the Spirit. Spirit-Life is unseen, but you see the effects of its influence. It's like the wind. You can hear it. You can see what it is doing. You can feel it; but you can't hold it in your hand, or limit it, or even define it. You don't completely know where it is headed. That is what Spiritual Life is like."

"Are you telling me that there is another realm, a spiritual realm? That it is co-existent with this one? I've wondered about that." The priest tried to wrap his comprehension powers around what he was hearing. "Is the realm of God is larger than what I can see? How is that possible?"

"Nicodemus, you are a leader and teacher of God's people. You don't understand that there is an eternal realm? You do understand that is the entire reason for creation; relationship with God; on God's terms; in God's realm of existence."

Journey

Jesus smiled at the priest. "You are part of that creation; designed to know and be known."

"I know that God knows *me*," Nicodemus answered. "That part isn't difficult for me. But I have always hungered that I could know *Him*. I think that might be why I wanted to pursue the priesthood; I mean beyond duty. I wanted to really know I was significant to Him."

"You are significant to Him. But know this, your significance and importance can never be centered in what you *do*." Jesus put his arm around the older man's shoulders. "It is because of who you *are*. You are created in the image of God. You are an image bearer."

"If that's true, then I don't think I bear that image very well," Nicodemus looked into the fire. "How can I be a part of an eternal realm, when I carry so many failings and faults within myself?"

"It is the Spiritual realm that is real and eternal, Nicodemus. This is the realm I understand. I came from that realm. I have come for this purpose. What's more, just as there was a sacrifice to save God's people from the plague of snakes in Moses' day, I have come to be a sacrifice; opening the door to relationship with God. Anyone who looks to me will experience the lifting of the plague of sin. What I do in healing people's bodies, is just preparation for what I hope they will allow me to do in their souls.

"I didn't come to disapprove, or criticize. I didn't come to compare or pass judgment on. I have come simply to give Life; to be the Light in the darkness. Those who want to live in the Light will come to me. Those who love to do evil, will hide in the darkness, and refuse to come to the Light. Those who don't think they need the Light, but can heal themselves; they will also hide in the darkness. But those who love Truth will come to the Light, and experience Spiritual Life."

They spoke together until streaks of light began to show themselves in the eastern sky. Journeying toward his home that morning, Nicodemus realized his heart was lighter, as though a cumbersome, long-carried burden had been lifted from his soul. His perspective was different, he realized, noticing the leaves blowing around him. He was aware of Something Greater. As the awaited rain droplets began to fall, he came to understanding. It was as though God Himself had washed him, cleansing the inner recesses of his heart and soul.

How could one night have changed everything?

How long had it been since he felt so good about just being alive?

In Galilee, Eleazar and Joseph had been spending the week working their way through the fishing villages along the shores of the Sea of Galilee. It was time to renew acquaintances and contracts for the coming year. Trade had been picking up in the cities on the north side of late. So much so, Eleazar had recently made a trip to the cities of the Decapolis. The Roman and Phoenician women in the developed cities on that side of the lake were certainly interested in the dyed silk fabrics selling in Jerusalem and Jericho.

It was strange, he considered; the need for material goods transcended all boundaries and status levels. People in every city, town, or village wanted to be comfortable, and to make a good appearance.

Travelling with Joseph this week, he realized how great his company's need was to hire second and third tradesmen who could travel with their own wagons. The demand for his goods was increasing. The taste of success was a wonderful thing!

Yes, it was time to expand.

Approaching the town of Capernaum, Eleazar recognized his contact for trade.

"Zebedee! You old man! How is your fishing business?" he shook Zebedee's hand heartily.

The old man laughed. "Well, it would be a little better if *both* of my sons would stay home. But I think we're doing all right. What brings you so far from home? Aren't you living down in Jerusalem now?"

"Oh, I came up north to renew trade agreements for the year, and to check on my sister. She runs the business for me in Migdal."

"I forgot you had a sister. But now I remember her coming through here with you, when we began working together. Where is she in Migdal?"

"She works in the linen and flax trade. She lives in the house that used to belong to Ebenezer, the caravan driver."

Zebedee's connection of the young tradesman standing with him, and his knowledge of Mary's reputation in the region came together as if in slow motion. In discussions with his employees, and with the soldiers from the garrison who purchased his fish at the market, the old fisherman had heard many accounts of men's experiences with the owner of the "Silken House," as Ebenezer's old home had come to be known. *"A man gets more than trade from her,"* was a saying he had heard more than once in regard to the woman.

How had this bright and honest young man come to have such a sister? What was their story, the old man wondered? Not wanting to hurt his young friend, Zebedee raised his eyebrows and looked down at the ground, continuing to listen.

Eleazar continued. "When Ebenezer died, he left me everything, and said I was the son he had never had. It was God's provision, because our own father squandered our family's livelihood after our mother died. When we were little, we lived in a large house, in EnKarem. Then, my oldest sister married. She and her husband live in the village of Bethany."

"Is she ill?"

"No, she married a physician, and they serve the village as best they can. I stay with them when I am in the south. A few weeks ago, I sat with a man while Miriam helped his wife have a baby. She has developed into quite a healer herself."

"That profession has to be a call of God. I don't have the patience to work with sick people. I can't stand the complaining," Zebedee commented.

"I don't know how they do it," Eleazar agreed.

"So, how did your other sister come to Migdal?" the fisherman wanted to know.

"It's a long story, I'm afraid. Our mother died the day she was born, and our father hurt her terribly. At one point she ran away to live with Abiel and Miriam. When I began the trade business she traveled here with me, and Ebenezer took care of her when I was away. But now, I am gone so much of the time. I worry about her." The young man's voice trailed off.

Journey

"What do you mean?" Zebedee could sense the young man needed to talk.

"Well, each time I come home to her, there is a man visiting. It is never the same one. Whoever it is always leaves when I arrive, as though it has been pre-arranged. Mary makes a pretense that they have been doing business. Each time, the man will pay her, and she will give him goods. She won't discuss it with me, or even tell me why or what she is doing. The last time it happened, I told her she couldn't live this way, and she had to stop. After all, it is my house. She told me she agreed. And then I came home this time…"

"Yes?"

"She had a lamp lit in every room of the house. When I first arrived, I couldn't find her. After I went looking, I found her sitting in the storeroom, huddled in the corner. She didn't respond when I spoke to her. Her eyes were glazed over; and there are scars on her chest and her legs, as though she has been cut. But I know she has had no attackers. Joseph has been to the house each week, to pick up wares for the trade route through the villages. He tells me that she is always up and working when he comes. She greets him, and helps him load his wagon."

"Did she cut herself, perhaps?"

"These cuts were not done by accident. If she did cut herself, she would have had to be doing it on purpose. I keep thinking about the two men they warn the sailors about in Gadara across the Sea," Eleazar nodded toward the other side of the Sea of Galilee. "It is said they cut themselves with stones and voices other than their own come out of their bodies. I am afraid for her, Zebedee."

"Have you spoken with a priest?" the older man asked.

"No," the young merchant sighed. "I'm think they would want to stone her. She certainly would come under judgment. I'm not sure what to do. She told me once that she had been having bad dreams, and I thought it was just a child's passing nightmare."

"Could you put someone in charge of the trade in Migdal, and take her to your family in Bethany? It sounds like she needs care."

"I have thought of that. But Mary doesn't want to be anywhere where our father might chance to see her, or even know where she is."

"Whatever is faulty is based in her thinking and understanding," the older man assessed. "It will take time for her to heal, whenever it happens."

"I wish I could reach her," Eleazar told him. "I'm afraid she has slipped away from me, and I don't know what to do. It's like something inside of her has snapped."

After a short, silence, he changed the subject. "Why are your sons not at home these days?"

"Oh," Zebedee responded. "James is here, but not for long. There is a young man from Nazareth who we think might be a prophet. He has been teaching in the synagogues in the area. When the boys and Salome went to a wedding in Cana, they came home telling me how he turned water into wine during the festivities."

"Water into wine?"

"Yes. The boys have changed since they met him; more responsible. That is a definite wonder, as anyone who knows my boys will tell you. They love life, and they want to experience it. I have had to realize that they might not want to be fishermen. They just aren't as involved with the fishing business as I thought they would be."

"John isn't here?"

"When Jesus, the young man from Nazareth, left to take his family home, John and a couple of his friends went with them. They should be back in a few days. Jesus is planning on setting up his business here in Capernaum. I'm not sure whether they found a home for him while they were here. I think his father was a carpenter."

"Has he done other miracles?" Eleazar asked.

"I don't know."

~~~

It was mid-day in Bethany. Miriam sat alone in the courtyard of their home, which was unusual. She had to have a quiet place to think things through. It had been three days since she had asked the villagers not to come to the clinic for treatment.

How long had it been since the sister of one of the lepers had brought her child to them for care? If Miriam could remember correctly, the little girl, three or four years in age, had presented at the clinic with what appeared to be a common cold. After a couple of weeks, the fever still remained, and a cough began to set in. Abiel had prescribed the common herbs and teas, and had advised the mother to keep the child inside, keeping her warm and giving her lots of fluids.

On the second visit, the child had begun to have difficulty breathing, and would experience coughing spells that ended with a chirp-like sound, similar to a chicken's cluck. Miriam tried to run through the symptoms in her memory, putting them in order.

Then, when nothing was bringing a cure, Abiel and Miriam began visiting the family at home, investigating to see if there could be a simple, practical solution to the illness. One day, when Miriam was delivering some teas, the little girl had experienced a coughing spell lasting for more than a two minutes. In the process, the child had turned purple; she couldn't get enough breath. She had then thrown up.

"Does this happen often?" Miriam had asked the mother.

"Every day, several times a day," was the reply. "She no longer can eat at all."

Abiel had been intrigued by the case, and had spent several nights in the family's home, hoping to observe something to tell him what medical remedy to offer them.

Nothing made a difference in the child's condition.

Then, two weeks later, Abiel had developed cold symptoms of his own. That had been three months ago. Miriam hadn't been concerned until the coughing spells had started; deep, long-lasting coughing spells that ended in the same bird-like sound. To make matters worse, nothing stayed on his stomach for long.

He too, could no longer eat.

Yet, Abiel's main concern was always his wife's well-being. Even in the midst of his coughing spells, and his subsequent weakness, he would insist upon their daily walks.

He still prepared her tea each morning.

His worry was for her; always for her.

Journey

That particular morning, Miriam had awakened to the sound of her husband gasping for breath. It had frightened her.

She considered. It wasn't unusual for a physician to come in contact with a patient's illness. Abiel and Miriam had lived and worked in their clinic for years. Both of them had always recovered. But this time it was different.

The little girl had died two weeks ago. Early in the morning, the mother had gone into the child's sleeping area to awaken her, and had discovered a lifeless body.

As a young wife, Miriam felt as though she were watching the child's daily condition reoccurring in the body of her husband. Somehow she knew.

It was only a matter of time until Abiel died also.

How could this happen, Miriam asked herself? Hadn't they done all the right things? Wasn't God supposed to bless people who did good for others? Why Abiel? Why not someone who was dishonest, or hard-hearted, or a criminal?

Why did she have to be widowed at such a young age?

Her thoughts took her to memories of Rachel, her mother, and the day of Mary's birth. She considered her father, the older Eleazar. Had he felt this way that day? Was that why he had stopped living; and had started drinking? Was that what had happened to him? Surely, he had locked himself away when his Rachel died.

How could God let things like this happen?

Was this the design of life; to suffer pain and fear; to walk through days abandoned?

What would she do now?

In the quiet stillness of the afternoon, Miriam felt tears fall from her eyes for the first time since her childhood.

Never had she felt so alone.

Two weeks later, the younger Eleazar returned home to find his older sister at home, alone and grieving the fresh burial of her young husband. After the neighbors and concerned friends retreated to their own homes, Eleazar decided to stay in Bethany with her for a few days. Sitting with her in the courtyard, under the sycamore tree, the brother and sister grappled with their sorrow.

Pain, their old, familiar enemy, settled upon their souls and manifested itself in a heaviness of spirit. The underlying hopelessness of the Village of the Poor and Afflicted had expanded its living space. And, although both of them worked diligently to evade the emotion and tone of Loss, the accompanying sadness had found a new home.

Eleazar watched her, and realized he had no tools or insight to supply either of his sisters with what they needed for living.

Miriam knew it would be a long time until she could find the power the smile again.

Sychar

Was she imagining things? It seemed so much hotter in Sychar today than yesterday. Ahava sighed. Checking the window with full view of the well, she decided it was finally safe to venture out. She needed to draw water for washing.

Perhaps she should just put up with the pain, she thought, and go when the other women were there.

How long had it been since she had felt free to draw in the cool of the day?

How many years? She sighed. Well, she wasn't in her twenties any longer.

Pulling up her head-covering to protect her head from the midday sun, Ahava mentally counted her steps for the afternoon. She lifted the water-pot; first hoisting it to her hip and then to her shoulder. She would have to work quickly today. Miklos would be bringing his friends home with him. She knew from past experience that to not have things ready for his enjoyment when he arrived would be met with anger and disappointment.

She did not want a scene tonight.

How long had she been with him? Had it really been almost a year?

How quickly time flew by.

How many others had there been before him? She had lost count. But why would she even want to keep track? What was the point?

Where had *that* thought even come from, she wondered?

Husbands were worth counting. At least *those* men had wanted her enough to marry her.

Five husbands. Two had died, and three of them had thrown her out on the street, for one reason or another. With each of those three, she had found herself beginning her life all over again. It had been difficult. All she had owned had been clothes she wore on her back.

By the time the third one had rejected her, she had begun sewing shekels into the hem of her toga, and hiding larger coins inside her head-dress.

You never knew when your life might fall apart.

It was always better to expect the worst.

Miklos had rescued her. It had been his smile that had hooked her, she thought. Just like a fish.... He had been so caring and full of charm when he had found her on the street. He had taken her to his home, and given her food and shelter.

She owed him so much. It was important to please him; to keep him happy.

And, as long as she pleased him, she felt safe and accepted.

To think of it, Miklos wasn't much different from her father and her brothers. It seemed that no man had ever thought she had value. She sighed. After all, she was a woman.

The priests and holy men wouldn't even look at her.

Journey

And to make it worse, she was a Samaritan.

A reject; avoided and suspected. And to be honest, Samaria was a land of half-breeds and idolaters, or at least, every religious-minded person in Israel said so. The people of her country had inter-married with foreigners. Even their worship was criticized. The Samaritans had tried to continue to worship on their own mountain, instead of coming to the Temple in Jerusalem each year. It didn't matter if their reasons were historical and made good sense to them, she considered. Never mind that Moses' Tabernacle still rested there. The Jews wouldn't even travel through Samaria, adding over 15 miles to a journey just to avoid the Samaritan border! She had once overheard a Jewish priest compare her people with those in the leper colonies....

Of course, most Samaritans had decided that God avoided them as well. Shouldn't they believe so? The so-called "righteous and accepted" taught their children that even God disapproved of and rejected people who didn't worship Him in the right way.

Ahava shook her head. Why was her focus on such negative thoughts today?

Moving outdoors, she ventured down the street toward the well. It was a square, stone structure, with a sitting ledge, or step, surrounding it in its design. The rope and drawing pail were fastened to a hook on the far side. She would have to go around again, she realized. Looking down, according to habit, the woman moved quickly to lower the wooden drawing bucket down into the open access to the water below.

She was so absorbed in her duties; she was unaware of the figure seated at the well, not even ten feet away.

"Could I have a drink?"

Ahava startled. She could tell by the man's accent he was from .... Israel? He sounded like he was from the north..... Was it a Galilean accent?

"Did you say something, sir?"

"Could I have a drink? I have no cup to draw with."

Well, at least he was a man with manners, and didn't just help himself, or drink from the drawing bucket, she thought.

"How is it that you, a Jew, would speak to a Samaritan? People like you don't usually talk to people like me... especially since I'm a woman."

"If you knew who you were speaking with, you would have asked *me* for water; water with Life in it. And I would have given it to you," the man replied.

Ahava was intrigued. "But I thought you said you didn't have a cup to draw with. Where would you get that kind of water from? Do you think you can do better than our ancestor, Jacob, who dug this well?"

"Listen," the man answered, "whoever drinks from this well will be thirsty again in an hour. The water I am talking about is alive. It will become a well of its own inside anyone who drinks of it. It will become a fountain that will satisfy a person's thirst forever. It will flow from the deepest part of your being."

"I would like to get my hands on some of the water you are talking about, mister," Ahava said. "I would like to never have to come to this well to draw water again."

Journey

"Okay," the man replied. "Go and get your husband and come back here."

Ahava looked down at the ground. "I don't have a husband," she murmured.

The man stood up and came close to her. He put his hand under her chin, and with one finger lifted her face so that she was looking up into the deepest eyes she had ever seen. "I know," he said gently. "You are telling me the truth. In fact, you have had *five* husbands, and the man you are living with right now, is not your husband."

Ahava felt as though his look had seen to the rock bottom of her life; past, present and future. She was transfixed; she didn't want to move. What was it about this stranger? His touch was different from any of the other men she had known. There were no sexual overtones in his touch; or his look…. It felt safe. His touch was a communication of care and concern.

Ahava broke from his gaze to look downward. "Sir, I get the feeling that you are a prophet." She tried to change the subject of the conversation. "If you are a prophet, tell me something. Where is the right place to worship; here on Mt. Gershom, or in Jerusalem? You Jews say that we can't worship God properly, and do it here in Samaria."

The man laughed, and stepped away from her, toward the drawing pail. "Let me tell you something, Ahava. People get focused on the wrong things when it comes to having a relationship with God. God's concern is that worship be from the heart, and that it be honest, complete and true." He paused, looking down into the well's opening. "God is not as concerned about *where* worship happens, as he is concerned about the condition of the heart it comes from. God is Spirit. *People* are the ones who worry about the physical things. *God's* focus is on the spiritual; the eternal. People were made in the image of God, to bear the image of God; so people are spirit as well. Those who worship God must worship in spirit and in truth. In fact, God seeks out people who will worship Him just that way."

He looked up once again at her and smiled. Suddenly, Ahava was aware of a Presence. She shivered slightly, realizing she was standing at a personal crossroads. Who *was* this man standing in front of her? Had she told him her name? How did he know her?

"Sir," she spoke quickly, as though desperate to get the words out, "I know that when the Promised Deliverer comes, he will show us all things. He will explain these things to us, and will help us to understand who God really is and what He is like…."

A few seconds of silence passed between them. Ahava found herself having difficulty putting her thoughts and questions into words. It was as though her emotions were just out of the reach of her vocabulary. When she realized she had stopped speaking mid-sentence, Ahava looked up. Surprised, she found the man's gaze fixed on her. Then he spoke.

"I am that Promised Deliverer, Ahava. My name is Jesus."

Something inside Ahava's being jumped. Involuntarily, she breathed in, as though gasping for air. Was it true? It had to be. She could feel it. Suddenly, all of her questions about her own life came rushing to the surface. She left the water-pot untended on the ledge and sat down next to this man; this Jesus.

For the next several hours, they sat together, sharing and laughing like old friends. As the time passed, the heavy veils of disillusionment and fear melted from her heart, long shut-away and abandoned. What was the Power this man carried? What authority and understanding was it? As the shadows lengthened, and the cool of the day approached, Ahava realized she didn't care if the women of the neighborhood saw her with *this* man. It didn't bother her *what* they might say about her *this* time. Let the gossipers draw their conclusions.

She had found her life.

Suddenly, there was no fear of Miklos, or of his friends, or even of their ability to put her out on the street again.

His anger didn't matter anymore. Her heart was at peace.

As the afternoon was coming to a close, Jesus' friends approached the well, looking for him, with packages of fish and bread in hand. They began to speak with him. "Eat something, Jesus," they offered.

"I'm not really hungry right now."

"Did someone feed you? You can't have eaten anything….. And why are you talking to a Samaritan woman?"

"I've had food to eat that you wouldn't understand. I have done what my Father wanted me to do. Just knowing that has taken my hunger away."

Wanting to give them room for their discussion, Ahava quietly retreated to fill her water-pot. Hoisting it once again to her shoulder, she carried it into Miklos' house. It was then she realized how late she really was.

Her benefactor was sitting by the window with the two friends he had brought home from the races in Caesarea. "Where had you been?" he wanted to know, a tinge of anger in his voice. "I thought I told you I wanted to eat at this hour."

"Miklos," strangely calm, she spoke as she put the water-pot by the fire. "You have to come back to the well with me. I met someone today."

His eyebrows went up, fully expecting her to tell him of a new-found love. "A man? Another one? That is why my bread isn't made, and the house looks like this? What are you trying to tell me, woman?"

"He is a prophet. He told me *everything* I had ever done. He just knew."

"Everything?" Miklos was surprised and more than a little concerned. "How?"

"I don't know," she replied excitedly. "He *says* he is the Promised Deliverer."

"*Here? The Jewish Deliverer?* In Samaria?"

"I know. I know. But yes, in Samaria." She looked around the room. "And yes," she paused for emphasis, looking him in the eye, "everything."

It took less than a minute for Miklos and his friends to gather their cloaks and sandals, and move outdoors to meet the man who was still sitting at the well. As soon as they left the house, Ahava made her way through the streets of Sychar, to the homes of the men she knew, and the homes of those she *had known*, in the city. At each door she repeated her astonished declaration, "You have to come and meet the man who told me everything I had ever done, without anyone telling him anything."

Journey

Long after sunset in Sychar, the townspeople sat by a well, to listen and dialogue with Jesus, the young man from Galilee. Long after the moon rose, and even continuing for the next few days, physical bodies were healed, hearts were mended, souls were freed, and lives were made new. Young and old alike opened their hearts to hear and believe the man who had asked Ahava for a drink of water on a hot afternoon.

In the middle of the darkness, Light had begun to glimmer in the hearts of a people who believed God had forgotten them.

Hope was breathing once again in Samaria.

It was the beginning of New Life.

~~~

The night-watch in Galilee was proving to be uneventful tonight.

It was close to two in the morning.

Justus Flavius was born a Roman citizen. Now that he considered, it seemed he had been a soldier in the service of the empire almost that long as well. As a boy, he'd served with his father on battlefields in the Roman civil war. Small and wiry, he was able to courier messages behind the lines without being discovered.

Justus smiled into the fire and rubbed his hands together, warming them. The generals encouraged him, even then, it seemed. He remembered standing in the middle of a gathering of great military minds; hearing someone comment how much he looked like his grandfather. How strange it was to be seeing flecks of silver in his own hair in these days, he thought!

Yes, the military had been integrated into the Flavius family history. Justus' grand-father served as a commander with the great Julius Caesar in the early days of the empire, some seventy years prior. His son, Andronicus, who was Justus' father, spent many hours with the boy, sharing stories from the battlefields and war-rooms.

How Justus had loved hearing stories of the battles in Egypt and Hispania; how the Caesar had fallen in love with the princess, Cleopatra! Not only was the conquest of a formidable nation appealing, but to the mind of a young boy, the conquest of a resistant princess drew attention as well. As a boy, Andronicus' stories swept his son away to worlds outside of his own, whetting his appetites to learn the strategies and ways of war.

To be a soldier for Rome was the mark of a man.

Justus became pensive as he considered his father's life. The Flavius family was not of the noble patricians, with wealth and privilege. Rather they were part of the middle, working class of the Roman citizenry. As such, his fortunes had risen and fallen with the conquests of his superiors: the harder the duty, the greater the pay; the larger the conquest, the larger the bonus.

As his pay scale increased; so had his rank and privilege. Now, after twenty-three years with the military, he was Centurion Commander of the garrison, and assistant to the Legion Commander, whose station was in Jerusalem.

Justus was considered a career soldier. As such, he was provided many advantages not allowed the common foot-soldier. One such privilege was housing being provided for his family, who followed him to whatever assignment he was given, unless the area were in a war zone. Food and medical allowances were also provided for his wife and children. Additionally, when he retired, his home became his own.

As commander of the area garrison for the empire, Justus drew the respect and ear of those in Rome who kept their fingers on the pulse beat of Israel's political situation. Many of such officials in the capital were long time friends of his family.

It wasn't a difficult assignment, really, he had recently concluded. After all, he could dictate his own schedule, as long as his men kept order, and maintained their reports to Rome, through the Syrian governor, and to Herod Antipas, the tetrarch. During his tenure, there had been time to learn new languages, and teach his children to read. There had also been time to finally work through the silent conflicts with his wife, Julia.

He had discovered his own heart in the process.

Yes, having a home to retreat to from the garrison made all the difference for the centurion. It was a haven, a place to rest and ponder; something he had been doing much of late. Life in the barracks was grueling. He remembered his early days as he stoked the fire.

Justus was the first in his family's line to own a house slave. And now, they owned four. Julia had doubled their investment by purchasing a young woman and her son off the block during the last growing season. So much help was needed around the house, to harvest the garden, and prepare food for winter storage. His parents had always hired servants, and hadn't believed in slavery. "It devalues a man, to make him a slave," his mother had said.

His mother had a keen sense of values, he considered. Sher would not attend the games, either, as they disturbed her "sense of peace." "Human beings should not kill each other *for sport*; nor should we; nor can we be *owned*. We are not cattle to be traded," she had told him. "These things will be the undoing of Rome."

He had not told his mother about his slave purchases.

He sighed.

This was one of the few good points to being outside of Italy, too. Some conflicts were meant to be avoided.

On the other hand, it was a good thing for Julia to have help around the house, he considered. Years ago, before his marriage, he had purchased Adelphos, a young Greek with education in languages and numbers, to be his companion and steward. What a tremendous relationship they had developed! Why, Adelphos was more of a brother now, than a slave. These days, the man took care of the household details, and handled his investments as well.

If it weren't for Julia and the children, he would have no need to come home, except to rest, he told himself. His steward ran things more efficiently than he ever could.

Having daughters meant not having sons to help with the heavier tasks around the house. Julia needed someone near with a strong arm to serve when he was away on duty. That had not been the case during his own childhood. Justus could remember having to carry the water for washing at five years of age. No matter, the hard work had prepared him for war.

"Everything in life is preparation," his father had told him.

Victoria and Helena, his daughters, did not need to be prepared for war.

They needed training for life.

Journey

Justus shrugged. Not everyone in the empire could afford to pay servants. Most of the empire had, out of necessity, become slave owners. It was impossible to live well without someone helping. In the long run, it was cheaper to purchase a life on the block than pay an hour's wage. Not only that, but the younger of his daughters, Helena, many times found herself alone, and needing a friend. The young woman's son would be a playmate and protector. After all, Helena's sister was so much older.

The new slave boy was about the same age his sons would have been.

The fresh gap in years between Victoria and little Helena was still a source of deep sorrow for Justus. He brushed away the sudden wetness from his eyes.

It had been difficult to bury his twin sons last year. The fever came upon the youngest son so suddenly; within a fortnight both were gone. It was almost a year to this day. For a time, he was tempted to withdraw into himself. Had there been a war to volunteer for, he would have tried to join them in death.

He was glad now to be serving in peace-time.

How he would have wronged his family! Suicide was a selfish man's escape, he had decided.

It had been his little Helena who had reached him in his dark pit. "Father, will you take me fishing?" She had pestered him until he had relented and had taken her out with her tiny net. Standing by the shore, her little arms had not been strong or long enough to throw the net into the deeper waters where she would catch even the tiniest bait fish. Independent in nature, she resisted her father's help.

Justus smiled. It must have been an amusing scene, to see a helpless centurion with a little girl at his side, standing on the shoreline. The town's fishermen were outfitting their tools and riggings that afternoon. Justus struck up conversation with one of the older men.

"You want to ride on the water, Helena?" Zebedee had invited. He had a need for net-making supplies and was crossing the water to a nearby village.

How had Zebedee become such a good friend to him? How unlikely that a soldier and a fisherman would find so much in common. In some ways, the crusty mannerisms of the older man reminded him of his father. Both were hard working men. Both had experienced the pains of life. Both had managed to stay alive and raise a family in difficult times in the empire.

It had been Zebedee who suggested he seek answers in a God other than the gods of Rome. It had been Zebedee who gave him a fatherly hug when the grief of the loss of his sons overwhelmed him. It had been Zebedee who taught him how to fish, a pastime in which he now found solitude.

Watching Zebedee, he determined to put his energies into raising strong and healthy daughters. He and Julia found themselves at the fisherman's home for dinner more than once.

He paused in his thought processes, looking around him.

The watch was going well. The sky was clearing. Justus added a log to the fire, and stoked it. He rose to stretch and check on his men. It would be daylight soon.

Journey

What was it about Zebedee that reminded him of his father? How did the two men compare?

Justus' father, Andronicus, had loved the soldiering life, beginning his career on the battlefields of the Roman civil wars; then later being assigned to the Praetorian Cohort in the Roman senate. Those had been dangerous days for a man in the Guard in Rome.

It was during his father's tenure there he had met his wife, the beautiful Geneva, daughter of a senator from Malta. They had married and continued to live in Rome.

Geneva's family had perfected a breeding process for a particular small dog. Completely white and tiny, the breed had become a status symbol for Roman women to carry in their togas. The expressive little black eyes could even be seen peeking from a satchel or two in the marketplace!

The senator from Malta, Geneva's father, had made a gift to Caesar Tiberius of a breeding pair along with a slave to raise them. As part of the Praetorian Cohort, it became Andronicus' duty to tend to the animals, and keep watch on the slave. When the dogs did breed, and then give birth to a litter, the soldier was afraid of damaging the tiny pups. Each one measured the length of a man's finger at birth. When concerned because they didn't seem to be eating enough, Andronicus appealed to the senator, who laughed and referred him to his daughter, Geneva.

And so, the love story had begun. As the years had passed, the little Maltese dog had become a necessary and comforting element in all of the Flavius family homes. Its breed had also proliferated throughout the empire!

Justus chuckled, thinking about the little dog. The tradition of keeping such a pet was such a deeply imbedded tradition in his heart, that here, even in Galilee, a tiny white dog lived in his own home! Even now, the centurion could picture his daughters with Julia, playing chase and tug with the little thing.

Justus smiled into the fire. He stoked the embers. When their family arrived in Capernaum, the little dog caused conflict in Galilee, it seemed.

Being Roman made it a small matter.

When had his father made the decision not to leave Rome? Justus was not sure. Over the years it had become evident to him his father had not ventured outside the capital since the murder of Caesar Julius.

How many Caesars had there been since Julius? Justus had lost count.

The army must be in his blood, the centurion concluded. It was a noble thing to serve one's country; bringing civilization to the far ends of the earth. Hadn't Rome brought bridges and roads to the entire world? And libraries? And universities? Yes, the world was better off.

Anything the empire brought to a place made it better.

Justus was halted in his daydream. Well, perhaps not *anything* the empire brought. Hadn't his concern over *some* things caused him to begin his friendship with Simon the Pharisee? Yes, and to support the building of the synagogue, too.

There was something different about the belief system of these people. Their God was the center of their lives; so different from the jaded and skeptical responses of his own people to the plethora of gods and goddesses provided by the empire. Justus could remember overhearing his grandfather's reaction to the Senate's decision to bestow the title "deity" to Julius Caesar.

"The man is no god," he told Andronicus. "If he *were* a god, he would live forever. I have watched him sick on the battlefield. Gods do not get sick. I have seen his selfishness. Furthermore, I have heard him pray *to* the gods *himself.* This is nothing more than someone's ploy for power."

He had paused, and looked around before continuing. "My son, there are dangerous things afoot here. You watch. He will die, and they will bury him one day. It is dangerous for a man to be hailed by so many. The tides turn too quickly and unexpectedly."

Justus had not fully grasped the truth of his grandfather's words at the time.

But then, as circumstances and relationships around the Caesar changed in days following, Justus marveled at the wisdom of his grandfather's observations. He realized now he had silently made a decision to be a better listener and observer because of what he had witnessed.

Many night-time discussions with his father by the fire taught him to choose his values early on.

Socrates said "the unexamined life is not worth living." Socrates also made the observation "The greatest wisdom is to accept one's ignorance." The phrases were well quoted in the Flavius family. Justus considered now, how those modes of thinking kept them all alive during the civil wars.

If there *was* one single Power governing the universe, did it hold a purpose for him, he wondered?

The Centurion Commander watched the embers, glowing under the split logs in front of him. The sun's embers were beginning to show themselves on the far horizon, and the wind was picking up a little. He stamped his feet, and looked out over the garrison wall. How nice it would have been to be at home this evening with his Julia! Just to sit with a cup of warm wine or tea under the grapevines, and look at the stars through her eyes.

Justus considered himself a blessed man. Wherever the blessing had come from, he reasoned, it certainly was not due to any good thing he had done on his own. Out of all the commanders in the garrisons in Galilee, who could boast their family had been willing to move to such a post? To Galilee -- with its primitive culture and backwards ways; with its dangerous bandits and limited advantages.... To the desert -- with its unbelievable heat and parched riverbeds in summer....

Never mind the ruthlessness of the rulers in the region. Herod Antipas all by himself was a danger. It was said he had recently beheaded a pious man, who many of his own people had called a prophet. And why? Because the man had taken issue with Antipas seducing and stealing his brother's wife! Justus could remember days when that action would have been a catalyst for a judgment from the Roman Senate. The man would have been removed from his office.

Journey

But now, so many things were shifting in the empire. It was better to be stationed in a remote location.

The prophet in question had lost his head because of a belly dancer, it was said. It was becoming unsafe to voice a reasonable moral judgment, Justus observed. The rulers were beginning to follow the example of the people, he reasoned, instead of things being the other way around…..

Looking down at his hand, he saw his wedding ring.

His wife's face flickered in his mind.

Yes, Julia was a treasure; a prize for certain. Who would ask such a gentle creature to give up her life of privilege for *this*? He couldn't wait for the end of the watch.

He would go home now.

"Commander! Commander Flavius!" The call came from Titus, one of his men.

"What is it? I'm heading home for a rest after the watch. Walk with me."

"I cannot find my partner, Atticus. He headed to Migdal two weeks ago, saying something about the festival at Panias. He told me he would send word to me as to his arrival there, and he has not. Now, two of the men who were scheduled to run safety patrols are ill, and battalion leader Farzin has commanded Atticus and me to take the assignment. His leave has been cancelled. I have no idea where to begin to find him. Did he speak with you? Do you know where I could go, or what I should do? I don't have permission to leave the regiment." Titus fell into step with his centurion as he spoke.

"Who is on barracks duty? Did he file a report on his planned travel before he left? Why wasn't this reported?"

"You know the men. If they meet a woman or if they go somewhere other than the location they have intended when they leave the garrison….. we always give them a little room for … well…extra time."

"Yes, I forgot, he's unmarried," Justus chuckled. "Where do you think he went?"

"The problem is, Farzin has scheduled us to begin patrol duty on the trade routes today and continue for the next couple of weeks. Atticus' satchel is not packed, and he is not here. We are due to leave in the morning. He won't be ready without notice."

"I see," the commander responded. "Well, Atticus is a good soldier; this *is* unusual. And you're right. I didn't realize so many of the men had fallen to the sickness going around the village. Let me send word to my wife I will be home a little later. I'll go with you to look for him." They stopped at Justus' office door. The centurion took a clay tablet from the stack on the shelf behind his table to send a note to his wife. He called one of the garrison slaves and sent him off as a courier. He didn't want Julia to worry.

Stretching his arms and back, he tried to ease a little of the stiffness which had set in during the damp hours of his watch duty the night before.

"Commander Justus, are you sure you want to go with me, sir? You have been up all night." Titus spoke with concern. The centurion was well loved. It was not unusual for him to take a personal interest in the lives of the men under his command. Another commander might have angrily filed a report on Atticus' irresponsibility and headed home. Not this man

He saw himself as a father to the younger men; the militia in his command. As a result his contingent responded with reciprocal concern for his welfare as well.

They were also more teachable, more workable, and had greater communication skills.

It had been hard work to get there, but the Galilee Cohort functioned as a team.

"Yes, yes," Justus patted the younger man's arm. "I've been up all night once or twice before now." Rubbing his hands over his face, he said, "If it begins to take too long, I'll send a courier for a replacement." He paused. "I'm sure he's fine, Titus. He probably just had too much ale, and is sleeping it off somewhere. Don't worry yourself. Besides, I know your battalion leader's Commander. He is a reasonable man."

Later that morning, Justus wondered why he hadn't simply countermanded Farzin's orders. Perhaps that would have been the best choice. Perhaps he had just wanted a little change from the normal routine.

But then, there was the other matter, he mused. It would have to be handled sooner or later.

The two soldiers paused at the garrison stables to obtain fresh mounts for their search. It would be easier to cover the ten miles to the Migdal tower more quickly on horseback. Checking the sundial's shadow on his way to the gate, Justus realized the market stands were opening for the day. So, as they began their journey, Titus and his Commander paused once again; this time at a food vendor's stand, to purchase bread, fruit and a wineskin to share.

It was going to be a long day.. or maybe even two or three.

Simon the Pharisee was uncharacteristically quiet during the trip home to Capernaum. Abigail watched him. It was obvious to her; even though as they left his parents' home he was cordial and made jokes with the children. He had changed somehow during this trip. He must be grappling with something of deep concern.

She waited as Judah and Simon loaded the wagon, making sure to create individual places of rest for the children, who would not be able to walk the entire journey. Hadassah brought out a basket of fish and bread she had packed them. She had even added a little fruit.

"Those boys eat too much bread and cheese," Hadassah told her. "They need some fruit, and a lot more vegetables in their diet."

Abigail laughed. "You can be the one to hold them down and feed them."

Simon and Abigail had five children; two sons, and three daughters. Stair-stepped in age, the children's genders alternated; girl, boy, girl, boy, girl. Elizabeth was fifteen now, and her mother's right arm around the house. David was eleven, in so many ways already acting like a man; he would be going to the synagogue day-school very soon. The distance in years between these two had seen the deaths of two infants, now waiting in heaven to be held by their parents. Dorcas, the middle child, was ten, followed by Daniel, who was both a comic and a terror at eight. Deborah, the youngest, still nursing her thumbs, was now five years old.

Where had the time gone?

Journey

Since the birth of her last baby, Abigail realized her body was showing signs of beginning the Change. No matter. Five children was a good number for any family. It brought their home to the number of blessing and completeness: seven.

"What is on your mind, Simon?" she asked, trying to open doors, or even windows, of communication.

"Oh I was just thinking about that prophet out in the desert. What was his name ….," he paused, trying to remember, "… John?"

"Yes, I think so. Your mother said he was the son of her great-aunt. Did she speak with you?"

"No, not really," he replied. "We didn't talk much this trip."

"You were at the temple more than usual, this time," his wife observed. "Did anything special happen?"

Simon looked at his wife. She was easy to talk to, he realized. So, why did he find it difficult to tell her his thoughts? Perhaps he just wasn't supposed to share some things, he considered. Yes, some things were better left unsaid. Well, he couldn't tell her about the high priest's fears, or about his newly acquired place of trust as an informant, especially in front of the children.

So he shrugged.

"Nothing much of significance," he answered. "What did my mother tell you about John?"

"Apparently, his parents were both from priestly families. There were angelic appearances around his birth. According to the grapevine, it was a story like Abram and Sarai of old. John was given to them by God in their old age. Zacharias, John's father, was an old man when he was born; and Elizabeth had been barren for some time. The angel told them that John would be a prophet, who would prepare the way for God's Deliverer."

Simon heard her, but had drifted away once again in the middle of her discourse. His mind had centered once again on the luncheon he had shared with Joseph Caiaphas. How was he supposed to gain information regarding the young prophet concerning Joseph? He would have to come up with a plan. He once again fell silent, and remained so for the majority of the journey.

Abigail sighed. How could she have a relationship with someone who never responded? What would happen to her life when the house was empty and the children were grown, she wondered? It was good, for now, to have five children to busy herself with, she considered.

Moving away to let Simon walk alone, Abigail took the arm of her oldest daughter. She began to sing songs and skip with the children. As she did so, her mind and heart came to a silent resolution.

She had waited long enough.

She would not pine away, waiting for her husband to become once again like the young man she had married. His nature was evident. Silently, she chose. It wasn't necessary to wait for Simon to show his approval or to communicate any longer. She needed friendship. She

Journey

was tired of living alone in her marriage. She was weary of working all the time, feeling like she was earning her niche.

She would not be unfaithful to him. No, he was a good provider, and was reasonably kind to her. He just never seemed to want relationship outside of the bedroom. Looking at her son's smile, listening to her daughters' laughter, she changed her focus. She would begin to pour herself into her children even more than before. She was disillusioned with waiting, getting her hopes up, and then being disappointed.

The cycle had repeated itself so many times she had come to *expect* disappointment. Oh well, she thought, it doesn't really matter. I can't do anything about it.

She felt drained; sick of the ache, weary of the burden, frustrated with the silence; Most of all, she felt the cold fingers of anger inside; squeezing the sense of identity from her heart. It was difficult to be so isolated, with no one to share with.

How could she work through these emotions alone?

Surely there had to be another woman somewhere who felt as she did….. perhaps even in Capernaum.

As she walked, she came to a resolve. She would find new friends.

She would not become a casualty to bitterness.

She would survive.

Caught up in his own world, Simon was oblivious to his wife's choices. Tugging on his beard, he felt a sharp pain move through his jaw. What was happening to his body, he speculated? He would have to drink some tea when he arrived home. Where had this new pain come from? Perhaps it was due to his sleeping position at his father's home. They had been in a different place the night before, after all.

He would not think about it just now.

There were more important matters needing his attention.

As a priest, he had much to do. Visiting the Temple in Jerusalem had brought him to awareness of so many weak areas in his leadership style. As ruler of the synagogue in Capernaum, he suddenly realized how slack he had become in his methods of relating to those under his care.

He had been far too trusting; far too easy-going.

To begin with, his new responsibilities had been delegated to him by Caiaphas, the high priest himself. Simon smiled to himself. He was now a part of Joseph's inner circle: the "Circle of the Friends of God." How could he best protect and serve the people in his care?

What Providence! Surely the uneducated, like Zebedee and his sons would be swept away in this new deception, had these things not taken place! Wasn't Zebedee's son, John, already following this man, leaving behind his duties as a son and heir? How could anything good come of such irresponsibility?

"O God," Simon prayed. "Show me how to help the people. Make me a good ruler. Teach me how to evaluate and judge those in my care. Help me to expose this man Jesus for what he really is. Help me to protect these people. Give me wisdom. I thank you that I am not

Journey

like other men; that I am holy and a just man. Thank you that I know your Law. Guard me. Guard all of us from the traps of deception. So be it, and let it continue. Amen."

Yes, that would do the trick. God listened when his priests prayed. Hadn't he been set above other men for a purpose? God would help him.

Wasn't Elohim *already* showing him approval and blessing, in giving him favor with those who were loyal in the Court of the Hewn Stones? Perhaps, he mused, *he* might become the very tool that would change the Court once again. *His* knowledge and wisdom might just be the missing link in the chemistry of the High Council. Yes, Joseph needed him; needed his input. There were gaps in even Joseph's leadership style. That was the reason for the division within the High Council.

He would store up instruction. He could tell them a thing or two.

Simon was resolved. He would work hard at his new post. Perhaps he would even earn a place to serve alongside his father, Judah.

He would someday be a part of the High Council.

What insight he had been given! What knowledge! Above that of other men! Yes, he was needed to bring change. And he would be faithful to the call. He was gifted, so gifted; and had so much to offer.

When the family arrived home, although it was late, Simon took a walk through the town of Capernaum down to the water's edge. He always felt closer to God when he could see the reflection of the moon upon the water. It occurred to him how his life was designed to be a reflection of God to for those entrusted to his care. Well, he decided, he had been lax in his duties. He would be more observant. He would be more vigilant.

He would become a better keeper and enforcer of the Law.

Walking past the garrison, he noticed Commander Flavius warming his hands by the fire. Justus must be on watch duty tonight, he observed.

Continuing his walk, Simon considered his own life and his relationship to the Council of the Hewn Stones. Wasn't he a soldier as well? Yes, he was a religious soldier in an unseen army of souls. He was a commander as well. Why had he not realized this duty before?

He might not have seen it before, but he could see it now. Without realizing it, during his journey to Jerusalem, he had stepped into rank.

What a fortunate happening it had been he had been at the Temple Mount at just the right moment! He had observed firsthand the spiritual battle at hand! And he had been faithful to follow those in charge.

That must be how God chose his leaders! He had stumbled onto something, Simon thought, and it was pivotal; with the potential to change his life. This new vigilance he could feel within himself had an iron edge. It was sharp, and ready to cut out those who infringed on what Joseph Caiaphas had called the purposes of God.

What better way to earn God's endorsement and approval?

He would do anything to gain God's approval, he told himself.

Anything.

Journey

Joseph had gained Simon's trust and involvement through a meal. That might just be the ticket, Simon considered. What if ….. yes……

It would take some time to plan, but it could be done.

He would speak to Abigail about hosting a dinner. It was good to have such a capable wife! He could invite the leaders of the synagogue, as well as this Jesus. Why, he would also invite Zebedee and his sons!

And perhaps Justus Flavius. He could afford to be generous. Justus might be a Roman, but he was most certainly not a pagan. After all, the man had practically built the entire synagogue! Yes, the Commander should come to dinner. He was in the midst of converting, if he hadn't already done so in his heart…..

Simon thought through his plans. Over the meal, he would find out just exactly why people were so enamored with this so-called prophet. Perhaps he could catch Jesus in his words; and expose the man to be no prophet at all.

Perhaps he could even help this young man to come into the True Light of God; get him to be a little more respectful …. and perhaps prolong his life.

But then, conceivably he might discover something more ominous behind all the so-called miracles.

No one was *that* good. There had to be a catch somewhere.

He would find it.

Yes, it was time to pull in the reins a little. He had been afraid to utilize his authority; but no more.

Too much was at stake.

Journey

Panic

A little over fifty miles away to the north, in the newly finished city of Caesarea Philippi, the lovely Dido sat in her salon, waiting for the first clients of the day. She was up earlier than usual that morning. There were so many extra preparations to be made during the festival; more than on quieter days. The city and temple were thronged with pilgrims coming to pay homage to Pan and his Court. And the festival still had ten days to go!

She took a sip of her tea, and glanced at the angle of the sun through the window. Just a little longer to enjoy the peace before they descended upon her; the swarm of comfort-seekers; the stressed; the entitled.

Her slaves would be bringing in the food trays soon. Why was it people always relaxed more easily when food was served? She smiled. It had been a good day when she had rescued the Greek mother and daughter, Sylvia and Syrene, at the slave market. Just behind her in the line of purchasers had been Adonis, steward of the Sacred Brothel.

The man was nothing like the god, she thought. The priests must have changed his name....

He would have taken the daughter in a heartbeat, she reasoned, just because of her long, black, silky tresses and slender shape. Dido remembered observing the steward's manner of examining potential slaves. He had been working behind her in line, making the women publicly disrobe, leering as he checked their teeth and bone structure. He had encircled one particular woman with his arm after making her disrobe. He had drawn her nude body to him. "You'll be amazed by what I can teach you, if *I* buy you," Dido overheard him breathe into her ear.

"No! No! No!" A high-pitched, nasal-sounding vendor had reprimanded. "You cannot touch the merchandise until you purchase it!" Dido giggled as the images resurfaced. The short, rotund and toothless slave trader had trotted from across the rows, shaking his staff and yelling. Out of habit the man had hit Adonis squarely on the top of the head, as well as on the shoulders, until he had released the naked girl. "Enough of that!" he had demanded. "Move on down the line!"

Adonis had recoiled and whined. "I was just seeing how they would measure up at the Brothel." He rubbed his head where it had connected with the man's staff. "I have to make them want it."

"You don't try them on unless you purchase them. If you do it again, you will be barred from any more purchases today. It isn't fair to the buyers who come behind you."

Adonis had looked around for support. His eyes settled on Dido to appeal. "You understand, don't you Mistress Dido?"

She was still amazed she had found the ability to speak civilly to the man. "Your appetites are best kept *inside* the Brothel, Adonis. The priests will not be pleased if you lose the ability to purchase today." The man had settled down after that.

She shuddered. She wouldn't want to be in that man's presence for an *hour!* Even when he was bathed she felt the need to wash after shaking his hand.... What must it be like to have him for an owner?

She thought of her own little girl, at home in the charge of her nurse. It was good she would never have to worry about becoming a slave.

Adonis had looked ahead in line, viewing Syrene. "Now there's one," he had said confidentially to Dido. "Look at her. Men coming to Panias to worship Aphrodite can imagine themselves in the arms of a goddess. Why, *I* might even have a go. She's young, too; but I like them young.... easier to break in... Of course, the young ones scream too much when we tattoo them with the image of the gods for the Brothel." He had laughed a sinister laugh, and jabbed Dido in the side. "Think she's a screamer, Mistress Dido?"

Dido had pulled back, repulsed. He had ventured to stand too close to her. "I'm sorry," she replied out of nowhere. "This is my second time to walk through the market today. I have already made the decision to purchase both the mother and the daughter. I need their hair for wigs for the salon. And, since I was here first, I have the right to choose."

Dido smiled as she remembered the man's obvious disappointment. "I'll have to remember that next month. I'll get here earlier," he had snarled.

Adonis' constant clutching would provide no life for a beautiful woman, especially a brothel slave, Dido reasoned. Syrene, at fourteen, would have been diseased within two years. Sylvia, the mother, would have died from burns, exhaustion, or worse, as part of the city's cleaning or laundry workforce.

Her eyes misted as she remembered Sylvia falling to her knees to kiss her hands and feet when the purchase was finalized. "Thank you, mistress," she said. "We promise to serve you well. We will serve you well."

Even when Dido had shaved their heads to harvest their hair for wigs and extensions, the two women had continued to express gratitude.

The next day, they had surprised her by baking delicate pastries, some with sweetened fruit or nut filling. They served her a breakfast before the sun rose. Since that time, she had given them a place of status in her household; that of baking for the salon. Each evening as the rest of the house was retiring, Sylvia and Syrene arose from afternoon sleep. They worked through the night to prepare fresh pastries for the next day's business. It was amazing, Dido considered. The simple addition of those dainty morsels had increased her clientele. Perhaps it was the favor of the gods for her treatment of Sylvia and Syrene. Now, other merchants had begun to request pastries from her as well. Perhaps it was time to expand into a new business....

Or maybe not.

She sighed.

She was tired of working, although no one could argue with her accomplishments.

Journey

Phoenician by birth, Dido prided herself on caring well for her slaves. Hadn't it worked well for her to allow them to experience the very therapies performed in serving her salon? They were better able to recommend potential treatments as well. She had worked tirelessly to see that each of her slaves were educated in *all* of the remedies offered. It had proven to insure personal and individualized care for each of her customers.

Over the years, she had learned to pair her clients with slaves of the opposite gender. Once a trained slave was assigned to a customer, they could walk from one therapy to another with that person, ensuring complete care and satisfaction. It also added a little sense of romance to their experience, she had found. Her confidentiality endeared her to her clients.

What happened at Dido's, stayed behind them.

This approach to business had caused her business to become vital to the epicurean nature of the city. *"Come to Panias, and experience Dido's."*

She stifled a yawn. Was it possible to succeed at something without becoming so weary?

Why did she push herself so hard? But then, the insistent voice in her head reminded her: the only way to continue the quality of her salon was to oversee everything herself.

Well, at least the money was good.

Was it this morning the Syrian governor's wife and daughters were coming in? Who else was on the list? She made a review. It would be time to appoint certain slaves to wait for their specific clients soon. She checked the list again. How many were needed? When multiple treatments were involved she had developed a rule: one slave per client per day. In this way, her slaves were rested and had strength to provide the excellent services she was known for.

Attentive slaves provided excellent services.

Excellent services meant excellent profits.

Dido began setting up her money changing table. It paid well to plan well, she considered.

Just styling the hair for the temple's sacred prostitutes had taken the total attention of three of her male slaves. She always assigned the same three to that task. It was easier in the long run, although those three male slaves were popular with all of her women clients. Each one was artistic in nature and could suggest styles and therapies. She was unsure as to their ethnic backgrounds; two were tall, and darker skinned, with dark eyes. The third was dark, but taller. He had blue eyes, and used lemon juice and cow's urine to lighten his hair to a whitish yellow. She had given him the oversight of the use of colorations. He had become a friend more than a slave.

It was too bad all three of their sexual appetites ran towards each other.

Dido moved to stoke the fire pits. She had built two fires before dawn; one in the steam sauna, and one for the hair irons. It took hours for the beds of coals to build up properly, and she had never been able to trust her slaves to do the job the right way. Everyone credited her beauty treatments, and her salon was known as a place where quality and guaranteed satisfaction took place on a daily basis.

It would never pay to have a client burned or made ill by improper preparations.

Journey

She stood and stretched, slipping her dainty feet into elegant golden sandals. This would be a long day. Walking through her facility one more time, she re-checked the readiness of her supplies. The water basins had been filled. Towels were folded, and ready for a busy day. Trays of essential oils and conditioning treatments were organized. Vials of colorations for nails and hair were re-filled, ordered neatly in rows on the shelf above the couches. Tiny saucers colorations, along with petite brushes for the eyes and lips were standing by for those clients attending the Proconsul's temple feast tonight. Tiny oil lamps in the massage rooms were also full, as were the lamps elsewhere, with wicks re-stocked, waiting to be lit.

Her musicians would be arriving soon. The veil hiding their playing platform covered a hidden niche built into the wall. At the moment, it was pulled back with a silver cord. When customers arrived, and the musicians were performing, Dido would loosen the cord. The veil would fall into place, covering the niche, so as to have music coming from a hidden source. Her slaves always played better when they could just improvise and be overheard, she reasoned.

She could hear the slaves laughing and talking, as they ate breakfast outside in the kitchen area. Even *they* were anticipating a busy day. And why shouldn't they? The dignitaries attending the festival were a special breed. Dido had even ordered wire hair frames from Rome, as well as powdered glitter. Additionally, strands of pearls and small jewels were always part of her hair designed; for those needing styles for endless festival parties.

They would remember her flair … an unforgettable experience.

She had discovered over the years how to spark a customer's appetite; to keep them coming back for more.

After all, Pleasure and Comfort were masters no one argued with.

~~~

After making the long journey north to Caesarea Philippi, Mary was uncharacteristically weary. Although she and Atticus made the journey on horseback, stopping periodically to eat, stretch and rest; her back and neck gripped her with pain: a persistently jabbing stiffness, as well as what felt like pulsating thunder filling her head.

Why now, she wondered?

Arriving several days before the festival, to do a little trading and shopping, the couple booked a room at the Inn near the Sacred Groves. The Groves were not of interest to Mary, nor to Atticus. Rather, it was the opportunity to experience the waterfalls, and the cool spring water bursting from the bottom of Mt. Hermon which drew them. These were the headwaters of the Jordan River. The waters were said to have healing properties, having been pulled up from the earth by the gods themselves!

Mary loved just sitting and soaking in the water. It was so peaceful.

There had been a day when she had prayed to the statues and images poised in their carved-out alcoves in the rock wall of the mountain. She had brought offerings of wool and linen, giving portions of her best, as she had begged to be relieved of her terrorizing visions.

There had been days when physical pain in her abdomen had stabbed her in the night hours, disabling her ability to function. There had been seasons when bloody, grotesque

Journey

flying insects, with faces of men, and bodies of reptiles had tormented her dreams and her daytime thoughts.

Always, there was the sense of snakes slithering over her body, coiling around her, pulling her down into the great darkness.

One year, Mary had even brought a lamb with her to offer to Pan in sacrifice, hoping its blood would pay the god's ransom for her peace.

But nothing the priests had told her to do had ever worked very long.

In the early days, she sought out the priests in Pan's temple for counsel regarding the frightening apparitions stealing her rest each night. "Pan is the mischievous god of sudden fears, my lady," they told her. "He terrorizes at night, when his face changes. You must do whatever it takes to experience the good side of the god. He will forever enslave you in the death surrounding him if you do not take the proper steps. You must come to the festival and make another sacrifice, perhaps of your firstborn. At least offer your body to the ravishes of his nymphs and satyrs, by going to the Sacred Brothel.

Then your Panic and fears will go away completely."

The priest looked at her with bloodshot and yellow eyes. "What have you not given to him?"

Given him. Given him, indeed. Mary snorted, just thinking about it, as she lay on her sleeping pallet. *Taken* was more like it. She felt consumed, and rav*aged*, rather than rav*ished*. It was obvious to her the temple priests had never really understood her distress. How could they? To them, it was all words anyway.

There were no *real* deities, she thought distractedly. Your life is just what it is. You have to make the most of what you have, and just survive; just try to stay comfortable until it is your time to die.

There were times when she looked for solace in the arms of men who visited her. She had visited the apothecary's tent in the Gentile marketplace in Jerusalem. The hemp and opium seeds had created strange-smelling incense when she used them. They provided a fleeting sense of lightness, but it had faded with the wind.

She had been hopeful.... but the fears returned.

Even the cannabis "drinking smoke" seemed like a viable solution for a time. It made her sleepy, but also removed her ability to function with sound reason. Besides, she didn't like the way it made her feel... dazed, silly, out of control; without her complete senses.

She had been offered ale and wine many times to drown her sorrows. The smell induced nausea; always taking back to painfully imbedded images of her father, Eleazar: The night he had thrown her across the courtyard; the night he had awakened her from sleep to rape her, stealing her virtue.

No, strong drink would have no more place in her life.

It had already stolen too much.... destroyed too much...

She could remember comparing herself to the camel dung the beggars used for fuel. She was at such a low point then. Now she knew she had to make her own way; make her own life. No one could help her. It was her own responsibility.

No.

She would not throw away what little dignity she had managed to scrape together since then. She would maintain control. She was strong enough.

As far as the festival was concerned, this year, Mary had decided to attend without trying to become a part of its experiences. She brought no sacrifice to offer. After all, she considered grimly, she couldn't see that it had really ever done any good, anyway. No, this year, she would go, and just enjoy the food booths, spending time with a lonely soldier who needed comforting.

At least *that* was something she was good at, she reasoned. Sexual comfort.

Why do I feel as though I have lost a piece of myself with each one?

Mary shook her head, seeking to ignore the thought darting like a red banner across her mind.

But then this headache had overtaken her. Why now?

Usually, in the days prior to the festival, she felt more rested, and experienced a lessening of her nightmares. That small relief was a part of the reason she decided to continue making the trek an annual event. Perhaps there *was* truth in what the Romans believed.

Pan only left her alone when he knew she was coming to the party.

Avoiding a man's anger, she thought, as she lifted her head to punch a little life into her pillow. *Why was life always about that for a woman? And was that really true?*

Would there ever be a time when she could just experience life without these fears?

Suddenly, she found herself thinking about her old nursemaid, Clio, and the stories the woman had told her as a child. Was it a sign? Would Clio be here at the festival, she wondered? Why was this coming to mind now? Perhaps it was just another way Pan was using to torment her mind.

Drained and frustrated, Mary drifted off once again into a fitful sleep.

Atticus had risen early, to go to the marketplace for breakfast foods, and to fill a water-pot with healing water from the waterfalls. Mary needed some fresh foods to help her head feel better. On his way back to the room, he stopped at the apothecary as well, for some ground medicinal herbs.

He would show her how she would be taken care of when he was with her.

Passing by the *thermae,* or bath-house, a thought crossed his mind. Why not take Mary to the bath-house, and get her a massage? There were always slaves there this time of day. Besides, a sit in the steam, followed by a dip in the cooler waters might help the pressure in her head to lessen.

Not more than an hour later, Atticus and Mary made their way to the bath-house. In the first room, a slave applied myrrh and a perfumed oil of their choosing to parts of their body they felt needed cleansing and attention. The mixture helped to loosen dirt and sweat from the body. Then, the same slave used the *strigil,* a curved metal tool attached to a small gathering cup, to scrape each of them clean. Then, after a steam, and a luxuriously warm

Journey

soaking, each of them were given a small bar of *nitre;* a relatively new discovery in Rome. Atticus turned the bar over in his hand.

"Wet it, sir," the slave told him. "Then rub it against your skin. It feels good."

"What is it made of?" Mary wanted to know.

"It is a mixture of ashes and perfumed oils. Our house adds a little salt to purify the skin," came the answer.

Mary put the bar into the water, and rubbed it up and down her arm.

"Look!" Atticus pointed. There was a trail of white bubbles tracing the bar's path.

Mary felt her skin. "It's softer," she told him in amazement. "I like this. Let's buy some and take it home!"

After a few moments, Atticus and Mary moved into the cooler water. As they sat together, the soldier noticed his travel companion was somewhat quiet.

"How are you feeling, beloved?" he asked. He contemplated the scars on her shoulders and upper legs from …. how had she cut herself?

There is much about this woman's life you don't know, he reflected.

Mary was uncomfortable with his endearment, and didn't want to encourage him. So, she acted as though she hadn't heard, by not answering immediately. She looked deep into the water, attempting to appear lost in contemplation.

Atticus repeated himself. "Mary, how are you feeling?" He spoke a little louder this time.

She looked up at him. "A little better. I think you are right about a massage. But I don't want one here. I want to go to Dido's."

At the name of the high-level salon, Atticus was surprised. "You have an appointment?"

"Oh, yes. Later this morning," she shrugged. "I go quite often, especially when I'm here to trade. I'll just add a stress massage to my regular appointment. She always has more than enough slaves to take care of everyone. And even when I have to wait, the music is wonderful. It's nice just to sit and listen to music, don't you think?"

"I'm not sure that I ever have done that, Mary. It's quite a luxury on a soldier's salary. Only noblemen have musicians."

"And salon owners like Dido," she commented, brightening. "Do you need a haircut, or a therapy? It will be a lot of fun, you'll see. Please come with me. I will pay for you."

And so they spent the day. The slave who attended Mary was the same young man who had attended her every year for the past nine years; fully acquainted with her needs. Atticus was given a beautiful female slave for the day, who massaged his body with oils, and cut his hair in the current Roman style. She even conditioned his hands with a Persian softening agent; cleaning and trimming his fingernails.

As the afternoon was nearing a close, Syrene entered the salon from the kitchen, carrying a tray full of pastries, and fresh fruit. Sitting with Mary, Dido called to her.

"Syrene, come here to me," she invited. "I want to introduce you to one of my long-term clients. I don't think you met her the last time she was here."

"No, I didn't," interjected Mary. "She must have been in the kitchen." Mary then spoke to Syrene. "Dido tells me you make all of these pastries yourself. Is that true?"

Journey

Syrene shyly spoke. "My mother and I make the pastries for Mistress. She is very kind to us." She self-consciously ran her hand over the very short hair on her almost bald head, and pulled her head-scarf up to cover the fact that Dido had recently harvested her for a black wig.

"I would think she would be. Dido, what a find to have a mother and a daughter who both bake like this!! I would have to re-think having slaves if I could eat like this every day!"

Dido's eyes twinkled. "No, Mary! You can't have them."

Syrene laughed carefully. "It is a privilege to have such a good and kind mistress," she said graciously.

At the sound of Syrene's merry giggle, Mary's emotions made an involuntary shudder.

"What is it, Mary?" Dido looked at her with concern. "Is it too cold? Do you need to go back to the steam room?"

Mary was visibly shaken. The hair on the back of her neck stood to attention. What was going on? She looked carefully at the girl.

"Where are you from, Syrene?" she asked quietly.

"We are Greek, Mistress. But we have been many places."

"We?"

"Yes. My mother and myself. I had a brother until several years ago. He was killed in the fields by our last master. He was whipped and his back became infected." Her voice trailed off, and she looked around the room, now rapt in attention, realizing she had said too much.

Mary was not offended. She was looking at Syrene strangely, as though she was seeing someone else. "What was your brother's name?" she asked quietly.

"Tychus."

The name of her long lost would-be twin "brother" released a torrent of emotion from Mary's heart. Suddenly, she felt as though something in her chest would explode. Struggling to breathe, she stood quickly from the couch she had been sitting on, and began moving toward the kitchen door.

Dido rose to follow her. "What do you need, Mary? How can I help you?" She spoke sternly to Syrene. "You have embarrassed me. We do not speak of our personal matters with clients. Her experience today has been ruined, because of your lack of decorum. Go to your room."

Surprised, Syrene moved toward the door. "I'm sorry, Mistress," she said to Dido. "I'm sorry," she said to Mary. "I didn't mean to…."

"Where is she?" Mary blurted out, interrupting her. "Where is your mother?"

"She is in our room, getting ready to go to sleep. It is our duty to sleep now, and work through the night for the salon to be ready tomorrow."

Mary looked at Dido. "I think I know this woman. This, this, … what was her name?"

"Sylvia."

"I think I know her, and it would help me greatly to find out. Can you take me to her?"

Dido was visibly uncomfortable with Mary's request. "My slaves need their rest, if they are to perform well tomorrow. I don't allow my clients into their living quarters," she answered.

"I will pay you extra," Mary offered. "Please, Dido. It would mean a lot to me. I have to know."

Syrene led the way, through the small kitchen area outside, across a courtyard, to a smaller, simpler building behind the elaborate salon. Dido and Mary followed close behind. Entering the building, they came upon a large square room with a firepot in its middle; vented through the ceiling. There were rolled mats against the walls, and small boxes that apparently held personal belongings. It was clean, but the sparseness of the room struck Mary.

"What is *this* room?" she asked Syrene.

"This is the general living area for all of the slaves, except for my mother and me," Syrene glanced at Dido. The Mistress did not seem to be disturbed by her sharing, so she continued. "Everyone else works during the day, but my mother and I work at night, and sleep during the day, so we have been honored with a private room."

It had never occurred to Mary that slaves would live in any manner different than her own level of comfort. "Do you like it here?"

No answer to the question came. The trio stopped at a closed door, behind which someone could heard to be humming a tune. Syrene knocked gently.

"Mama? Can we come in?"

Sylvia answered. "Who is *we*, child? I'm getting ready for sleep now."

Dido spoke, her voice flat and devoid of emotion. "A friend of Mistress Dido thinks she knows you, and wants to meet you."

Sylvia opened the door quickly. "Yes, Mistress. What can I do for you?"

"This is Mistress Mary, Sylvia," Dido made the introduction. "She was so impressed with your pastries she wanted to meet you."

Grasping her wrists behind her back, Sylvia nodded. "It is good to meet you, Mistress. How is it you think you know me?"

Mary was suddenly at a loss for words. "I, uh, well, there was a woman once who used to tell me stories when I was little, and she used to laugh, and my mother died...... I was a baby, and she nursed me...." She halted, and then finally finished, ",,,and she had a son named Tychus."

Sylvia's face was impassive; her tone cool. "What was her name, Mistress?"

"Clio. Her name was Clio."

"My name is Sylvia, Mistress." The slave looked at Mary evenly. "I do not have that name."

"Oh, I.... I see," Mary stammered. "I'm sorry... my mistake." Tears began to stream down Mary's cheeks, as she contemplated the meaning of the negative response.

There was an awkward pause, everyone staring at Mary; waiting for her to say something; but the usually confident and self-assured mask had been lowered. This was a woman no one knew.

Journey

The core of Mary's life was exposed. She could feel it.

She began to shake involuntarily.

Finally, Dido put her arm around Mary, her voice conciliatory. Without knowing it, she was using the same tone of voice she did when her own young daughter was upset, and in need of comfort. "I didn't know all that about you, my dear. What a difficult life you have led... You know, I would come to a salon every day if I were in your shoes, I would have to. I might even need to spend time at the apothecary!" With her arm around Mary, she drew the shaken woman around, so as to put their backs to the doorway of her slaves' bedroom. She herded Mary back into the general living quarters of the house.

"No matter," she cooed. "It will be all right. Come with me back to the couches. Let me get you another cup of tea, or perhaps some wine. I will have your slave add another treatment to your package – at no cost." She glanced with warning disapproval over her shoulder at Syrene. "This has been a horrible day for you, and you are one of my best clients. I feel so responsible. But we will make it right. You'll see. Would you like to try one of our new Persian facials, perhaps? Each one has a different aroma." Her voice trailed off as the two of them moved further and further away. "I think the eucalyptus, or the jasmine... both would release these deep emotions you feel. I will have your slave hang a crystal over you as he works as well..."

As Dido ushered Mary back to the formal areas of the salon to complete her treatments, Syrene moved into the room she shared with her mother, closing the door. "Why didn't you tell her?"

"Tell her what?" Sylvia spoke more lightly than she felt. "We may be slaves, but some parts of our lives are still private, Syrene. I, for one, am going to maintain my dignity." Sitting on a stool, she began smoothing her skin with oils.

"But she needs to know!"

"Needs? A woman like that? You have a lot to learn about life."

"Mother, why didn't you tell her that the owner who fathered me changed your name to make you more saleable? *Why* didn't you tell her that *you are Clio?*"

Sylvia laughed a brittle, bitter laugh. "What difference would it have made? After all, I'm not sure it would be good to be known as her friend. She's not a patrician, Syrene. She's a Jew. We are in a better position here because of Dido, than anywhere we have ever been. I don't want to jeopardize that."

"Jewish.... Are you sure? She looks like a rich Roman merchant to me. And she is so beautiful!!"

"Believe me. I nursed her. I taught her to speak, to read, to write. I don't know what happened to her after she was five; nor am I sure I want to. You're too young to understand, Syrene. Looking at her robes, she is still the rich merchant's daughter. She could kill me on a whim. Think about it.... Would you trust someone who becomes that emotional in a public place?"

Syrene sighed, put on her nightdress, and hung on a hook the exquisite working gown she wore in the salon each morning, making sure it's soft and sheer folds hung properly.

Journey

Sixteen now, she had no illusions about her position, or her value for that matter. The robe itself had cost more than Dido had paid for her entire life in the slave market. Carefully she put the loop sewn into its neckline on its hook on the wall.

She said nothing, but her mind was working, musing over her mother's words. Syrene would have liked to have known more about her mother's life before she was born. She would have liked to have had a sister. But slavery was all she had ever known. Oh, well. It didn't matter now. She needed to sleep. The time to bake again would be coming quickly. Unrolling her mat and setting it against the wall, Syrene lay down and pulled up the thinnest of blankets over herself, silently watching her mother from across the room. She folded her arm under her ear, to create a sort of pillow, and pulled the cover up over her head to shut out the late afternoon light.

She tried not to wonder why her mother had lied to the nice lady named Mary who was friends with her Mistress.

Why had Mary suddenly cried? Why had she been so upset?

Lying on a mat across from her, Sylvia was quiet as well. Intuitive to survive, she had become aware of the storm back-building in Mistress Dido's eyes during Mary's brief breakdown. She had noticed her owner's barbed looks at Syrene.

What would she do if she lost the only child she had left?

It was in Dido's power to do anything she wanted to with her slaves, without fear of repercussions.

What would Dido do to Syrene? Yes, she was a merciful owner, and generous, but she was also given to private rages; sudden temper tantrums, provoking unspeakable actions the Mistress always regretted after the fact. Sylvia had comforted her many times with pastries and light conversation, helping Dido to laugh.

But now the offender was her own daughter. What if she blamed Sylvia as well, and sold them both? What if the child had fallen under Dido's "evil eye," as the household's community of slaves referred to it.

It was within Dido's power to sell them to Adonis, she remembered grimly. Well, she would do whatever it took to prevent that from happening; even if it meant running away.

Sylvia resolved to give Syrene warning and teaching as they baked this evening. For now, she had to sleep. The old ache between her shoulders was screaming for relief. She fleetingly wondered how much longer she could maintain her life.

She was getting too old for this. She wished for the return of happier days.

She folded her arm under her, and, as she did each night, kissed the image of the chariot driver, tattooed into her forearm; her dead husband's ashes. She folded that arm under her, so her memory became her pillow. As she closed her eyes, a silent tear, and then another, crept from below her eyelids to the stone floor below.

A few hours later, mother and daughter rose from light sleep, as they heard the general slave quarters fill with noise once again. It was time to rise and labor through the night once more.

Journey

Mary was quiet the rest of the day, withdrawn into a world where Atticus could not reach her. She had been so sure….. and hadn't Syrene's giggle sounded just like Clio's? It was one of her favorite memories. She hadn't heard that laugh in two decades, yet she would have recognized it anywhere!

Hadn't her heart jumped at the sound? How could she have been so wrong? Perhaps the headache had clouded her judgment.

As the couple walked away from the salon, working their way down the street, sampling various festival foods, Atticus suddenly startled. He grabbed Mary's arm.

"Mary, look!" he exclaimed excitedly. "It's my Commander. I wonder why he is here. And Titus is with him!" Taking Mary with him, the young foot-solder made his way through the crowded street to where his friends were standing.

The Commander saw him coming and smiled. Justus Flavius decided to give his subordinate a ribbing hard time. "Why aren't you in uniform, soldier? Are you ashamed of your unit?"

Atticus saluted his centurion. "No sir! I….We were at Dido's salon all day." He looked at Titus, and then back to his commander. "What brings you to Panias? Here for the festival?"

Titus responded with a laugh. "Oh yes, and I came with the Commander. We have planned this trip for months together, haven't we sir?" He looked at Atticus. "Are you crazy?"

Justus played along in jest, chuckling. "Yes, Julia was unavailable, so I came with a man. No, not hardly!"

Atticus hit Titus in the chest. "Well, it's just that I know what a difficult time you have finding a pretty woman who *wants* you."

"Thank you for that." Titus laughed and then spoke more seriously. "Paul and Aquinas have fallen sick to the village illness. They cannot run the trade routes. So, Battalion Leader Farzin has rescinded your leave. You and I have been assigned the patrol routes beginning tomorrow. The Commander came with me to find you."

Atticus' eyebrows went up. The Commander travelled with Titus? Why not another soldier? He looked at Justus.

The centurion explained. "I needed a sense of adventure. It's been too quiet of late." Justus Flavius patted Atticus on the shoulder. "I'll make it up to you, my boy, when the illness passes." He winked at Mary. "And who is this lovely young thing you are with?"

Atticus put his hand in the small of Mary's back. "This is Mary. She is a fabric merchant from Migdal. I accompanied her to the festival. We have been having a wonderful time."

Justus reached out his hand towards her. "It's great to meet you Mary."

"Thank you," she responded, shaking his hand.

The Commander looked at Atticus. "Tell you what, my boy. Titus and I will wait while you get your belongings together. I will send a hired courier ahead of you to Farzin with my seal, to delay your duties until you return to Capernaum. You and Titus can leave now. If you ride hard, you will be back at the post by tomorrow evening. I will make sure Mary makes it home safely."

Journey

It was a more than generous offer for any superior to make given the circumstances. Everyone knew it. They also realized it was more a command than a suggestion.

"Mary," the older man continued, "if you wish to remain at the festival without Atticus, I'm sorry I cannot stay. However, I *can* hire an escort to ensure your safety for the next few days here in Panias. Then, I will petition the Commander of the regiment here to assign a soldier from their unit to accompany you home after the festival. On the other hand, if you do not wish to stay here alone, and you are willing to leave Panias now, I will escort you to Migdal. It is only a little detour on my way home."

Mary looked at Justus Flavius, assessing him. Enough had taken place in the past hour, she was unsettled. Looking around at the festival, she realized abruptly, a deep yearning to go home. Then again, no, perhaps not even to Migdal….

…Perhaps to find Miriam and Eleazar in Bethany.

How had it happened?

In a short matter of hours, the mystery was gone. The appeal had vanished.

And, in its place was the Abyss, the Void; the great and empty gloom she had been running from since childhood. She could not remember ever feeling so alone; or raw; or vulnerable. The ever-present fear hovered, watching; as though waiting for something.

Only now there was no place to hide. What safety was there?

The blackness threatened to overwhelm her again. She shook her head slightly.

She could not allow herself to be alone. Not now.

Outwardly, she smiled lightly and shrugged.

"I think I have done all I came here to do," was all she said. She looked at Justus Flavius. "Thank you. I would be honored if you would accompany me to my home."

An hour later, Titus was fed, bathed, shaven and changed. He and Atticus gained fresh mounts from the military offices at Panias, and headed towards Capernaum. Atticus did not leave, however, without seeking Mary out and promising her another opportunity to experience the Panias waters; this time without interruption. Would she forgive him for this intrusion? Such was the life of a soldier, he explained.

Mary assured him all was well with the world; she looked forward to another excursion. He left, satisfied he had kept her interest, if not her love.

Mary and Commander Flavius, however, took a little extra time to begin their journey.

For one thing, Justus was tired. He sent a second message by courier to his wife, and rented a room. He then headed to the bath-house for a soak, a swim, and a massage. After a nap, and a meal of festival foods, he decided they would wait until the following morning to leave Panias.

In the end, Mary found she needed to hire a camel driver and two camels to transport the Phoenician and Syrian fabrics she had traded for prior to the festival. Her wares had been accumulating in the corner of the room she had shared with Atticus. She hadn't realized…

Journey

Her experience had taught her well, she reasoned. Mary had discovered long ago Panias was close enough to the Phoenician and Syrian borders so as to allow for inexpensive trade. She would make a lot of money because of this trip, she was sure.

Flavius watched her as she conducted her business dealings. She was a formidable force, to be sure. How had one so young, and so delicate, become so matter-of-fact, and bottom-line oriented? Was she hard-hearted; or brash; or brazen?

No, he didn't think so. He had watched her with Atticus. The man was smitten.

He had to admit; there was a sort of personal helplessness exuding from her, even though she was smart and savvy. Was it genuine?

She seemed sincere;

Apparently, his foot-soldier though so.

Flavius was not sure Mary shared Atticus' depth of emotion.

Why didn't she? Atticus was a good man; and good looking.

He found himself wanting to know her story.

And so it was, as they journeyed south to Migdal, Mary found herself uncharacteristically discussing her own life, rather than the life of the man she was with. She began thinking of Justus as a father figure; a relationship she had not experienced in a long, long time. Unconsciously, she compared the centurion to the old caravan driver, Ebenezer, who had deeded his home and camels to Eleazar and to her.

For his part, Justus shared with Mary descriptions of his boyhood home in Italy; his family life during his formative years. He shared funny stories from the battlefields. He told her little-known trivia, learned from his father's years in the Praetorian Cohort. He also shared with her about his life with Julia, and his daughters in Capernaum.

All the while, he kept his heart close to himself, under guard.

Mary was fascinated. She admired this older, distinguished man. How nice he had been to take time from his Command, helping Titus find Atticus. And now, to see her home! Did all commanders take such an interest in their men's activities?

Unknown to Mary, Commander Justus Flavius was not a man who usually dealt in trivialities. Nor was he derelict in his duties when it came to the health and morale of the men under his authority. When Titus mentioned Migdal as Atticus' destination, the centurion's attention was piqued. More than once, he had observed Atticus' practice of finding a pretty female jewel to decorate his arm on his free evenings. He was also aware of the young man's appetite for ale. Quickly, he had surmised the purpose of Atticus' holiday trip during leave. Putting the puzzle pieces together, Justus made an astute guess as to what company the boy would be keeping. Mary's reputation preceded her, and Justus knew Atticus to be a man who felt driven to respond to a challenge.

Those two elements were not a good combination.

It had not been a hasty decision to go with Titus. It was simply the right opportunity. It was time to curtail this woman's power over his men. Too many of the young ones had been rendered ineffective in duty because of her casual attitude toward relationships; or perhaps, her lack of committed response to an earnest proposal. He had determined to go with Titus, to

146

Journey

find out for himself what drawing factor Mary actually possessed, what allowed her to continue these behaviors.

As Battalion Commander, Justus mused, it was also his duty to protect the community where he served. Hadn't the stories he heard about her been part of his concern in assuming his post in Galilee?

Yes. It was high time.

Mary had been a topic of conversation during his walks with Julia on more than one occasion. "There is a story there," his wife told him, expressing a mother's care for Mary. "Someone has abandoned her, and she is just doing what she can to get by. Perhaps we could help her, Justus."

Grimly, he had disagreed with his wife. "This woman is garbage; street rabble, elevated only by a full purse," he had retorted. "You'd feel differently if Helena was old enough to know her, or be privy to her business dealings."

"Perhaps you are right," Julia had conceded. "But if everyone who has made bad choices becomes the garbage of the empire, who will be left to clean the streets? I'm just saying I would like to be part of the solution when it presents itself."

And now, as Justus sat in the saddle behind Mary and the camel driver, he realized he was thinking differently; more along the lines of his wife. He had expected to find... well, not this.... a powerless, defenseless child in a woman's body... She drew a person in with her generous and endearing nature.

It was amazing she wasn't full of disease! She certainly didn't *seem* to be the hardened hussy and whore he had anticipated...

Just how would one go about beginning to help her gain the proper virtues for healthy respectability? He knew from parenting his own children those foundation stones were set into a child's character early on. How would you help someone who grew up without a family? Or a father? How would you instill the solid knowing and confidence that came from belonging and being loved?

Perhaps that is what Mary is really looking for. The thought came, unbidden.

It would be like trying to add salt to the dough after the bread was baked. Could you just sprinkle it on top, and have the end result be the same, he wondered?

Probably not.

But if not ... then how?

On the second day, as they were nearing the town of Migdal, the conversation between them took a serious turn.

"I've never been part of a family like that," Mary told him. "I have always felt alone, except for my sister and my brother."

"You should come to our home, Mary," Justus told her. "Our girls would love you. You have had a lot of life experience, but you really are not very old in years. You would enjoy sitting under our grapevines, and watching the children play with the dog."

"You have a dog? In your home?" Mary was surprised. "I didn't know that was allowed in Palestine."

"We are not Jewish, Mary," Justus reminded her. "We are Roman. As such, we are subject only to Roman laws."

"I didn't think about it, I guess," she responded. "I grew up thinking there was something wrong with everything ... especially me."

"What about you and Atticus? Are you and he considering a future together?" he probed.

Mary smiled. "No, not really. He is just a diversion in a long line of diversions."

"Does *he* know this?" Justus was not surprised.

"Probably not," she answered, laughing.

"Don't you think you should tell him? I think he is swimming in the deep end of the pool when it comes to you." *Many men have.* He thought it, but did not say it.

She giggled. "I'm sure he will find out soon enough. They all do."

"Why are you afraid to give yourself away?" He asked, before he really thought about the depth of the question. "Who hurt you so deeply? I would like to help."

He could tell by the silence following, he had said too much.

Mary pulled her horse to a stop. She turned around in the saddle to look the centurion square in the eye. It happened so suddenly, Justus had to rein his horse quickly to avoid running into her. She spoke with grit, determination, and no small amount of defiance.

"Commander, I have been hit, slapped, cheated, raped, beaten, used, stolen from, spit upon, and used for entertainment by men of many different races, creeds, beliefs, philosophies, practices and value systems. I am weary of it. I do not need a man in order for the world to be right with itself in my eyes. I am *alone*. I live *alone*. I do business *alone,* and I have come to the conclusion, with no lack of struggle, that I will most probably always *be* alone. Additionally, if we want to discuss my relationships with other women, my own mother died giving me birth. Since that day, *other* women have abandoned me, rejected me, lied to me, judged me, neglected me, gossiped about me, ignored me, and tried to win me over with false compliments for their own purposes. I have been lectured, ostracized, cursed, threatened, and left to rot by those who *say* they love God; those who *say* they live in His mercy every day."

She paused to take a breath. "For myself, I am not sure there even *is* a God, and I see no purpose whatsoever in religion. Although, if there is a God, He knows there are man-made, rules-oriented counterfeits aplenty to choose from. If He *does* exist, He will have to gain my attention in an unmistakable manner. He is a man, I assume, so He will have to prove Himself to me."

She paused in her tirade, taking a breath. "I have never had a family, except for the years I spent with my sister and her husband in Bethany. Even then, *they* were bent on changing me and bringing me into the realms of what they considered acceptable behavior ... And now, you come...seeking to solve the deepest private issues of my life, and mend my soul... during a horseback ride? I don't know you, nor do I trust you."

The Commander opened his mouth to speak. Mary lifted her index finger to indicate she had more to say.

Journey

"If I wanted my fortune read, I would have gone to a sorcerer's booth at the festival. If I wanted the advice of a wise man or a prophet, I would have spoken with an astrologer or a diviner. I certainly would not have bared my life to *you*, especially in this setting. Now let's cut to the end of the issue at hand. What do you want in exchange for seeing me safely to my place of residence?"

Commander Justus Flavius was taken aback. Astonished at her frank directness, he responded quietly. "I'm sorry I offended you Mary. I don't want anything from you."

Mary was somewhat chagrined but not convinced. "Every man wants *something* from me," she persisted.

"Not me, young woman," he lowered his chin with an even gaze. "My needs are met. I have a wife at home."

"So do most of the men I have spent time with," she bitterly countered.

They continued their travel in silence.

This was not at all what the Commander had expected.

Travelling in company, on foot from Nazareth, John was deep in thought. The spring rains had not lasted long in Jerusalem. It would be summer soon. It was a good thing they were heading north. It was always cooler near the Sea of Galilee. So much had happened in the past few weeks, it was hard to put it all into decipherable order.

They had celebrated the feast in Jerusalem. Many had come to speak with Jesus, during their stay there. Scores had been baptized! He, Philip, Nathaniel and Andrew had been so busy. There had barely been time to eat! Those who needed healing and advice had come at all hours. The image of Nicodemus' midnight visit flashed before him. Remembering the past few weeks, he rotated his shoulders, trying to ease the tightness from them. He rubbed his face with his hands. A realization hit. He was tired.

Working with Zebedee, his father, might just be a welcome break when he arrived home…..

John could still remember the eyes of Josiah, his aunt's neighbor. Josiah and his family had lived in Capernaum for generations, and now were part of the ruling class of the citizenry. For many years in their marriage, Josiah and his wife had tried to have children, to no avail. Then, as Josiah was approaching his fifties, his wife her forties, they had discovered she was pregnant. It was a hope-filled story of God's greatness, still used by the rabbis (and sometimes, even Simon the Pharisee himself), to encourage barren couples in their persistence to raise a family.

As their entourage had approached the home of Jesus' uncle in Cana, the family whose home had hosted the wedding had been held several months prior, Josiah had run out the front door, covering the distance between the travelers and the house quickly. The man had fallen down in front of Jesus.

"Master," he cried. "My only son is at home sick. He is dying. We waited for God's goodness so long, and now it is being stolen from us!"

Journey

Jesus stopped, bending over to help the man to his feet. "Take heart, friend," he said, his voice full of compassion. "What is it you want from me?"

"Please heal my son. Come with me to my house, and give him back to me."

"Is this why you believe?" the rabbi asked him, "Because you need a miracle?"

Josiah's shoulders stooped. He murmured as if in protest. "He is my only child."

Jesus continued. "I know that Josiah. Just consider…. Do you need a miracle in order to believe? Are you one of those who need things to go their way before they trust me?" Jesus asked him.

"Please come before he dies." The plea had become desperation.

"Josiah, look at me," Jesus took him by the shoulders. "Healing is the children's bread. Abba Father does not practice favoritism, nor does he withhold. Take a deep breath. I heard your cry; I was listening. Rest a moment. Get something to drink. Then, go home to Capernaum. Abba Father does not give gifts just to take them away again. He does not change Him mind. Go back to your house. Your son will live."

It took a moment for Josiah's mind to catch up with what Jesus said to him. Then, as if his thoughts had taken flight, he ran back to the house. "I have to gather my things," he told his servant. "Let's go home."

"But, Master, what did he say?" his servant queried.

Giving the man a nudge, he responded. "Hurry! He told me to go home. So, let's go see what's happened."

The two men scurried out so quickly, they were gone before Jesus had his sandals off for much needed foot-washing upon their arrival.

The next day, two of Josiah's house-slaves arrived, bringing a message to Jesus. On the nobleman's way home, they had met him, with news that his son was restored to full health.

"What time did he take a turn for healing?" was all Josiah wanted to know.

When he compared the time of his son's recovery with his own timeline, Josiah discovered, it had been at the exact moment that Jesus had spoken the words, "Your son will live."

Josiah had sent his servants on to Cana, to share the outcome of the story, along with a second private word for Jesus from the nobleman. Hearing the message, Jesus threw his head back and laughed with great enjoyment. "I trust you," was all it said.

In sharing conversation, Philip, Andrew, Nathaniel and John decided they themselves had needed the encouragement of Josiah's response to his son's miracle. It had prepared them for the rejection that had taken place just days later in Jesus' hometown of Nazareth.

John wondered. Was what happened in Nazareth a sign of things to come? He had not seen it coming.

It had begun the morning of the Sabbath. Thinking to honor Jesus, the Pharisee ruling the synagogue had given the younger rabbi the coveted responsibility of reading from the prophets during the gathering. Opening the scroll from the book of Isaiah, Jesus begun to read,

"The Spirit of the Lord is upon me,

He has anointed me to preach the good news to the poor;
He has sent me to heal the broken-hearted,
To preach deliverance to the captives,
And the recovering of sight to the blind;
To set at liberty those who are bruised.
To preach the acceptable year of the Lord."

Then he closed the scroll, and looked at the crowd gathered for this time. After a short pause, he had spoken.

"Today, this Scripture is fulfilled, in your hearing." He had talked about the necessity of trusting God when it came to discovering relationship with Him. The reaction within the crowd had been one of anger and rejection; especially among the religious leaders.

John had overheard several of them talking. "Who does he think he is? This kind of talk might work somewhere else, but not here. We've all grown up with him. We know his family, and his history. He can't be anything more than where he came from…." And so it went.

That evening, in Jesus' childhood home, they had discussed the matter together. Jesus listened as everyone else seemed to be seeking an answer to avoid creating more conflict. For his part, John had been surprised by the off-handed rejection of the religious rulers. Didn't the miracles and the wisdom Jesus carried count for anything?

"It would require change," Mary, Jesus' mother, had said. "Change scares those who lean on tradition for their security."

Walking with beside her on the road, John contemplated those words. She certainly wasn't a woman afraid of change, he decided. They were traveling with a wagon filled with many of Mary's possessions, as well as some of her deceased husband's tools.

"Jesus will need them," Mary confided to John. "He is quite a craftsman. He will use them to create furnishings his home. I left the tools that my James and young Joseph would want. But both of them are grown now; still living at home. It will be some time before either of them chooses a wife. Jesus is beginning his new life now… alone. I want to help if I can."

Jesus had decided to move to Capernaum now, and find a home there. Mary seemed to think He would just have to take possession of the house they had found earlier than expected, that was all. In addition, Mary had decided to leave the other children at home in Nazareth for a time, while she helped settle housekeeping for Jesus in his new venture.

Andrew had teased her. "You just want to see what is going to happen with him. Some mothers just don't let go."

She had responded with a gentle smile. "It's true. I have pondered so many things for so long. I would like to see how they come to pass." She looked at them, her eyes filled with hope. "He is not just my son, you know. There is something eternal about Him. The angel even told Joseph so during our betrothal."

"The angel?" John inquired.

For the rest of the journey, she shared with them the story of how she had conceived Jesus. She told them of the appearance of an angel named Gabriel, who told her she would be

Journey

with child, without having been with a man. She told them of her cousin, Elizabeth's, miraculous pregnancy with John, whom they called "The Baptist." She told them how she had read the words of the prophets, and had discovered that all the words of the prophets had been fulfilled regarding both babies….. She shared about millions of angels appearing in a midnight sky in Bethlehem, shouting and singing praises to God; of shepherds visiting in a cave, of eastern wise men and a star; of Joseph, her husband, and his dreams.

Her conviction was compelling, John considered. He remembered the words of the prophets and Moses concerning the Promised Deliverer. It was clear Jesus was a prophet; a teacher sent of God to reach the generation of his day. Now, he was reflecting on the prophecies of the Deliverer to come. The Torah said that he would be "the seed of the woman," and "born of a virgin." Wasn't that what Mary was saying? She had remained a virgin until after Jesus was born?

"Listen to his teaching if you want to know God," she told Andrew. "Get to know Him. You will not have this opportunity forever."

That was all she would say. John noticed whenever Jesus spoke, Mary looked at him differently than most mothers looked at their sons... certainly different than the condescension and controlling "suggestions" he felt from his *own* mother! With Mary, there was none of the "I taught him that" demeanor many women carried. There was no hint of "I'm so proud of him; look how we raised him" in her communications. On the contrary, Mary treated Jesus with deference and … what was it? Almost a reverence, he decided, as though Jesus was a rabbi, and she was one of his students. She felt free to ask him questions, which was refreshing in their culture, especially when it came to religious matters.

Yet, Jesus was anything but religious, he considered.

It made John want to learn more too.

He could hear her now as she was speaking to Jesus. "Would it be possible to stop at some of the fabric merchants in Migdal on the way to Zebedee and Salome's home? I would like to do some weaving while we are there." Everyone knew Mary had woven the tunic Jesus wore. The design she had chosen was seamless, utilized by the more skilled Egyptian weavers, praised by those who created intricate designs and layered tapestries. The end result had been an exquisite robe with designs in the weave around the bottom hem and sleeves.

Thinking about it, John realized her loom must have been constructed by her husband, or her son.

"I hear there is a place where I can purchase some of the new fabric everyone has said is so wonderful… silk?" Mary was saying to Jesus. "It would be nice to see what it looks like, even if we can't afford it. I have heard it can be purchased in many different colors."

Jesus answered. "Do you want to go to the marketplace?"

"I don't know where it is sold," she replied. "Perhaps we can ask when we get closer to town. I don't want to add unnecessary time to the trip; it would just be nice to make a gift for Salome. She has been so kind to me."

Towards the end of the second day after leaving Nazareth, Philip stood in an inn courtyard in Migdal, bartering for rooms to house them all for an evening. The innkeeper was thrilled to have a group of so many come to stay at his establishment. He was a middle-aged, robust man, with a crooked grin, and an honest demeanor. Andrew took a liking to the fellow, and sat with him for a long time, laughing and talking. They discovered his name was Sol, from Solomon, which meant "peace."

"Is there anything else I can get for you before I leave you?" he asked after bringing bread, fish and cucumber sauce for their evening meal.

"You have been more than kind to us," Philip replied. "I'm sure we have everything we need." He looked around at his companions, considering. "On second thought, Sol, perhaps some extra towels… and a wash basin or two?"

Involuntary laughter erupted. "Are you saying we are all filthy? How could that be?" John thumped Philip's chest as he spoke. Smiling, Sol nodded and moved to fulfill the request.

It wasn't long before he returned with a stack of freshly folded towels and two large wash basins for bathing. "The well is just outside in the courtyard," he said. "Our cistern is full of fresh water from an underground spring year-round. Feel free to take as much as you need. There is also a fire-pit in the courtyard, should you need to cook or heat some water for washing. The drying rock is in the corner." He pointed. "There." He pointed to a large, waist-high boulder, set in the middle of the courtyard, next to the animal pens.

"Sol, are you familiar with the fabric industry in the area?" Jesus asked.

"There are many merchants and weaving houses here," Sol replied. "The linen for the temple priests is woven at the top of Mount Arbel, just above your heads. Would you like me to find a guide for a tour?"

"No, nothing like that," Jesus answered. "My mother is interested in finding a new fabric known as 'silk' and heard it could be purchased from merchants here in Migdal. She also needs to find some thread and yarn for weaving."

Sol brightened. "I know just the place." He lowered his voice. "There is a woman who is a merchant a little south of the city…. in the area where the caravan drivers live. I will draw you a map in the morning. I've heard it said she has silk yardage most of the year, depending upon her trade. Her name is Mary."

A quiet ripple went through the room. "That's *my* name!" Jesus' mother exclaimed. "I can't wait to meet her!"

"Yes, my lady," Sol bowed. "She is not of our beliefs, but she is a nice woman. I have purchased her fabrics for coverings here at the Inn." He lowered his voice, and looked around the room to the men with sense of conspiracy. "But guard your virtue," he murmured, looking at Philip and Andrew. "She lets very few men get away."

~~~~~

Just south of Jerusalem, in the village of EnKarem, a lonely man sat looking out an open window. He was thinner now. His hair was gray and his skin was sallow. The effects of his alcohol addiction were dissipating, day by day, but he still experienced difficulty concentrating. Where had the time gone? When had he last sat here? Had it been the day of

Rachel's death? Her face flashed across his mind. He could feel Grief, crouching close by, waiting to overtake him once again.

He shook his head. He had to get through this.

He had to stay strong.

He would *stay* sober *this* time.

Looking down, he noticed the nervous shakiness from his legs had transferred to his hands.

How could I have lost it all? What will I do now?

With regret, he remembered.

The children were gone….. grown.

He recalled Miriam's wedding. How beautiful she had been! Had he told her? Or had he been taking refuge, hiding in the wineskin?

He wished he could remember more clearly.

He remembered his son, Eleazar. The picture of the small boy walking behind him with tablet in hand, saying "How many, Papa?" filled his mind.

Where were they now?

His son, Eleazar, had come to see him. He somehow remembered that. When was that? They had talked; rather, his son talked.

It seemed like a distant shadow. The young man was a trader now….

Even if I did begin again, would my son want the business?

They wouldn't want anything to do with me now, he thought dismally. *No, that is one thing I am sure of.*

His thoughts felt like sand on the wind; out of reach; out of touch. Something was missing still … something important. What was it? For several hours, he anguished, trying to concentrate, re-gathering the timeline of lost years.

No…. it wasn't some*thing*. It was some*one*.

Then it emerged, without warning. With horror, he remembered. Terror filled him, as the knowledge of his own actions returned…

Mary! Was she real? Or had he imagined…. She had looked just like his wife…. What had he done to her?

Surely it couldn't be true. Surely these memories belonged to another man's story….. had he been sober….

She must hate me. She just disappeared. Did she die?

And later,

She must hate me. I am a monster. How could I have done those things? Surely it was all a nightmare…. Yes, a horrible nightmare…… I would never…..

But *I am a good man.*

His mind and heart battled to defend his intentions. Finally….

No, I am a weak man, he admitted. *I am flawed, and I have failed miserably.*

Then he realized. It *was* true. Mary's birth had been the reason for Rachel's death.

Journey

He hadn't wanted to *live* without his beloved Rachel. *She* had been the center of his world, his reason for living. How could he have blamed; blamed a child; a *baby?*

How could he have ignored, or perhaps destroyed, the lives of his children?

Had he caused Mary to not want to live also?

I should just end it all ... right now....

Now there is nothing.

He looked through the empty house, looking for a way to end his life. Where were all the knives? Without warning, a Voice spoke into his despair.

You shall not kill.

Had someone spoken? He looked around the room…. No. He was alone.

It was unlike the voices he had heard during his drinking years. Who had spoken? Was he really going crazy?

*You shall **not** kill.*

Silence surrounded him. He shook his head. Would the Spirit of God speak…..*to him?*

"Oh God," he whispered, looking at the ceiling. "Can you hear me? Are you still listening when I pray? I will do anything you want." His eyes welled up and overflowed to his cheeks. His tears released a pain, physical and deep, in his chest.

Covering his face, he cried out in distress. "I know I have done this to myself! This is my own fault. My own choices have brought me to this." For long moments, the only sounds in the room were his sobs and wails.

"Forgive me for blaming you, God. I was wrong."

For another hour he wept, alone, contemplating his past, afraid to embrace it, afraid of impending doom and judgment.

Fitfully, he slept, huddled on the floor, exhausted. Waking in the middle of the night, Pain still absorbed his attention. Once again, he spoke. "I don't know what to do, God. I have lost them. I have lost everything. Even my steward has forsaken me."

Scenes of the warehouse in Jerusalem flashed before him. Was it still there? Had the city's elders deemed it abandoned and saleable?

You will have to find out. It's time.

In the silence, Peace began to rise … Isolation began to turn into Solitude.

The Spirit of God was hovering over him, breathing Hope into his submitted soul.

"Show me what to do. How do I begin again?" he asked, overwhelmed at the thought. How would he do it alone? "I'm afraid. Send someone … … Please God …."

The sun was beginning to descend in the horizon when Commander Flavius and the younger Mary arrived at her home in Migdal. Joseph Barsabas had just finished unloading the trade wagon for the week, and feeding the donkey. He was cleaning out stalls, and preparing for the next day, when they arrived. He greeted her with a broom in his hand.

"Mistress Mary! How was the festival?"

Journey

"We had a good time. The food was wonderful, as usual. I had a chance to get a massage, and couple of other treatments at Dido's. I brought home two fully-loaded camels. How was your time in Galilee?" She slid off her horse, and handed him the reins.

Joseph smiled at her. "I have just returned from taking a second load of fish to the Tower. The coin we gained is on the table by your lamp and the papyrus scrolls." He nodded his head toward the house. "Do you need me to stay and unload the camels?"

"Could you, Joseph? I would be so grateful." Mary sighed wearily as she spoke. "The Commander will be taking these horses back to Capernaum with him." She paused, and looked at him. "Have you enough money for your needs?" It was a question she habitually asked, but tonight it held more concern. She was remembering the sparse sleeping room provided for Dido's slaves. For some reason, she felt a twinge of guilt. Suddenly, she realized. She had never been to Joseph' home, nor had she met his wife in the six years he had been indentured to her. Was *she* like the slave owners, she wondered? She shook her head as though to answer the question.

"I haven't taken any money since the last time you gave us provisions, Mistress," he answered respectfully. "My family is managing. We are fine."

Silently, Mary calculated. It had been at least a month since she had given him money. What were they eating? Surely his children had grown. Yet, he had never asked for anything.

Were you waiting for him to ask? The thought emerged without warning.

Mary walked into the house. Finding the purse Joseph had described, she counted out a generous amount. Then, she rummaged in a basket on a shelf in the corner for a smaller purse. After re-counting the money into the small purse, she pulled the drawstrings to close it. Walking through the storeroom, she noted additions in the stockroom made in her absence. She assessed where the new bolts she had brought from Panias would be placed. Stopping at a collection of bolts of fabric, she chose a linen bolt in a brilliant blue, and another in sheer Roman white. Joseph's wife would like these, she decided. She placed them on the table by her scrolls of accounts.

Arriving in the courtyard, she spoke once again to Joseph. "When you have finished unloading, I need to speak with you in the house, Joseph. I have something for you."

"Yes, Mistress," he answered. She moved back inside to her bedchamber, and began the task of washing her feet; changing into more comfortable clothes.

Justus Flavius was working with the camel driver to unload the camels. "Where would you like these fabric supplies to be put?" he asked, his arms full of bolts of silk fabrics. He walked into the house.

Hearing his voice, Mary emerged from her room. She saw Justus and began to laugh.

He stopped at her response. "What? Why are you laughing?"

"Look at you!" she giggled. "Turn around and look!"

Justus looked down. In his effort to help, the centurion had sought to bring in as much of the goods from the first camel as possible. His arms were laden down with more than five bolts of fabric, as well as additional items piled on top. Behind him, a trail of white linen had intertwined with another trail of woolen goods. The twisted fabrics had been dragging behind him since he had taken them from the camel, and now were stretched across the courtyard.

"Are you trying to create laundry for me, before I even get a chance to eat a meal?" she laughed. "Here, let me help."

Together they turned the wooden spools until the fabrics were once again in storable condition. Then they moved to the storeroom, to put the goods away.

"Thank you for your help, Commander Justus," Mary spoke quietly.

"No trouble at all," he replied. "I do need to be going soon. I've been away from the barracks longer than planned."

"I understand." She paused. "Could you ask the camel driver to come and see me when he is finished unloading? I have some goods to send to Jerusalem in the morning to the dyeing house."

"Surely," Justus replied. He moved toward the door.

"Commander?" Mary called him hesitantly.

Justus turned to face her. "Yes?"

"I'm sorry. I'm sorry I threw fire in your face, with my words."

The soldier spoke carefully. "I'm sorry too. I shouldn't have tried to talk with you about your private matters. You're right. You don't know me well enough to trust me."

"I would like to." Mary spoke simply, without affectation. "I realized afterwards I don't trust anyone, not even myself." She pulled up her sleeve to show him the scars on her shoulder. "Look at what I do. I saw Atticus looking in the bath-house. Sometimes I just want to know what I can do to *feel* something. I am always so numb inside."

The older man felt compassion rise for this young woman. "You cut... *yourself?* Why?"

"I don't even know. I will catch myself doing it, instead of letting myself weep. It keeps my mind off of the night visions."

Then she told him, as they sat on bolts of fabric in the storeroom; the first person she had told since confiding in her brother, Eleazar, years prior.

In contrast, Justus listened quietly, making no comment until she was finished. "Do you know when they began?" he asked.

"Y-y-yes." Mary nodded. Slowly at first, she began to shake. Although she tried to speak, the words would not come. It was difficult to breathe. Were the walls moving inward? Her throat hurt, suddenly. She put one hand up to guard herself from the falling walls, and the other hand to her throat. Out of the blue, she felt as though she was choking, and her vision went black. She fell to the floor, convulsing and screaming in pain, holding her stomach.

Commander Justus was a warrior, trained and honed for battle in the Roman army. He had experienced war, and knew the fear of being ambushed. By sheer practice, he had learned to live on the alert against all dangers. Unexpectedly, he realized he was in the midst of a conflict; a conflict for which he had received no training.

"Joseph!!" he called for help.

By the tone of his voice, Joseph knew that Mary was having another episode. He dropped everything and ran immediately into the house. "What is it? Where are you?"

Journey

Justus shouted. "In here! In the fabric room!"

Mary was looking at Justus with wild eyes when Joseph entered the room. She had backed up into the corner, her knees doubled under her. Foamy dribble erupted from her mouth. The atmosphere of the room had changed. Was it darker than before, he wondered? Perhaps it was just the fact the sun was setting....

Then, without warning, a guttural form of Mary's voice came from her being. "She's mine!" it said. "You cannot have her!"

Involuntarily, Justus spoke. "Mary, stop it! You don't have to put on an act for me."

In the corner, she began to heave and sob, while an unearthly laughter came from her voice box. "Mary's not here anymore," it said. "We have taken control."

The reality of the demonic manifestation struck the Commander. "Who are you?"

"We are seven. And we have a legal right to be here. She has given us our place."

Joseph shuddered. What unspeakable things had Mary done to invite such a presence into her life? What could *he do*? Abruptly, he was overwhelmed with a great desire to go home to his wife and children.

You can't do anything more here. Go home. You're tired.

"I can't do anything more here, Commander," he parroted. "I need to go home to my family. It's been a long day. I'm really tired."

"No, don't be afraid, Joseph. You need to stay."

Whose voice was that? Justus and Joseph looked at each other, and realized neither one of them had spoken. The sound had come from just outside the storeroom. Looking outside the doorway, Joseph discovered a group of people standing in the main room of the house. He recognized one of them as a fisherman from Capernaum. It was one of Zebedee's sons.

"I'm sorry," he said. "You'll have to come back later. We are in the middle of something here."

"I can help." One of the men stepped forward from the group, and came to the doorway where Joseph was standing.

"What can you do?" Joseph asked, defensively. "We've been dealing with this for years."

"Years?" Justus interjected the question. "How long is years?"

"Five or more; ever since I've known them," Joseph answered. "I became indentured to her family years ago."

Jesus moved into the room, and crouched next to Mary's limp form, laying still on the floor.

"Is she dead?" Joseph wanted to know. "I've heard of situations where demons have killed people."

"She isn't dead," Jesus replied calmly, looking at Joseph over his shoulder. "The demons are trying to go into hiding."

"Why?"

"Because I'm *here*." He turned his attention to Mary. He spoke to her. "Mary, I know can hear me. Don't be afraid, little one."

Journey

Then he stood and moved back to the door of the room. "John, Andrew, Philip, Nathaniel, I want you to pray. Pray for Abba Father's will to be made the first priority in this house. Pray over the property. Just pray with me." He looked at his mother. "Would you pray too, please?" Mary moved with the rest of his followers to the outside of the house, where they all began to pray for the other Mary, who was lying in the storeroom, still and unmoving.

Inside the house, Jesus moved back into his prior position, crouching next to her. "What did they say to you?" he asked Justus.

"They said they are seven, and that she has given them a legal right to be there. They said that she is not here anymore."

Jesus smiled at Justus. "Oh, she's here." He stroked Mary's head. "She's here." He looked at Joseph. "Her will is strengthening now. It has been badly bruised."

Looking at both men, he continued. "Let me spend a little time with her alone. She'll be fine."

Joseph shifted uneasily. "Her brother charged me with her care, sir. But I will do as you ask."

Justus and Joseph both left the room, and went out to the courtyard, where they helped the camel driver finish unloading goods, and care for his camels.

When the room had cleared, Jesus sat down on the floor next to Mary. She was still motionless and silent. "Mary," he spoke to her again. "I'm here. Keep standing your ground. It's time. I'm with you."

Inside of her being, Mary was huddled into a ball. She could see them; the same reptilian creatures that had invaded her dreams. It was as though every fear she had ever experienced was magnified and present around her. A thousand eyes were watching her, mocking and heckling, criticizing and threatening. Every act she had committed, every relationship was exposed.

And she was alone.

Before her and around her was a mob of evil enemies, like walking dead. They reached towards her, and Mary recoiled into a wall.

"You have given us the blood-right to your life," the largest one told her. "*This* is your life now. We own you. You are our slave."

Although unable to speak or move volitionally with her physical body; Within her, she raised her head from her hiding place. She eked out words towards the demon. "You do *not* own me. I will *not* be your slave."

"You are wrong. We have a legal right to be here. You have opened your heart to us."

"How? I would never have done so. You must be wrong."

The demons laughed at her, sinister and demeaning.

"Anyone who refuses to make a decision for the Right; who allows their life to become passive; Anyone who buys into the belief they can rule their own life, or make their own way; Anyone who chooses the independence of Self above the Creator's plan for the

Common Good; These are those who open their hearts to us. We were given the right to rule the planet – and *you,"* they spat, "from the days of antiquity."

Mary's mind was racing. "By *whom?*" she wanted to know.

There was no answer.

Inside her soul, she stood to her feet. She screamed. "*Who* gave you the right?"

The eerie laughter surrounded her, accompanied by a hollow, raging, fiery wind. Looking down, she saw leeches and spiders intertwined with snakes. The mass of them was crawling around her feet, and making their way up her legs.

When she opened her mouth to cry for help, no sound would emerge.

Still physically motionless, her soul repeated the question. "*Who* gave you the right?"

"Adam." The name reverberated with countless echoes.

"Eve." Once again, the reverberation and wind.

"Your father, Adam."

"Your mother, Eve."

"You are ours."

"You can never leave."

The sound became louder and more defined. It echoed around her, as the demons chanted, repeating the lines over and over. They were tormenting her, coming closer and closer. She could smell Evil. It was putrid, and decayed. It carried the odors of disease and decomposition. It filled her head. She began to gag, fighting to breathe.

She saw her own form within her, doubling over.

No. She would not yield. Not to them. Not again.

Suddenly, Mary understood. Before her she saw an endless line of people; from every ethnicity, every nation, every language, and every culture. It stretched back across the ages. Simply by being born on the planet, she had entered into the family of Adam. There were no exemptions. The binding tie was the blood of humanity. Watching the image, she came to awareness. The face of her midwife, Anna, became known before her. She saw herself as a tiny child sitting with Anna, listening to stories; stories Anna had told her were true. Unbidden, the accounts came rushing before her; of Moses, of Samson, of David; of Deborah and Esther.

She saw herself as a young woman, mocking those accounts, rejecting them.

As her mind began to consider these things, she saw a giant, closed door. Behind the door was a streaming, blue-white light, evidenced through the cracks around it.

"I choose Anna's God," she whispered in her inner soul. It was all she could do. It took all of her strength to do it.

She was unaware; a rock platform began to appear under her.

In the storeroom, an hour had passed. The camels had been fed and put down for the night. Justus had sent the camel driver to the Inn, and had left for his home. Joseph had gone home to his family. He had left a tablet with a message for Mary. He would come by in the morning to finish whatever she had needed. Jesus had sent his friends and family back to the Inn with the camel driver.

Only He remained.

Inside her soul, Mary had regained her strength. She repeated the statement again within her being, this time with resolve. "I choose Anna's God; Above Everything." Once again, it was all she could do. But this time, it had not removed all of her strength to do it.

The Rock platform rose higher under her, and she began to see from a different perspective.

Another hour passed in the storeroom.

Still unable to speak, or move her body, but once again with strength rising within her soul, she still stood facing the closed door that hid the streaming light. With a sense of fortitude she had only experienced when angry, she shouted within herself; still unable to move or speak with her physical body. "I choose Anna's God, the Creator of All."

Suddenly the Rock platform became a mountain, and a part of her feet.

She did not know it, but the Spirit of God was speaking to Jesus, who had been waiting with her, simply praying.

"*Now!*" the Holy Spirit said.

Jesus spoke to the demons. "Leave her. Now."

The demons used Mary's voice to speak once more. "We have the right to be here. Have you come to torment us before the time?"

Jesus never wavered. "Your right to torment her has been broken. This is the day the prayers over her life are being answered... *right now!*

Within her being, Mary stood, focused on the door with the streaming light behind it. Swiftly, the Door swung open wide. Through the door came a Man, dressed in a white robe, with a golden belt around his waist. She somehow knew that he was a mighty warrior. He was carrying a shining sword. As she looked at the sword, she saw slave-chains and iron shackles attached to her wrists, her neck, and her ankles. How had she not seen or felt them before now, she wondered? Then it hit her. She realized how very tired she was of carrying them.

Behind her, the laughter of the demonic monstrosities had turned to whimpering and wailing. The light streaming from the open door began to grow in intensity, until it filled the entire room. She began to see her surroundings.

The room was bare and empty, similar to the slave quarters at Dido's salon. Except this room, she understood, was the definition of her identity and personhood in the unseen realm. It was without color, without furnishing, without design.

Mary looked to the walls, hoping for an affirmation of her accomplishments, looking for a sign of her development as a woman, but all she saw was blankness. All at once, she was filled with perception. This was what her isolation, her lack of bonding, and the absence of attachment had done to her.

She had not opened her heart to develop before now, she realized.

She hadn't known *how*.

This was why she had not been able to feel.

Journey

Without a word, the Man in White lifted the shining sword over his head and swung at her chains. Immediately, they began to turn into sand, and were driven away by the fiery wind.

As the chains dissolved, simultaneously, the demons began to wail and moan, swirling around her. They sought to knock her over; but her feet were melded into the mountain of rock below her.

Then it was calm. Mary stood, free from her chains, looking at the Man in White. She felt her attention drawn to his eyes.

Then, she looked down. He was holding out His hand to her. "Come with me."

"Mary," the Man said. "Mary? Can you hear me?"

She could feel the scene was about to change. She didn't want to go back. Couldn't she just stay here with the Man in White? She had never felt so safe or so secure…

Not wanting to leave the vision of the Man who had freed her within, Mary struggled to stay with her Rescuer, afraid she would lose the freedom she had gained. Time didn't matter here, in this realm.

In the storeroom, she stirred.

"Mary, open your eyes," Jesus said.

Mary relaxed. The fear was gone. Completely *gone*.

It was good to feel this way, she noted. *Good to feel*.

Looking intently at the Rescuer who was holding her hand, she tried to memorize his face. Perhaps He would visit her again in her dreams. She felt strangely different, yet, in a good way. She opened her eyes.

To her surprise, she saw the face of the Man in White sitting in front of her.

"You…. you came to my prison… you destroyed the chains…. how…." She stammered.

"It will take a little while for your head to grasp what has happened here. Perhaps a couple of days," Jesus told her. "It would be good for you to rest now."

"But," Mary spoke carefully, "I need to ask you…"

"Yes?" Jesus answered.

"What happened to me?"

Jesus sat with Mary in the storeroom, helping her sift through the new understandings she had received during her deliverance. And that is how Joseph found them the next morning, still in the storeroom, still talking.

Mary stood to greet him when he came in.

"Good morning, Joseph," she greeted him.

Joseph didn't know how to react. She had stood to greet him. Well, perhaps she was covering her tracks again. Next, she would tell him that the man had bought some fabric. Mary was known for keeping men overnight, just so she wouldn't be alone.

He was halted in his thought pattern.

Journey

No. This didn't feel the same. Somehow, this was different. He looked at Mary. Yes, she was disheveled. Had she had another sleepless night? Perhaps, but there was a different sense about her.

Her eyes had changed.

She was different.

He looked from Mary to Jesus, and noticed that Jesus was sitting on the floor, just observing *him* as he watched *them*. Why was he smiling?

"I want to give you something, Joseph," Mary was saying. She moved over to the table where she had left the bolts of fabric and the purse of coin the night before. "I want you to have these things, and I've been thinking since last night. I want to help your family. I want to forgive your debt."

"What did you say?" Joseph wasn't sure he heard her.

"I want to forgive your debt. I want you and your family to move into this house, and take over the business for me. I will pay you a percentage from the profits to be my steward. I want to take a break from doing this for awhile."

"Uh, thank you, Mistress," Joseph was stunned. "What…. Why?"

"I'm free," she answered simply. "I met Jesus, and my life is changed. I will never be the same."

"Okay," Joseph said slowly, still not really comprehending her. These were words she had said before, about several different men.

Seeing the look on his face, Mary put her hands up in protest. "No, no, it's not what you think," she said. "I've been in a prison inside for my whole life. I've always been alone. I've been running. This business was part of that life. This business and…. the other.. you know."

Joseph was amazed to see an embarrassed blush creeping up into Mary's face, and tears welling in her eyes.

Mary looked at Jesus. "But I'm forgiven now. I'm free." She seemed to be at a loss for words.

"What will you do, Mistress?" he asked.

"I'm not sure. I'm not sure my mind has caught up with everything that has happened." She smiled. "And that's alright. From what I understand it's going to take a while…. We were up all night talking, Joseph… Just talking… Isn't that amazing? I feel like …. well, open. It's so new to me…."

Joseph had never seen Mary like this before. She had always been so self-assured and in control. Usually on a morning after the lesser episodes he had witnessed, Mary was defensive and irritable. She had never looked like this on a morning after…

This really *was* something new.

Even her eyes were shining.

"What happened after I left last night?" Joseph looked at Jesus. "She's never been like this before."

"Mary and I fought a battle together," Jesus answered. "Do you remember, Mary?"

Mary's eyes were wide. "I will never forget it."

"What kind of battle?" Joseph wanted to know.

"A battle for her *soul*," Jesus explained. "It happened *inside* her."

Mary looked at Joseph. "I never could tell you before. Those things.... They were horrible... I heard their voices all the time.... and I had chains on my neck like a slave.... I felt so powerless...they threatened me and lied..... But then *He* came....He had a sword, and he turned the chains to sand.... And the light filled the room... it filled .... *me.*"

"Who *are* you?" Joseph asked Jesus the question, without thinking.

Jesus had turned his attention back to Mary. "Do you remember what caused the beginning of your freedom?"

There was a quick pause as Mary considered. "I chose. I chose Anna's God."

"That caused Truth to begin to become your foundation. The Rock that became part of your feet is Truth," he explained.

Jesus looked at Joseph. "I am Truth," he said.

Joseph did not know where to take the conversation after that. So he said, "Mistress, what are your plans now?"

Mary smiled. "I don't know, exactly. At some point, I think I'd like to visit my sister in Bethany. I haven't seen my brother for a long time." She paused. "I have a lot to learn, I'm sure. I don't even know what's missing, but I know there is a lot. I wish I had a mother...." Her voice trailed off.

"I know someone who can help you, Mary," Jesus spoke from his seat on the floor.

And so it came happened that Mary left her business, the life she had known, behind her. That afternoon, she packed a satchel with as many things as she could carry for travel. After all, if she needed more, she could also send for it. In the midst of her task she remembered the last time she had left her home with nothing but a satchel full of goods.

Only this time she wasn't running away *from* anything.

This time... she was not alone.

Journey

Prologue 3

**Flavius Vineyards – Galilee
29 CE
Day Forty- Eight**

Had it been five days already?
Justus Flavius lay back under the grapevine arbor, looking up at the stars. It was strange how he could always still see them through the arbor. Even when he couldn't' see them, they were still shining, he considered. They remained constant, no matter what he thought... or did.

His wife, Julia, entered the outer living area with a tray. At her heels was a small, white dog, who was watching the tray intently, expecting something worth eating to fall into her realm. Justus smiled as he remembered the last time Julia had worked with the barbering tools to cut the dog's soft hair into the short fluff it was at the moment.

"If I cut the hair closer to the skin, there is less chance of matting," Julia had declared. The dog had submitted to a bath, but had nipped at the scissors and comb. Yet, everywhere Julia went, the little animal followed, looking on with adoring, black eyes.

"I brought us some food for talking, and little wine," she said, setting the tray down on the stone table next to him.

He looked at her with eyes of love and grinned. "You are good to me," he said, and reached for her hand. She gave it, and he drew down next to him. She snuggled in, laying her head on his chest.

"How was your week on duty?" she asked him. "It's good to have you home. I love having time to catch up on our lives together…You don't have to go back for awhile, do you?"

"No, I've taken an extended leave. I need some time…." His voice faded away.

"Are you all right, my love?" her concern showed.

"Honestly, Julia, I need the break," Justus told her. "All at once, I feel as if I am living in a new world. I have become so aware of things I had never seen before this past two months. There is so much corruption around us, and the rumors I am hearing from the Roman Senate do not promise a better life."

"Are you wanting to go back to Rome?" she asked carefully.

His response was quick and decisive. "No; never…" He paused, and then continued with a gentler tone. "Not unless God wills it. We both know our lives took a turn the day we decided to become disciples of the Master. I want to stay here. I have found my life here, with you and the girls…"

"Me too…" Julia hugged him closer. "Let's just stay right here forever."

There was a short pause before Justus continued. "But I do I think I'm ready to retire now. Perhaps we could find a way to help the poor; or even the not so poor."

Julia smiled, her head resting on his arm. "Do you want to open an Inn, perhaps?" she teased.

"No," he said seriously, "I don't think so….Are you ready to become the wife of a vineyard owner?" he asked. "It's time for a life change for us; a real life change."

She chuckled. "I thought we had done that already… especially with all the homeless people you have brought me over the past couple of years…that's what made me think you wanted to open an inn.."

Justus lifted his head to look down at her. When he did not comment, Julia looked up to his ever-evaluating eyes. "Don't misunderstand. I wouldn't have changed a thing," she continued. "I know our servants especially are grateful to you….and we are all so much happier. Sometimes, I just missed moments like these during those years. I love having the opportunity to spend time alone with you."

He lifted his arm to stroke her hair. So many things had happened; so many changes. He was not the same man he had been. He smiled. Nor, for that matter, were any of them.

"Helena and Victoria went with Mary and Salome to Jerusalem?" He asked the question more matter-of-fact, as though requesting confirmation of a status report from one of his men.

"Yes. The girls went with them to Galilee, to see Jesus one last time. Afterwards, Zebedee sent word Jesus had asked them all to go to Jerusalem and wait. You know they take care of both of them like grandparents."

Justus was not concerned, although he was curious. "Wait for what?"

"Zebedee didn't say. I wondered what Jesus had in mind, too. From what Salome said, it sounded as though they were waiting for someone whom Jesus would be sending." She paused. "Do you know?"

The old soldier shook his head. "No, I only know the same things you do." Something stirred inside of his chest. He had learned to listen to those stirrings now. "Do you want to go to Jerusalem?" he asked his wife. "I couldn't leave the garrison until I was off-duty."

She lifted up on one elbow to look him in the eye.

"The servants have us all packed," she replied. "I was going to ask your permission to go… but you are packed as well, if you would please go with us…. Oh Justus, please let's go. I don't want to miss anything….. I just want to be a part of whatever new thing Jesus is doing." She clapped her hands together. "I'm so excited to see everyone!"

"You could have gone with them, Julia," he smiled at her enthusiasm.

"Not without you."

Their household steward, Adelphos, poked his head out from the back entryway. "Master Justus?"

"I've asked you not to call me that anymore."

"Sorry, sir; It's a longtime habit."

Justus chuckled. "What is it?"

Journey

"I just wondered if Mistress Julia had told you yet about us leaving for Jerusalem. There are several of us who want to ask to join you."

The Roman Commander winked at his wife. "Told me? I am so glad I came home to fit into your plans, Madam. Please, how soon would you like to leave?"

Julia pinched him. "Immediately, Master Justus," she teased. "How about at the first light of day?"

Nonplussed, Justus stayed in his prone position, his arm around his wife's waist. He looked back at Adelphos. "The Battalion Commander has decreed to me that we should leave at dawn," he jibed. "Tell the servants that as many as wish to go may do so... And Adelphos?"

"Yes, sir?" the slave answered.

"Don't be late! You know what a taskmaster she can be!"

"Yes sir!" Adelphos responded with a mock salute of tribute to Julia, and withdrew back into the house. As usual, laughter could be heard through the windows, renewing itself each time the story of their conversation was repeated.

They would leave in the morning.

~~~~

In Jerusalem, Abigail sat in the corner on her sleeping mat, with two five-year-olds: her own daughter, Deborah and Helena Flavius. The little girls were snuggled next to her. Tired, Abigail straightened her shoulders. She leaned back, feeling the refreshing coolness of the stone wall. She surveyed the room. Things were becoming quiet now. One by one, lamps were being extinguished, as families were going to sleep.

Over the past five days, life in the Essene Quarter had developed into routine activity; each of them finding a place to serve. Over that time, her children had drawn her into the circle of their companions, whose parents were also waiting with her and Simon.

Abigail considered. It was a wonderful way to get to know people; sharing living quarters for a few days. She had made several friends during the past few days; women she would have never met otherwise.

And now.... She realized her personal experiences with Jesus had become shared memories with each of the people in this room. Their experiences had become the binding tie between them. Each of them were forever different.

What would they all do now, she wondered?

"Mistress Abigail, Mistress Abigail," Helena whispered, tugging on her sleeve. "I have to go."

"Me too, Mommy," Deborah nodded.

"Does anyone else have to go?" Abigail looked around to the circle of children. Needs had been taken care of over an hour ago, but a mother never knew. Somehow, she had become the adopted parent to these new friends of her children.

She was glad Simon had chosen this corner. It was closer to the door. Like a piper leading a dance through the street, Abigail herded the children out the door, down the stairs,

Journey

and out to the facility; all the while reminding them to maintain quiet out of consideration for Ezra and the others who had allowed them to stay in their community.

As she helped the children settle back down for sleep once again, Abigail realized how much she missed her own home. How long would they be here, like this? There were so many tasks waiting in Capernaum... and the children would be needing to resume their lessons soon...

Simon stirred as she lay down. "Are you all right, Abby?"

"I'm really fine," she responded. "I just miss my home."

Her husband encircled her with his arm and pulled her closer. "I know things will happen soon .... I don't want to miss this. I can feel it; something wonderful is about to happen. I'm sure we will be home again in Capernaum soon enough."

"I feel that way too," she responded. "It's hard not knowing."

Simon reached up to stroke her hair. He whispered in her ear. "I love you."

"I love you too," she answered. "It's hard to find moments alone here as well."

"Jesus asked us to wait. This is the least I can do...." Simon spoke gently. "If you and the children need to go, I understand."

"No, it's not like that, Simon. I'm just tired, that's all." She kissed his hand. "Let's just get some sleep while we can."

Although no one said anything, the question had posed itself in everyone's minds. When would the One whom Jesus had promised them show himself? How would they know? How long would they be waiting?

It would be the Feast of Weeks in two days; a holiday. It was a day set aside to remember the giving of the Law of Moses; the day set aside to remember ElShalom giving water from the Rock at Mt. Horeb. That Law had become the basis of their national existence. It was an important day. The city was already filling with travelers and pilgrims from all over the world. Why had Jesus put them here?

Was the one he was sending coming from another land, perhaps, to the feast?

All they knew was he had asked them to wait.

"I just want you do one thing for me," Jesus had told them. "Wait in Jerusalem. I will send you enablement. You will receive power, and the Kingdom will spread over the entire earth."

Jesus had spoken cryptically many times, Abigail considered. His parables had changed her. The more she thought about the meaning behind his stories, the more she became aware of attitudes and values within her own soul needing to change. Knowing Jesus had altered her approach of looking at the world, her home, even her methods of relating to other people. She had become more understanding, and patient, for one thing. She had seen it in her relationships with her children; and with Simon.

"You will receive enablement. The Kingdom will spread....." What did those words mean, she speculated? She blew out the lamp.

"Mistress Abigail?" a young woman's voice whispered just a few feet from her.

"Yes?" she replied. "Who is it?"

168

Journey

"It's Leah, mistress," came the voice. "I was just wondering..."

"Yes, Leah?" she replied.

"How will we know when He comes?"

"I don't know, dear. He just asked us to wait. Wait and pray."

"I'm afraid I will miss it."

Abigail reached out into the darkness, and rubbed the arm of the young woman next to her. "Don't worry," she said, "He promised he would never leave us."

We are all children, she considered. No one knows the future. We have to trust Him. Wasn't that part of the lesson she had learned?

Abigail felt her husband's breathing settle into a relaxed rhythm beside her.

Jesus had healed her family, she reflected. Even Simon....

No.. especially Simon...

She settled onto her side and adjusted her pillow.

Considering these things, she waited for sleep to come.

He had listened to Jesus speak, but only for the purpose of trying to find him guilty of a crime. How could he ever relate to these people; those who had trusted Jesus all along? But he did believe in Jesus now. That was one thing he knew for certain. How he wished he could go back and live the past three years over again!

Malchus, former servant of the high priest, reached up to pull on his ear lobe. He stopped. This was the ear the Master had touched in Gethsemane, the night he was arrested! He felt around it. It still amazed him that there was no scar. Was it his imagination, or could he hear out of it better as well?

Simon Peter was watching Malchus from across the room. He stood up and moved over to him. "Hello Malchus," he said.

The man looked up at Simon Peter. Seeing who it was, he was responded carefully. "Uh...,hello., I was just sitting here thinking."

"About Jesus?"

Malchus nodded. "You know, he healed my ear when I didn't even believe in him."

Simon Peter sat down next to the man. "He did that all the time. I think it was because he doesn't wait for us to be perfect or have it all together before he can use our lives." He paused. "Say, do you remember what happened in the Garden that night?"

"I do remember." He looked at Simon Peter. "You were the one who cut my ear off."

Peter looked at him. "I know I was. That's why I came over here. I was wrong. It wasn't how he wanted things done. Would you forgive me?"

"With all my heart," Malchus replied. "Just think about it: had I not lost my ear, Jesus wouldn't have healed me. Had I not been healed, I'm sure I wouldn't have believed. I would still be trying to gain Joseph Caiaphas' favor." He looked at Simon Peter. "Thank you for cutting off my ear, Simon. I appreciate it."

Then, Malchus' face broke into a grin, and then a chuckle.

"Glad to be of service," Peter responded, joining him in laughter.

Journey

In a quiet corner under the windows, two older men, Ezra and Eli, sat under the windows, reading. Occasionally, they would lift their eyes from the scroll they were sharing, and whisper in discussion. The two older Essenes were surrounded by three younger apprentices, who were also studying. Quiet and non-intrusive, Eli and the three younger men had been part of the company during the majority of Jesus' ministry, and had been part of the seventy whom the Master had sent out as emissaries.

Ezra, the overseer, had been Eli's mentor and friend since his youth. The two men had spent the majority of the past several days catching up, and sharing their discoveries with each other. It was good to have this time, they decided.

One of the younger men looked up from his scroll, to gaze at the old scribe.

"When will it happen?" he asked. "It's been five days. Aren't there other things we could be doing of more value?"

"I have waited my whole life for the Deliverer, Issachar," Eli looked at the young man, and then at Ezra. "Now that I have found Him, I can't afford to be impatient when He asks something of me. I don't want to miss anything He has planned. Do you understand?"

The younger man smiled in response and nodded.

Eli patted his arm. "We can wait a little longer."

Oblivious to the exchange, old Ezra had been continuing to read. Looking up at that moment, he caught Eli's attention, and pointed to a place in the scroll where he had been reading.

"Here's another place where the prophets knew!" he exclaimed.

A roomful of sleepy people involuntarily made the same noise. "Sshhh!"

"Sorry!" Ezra spoke to the room. He looked at Eli, his eyes bright, and pointed to the scroll. "It's just <u>right here</u>!" Ezra responded, lowering his voice to a whisper. The two men continued their studies together.

Journey

Images

In the southern wilderness of EnGedi, some twenty-five miles east of Jerusalem, a scribe named Issachar sat on a stone bench in the Scriptorium, working by lamp-light to finish copying a scroll. There were only a few more characters to go…

He stopped to shake his hand again, quelling the cramp in his forearm. It was imperative he finish this particular scroll before the sun began its descent into the horizon. Bedouin shepherds would be arriving at the Qumran Community for the evening meal soon; a meal they shared monthly in exchange for transporting shipments of scrolls to the Temple in Jerusalem. In addition to this service, the shepherds also brought communications and foodstuffs from the brothers in the Essene Quarter of the city.

The intrinsic arrangement between the two unlikely social groups had evolved into one of friendship and understanding. The Bedouins not only transported the scrolls each month, but also brought animal skins and papyri to the settlement, all of which were eventually fashioned into scrolls.

The skins were transformed by the community's monks into high quality parchment; the tannery at Qumran was known for holding and meeting the highest quality standards in Israel.

Materials delivered to the community were returned to Jerusalem much later, as scrolls; designed for use in the Temple's rabbinical school. Those not used in the Temple were distributed throughout the nation; to synagogues, to libraries, and homes.

Eli, the Scribe Overseer, sat in the corner, dozing. In the corner, two additional, younger scribes were working on their own assignments, working diligently to create meticulous duplicates of originals. The original scrolls were made of the more durable animal skin parchment. Most had been kept at the Essene settlement since before Eli's birth. The blank scrolls, however, were made of papyrus, as that material was more cost effective for trade.

Accuracy and exactness were the code within the Qumran settlement. "A wrong interpretation by the wrong person, could lead thousands to destruction," Ezra, Eli's own Overseer, had told him, in days when he himself had held the stylus. In fact, he mused, he had worked at the very desk where young Issachar toiled now.

He could still hear his old overseer. "There will be no talking! If you look away, you will lose your place, or worse, ruin an entire scroll with one mistake. Concentrate on your work!"

The Essene scrolls were the most accurate of all.
To read an Essene scroll was to touch the Continuity of History.
It had always been; since the days of King Josiah; since the days of Ezra the Translator.

Journey

Issachar moved his shoulders in rotation, trying to get the ache out of them... five more lines.

"Master Eli," two other young men, who had been working in the corner called the overseer, breaking the silence. They rose to their feet. "The book of Psalms and the second book of Moses are completed. Where do you want them?"

Eli stood, stretching. "The rest of the shipment is in the stockroom. You can't miss it. It is the pile of rolls on top of the open saddlebag."

The two men nodded. They were done for the day and were eager to see their families. Moving into the stockroom they found a pyramid of papyrus rolls, resting in the middle of a circle of tanned leather. A leather strip was woven through slits around its edge. When the shipment was completed, the leather strip would serve as a drawstring. It would be pulled tight, forming a saddlebag for caravan travel.

As the two men left, Eli walked over to where Issachar was working. "How close are you to being finished?" he asked.

"The book of Isaias *is* the longest book," Issachar responded. "I thought I would probably be the last one to leave today. This one copy has taken me more than three weeks to complete."

"I remember the first time *I* copied that scroll," Eli reminisced. "My hand ached for days afterward."

"It is so long!" Issachar agreed. "And there is *so much* good, to learn, in the book." He lowered his voice. "It probably added time to my task, but I took some scraps of papyri from the storeroom, and wrote down the best of the prophet's words that fed my soul."

"What did you write?"

"They are just fragments; phrases and paragraphs that brought meaning to me as I was working."

"I would like to see." Eli was intrigued. It had been many years earlier he had done exactly the same thing; while transcribing the very same book.

Issachar fumbled to find the loose sheet he had written on. "Where is it?" He fumbled in the lamplight, finally finding the sheet on the floor, where it had fallen earlier. "Here it is." He began to read.

"Behold my servant, whom I uphold, My chosen, in whom my soul delights;

I have put my Spirit upon him; He will bring forth justice to the nations. He will not cry aloud or lift up his voice, Or make it heard in the street; A bruised reed he will not break, And a faintly burning wick he will not quench; He will faithfully bring forth justice. He will not grow faint or be discouraged

Until he has established justice in the earth; And the coastlands wait for his law."

"This is speaking of the Promised Deliverer. Is that right?" he asked.

"Yes," Eli answered. "You know it is."

Issachar continued.

"Therefore I will divide him a portion with the many, And he shall divide the spoil with the strong,

Journey

Because he poured out his soul to death And was numbered with the transgressors; Yet he bore the sin of many, And makes intercession for the transgressors."

The younger scribe paused and looked at his superior.

"Again, the prophet is speaking about the Deliverer," Eli motioned with his hand. He wanted Issachar to continue.

"Come, everyone who thirsts,
Come to the waters; And he who has no money, Come, buy and eat! Come, buy wine and milk without money and without price."

"What does the prophet mean, here?" Issachar asked. "How do you buy without money?"

Eli shrugged. "We spend ourselves daily."

"So, it means, that my soul can be hungry and thirsty?"

"Yes," the older man nodded.

"How do I buy the right things to feed my soul? How do I know?"

"It has to do with the Source, Issachar. You have learned over the years, have you not, how to distinguish fouled meat from good meat, haven't you?"

Issachar nodded.

"It is the same with your soul. You learn the things that really satisfy." He paused. "What else have you written there?"

"One more about the Deliverer," Issachar answered. "Do you want to hear it?" Eli nodded.

"And a Redeemer will come to Zion, To those in Jacob who turn from transgression," declares the LORD."

"Does that mean I could miss him?" Issachar wanted to know.

"He comes to Zion, to those who turn from transgression," Eli quoted Isaias' phrase. "That means when you learn something is wrong, you turn from doing it again."

"That's hard," Issachar said.

"But Adonai looks on the heart, son," Eli comforted him. "He sees your motives, and what you mean to do as well." He stood and stretched again, changing the subject. "Is the scroll of the prophet completed?"

"Yes; almost. I have a few more characters to go." Issachar looked at him hesitantly.

Eli could tell the younger scribe had another question. "Yes?" he smiled.

"Can I ask you something?"

"Go ahead."

"When I came here to study," Issachar began, "I became friends with a young man who had been brought to Qumran when his parents had died. He was here sometimes, and with the Bedouins sometimes; but he wasn't a scribe."

Eli knew the man Issachar spoke of. "You mean John. His father was a priest in the hill country. Both of his parents were very old when he was born. His father, Zacharias, died first, and then his mother. He was only eight when his neighbors brought him to us. It was his father's wish he be taught the Word of God in the right way.

Journey

"He left here several years ago, and began preaching in the desert. He would come by once in a while, and we would talk."

Issachar became more animated in his communication. "You took us all to hear him. I remember. But listen to this...." The younger scribe began to read once again.

"Comfort, comfort my people, says your God.
Speak tenderly to Jerusalem,
Cry to her that her warfare is ended, That her iniquity is pardoned, That she has received from the LORD's hand Double for all her sins.

A voice cries: "In the wilderness prepare the way of the LORD; Make straight in the desert a highway for our God. Every valley shall be lifted up, And every mountain and hill be made low; The uneven ground shall become level, And the rough places a plain.

And the glory of the LORD shall be revealed, And all flesh shall see it together, For the mouth of the LORD has spoken."

"Isn't that what John was preaching in the desert?" Issachar wanted to know.

"Yes, I heard him speak several times," Eli answered.

Issachar paused. "Was *John* the voice the prophet was speaking of?"

Eli was silent for a moment, thinking. "I don't know. I hadn't given it any thought before now," he answered. "It could *be*." He patted the younger man's shoulder. "Come and finish your work, Issachar. We will miss our chance to eat if we keep talking."

Issachar moved quickly to pick up his stylus and dip it into the ink. "I'll be done in a moment, Master Eli," he said, as he renewed his duties.

Issachar's question burned in the older scribe's mind. Was John the one who had been foretold; the one who would prepare the way? Suddenly, Eli remembered another phrase he had copied years before. What prophet had it been? He moved to the stockroom, and began looking through the animal skin scrolls. Where was it? He moved the rolls resting on top, indicative of the work most recently completed. After several moments of searching, he found the scroll he was seeking. He moved to the table against the wall to open it and read it.

"Behold, I send my messenger and he will prepare the way before me.
And the Lord whom you seek will suddenly come to his temple;
And the messenger of the covenant in whom you delight,
Behold, he is coming, says the LORD of hosts."

As the realization of Truth dawned upon him, Eli reeled within. If Issachar's discovery was viable, that would mean that God Himself was walking among men. He would come to the Temple. He would make covenant with man. It would happen suddenly.

For Whom had John been sent to prepare the way? How would he know? What if he missed him?

Without thinking about his tasks and duties, Eli ran to the synagogue. He had to pray.

He had to be ready.

~~~

Holding his camel's reins, Shakah stood on the shoreline. He pulled his head-covering around his face, shielding his eyes from the blowing sand. He squinted into the descending sun. The leaders at Qumran would be waiting. He really should hasten his pace, he thought, taking one last look at the Dead Sea. He had spent the afternoon splashing in its waters, enjoying the fact that it was impossible to sink, being careful not to get its biting saltiness into his eyes.

It had been good to get away from the rest of the tribe today.

He had needed time to think.

Lately, he had been having flashes of memory; pictures of himself in another life. He didn't know where that life had taken place, or even if it had really been. The only memories he could count on were those of life in the Bedouin tribe. That life had begun some fifteen years ago or so. Up until now, his efforts to remember his life prior to that time had been fruitless and frustrating.

Abram had found him; bleeding and unconscious; left for dead in the Valley of the Shadow. Someone had dumped his body on the road between Jericho and Jerusalem. How had they discovered him?

Shakah still marveled at the miraculous. One of Abram's nanny-goats had nudged Shakah with her nose, and begun to bleat, apparently complaining about the injured man lying in her path. All he had left to his name was his loincloth. The thieves had taken everything.

Abram had taken him home to the tribe, to his family tents. There, in the care of itinerant shepherds, he recovered from his wounds. Over time, he became strong and able to run again. He had *not* recovered all of his memory, however. Still unable to tell anyone his name, where he was from, or even what had happened to him, he had eventually melded into the tribe.

Shakah smiled. He was thankful they had accepted him, even though his skin was a lighter color. After several months, it had become evident he was truly a lost man. So, Abram named him "Shakah," meaning "forgotten." The old Bedouin was sure no one would be coming to rescue him.

Shakah rubbed his temples. It helped to stave off the inevitable headache since his bludgeoning. He sighed. He still experienced periodic moments of dizziness. He held the camel's reins to steady himself. But it had been needful to get away today.

It was necessary to find a place to think alone. He had begged Abram to be allowed to venture out to Qumran and then to Jerusalem. Abram agreed, and then sent him with two other shepherds, just for safety.

Those two had gone on ahead of him. Qumran was only a mile or so away.

Why did this land look familiar to him, he queried himself? Had he seen it .... before?

It was frustrating not to be able to remember....

Did those he knew before think he was dead? If he went back, would there still be a place for him? Surely everyone else had moved on with their lives.

It was strange, he considered. He retained his abilities to understand and converse in several languages. His knowledge of numbers and letters had remained. Abram had given him a trusted place in the tribe. He now was Trade Administrator.

Of late, though, Shakah had been experiencing unbidden intrusions of faces and places he didn't recognize, but somehow felt familiar. He had experienced several dreams; pleasant enough, but disturbing for a person with no ability to chronicle his life.

He had been afraid to marry. After all, what if he already *had* a wife somewhere, or children? But then, how would he even begin to look for them, if they did exist?

His thoughts fell on Leah. She was so beautiful, and had been his friend since the first day. Silently, he considered her.

He *had* fallen in love.

"I can't make you any promises until I know my roots," he had said to her.

"I will wait for you, Shakah. I have begged my father not to give me to anyone else." Leah was Abram's daughter; and the one to help him as he learned to walk again.

How much longer will it be, God, he wondered?

His heart held so many questions. Did he *want* to know where he had come from? It would be so much simpler if he could just walk away. After all, what good would it do to go back now?

Then had come the last dream; two nights ago. He had seen himself, as if in another life; dressed in fine linen, with tooled sandals on his feet. There was another man; an older man in the dream... His father? His teacher? As the dream had retreated into daylight, Shakah had heard the man's voice, calling him.

"Help me." A voice he realized *should* be familiar was indistinct, and yet as he reconsidered it, the dream had become imprinted and real. "Come quickly."

He had awoken with a chill; beads of sweat forming on his forehead.

Come, he questioned? Where?

"Your memory is returning, my son," Abram had told him. "Give it time. God has His ways."

Shakah looked out again over the still waters. Yesterday, awakening from sleep, he had had an impression of himself loading a wagon with supplies. He strained to see what the supplies were he was loading. Had he been a merchant? Had he been a thief?

Perhaps he had been a slave, he thought. What if his owner had him tried and executed for running away?

How much longer until he knew?

Perhaps it was better not to know. How would he know what was true?

He would ask Eli.

Pulling on the camel's reins, he continued his journey towards Qumran.

~~~

In the village of Bethany, Miriam worked to clean and organize her home. It had been a long time since she'd had open-ended opportunity to structure things... It was amazing how cluttered a home could become, she considered, each time she assessed the untidiness of her shelves.

Especially when a person has no motivation to keep going, she told herself.

Journey

It was always better to be busy, she decided. It helped to be able to work. Although the grief of losing Abiel continued to come in waves, like seas on a tide, the intensity of her pain was beginning to lessen. She was able to talk about it some now, and for the most part, able to function normally. Some days, however, she still had to remind herself to breathe, to move, to function. Some days the black hole of memories loomed over her, threatening to overwhelm her soul.

Such had been her experience this morning. She had forced herself to get out of bed.

"Can we go to into Jerusalem, Eleazar?" she had asked that morning. "I would like to go to the market there. I need a diversion."

Eleazar smiled at her, understanding. "Absolutely, he answered. "I need to visit Lucius this week anyway. A courier arrived from him this morning, with word that Mary has sent him a large shipment of raw silks needing to be dyed. He asked for help in the color selections. You wouldn't want that job, would you? You could go with me."

Miriam was eager to help; anything to get out of the house. She felt a deep need to do something useful.

"Were you planning to open the clinic this week?" Eleazar had asked. "Don't you have people coming?"

"No, not yet," she answered with a sigh. I'm not ready to open it again. Besides, I'm not even sure I want to; …. even though, people *do* keep asking me for herbs and teas." She looked at her brother. "I don't know if I could do what Abiel did. He had a second sense when it came to knowing what to do when people were ill. The best I ever did was just to serve as his helper. I wouldn't know where to begin! How could I possibly run a clinic?"

"You have more ability than you realize," Eleazar told her. "He was always teaching you, training you. Besides, you'll never know unless you try."

Miriam paused, looking at her brother. "I need a little more time. I feel stuck, somehow; nothing that needs doing appeals to me." She looked at her brother. "What do I do? I know I should step back into my life, but….. well….. I find myself without any motivation at all… or even desire?"

"I'll do whatever I can to help you get on your feet."

At the gentle answer, her eyes had filled with tears once again. She had grabbed his hand. "Thank you, Eleazar. You are a kind man."

"For a brother!" he had responded with a smile, jabbing her with his elbow; hoping to invoke a sign of recovered humor in her. But none came.

Thus they traveled to Jerusalem. Miriam enjoyed the larger marketplace, with its animal merchants, and hawkers. It was mid-afternoon before they made their way to the weaving house. Lucius greeted them warmly.

"Peace, my friends!" he cried, warmly hugging them both. He was a hulk of a man, and his brotherly embrace locked one arm around Eleazar, while the other encompassed the petite Miriam. He looked into her eyes. "How are you doing, little lady?" he asked, looking into her eyes with concern. "Abiel was a great man. I admired him a great deal. We will miss his smile."

Journey

"Me too," Miriam answered.

"I lost my wife years ago," he comforted her. "Just wait. It does get better with time. Life will continue; the days will become easier to manage."

"I hope so," she smiled at him. "Eleazar has been kind enough to include me in his errands today. I needed to get away from the house."

"I imagine so." Lucius studied her for a moment, and then looked at his friend. "Eleazar, I need your help choosing the dye colors for the next shipment of silks. Your sister, Mary, is quite a tradeswoman; although, from what the camel driver tells me, she has been ill of late."

"Ill? Mary?" Miriam was concerned.

Lucius rubbed her arm. "I'm sure it was nothing, little one. I'm sure it has passed by now."

"What happened?" Eleazar wanted to know. "Did she have another one of her episodes?"

"I'm not sure, exactly," Lucius responded. He nodded his head toward the back of the house, making indication. "The driver is still here, loading a caravan for Egypt. Why don't you go and speak with him?"

Eleazar thanked him, and moved towards the back of the building with Miriam, where the camels were being fed and watered; prepared for travel. Lucius moved back into the building, seeking to spur his workers on in finishing a special order.

"This order was prepaid, so I feel obligated to hurry to finish it," he explained, apologetically. "We are almost completed. I'll be with you soon."

As they waited, Miriam and Eleazar listened to the camel driver's account of Mary's encounter with Jesus in Migdal.

The man had not been in the house at the beginning of Mary's encounter. "I came in to find the Commander, and saw her in the storeroom on the floor. I think she had passed out. Perhaps she was tired from the journey," he told them. "But then, the next morning, when Master Joseph helped me load my camels with the silks, she was fine; really fine. She even paid me extra for having to wait. I thought *that* was unusual." He looked at Eleazar, and paused before he continued. "I have transported items for your company before. I saw her before."

"Before what?" Miriam wanted to know.

"Before she became free of her fear. She told me she feels like a different person since that night. She is happy. She was even smiling!"

"That's wonderful," Miriam commented. "I'm so glad she's happy."

Eleazar responded carefully, looking at his sister. "I'm not so sure. She has a way of getting into trouble in her relationships. These episodes have happened before, and then gone, like a passing storm, as soon as she has a new man in her life."

"What do you mean?" Miriam was unaware of Mary's personal life since leaving Bethany. "Has she been ill like this before? What do you mean, 'a new man'?" Eleazar had been certain it would break her heart, so he had kept it from her.

Journey

"Nothing. I'm probably just being overly critical. I just hope that she is being wise with her life, that's all," he answered evasively.

Miriam sensed his elusiveness, but said nothing. Watching her brother, she settled into quiet thought as the men continued their conversation.

I want to see her again, she thought. *We used to have such good talks.*

As the shadows lengthened in Jerusalem, the workers began leaving the weaving and dyeing house for their homes. Most had stayed longer than usual to help Lucius in finishing the order of fabrics leaving by caravan at dawn.

After the building was secured, Eleazar and Miriam accompanied Lucius to his home.

"You know, Eleazar, I have a new caravan of wares going to Egypt in a few months," he began.

"What are you trading?" the younger man asked.

"I want to try to trade some of the dyed silks there. We have done well in Phoenicia and Syria. The Roman women love the feel of the fabric, and how it shimmers. I even sold a bolt to a Bedouin tribe not long ago." Lucius paused. "I wondered if you would like to lead the caravan, and add some of your wares from the Galilee area."

"How long would I be gone?" Eleazar wanted to know. He looked at his sister, appraising the effect of his absence.

"Several months," Lucius replied. "I would pay you well, and you would make a good profit on your own goods." He looked at Miriam. "It would take us several months to gather all the essentials. I want someone I can trust to oversee the venture. You understand."

Eleazar did understand. He nodded. "Give me some time to think about it," he responded. "It is important to me Miriam be well settled before I leave her for any long period of time. Can I let you know in a few days?"

"Surely," Lucius answered. He clapped his hands and rubbed them together, "Now, what would you like to eat?" he asked.

"What is there to choose from?" Eleazar asked.

"Whatever is still being sold this time of day," the businessman laughed. "With the shipment coming in, I didn't pay attention to food. I didn't eat either." He began rummaging through the baskets on the shelves. "I might have a little bread left from yesterday."

Miriam looked toward the horizon. The sun had not yet set. Perhaps a few of the vendors were still open in the marketplace. She spoke. "Why don't you two work on the colors for the fabrics, and I'll quickly run to the market?"

"That's a great idea, sis," Eleazar responded.

Later that evening, the three of them sat in the living area of Lucius' home, sharing and laughing together. Miriam had offered to excuse herself to allow the men to dine alone, according to custom of the day, but Lucius would have nothing to do with it. "You went to the market. You planned our meal. Then, you not only cooked the meal, but you made fresh food for me for the next couple of days! Besides all that, my home has not been this clean or ordered in months. Tell me, Miriam, do you do everything this well?"

"She *does!*" Eleazar teased, chuckling.

Journey

Miriam blushed. "I just was trying to stay busy, Lucius," she answered.

Lucius continued to watch her with interest. More than once that evening, Eleazar noticed his friend's gaze being fixed on his sister. He smiled to himself. It had been a little over a year now. She might be ready for a friendship with someone new.

Miriam however, was unaware of Lucius' thoughts. It was so good to break away from deeper pain and memories. She felt light and almost giddy. She laughed gaily, and joined her brother and Lucius' in conversation. Ever a gracious host, Lucius gave Miriam the small enclosure on the roof for her sleeping quarters that evening. She retired gratefully, and fell asleep quickly.

"She is a wonderful woman," Lucius confided in Eleazar as he lay in the dark, thinking that night.

"I don't know if she is ready for a new relationship yet, Lucius," Eleazar replied. "She is still grieving." He paused. "How much older are you than she?"

"I don't know," Lucius replied, "twelve or fifteen years, perhaps. Arranged marriages have are made every day with even more of a difference in ages." He paused for a few moments, reflecting. "But I can tell you this. I have loved her from the day I met her when she was fifteen. I would pledge my life to take care of her. You don't know this, but no other woman has had my interest since my wife died. The difference in our ages doesn't matter to me. There is no difference in the ages of our hearts….. Eleazar?"

Eleazar was silent. Was he thinking? Had Lucius offended his friend? He followed his confession with a hastily uttered conciliatory.

"I will wait until she is ready." When there was still not answer, he added, "I will wait until you agree."

"Eleazar?"

When his friend continued to say nothing. Lucius began to wonder if Eleazar had even heard his initial declaration.

The younger man had begun to snore.

~~~~

In EnKarem, the older Eleazar loaded grapes into a handcart he had found on the property. It hadn't taken long to repair its wheel, once he located the wood and tools. He had also discovered his gardening equipment.

It was amazing. Everything had been left in order, he considered. All that was required was washing the dust off his tools; one or two of the wooden handles had needed replacement or repair; nothing more.

As he worked, there was plenty of time to think how his life was in the early years. Those who left his employment years ago had done so one by one. He couldn't remember speaking with any of them. Had he just ceased to exist, allowing the beer and wine to take over? Now, he could see he had allowed the drinking to become his comfort, his counsel; his escape.

In return, the addiction had stolen his life.

Eleazar had spent the last six months weeding terraces and pruning vines. It had taken one entire month just to set trailing lines above the vines once again, digging around the larger roots to add fertilizer. Some had become like tree trunks during the years of neglect! In the process, he had harvested wild grapes. These were the clusters he was loading into the cart.

He had discovered barley grain also, and planted a several terraces for a crop. Grain for a wheat crop had also been found in storage; waiting for him. He had pruned olive trees, gathering olives to put away. The date tree offered him its goodness as well.

It felt good to cultivate the ground again.

Perhaps the soil of his heart was becoming good too, he considered. *He had been hard-hearted for a long time. It would take some effort.*

He was not as young as he used to be; and it was tedious and exhausting to do the physical work alone. He had always enjoyed the company of others, even if he had not participated in community with his heart. As he worked, he found himself talking aloud, verbally processing his life, directing his words to God.

It was healthy to practice contemplation. He had never thought about himself or his life in this way before. Come to think of it, he had never *ever* reflected deeply before, beyond admiring his own accomplishments.

How shallow he had been! What substance he had evaded with ambition!

Well, there was nothing to be proud of any longer.

He would not beg again.

He wanted to be able to *give;* to help; to be a benefactor.

He could still remember the moment he realized just how far down the spiral he had slid. His reckoning with himself had occurred in Jerusalem. Living on the street once morning, he awakened as the subject of a conversation between a little girl and her older brother.

"Why is he sleeping in the street?" she asked.

"I dunno," the brother shrugged. "Maybe he doesn't have anywhere else to go."

"Why does he smell so bad?" she wanted to know.

"He probably doesn't care. You need to stay away from him. He might kill you."

The little girl had walked over to Eleazar and put out her hand. "You aren't going to *kill* me, are you?" she asked.

Eleazar had not known what to say. He had just shaken his head.

The boy had grabbed his sister's arm, pulling her away, but not before she threw several coins into the cup on the ground next to his head.

"I don't know why you beg," she said, looking Eleazar in the eye. She looked so much like his own daughters; he had stared at her with fascination. "You probably have a family somewhere. They might be looking for you. Why don't you go home?"

"Dorcas!" the brother had admonished. "You need to come with me now! Grandmother sent us to the market for bread, and we need to get home."

The little girl had looked once again at Eleazar, her eyes full of compassion. She looked at her brother. "Do you think *he* has had any bread?"

Her brother seemed to be considering something, and then spoke to Eleazar. "Are you hungry?"

Journey

The beggar nodded.

"Follow us home. Our grandmother is the best cook in town, and we always have people in for dinner."

Eleazar had followed the children home. The home they spoke of was a priest's home, apparently a man of great responsibility. The children were visiting their grandparents, and had left the next week. But Mistress Hadassah and her house staff had insisted Eleazar stay until he was on his feet. They fed him, clothed him, and had been true friends to him. They had allowed him to stay, in exchange for household chores; even preparing a sleeping area for him in one of the animal stalls. He had stayed several months, finally finding himsef sober.

As memory returned, his desire to return to EnKarem had come with it.

He remembered the morning he told Mistress Hadassah of his plan to leave.

"You have done so much for me here." He had been close to tears, trying desperately to maintain his dignity.

"The grandchildren found you. You are a treasure they brought to our house," she laughed. "We just do what God tells us to do."

"Please thank your husband for me," Eleazar told her. "I know he will be at the Temple all day."

"Judah will be sorry to have missed the chance to say goodbye, Eleazar," Hadassah told him. "When will we see you again?"

"I want to make some things right in my life. I will send you word when I can," he promised.

She had hugged him. "Stay away from the strong drink. Try to remember that you don't need to run from Pain. God brings good out of it, to bring us to Himself. You can always come back here. We will be a home for you."

Pain **had** deepened him, he realized. *If only he had worked with the Pain and not tried to escape it in the beginning…… If only he had listened to those around him who had given their advice when she died…. If only he…*

He stopped. No. He would do this today.

He loaded the last of the grapes and began his journey to the Temple. It would take him a full day. He would find the old warehouse, and speak to the city's elders. He would make amends.

He would make sure the blessing of God was resting upon the rebuilding of his life.

This was his first-fruits offering.

He smiled, as he thought about little Dorcas' coins, still in his possession. It was time to offer a sacrifice too. He needed to seal the change in his heart.

He would use the money to buy a lamb.

~~~

In the outdoor kitchen area of Zebedee's home, a group of women worked to prepare small baskets of food. As they did, conversation and laughter were heard, on the breeze. Seven children played in and around the yard, continually coming in and going out.

Journey

Eight-year-old Daniel darted into the cooking area, where Abigail, his mother, was helping Salome, Zebedee's wife, at the grinding stone. "Master Zebedee says he will take us on the boats today!" he announced, coming beside his mother. "Can we go? Can we go?"

Abigail looked at him with a smile. "Who is 'we', son?" she asked.

"David wants to go too. Dorcas wanted to go, but I told her she couldn't because *she's a girl*."

Fifteen-year-old Elizabeth was working with Julia Flavius, wrapping small loaves of barley bread. "Girls can do lots of things *you* can't do. You just don't want her to go, because she'll probably *out-fish* you," she retorted to her brother.

"Elizabeth!" her mother reprimanded. "Be kind."

"Oh, mother, honestly," Elizabeth complained, rolling her eyes. "Ever since father told David the boys could go with him to the Temple, they both have been positively unbearable!"

"Mother," Daniel rejoined, "why don't we marry *her* off to some old man who has no teeth?"

Abigail sighed, as she glanced at her son. "Daniel, we are working here. A large group of us are going out to listen to Jesus today, and we are making food to take with us. You can't come in here and disturb the peace with your sister…Yes, you can go with Master Zebedee… please… please go… have a wonderful day." She hugged her son. As she watched him go, she groaned.

An older woman across the outdoor cooking area looked at Abigail. "My boys used to act the same way," Joanna comforted her. "Jonas used to get so angry with them. He sometimes would make them mend nets all day just to keep them quiet and out of trouble. One time, when my Simon was about your Daniel's age, he thought it would be funny to tie all the nets together, and make a sphere for playing kickball. Jonas came home from the marketplace to find Simon and Andrew kicking a ball of nets up and down the hill next to the dock. They had become so distracted in their game none of the nets were mended." She laughed gaily as she spoke. "His face was not a pretty sight."

Even Elizabeth giggled. The thought of the two, husky, grown men as boys, getting into trouble like her brothers, amused her.

Elsbeth, Simon's wife, winked at Elizabeth. "When you meet your husband, take note of those things, Elizabeth." She smiled. "Simon, or should I say, '*Simon Peter*,' is the same now as he was then. I remember him taking all of my cleaning rags to make a kickball for our boys a while back. When we lived in Bethsaida, he and Andrew would gather all the children in the village out to play in the field. They have used that ball for years. I even think it came with us when we moved here to Capernaum." She looked at Joanna, her mother-in-law. "Some things never change."

Simon Peter and Elsbeth had moved to Capernaum within the past year or so, just after the death of Elsbeth's elderly father. She was glad to be back in village of her childhood, once again living with her mother in the house she had always known. For his part, Simon

Journey

had discovered a friend and business partner in Zebedee. The affiliation between them had grown of late, as their wives had become fast friends.

Soon after they relocated, Andrew had followed. "Is there room for your bachelor brother?" he had asked. "It's too quiet in Bethsaida without you."

And so, a fishing partnership had begun between Simon Peter and Andrew with Zebedee and his sons. Zebedee was glad for the additional nets and boats. Everyone was glad.

Especially now, since Jesus was travelling more and more.

Elsbeth looked over to her mother, Susanna, who was broiling fish with Mary, Jesus' mother. Adding fish to the lunch baskets was the completion step in the preparation process. "How are you feeling today, mother?" she inquired.

"Never better," Susanna smiled as she responded. "I don't think I have ever experienced a fever like that in my entire life. It came on me all of a sudden, with chills… and such weakness."

"I know," the daughter replied. "I was afraid we were going to lose you. You know you were sick for three days? I'm glad you feel well. I was just checking. I don't want to see you overdo things."

"Elsbeth, I'm fine. Really fine," Susanna responded. "In fact, the night Jesus came to the house with Simon marked a change in many ways for me. He not only healed me of whatever sickness I was suffering from, but something changed inside of me as well. I'm not afraid anymore. In fact, I finally have been able to feel peace for the first time since your father died." She paused, looking at the other women in the circle. "You know what I mean, don't you? Something inside of me is better, happier, more able to trust….. Does that make sense to anyone but me?"

A murmur of agreement rippled around the gathering.

Julia moved to Susanna, placing an arm around her shoulders. "I do know, exactly. I just can't express it completely either," she said. "Justus told me about his conversation with Jesus the day he asked him to heal our steward, Adelphos. The man has been Justus' companion since long before we were married. The physicians, and even the apothecary, had told us to prepare for his death, he was so sick."

Most of the women had heard the story before, and were nodding in agreement.

"What happened?" The voice belonged to eleven-year-old David, Abigail's son.

"Daddy didn't want to lose Adelphos," little Helena interjected. "He cried."

Julia stroked her daughter's hair, and continued. "One of the servants told Justus we should ask Jesus to heal him. So Justus went to search. He found Jesus just outside the village of Nain."

"Was that the day he raised the widow's son from the dead?" Joanna wanted to know.

Julia nodded; "Just before. Jesus said he would come to the house, and Justus said, 'Sir, I am also a man under authority; I tell my men what to do and where to go and they obey me. Just say the word, and I know Adelphos will be well.'"

"What did Jesus do then?" David asked.

"He told Justus that he hadn't seen anyone trust him like that; that completely, you know. He told him our steward would be healed. He told him to go home." She looked around the group. "Adelphos got up and went back to work in the same hour that Jesus spoke."

Listening quietly to the exchanges taking place around her, Mary once again remembered the night of her own deliverance, and her conversation with Jesus afterward. Hadn't Commander Justus been at her house in Migdal that night? He knew as well as she the amount of strength and authority that Jesus carried.

A man *under* authority…..

Jesus had waited until the proper time. How had he known? Whose authority was *he* under? She made a mental note to ask him the next time she saw him.

Looking around the circle of women, her mind went back to the day she arrived in Capernaum. Salome and Zebedee had opened their home to her at first. And then, she had met Julia, and was invited to stay in the Flavius' home.

Julia had become like a sister to her.

All of these women were good friends, she realized. She had never known a community of relationship like this before. Did *everyone* have this kind of safety with others, she wondered? She knew she was truly blessed.

So many things had happened since the night of her liberation.

She had watched the lesions disappear from a leper's face and hands. Jesus had healed him.

She had watched four men tear the roof tiles off of a house, when they couldn't get through a crowd, and Jesus was inside. The four had carried a paralyzed friend several miles on a stretcher. They had let him down through the roof. Jesus had healed him.

She had seen a man roll up a bed he had lain on by the pool of Bethesda for thirty-eight years. Jesus had healed him.

She had seen a man's hand fill with life, like a wineskin being filled; beginning to bulge. All Jesus had said was, "Stretch out your hand." At first, she thought Jesus was asking the impossible. But then, the man had attempted to do what Jesus had asked him to do. As he made the effort, suddenly, his withered hand and arm both strengthened, becoming usable.

Jesus had healed him – completely!!

And who could forget the day in Capernaum when the people had kept coming and coming? The sick, the blind, the lame, the deaf, the unclean… the demonized – like her…..

Jesus had healed them… *all.*

She did notice the priests hadn't seemed too happy. They didn't like his timing. And yet, Mary considered, he had waited for the perfect time when it had come to her.

Perhaps there was a difference between what happened outside a person, and what happened inside….

Were the men who had difficulty in accepting Jesus only worried about what things looked like on the outside? What was really the most important? What did God think was more important?

How would you know who you were supposed to be?

Journey

Was a person defined by the outside, or by the inside?

Suddenly, a picture of the sealed jar of ointment, given to her by her father years ago, flashed in her mind. Was it still in her satchel? She remembered her father's words, spoken to her and Miriam so many years ago as he had given them each an identical jar:

"These are very valuable. Please take good care of them.... If you ever have a need that I cannot meet, sell these......I put the nard in alabaster because it reminds me of the texture of your mother's skin; so clear; so beautiful... She was perfect in every way, and we were so happy. I want these bottles to remind you girls of what you can become. Each time you look at them, think of the perfection she was to me. If you ever open this bottle, just a tiny drop will fill the entire house with fragrance, just like your mother filled my life. You have a lot to live up to, now. Never forget that. When you see your bottle, I want you to see your mother looking back at you. You have a responsibility to become the woman she would have wanted you to become. There is no better model you could copy. She is the image you are to become."

She is the image you are to become...... *she* is the image..... The words echoed in her mind. Was *that* the reason she had brought the jar with her continually? Was that why it had always found its way into her travels; being placed in prominent places in her living spaces?

I never knew my mother, she realized. But my father wanted me to be *her*.....

Is that my purpose? Is that my goal?

I don't even know where to begin!! I have failed so miserably...... It is too late to go back and do things over again..... this emptiness is too deep to see real change come... it's too late for me....it is all ruined....I am damaged goods...

Standing, she turned away from the others. She walked down to the water's edge of the Sea of Galilee. Tears once again trickled down her cheeks. What was she supposed to do?

I have good plans for your life; a Hope and a Future.

She recognized the Voice of the Spirit of God.

She could sense an impending choice before her.

Suddenly, Mary understood. She knew what she had to do.

~~~

Some days later, Abigail and her children were working together, preparing the central room of their home for a large dinner gathering Simon the Pharisee was giving that evening.

"Mommy, how many are coming?" Dorcas asked, pullling on the legs of a reclining couch, hoping to help.

"Oh, Dorcas, let David and Daniel do that," her Mother hurried over to the little girl, and reached under the couch for the small eating table nestled under it for storage against the wall. "You can carry the tables."

"Why do we have to set up all these couches?" Elizabeth sighed. "They don't eat on couches at Zebedee and Salome's house. They just have one long table. Everyone sits on cushions on the floor when people come over."

Journey

David sneered at his sister. "They are just low-class fishermen. They eat like the sheep-herders. *We* are more civilized than that. *We* have better manners. Besides, Father likes the Greek couches. It keeps him separated from the sinful."

Abigail was shocked by her son's expressions of superiority and prejudice. "David bar Simon!" she corrected. "*We* eat at a low table and sit on cushions when *we* have no guests! Why, the girls and I sometimes eat in the kitchen area with a rug, like a picnic."

David pulled himself up, trying to give more height to his stature. "You are *women*," he stated, matter-of-factly. "Besides, I am going to be a Pharisee. Pharisees are not allowed to even touch those kinds of people. If I know where I'm going, and what I'm going to be, why should I *wait* to live by the rules? What is the difference *now?*"

Abigail was at a loss for words. It was difficult to hear her husband's viewpoints on religion and daily life being touted by her son. Somehow, it shattered her sense of safety; it was a signal. Her days of influencing her son's values and choices were coming to a close. She stared at David for a long moment, and then spoke. "My son, someday you might need help from those people. If you alienate them, you will be alone. Salome and her family have become my friends."

"If I do need help, I certainly wouldn't receive it from Zebedee," her son argued. "He and his sons have taken up with that Jesus, who calls himself a prophet."

Abigail was surprised. "But I thought you enjoyed spending time with the fishermen. Besides, Jesus doesn't call himself a prophet. Others do. What about the miracles?"

"Father says he is an insurgent, and we must be careful of him," David said, without thinking. He looked around quickly, realizing he had said too much.

"If that's true, then why is Father having him to dinner tonight?" Daniel wanted to know.

"I didn't know Jesus was coming!" Dorcas clapped her hands and jumped up and down. "Can we sit by him? Can I talk to him?"

"Of course not," David retorted. "Women and children eat in the kitchen. You get whatever we *men* leave for you to eat." He paused, and looked at his brother. "Where did you hear that Jesus was coming tonight?"

Shrugging, Daniel answered. "Father was talking to Commander Justus about the meal. The commander is coming too, and Eleazar, and Zebedee, and his sons." He was counting on his fingers. "It's going to use all the room we have."

David smiled smugly. "I know what Father is doing. He's gathering evidence."

Abigail worked the rest of the afternoon in troubled silence. She had thought Simon had been showing signs of cracking his hard exterior. She had misunderstood. His reasons for befriending Jesus and his companions apparently were something she had no knowledge of. She sighed.

This was yet another sign of Simon's pride and distancing.

Hadn't Jesus been going through the countryside, helping people? Simon had even asked him to speak in the synagogue! Why would he be so dualistic? Didn't he realize he was being dishonest?

He certainly wasn't the man she had married any longer. They had grown apart.

Journey

Suddenly, it no longer felt like an honor to be a Pharisee's wife.... or a Pharisee's mother, for that matter.

She could feel her heart being torn. Where did she want her loyalties to be? What direction should she take? She stopped, and looked through the open doorway to the outside.

Jesus. Unbidden, the name rippled through her like a shockwave.

Choose. Was it a voice, she wondered; or a nudging?

An image she had witnessed some weeks ago blazed into her mind. Jesus had been walking along the shore of the Sea of Galilee one morning. Simon Peter and Andrew had been mending and washing their nets close by, having come in from fishing through the early morning hours. Abigail had been returning home from the market with the smaller children; Daniel, Dorcas and Deborah. Daniel had seen a crowd gathering.

"Look! Can we go too?" he asked.

"Can we see, Mommy?" Deborah had asked. "Jesus is talking."

Abigail had nodded, and all three of her children had instantaneously deserted her, pushing through the crowd to get to the front. Why was it they always wanted to be near Jesus, she wondered? It was never so with their father. With Jesus, the children's responses always surprised her.

That particular day, she stood for a short while listening to Jesus' words, before realizing the man was not standing on the shore. Rather, he had stepped into one of Simon Peter's boats, and was speaking from a short distance off the shore. His voice echoed off the surface of the water, helping to amplify the sound.

When he finished, as the crowd dissipated, Abigail began looking for her children. She found them, watching Jesus from the water's edge. He was speaking to Simon, who at some point must have gotten into the boat with him. Andrew was with them.

"Thank you, Simon," Jesus said. "Let's go out a little deeper, and let down the nets for a catch of fish."

Simon Peter frowned. "Master, we worked all night long. We didn't catch anything. Andrew and I just finished washing our nets. I was...."

He stopped mid-sentence. Abigail had been unable to tell, but it was obvious he must have seen something in Jesus' eyes. Perhaps it had been the smile; or there had been a twinkle in his eye. She had been too far away to know for sure, but Simon had changed the direction of his words.

"It doesn't matter. You know what? I trust you. Just because you say to, I will let down the net."

Simon and Andrew had then maneuvered the boat into deeper waters, stopping where Jesus indicated they should. Unfolding and spreading the largest of their nets, the two weary fishermen worked together to cast it into the waters, and then pull it up, looking for a few fish they could bring in for cleaning. Abigail had turned to leave, but the children had continued to watch, captivated for some reason.

Then Simon began to call for help. The net was breaking! James and John had run to leap into their own boat, pushing out into the deeper waters as well. The five men had worked

Journey

together for almost an hour, retrieving and distributing fish into both boats. In the end, both boats had been filled to capacity with fish; so much so, they began to sink.

Where had all the fish come from? How had Jesus known?

Abigail had been amazed, but what struck in her memory were the actions she witnessed following the catch of fish.

They had been working together; Jesus hauling in the net aside Simon Peter. As Andrew turned the boat toward the shore, Simon had dropped to his knees in front of Jesus. He had been overwhelmed with an awareness of Jesus' power. He told his mother, Joanna, later that as he watched the net filling with fish, he became aware of how weak it was. "It couldn't hold all it had caught," he told her. "Then I saw the net of my own life, and how weak I am myself. It occurred to me I was not strong enough to be able to carry what God was bringing me into."

Abigail had heard Simon's words to Jesus over the waters that day. "Get away from me, Jesus. I'm a weak man; full of sinful desires. I don't think I can do this."

Jesus had put his hand on Peter's shoulder, and looked him in the eyes, laughing. "Don't be afraid, Simon. You think this is a good catch? From now on, you will be catching *people.*"

When they arrived at the shore, Zebedee's other workers began the task of sorting and cleaning the fish. Jesus had looked at the four fishermen, each one squarely, as if assessing them. "Come and follow me," he said.

One by one, Peter, Andrew, James and John had left their nets.

They had travelled with Jesus since that day; and they were becoming different men somehow. Elsbeth, had confided in Abigail about the changes in Simon, and in Andrew.

"He is gentler, somehow," she had said. "And we eat *together* now."

Abigail moved the tables into their positions, inside of the circle of couches. In this arrangement, she considered, the guests could recline, placing their elbows on the headrest, eating from the table in front of them. It would be easier to serve this way also, she reasoned. She and Elizabeth could bring the food in on trays, walking in the center of the circle, allowing each man to take the portion he desired.

She looked out the window. The sun would be setting soon, and guests would be arriving. She placed the lamps in their alcoves around the room, and filled each one with oil. As she did so, she heard her husband's voice behind her.

"Well, wife," Simon spoke, surveying the final preparations. "How are things coming along? Are we ready for the evening?"

Out of habit, Abigail bowed her head in deference to him. "We are almost ready. Elizabeth and Daniel are preparing some trays with fresh pita and hummus. We will bring them in as soon as everyone has arrived."

"Did you buy the meat?" he wanted to know.

"Yes, just as you asked. We are slicing the beef into slabs, and we will put them on the fire as soon as the guests begin arriving. I have a cucumber and leek salad prepared, as well as cabbage with sesame vinegar dressing. We also have some nuts and olives."

"Did you make your cucumber sauce?" Simon asked. "You know how much I like it."

Journey

"No, I didn't really have time. I made hummus instead."

"I'd like you to make cucumber sauce as well."

Abigail noticed he was shaking his left hand periodically.

"What did you do to your hand?" she asked.

"It's been giving me a little trouble of late," he answered. "Sometimes it goes numb when I work on the scrolls too long."

"I see," she replied. "Well, I'm headed back to the marketplace, if they are still open."

"Why?"

"I have no cucumbers for your sauce, or garlic either, for that matter. I will have to go to the market and then come home to prepare it. The meal might be a little late, if that is all right with you."

"Send David. You stay here and finish," Simon ordered.

Abigail hesitated. "Husband," she began. "Can I ask you something?"

Simon shrugged. "Go ahead."

"Well….." she paused, not sure where to begin, "lately when I ask David for help he is less than willing. This morning he told his sisters he was going to be a Pharisee, and didn't want to lower himself to touch those beneath his station."

Simon smiled. "It sounds like he is heading towards the priesthood, to me."

"No," she continued. "Is is true that you are having this meal tonight to gather evidence against Jesus? Who are you gathering it for?"

Simon's eyes narrowed. "Did David tell you that?"

"Yes, he did. He said you consider Jesus to be an insurgent."

Simon responded coolly. "I don't know what I believe, Abby. After all, if Jesus is what everyone says he is, the Promised Deliverer, then he will be setting up his rule soon. If he is not that Deliverer, then we will all be in deep trouble with the Roman government. Anyone who has had anything to do with him will be brought into the center of the Prefect's judgment hall for questioning. I'm just trying to secure our future, that's all."

"But you *do* believe Jesus, don't you?" she pressed.

"I believe the dinner will be late if you don't get a move on, woman!" Simon motioned with his hands to shoo her out of the room. He called out, "David! Come and help your mother! She needs you to go to the market!"

Disheartened yet again, Abigail left her husband's presence. It was becoming increasingly difficult to read his moods, or his expressions.

For his part, Abigail's question had caused Simon to question himself, even though he would never stoop to allow her to know so.

He was hoping conversation over the meal would provide greater insight into Jesus. He was anxious to discover Jesus' claims about who he was. He had heard the man's teachings. They each seemed to carry a common thread; the road to the finish line always caused a person to think about his life.

Journey

How could a young man, a carpenter yet, possess so much perception and wisdom? In addition to garnering information for Joseph Caiaphas, the high priest in Jerusalem, Simon found himself wanting to understand. "What is true, God?" he had prayed.

There had been so many miracles happening through Jesus. Of special interest to Simon was the man who had been delivered from demon possession. It had happened on the Sabbath, in the synagogue. Simon had known the man had the problem before…. He had assumed the problem was physical and would have to be tolerated.

Why had Jesus broken the Sabbath to heal someone; especially someone of such a low class?

Simon had never heard the prophets, or the Law explained in such simple terms as they were when Jesus taught them. Over the past couple of months the priest had experienced several discussions with Judah, his father. Each one had centered on statements Jesus had made. The Pharisee had become particularly focused on Jesus' repeatedly used phrase, "kingdom of heaven."

Simon was convinced the empire Jesus spoke of was a physical replacement of Rome. Judah, on the other hand, held the view that the Kingdom of Heaven was a spiritual realm.

"If it were physical," the old sage maintained, "the rest of Jesus' teachings would be centered on power and authority. They are not. This man's words focus upon God's relationship with man, and God's attitude toward us. He reviews the Law and the prophets. He teaches the virtues of character, and the value of serving others. These are not the messages of a man who is looking to overthrow or rebel against authority." Something in his father's simple logic had left Simon shaken.

He had thought; no, felt *certain,* Jesus was an insurgent.

Now, he wasn't sure.

Nevertheless, he had made a commitment to the High Priest. Caiaphas was closer to God. Simon smiled grimly. *He would follow through.*

Contemplative, he walked around the room, mentally deciding which of his guests should sit where. He wanted to be able to assess their responses tonight. What he learned tonight would be pivotal. He could sense it. He would have to stay alert.

Tonight had the potential to revolutionize *everything*; from top to bottom.

Justus Flavius stepped into the garden behind his home. He had left the garrison early today, in order to get ready for Simon's dinner. Julia and Mary were weeding together, while the little girls played with the dog. It was good to be home, he thought.

"Hello, my love." Julia's rich voice greeted him first. Then the children were upon him, with Mary close behind. "You are home early. Are you hungry?"

"No, I don't need to eat. I am going to that dinner at Simon the Pharisee's home this evening. I came home to bathe and get ready to go over there."

Julia smiled. "I'm glad you're going. Abigail is such a good friend. But it's odd. As much time as we have spent together; I have never met her husband. He seems …. What?" she looked at Mary, looking for words. "Removed? Unavailable?"

Mary looked at her blankly. "I wouldn't know. I've never met him either."

Julia stood and brushed her hands together. "Well that's enough weeding for today. Is the invitation for you only?" she asked her husband.

"It is, although I am toying with the idea of taking you with me, just to shake the man up a little. You know, mess with his severity. The worst he could do would be to ask me to leave."

Julia laughed. "He won't do that."

"I didn't think the Pharisees would eat with people unless they are part of their social group," Justus said.

"Usually, that's true; at least of Simon," Justus commented. "I'm not sure what brought this sudden change in his attitudes."

"Perhaps Jesus' teachings are getting to him," Julia offered, as they moved inside.

It was strange, Justus considered. He had always thought of the Pharisees as a group disinclined to break bread with gentiles. There must be a motive, he reflected. Why now, and why such a large contingency of those who were closest to Jesus?

Perhaps he is just curious, he reasoned.

After all, Jesus' teachings and miracles had more than disrupted the day-to-day rhythms of the region. It was impossible to go anywhere in Galilee and not hear some sort of account of a miracle in someone's life. Justus wondered about his friend. How was Simon handling Jesus' popularity?

He was glad to have been invited to the dinner, although in Roman culture, his wife would have also been invited. Perhaps he *would* take her along, so she could spend time with Abigail. Mary had said her brother, Eleazar, had also been invited. The young man was spending the day working on new trade agreements with Zebedee. He and the old man were going together to the Pharisee's house.

Perhaps it was a meeting to discuss trade arrangements.

Perhaps Simon needed more money. Maybe the synagogue needed repairs.

It didn't matter why Simon had invited him, Justus concluded.

He would leave in an hour, and he *would* take Julia with him.

As soon as Justus and Julia left the property, Mary went looking for Adelphos, the household steward. She found him pruning grapes in the vineyard, with the two little girls and another slave's son playing close by.

"Adelphos, could you take me into Capernaum?" she asked.

"Do you need to go to the market, Mistress?" the slave questioned. "The sun will be setting soon. I'm sure the merchants have gone home for the day."

"No, not that," she answered. "I need to see a friend. Could you take me there, and wait for me?"

"Surely, Mistress." Adelphos walked to the well to wash the dirt from his hands, and then made his way to the horse stalls. "It will take me a few minutes to prepare the Commander's chariot." Then he said, "I will have the horses ready when you want to leave. I just need to take the children inside. Ann will need to take care of Victoria and Helena while we are gone."

Mary scarcely heard him. She was headed into the house to her room. She was on a mission. Hurriedly, she packed a small bag, and changed her sandals. Looking through her garments, she found the most ordinary toga she could find; one that didn't accentuate her figure; of a plain color. She removed her earrings and headdress. She combed her hair and washed her face and hands and feet.

It was time.

She was silent as Adelphos helped her into the chariot. If he was surprised at the change in her appearance, he said nothing. Standing next to her, he picked up the reins.

"Where am I taking you, Mistress?"

"I need to go to the dinner at Simon the Pharisee's house," she replied.

Adelphos looked at her, and noticed she was clutching a small bag close to her chest. She seemed preoccupied. Remembering his master's instructions regarding her care, and the stories surrounding her, his heart filled with concern. "Are you all right, Mistress?" he inquired.

Mary looked at him and smiled. "I have never been better, Adelphos. Can we go now?"

Inside, Mary was contemplating her next move. She wasn't sure exactly how she would go about her plan. She knew the men would be eating by now. The women would be serving.

She struggled inwardly with an inner dialogue.

What will they think of me, she wondered?

Don't embarrass yourself. You don't have to do this now. Do it later.

All I'm going to do is give Jesus a gift, she reasoned. I will hand him the bag, and tell him "thank you" and then leave. I can always go into the kitchen with Salome and Julia.

You are violating your place. You are better to keep quiet. He knows you're thankful.

No. I have violated my "place" for the wrong reasons, and for too long. I am going to give Jesus a gift. It doesn't matter what they think about me. I stopped caring about that long ago.

I made sacrifices to Pan and Zeus, and they did nothing for me.

He cut my chains completely. I will make this sacrifice.

When they arrived at the house, Adelphos stepped down, and placed the stepstool on the ground for her. He took her hand and helped her out of the chariot. "I will be right here, Mistress. I will wait for you. And if you need to fly, we will fly back to safety."

Mary could have hugged him. "Thank you for being my friend," she said.

When she arrived at the door, she found it open. *It would disturb their talk and draw more attention to knock. I will just go in.* She took several deep breaths, to still her pounding heart, and moved forward. Following the sound of the conversation, she moved towards the center of the house, where Simon was entertaining his visitors.

The couches were set up in a somewhat oval pattern, with an open area in the middle of the room. At the end of each couch, towards the center, was a small table, where food and

Journey

drink were placed for each guest. She had seen the arrangement before, at other dinner parties and gatherings she had attended. Usually the host hired dancers or entertainers for his guests, but Simon had none. Abigail was standing in the circle with a tray of sweet foods, apparently moving from table to table, serving. Each individual could then choose what they wanted.

The meal is almost over. Just say you needed to talk to Abigail. It's not too late.

Mary shook her head to clear it. She looked around the room, and noted who was there.

Eleazar and Zebedee were seated on one side, with James and John. Peter and Andrew were sitting with Levi, a former tax-collector who had joined Jesus' group recently. Apparently, the rest of the twelve had not come. Justus Flavius was seated next to Simon the Pharisee, with a few men she hadn't seen before. On the other side of Simon, was Jesus. She began moving toward his couch.

At the sight of her, her brother, Eleazar spoke. "Hello, Mary," he said.

Every eye in the room moved in her direction, expectant. All conversation stopped. But Mary said nothing. Her focus was on trying to get to Jesus. Why did her feet feel like iron?

The Commander spoke. "Was there something you needed, child?"

Mary glanced up at him. He smiled. Then her gaze moved to Simon the Pharisee. There was no smile in his eyes. Suddenly, she felt the weight of years upon her. She sensed the darkness.

You are out of place. Go away. Run now to Adelphos. He's waiting.

Her hands were shaking. She opened the small bag, and drew out the dreaded alabaster jar, still sealed with wax and a golden seal. Seeing it anew, the memories of lost years overwhelmed her.

It represented her life; her failed life; the woman she would never become.

The image of impossible perfection.

The mother she had never known; her quest for acceptance.

It represented unspoken expectations, and unsatisfied demands.

Her tears began; a trickle at first, and then a stream. Weeping overtook her. She struggled to remove wax seal. It was old and hard, and wouldn't budge.

She wanted to, she had to, just give it away….

The room full of men was still silent, watching, transfixed, not knowing how to respond.

She look down and saw the dirt on Simon the Pharisee's feet, and then on Jesus' feet.

Frustrated, she took the jar, and lifted it up. She brought it down hard on the edge of the couch where Jesus was reclining. It didn't break at first, so she tried again. This time, the fragile alabaster shell, concealing the ointment within, cracked open. Spikenard oil began to drip through the opening.

When the jar cracked open, Mary felt as though something within her had broken open as well. It was as though a dam had burst within her. Even more emotion roared from the depths of her soul to the surface. Where had it come from, she wondered? A torrent of sobs erupted.

Unable to continue to stand, Mary dropped to her knees at the end of Jesus' couch. He had turned around to face her, now. His feet were now on the floor. Disheveled and full of desolation, she looked at him. He smiled at her, and touched her arm. She began to weep even more vehemently.

Suddenly, she noticed his feet were wet. Were those her tears on his feet? She tried to wipe them away, but her hands were full of nard. Laying the jar aside, she gathered her hair in her hands, and began to use them as a towel. As she did, words began to stream from her lips.

"Thank you, Jesus …… you rescued me……..oh God…." Her words were interrupted by her involuntary sobs.

Simon the Pharisee watched in derision and disgust. Who had left the door unlocked? Didn't this woman know her place?

This is an important meeting; we are conducting important business here, he said to himself. *This is no place for a woman. She doesn't know her place. It's obvious this Jesus is not a holy man. If he were, he would know what kind of a woman this is. He should know her reputation. He wouldn't even let her touch him. She is a sinner..... If we still had the authority to pass sentence, she would have been stoned long before now...*

The priest looked up, and saw Jesus watching him. "Simon, I have something to ask you."

Perplexed, Simon looked at Jesus. Didn't the prophet even know that the woman was still down there, washing his feet? Couldn't he hear her? Did her touch disturb him? Simon answered, "What is it, Master?"

Jesus looked around the room. "I want to tell you a story. There was a man who loaned money to others, a creditor. He had two men who owed him money; one owed him a hundred *dinar*, and the other owed him fifty. When they had no way to pay him back, he forgave them both completely." He paused, and looked down at Mary. "Tell me what you think, Simon. Who will love him the most?"

Simon was stunned. What answer should he give? He stuttered. "I suppose the one he forgave the most."

Jesus looked at him squarely. "You are absolutely right." He looked at Mary, indicating her actions. "Do you see this woman? When I came into your house, you didn't give me water to wash the dirt from my feet. She, on the other hand, has washed my feet with tears, and wiped them with the hairs of her head. You gave me no customary kiss of greeting. She, on the other hand, is kissing my feet! You did not give me oil to anoint and bless my visit with you. She, on the other hand, has anointed my feet with costly perfume."

He paused. Around the room, each guest was breathing in the fragrance of the nard. It had filled the room, and had drawn everyone's full attention to what Jesus was saying. The women had crowded in at the door, watching and listening.

A sense of awe had overtaken each of them.

Jesus continued. "I want all of you to understand this. Her sins, which are many, are forgiven. She recognized the state of her soul. Because of that fact, she has loved much." He looked at Simon. "Those who think they need no forgiveness, cannot see the state of their

Journey

soul; the state of every soul. They are closed, and able to receive very little forgiveness. As a result *they love little*."

Simon didn't know what to say. Was Jesus saying he had the power to forgive sin, he wondered? Looking and listening to Jesus, he felt compassion welling up for Mary. What was this? He had never felt like this before… He stopped himself.

Don't be drawn in by him. The voice spoke loudly in his head.

So great was the struggle within his heart, Simon was unaware of the events immediately following Jesus' words.

Standing to his feet, Jesus took Mary's hands in his own. "Thank you, Mary," he said. "It is your trust and relationship with me that has rescued you. Go on from this point in Peace."

Looking at him, Mary smiled. She looked around the room, and realized that those she knew in the room were smiling also. "I'm free," she said. She looked at Julia and Salome, who were standing in the doorway, and repeated herself. "I'm really free!"

She ran out of the house, surprising Adelphos. He sprinted into action, thinking she was in distress. "Let's fly, Adelphos! God has given me wings!" Glancing at his concerned face, she quickly added. "It's good. Really good; for the first time in my life I can really breathe!"

Changing into his sleeping gown that night, Simon the Pharisee looked down at his left arm. It had been aching strangely more and more all day. He hadn't realized it until now, but his entire arm was now numb between his shoulder and his elbow. His back felt odd as well; tingly.

"Abigail," he called. "Come here!"

"What is it, Simon? I was half asleep."

"Come here now, woman," he demanded. "My arm is numb again. Do we have any salve or ointment to relieve the pain?"

Sleepily rising from the bed, a weary Abigail trudged into the room where her husband was standing. The preparations for the dinner party had been her responsibility. Subsequently, she had worked late into the night over the past few days, retiring after her husband, and rising at dawn. She had not seen his bare back for several days.

Coming through the door, she gradually became aware. Staring, wide-eyed, at her husband's back, she raised her hand to her mouth and stifled an involuntary gasp.

Hearing her, Simon turned, impervious to her weariness. "It's about time." Then he saw the look on her face. "What is it?"

Abigail backed up against the door. "You have a lesion on your back."

"What?" the priest responded. "It's probably just dry skin."

"No, it's *not* dry skin." Abigail moved away from her husband. "It's something much worse. I can feel it." She went to the bedchamber and began gathering her sleeping mat, her coverings and her pillow. "I will be sleeping in the courtyard tonight, Simon. You need to see the physician in the morning."

Simon shrugged. As far as he was concerned, Abby's response was yet another indication of womanly over-reaction. Still, it would be good to finally discover what had

Journey

been happening in his body over the past year. He continued dressing for bed, and retired, without giving his wife another thought.

Perhaps he would see a physician. He would see if he had the time.

Everyone knew that women worried too much.

The next day, Simon was surprised when his physician confirmed Abigail's concern. The spot on Simon's back was indeed concerning. After performing several tests, and asking the Pharisee some key questions, he made a diagnosis.

Simon was carrying a contagious disease. Apparently, it had remained dormant in his body for more than a year. It was the cause of his sensitivity to bright light, the numbness in his hands, as well as the continual ache. The disease was spreading, and would eventually take his life.

Simon did not seem to absorb the meaning of the words spoken to him until the physician came to the end of his consultation.

There was no cure.

Simon the Pharisee…. had become a leper.

Everything was about to change.

Journey

Bethany

In the middle of his trade route through the villages, Joseph Barsabas stopped to hear the Teacher. He had sought Jesus out to hear his teachings as much as possible, since the night of Mary's encounter. He realized there was much he needed to learn.

Most of all, Joseph loved listening to Jesus' stories. Seeing the usual crowd gathering ahead, the tradesman pulled his wagon to a stop. He reached into his supply duffle, and pulled out a wrapped loaf of bread, some dates, and a wineskin full of water. He would take his lunch break here, he decided.

He could see Jesus sitting in Simon Peter's boat once again, speaking to the crowd gathering on the shore.

"A farmer was planting seeds one day, reaching into his bag, and throwing the seed into his plowed field." Jesus made the motion of the sower as he spoke.

"Now, when this man threw seed, it fell in all sorts of places; on all sorts of soil. Some of the seeds fell on the side of the road. That ground was hard ground, and the birds came and ate up all the seed. Some of the seed fell on stony places. In fact, that ground had more stones than soil. But the seed did its job; it put down roots where it could. The problem was, there was no depth of soil. The roots couldn't go anywhere deep. So, when the sun came up, the heat scorched the plants because they didn't have good roots. Those plants withered and died.

"Some of the seeds fell where there were thorns and weeds. When the plants tried to grow, the weeds stole their nourishment, and the plants starved and died.

"Finally, there was seed that fell into the good ground. That seed put down deep roots, and grew to maturity. It gave a good harvest. Now, as with most farming, the results varied: some of the crops increased by thirty percent; some by sixty percent; some by one hundred percent.

"If you have the heart to understand what I have said in this story, you will hear the Voice of the Spirit of God. Listen to what He says to you."

Joseph was so caught up in the story he was hearing, he failed to see Justus Flavius walk up beside him. When the centurion spoke to him, he was so startled he jumped, emitting an involuntary sound of alarm.

Justus laughed. "What's wrong, Joseph? Sorry if I scared you."

"It… it's okay," Joseph replied, glancing sideways at the commander, who was in full Roman uniform. "I'm not used to seeing you like that."

"How is the trading going this week?" Justus wanted to know. "We have been dispatched to keep an eye on the crowds that Jesus draws these days. I thought I would come today, instead of one of my men." He nodded towards Jesus. "I always enjoy his stories."

Joseph looked at Justus, assessing him. Should he ask, he wondered? He had been holding a question for some time now.

Justus sensed the man's eyes on him. "Did you have something you needed?" he said.

The younger man paused. "I just wondered…" he began and then stopped.

"What?" Justus smiled at him. "I won't bite."

Joseph took a deep breath. "Well," he said, "I was just wondering where you stand with this whole thing. I mean, with Jesus, and the way we worship God. You're Roman, you know, and…."

Justus chuckled at the man's discomfort. "You mean, why did I finance the building of the synagogue when I'm not Jewish? Or, why am I so drawn to Jesus, if I'm a Roman?"

Joseph swallowed his water and nodded. "Yes, something like that."

The Commander responded. "Well, the Roman gods I was raised with have always promised prosperity, and blessing. There are so many of them, and as I was growing up, my mother would keep me in line by saying things like: 'Don't go into the river, you will make Poseidon angry;' or 'When you fight with your sister you make Mars angry.' I grew up always looking over my shoulder for some unknown deity to come after me; threatening to kill me or punish me if I didn't keep them appeased.

"When I was a young man in the infantry, the Roman senate decided to declare Julius Caesar a god. My grandfather had served with him in battle, and knew him well. I suppose I came to awareness those gods were not real. The things they promised; the miracles the priests would credit them with…. never really happened."

He paused, and looked at Joseph. "Does that make sense?"

Joseph nodded. "Yes, it does. I have wondered about what it would be like to grow up that way."

Justus continued. "Then, when I was stationed here, as garrison commander, I found myself watching the people here in Capernaum. Life is much simpler here, and so much richer, even though the people are poor. I still don't have words to explain it. The longer Julia and I have been here, the more I have discovered I do believe that there is one God, instead of many, and that He is the Giver of life. He is the Creator. It is the only belief system that makes real sense to me."

"Is that why you gave so much towards the synagogue?"

"Yes; and because one day I realized … I didn't sense fear when I thought about *this* God. I sensed acceptance, and invitation. I felt Peace."

"So, what is it about Jesus that draws you?" Joseph wanted to know.

"I have read the scrolls of your prophets. Simon was kind enough to allow me to borrow them. Did you know that Jesus' message and how he was born were foretold by the prophets? That means he is something, or someone more than just a prophet. If he is the one the prophets saw coming to us, then he is God."

"What are you saying?" Joseph was surprised. "Are you saying Jesus is a god?"

"No," Justus spoke carefully. "I am saying that we must pay attention to what is happening around us; and, if his life continues to fulfill the prophecies written down so long

Journey

ago; Jesus is the Promised Deliverer. He is not just *a* god; He *is* God: the God of your Torah; here, in flesh, walking with us."

The young man wasn't sure what to think, or to say.

Justus looked at him. "Well, I had better get back to work. Enjoy the rest of your day, Joseph. It was good to talk with you." He moved away, once more in soldier mode. Out of habit, the commander patted the rump of the horse tethered to the wagon. The horse began to move.

"You too," Joseph picked up his reins and moved the wagon back on to the open road. He could not get Justus' words out of his mind for the next several days.

―――

EnKarem was still a beautiful place to live, Eleazar considered, especially at sunrise. He had slept inside the cave the night before, simply because it was cooler. He wanted to get a good night's sleep prior to his walk to Jerusalem today.

After filling his wineskin with fresh water from the stream, he slipped his sandals on, and picked up the handles to the pushcart. It would still be a long day. He hoped by starting early, he would avoid the intense midday sun.

In spite of all his best efforts, it was mid-afternoon when Eleazar arrived at the Temple. Making his way to the outer court, he looked for the priest on duty. After waiting his turn in line, he stood at the door of acceptance. "Is the Great Council in session?" he asked, using his head-wrap to wipe the sweat from his face and neck.

The young man looked him up and down with a skeptical glance. "Why would *you* want to know, old man?"

"I have a friend on the Council. His name is Master Judah." Eleazar paused. "According to the Law, I brought the first-fruits from my vineyard as an offering. I am still allowed to choose the Levite family I want to give it to, am I not?"

"Master Judah doesn't need your grapes. He is a wealthy man," the young priest retorted. "Why don't you just put them in with the general offerings?"

"No," Eleazar spoke with conviction. "I need to see Master Judah. It is my right."

The younger man sighed. He motioned toward a stone bench against the courtyard wall. "Oh, all right," he groaned. "Wait over there. I'll be right back."

Eleazar moved to the bench indicated and waited for several minutes. When the young priest returned, Judah was right behind him. The older man was speaking, "Who was it, Saul? Where is he? He said he is a friend of mine? Why didn't you bring him to the library?"

"Master Judah, it is my responsibility to protect your time. Prince Caiaphas said that…." At the sound of the new title the high priest was requiring be used when he was referred to, Judah cut the boy off.

"I know, I know, but we are called to serve the *people* before we serve *ourselves*," he said. Looking ahead, the sage saw Eleazar, and recognized him. His face lit up with a great smile.

"Eleazar! My friend! It is so good to see you!" Judah crossed the courtyard quickly, in bounding steps. "What a privilege!"

Journey

Judah looked at the young priest, who had sought to keep the two men apart. "Next time, when a friend of mind comes to the court, bring them to me, wherever I am," he corrected.

Saul looked at Eleazar, and then at Judah. "Yes, Master Judah," he replied meekly. "I'm sorry. I was just trying to do my job."

Judah patted Eleazar's shoulder. "No matter, no matter, now." He looked into the old man's eyes. "You are well? What can I do for you?"

Eleazar was thankful for such a warm reception. "Master Judah, you and Mistress Hadassah were so good to me. I have been working my ground in EnKarem, and I brought you the first-fruits offering from the vineyard. I know you probably don't want it, or need it," he paused and glanced at Saul.

Judah followed his glance, perceptively picking picked up on what had taken place before his arrival in the courtyard. "Nonsense; I am grateful you would think of us. Hadassah loves fresh grapes. In fact, I will send them home to the house right now with a message." Calling for a runner, the priest quickly inscribed a message on a clay tablet, and then sent the grapes to his wife.

Eleazar once again wiped the sweat from his face and neck. "Thank you for your gracious response to my offering," he said.

The sage had been assessing Eleazar's condition as they had been speaking together. "Did you walk all the way from EnKarem today; all at once?" When the old man nodded, Judah spoke, "That's too far for you to walk in the heat, my brother. You need something cool to drink, and time to sit against the cool stone walls. Come to the Rabbinical School Library with me. We will talk and catch up on each other's lives. You can rest there, until the runner returns with your cart."

As the two men moved down the hallway, cooler air descended inside the shade of the Temple's stone building, and helped to lift Eleazar's weariness. By the time he had shared some food and drink with Judah in the Library, he was beginning to feel his strength return once again. While Judah continued working, the landowner found a small pillow. He put it behind his neck on the wall, and leaned back against the stone, quietly dozing off to sleep.

"Master Judah." At the sound of Saul's voice, Judah turned around and put his finger to his lips.

"Ssh. My friend is resting," he warned.

At the sight of the poorer man sleeping on a Temple bench, Saul bristled slightly. "The Bedouin shepherds are here with this month's scroll shipment," he whispered. "Do you want me to send them up?"

Judah stepped into the hallway to speak to Saul quietly. "Just send *one* of them, and warn him to say nothing. Take the others to the courtyard and feed them. See that their animals are tended. They will be resting in Jerusalem tonight."

"Yes, Master," Saul responded. "Also, the runner has returned with your friend's handcart."

"Keep it close to your station in the outer court. I will take it home with me tonight."

"Sir?"

Journey

"Eleazar will be coming to my home this evening. Did you think I would do something else?"

Saul smiled. So, he really *had* misunderstood. This man really *was* Master Judah's friend; he just didn't look the part. "I'm sorry," he said. "I didn't realize."

"I forgive you," said Judah. "Just try to remember that it is our responsibility to honor all people. *All* lives are valuable. We each carry the image of the Creator within us. He made us in His image. Some carry the image poorly, to be sure, while some carry it well. Whether we realize it or not, we each represent the One who made us. Not only that, but we are each on a journey *towards* the One who made us."

Saul wasn't sure what to say. He knew he had just been given a great lesson. "Thank you, Master Judah," he said. "I will try to absorb those words into practice."

As he left the room, Judah smiled. The words he had spoken to Saul had been repeated from Nicodemus' encounter with Jesus sometime prior. He and his friend had discussed the wisdom they contained several times since.

Moments later, a Bedouin shepherd stealthily entered the room, carrying an enormous leather saddlebag over his shoulder. Judah greeted him.

"Hello, my friend!" Judah whispered. "What has old Eli sent us this month? How many?"

The Bedouin also whispered. "The saddlebag is full. I'm not sure, but he placed the papyrus with the total count on top. Let me get the bag open for you."

Quietly, the young man maneuvered the bag from his shoulder, drawing it around to lay it on the floor. As he did so, he looked up at Judah. "Why are we being so quiet?" he breathed. "Who is asleep?"

Judah motioned towards Eleazar, still dozing on the bench. The Bedouin's eyes followed the direction of his hand. As soon as his eyes fell on the old man, he let out a loud, involuntary gasp.

"That's the man!" he said in his normal voice. "That's the man in my dream!"

Judah was surprised. "Shakah, what are you talking about?"

"I have had dreams of late, Master Judah; dreams of myself in another life; dreams of the past I can't remember. This man…" he paused. "Who is he?"

"Are you sure?" Judah wanted to know.

The sound of the two men's voices stirred Eleazar. He opened his eyes. At first, he saw only Judah, and then saw the second man. As he came to wakefulness, he also came to realization. He *knew* the young man standing with Judah, his friend. Who was it?

Why was it so hard to remember?

"Thank you for letting me sleep, Judah," he said. "I didn't realize how much the day of travel had taken out of me."

"I'm sorry we woke you," Judah replied. "When he brought in the scroll shipment, we tried to be quiet."

Shakah was standing in the middle of the room, just staring at Eleazar.

Journey

Quickly, Judah explained the man's actions to his friend. "This man thinks he knows you, or has seen you before."

Shakah spoke to the Eleazar. "You were in my dreams three nights ago."

The older man responded. "When I opened my eyes, I thought I knew you. It has been many years. Were you part of my life before I began drinking? There are only some things I can remember readily. The rest I find I have to work for."

The Bedouin was hoping to find the answers he had been seeking. "I understand what it means to have veiled memories as well. In my dream, you said, 'help me,' and then 'come quickly.' I've also had images of myself loading a wagon with some kind of supplies. In the dream I wore fine linen and tooled sandals."

"What happened to you?" Eleazar wanted to know. He had noticed an ugly scar on the Bedouin's forehead.

"Well," said Shakah, "apparently I was robbed and left for dead on the road between Jerusalem and Jericho. The thieves took everything, except my loincloth. They dumped my body down the side of a hill and left me there. Abram, the chief of our tribe, found me while he was herding goats. He took me back to his tents and took care of me. I have lived there since. They didn't know my name when they found me, so when no one came for me; they called me, "Shakah," which means *forgotten*."

He stopped and watched Eleazar, waiting for a reaction. There didn't appear to be one. He looked at disappointedly at Judah. "Oh well, I thought there might be a connection. I have become used to these false hopes. It's strange though. I asked Abram to allow me to come on this mission, because I'm desperate to find answers. I thought this would be the time God would choose. It is difficult to live with so many issues unanswered in my life."

"I understand, son," Judah spoke kindly. "Let's let him wake up fully, while we work on the shipment together. Then, perhaps we can discover why he was in your dream."

The priest and the shepherd leaned in toward the saddlebag. Shakah began to read the names of the books printed on the outside edge of each papyrus roll. As he read each one, Judah checked them on Eli's shipment list, and placed them in proper order on the library shelves. The two men had been working for some time, when Eleazar began to speak.

"I think I remember now," he said softly.

Shakah did not hear him, and continued to call out scroll names. Judah, however, had heard, and responded.

"What is it you remember, Eleazar?"

The two men stopped working to hear, as the older man's voice began quietly, with a sense of great discovery.

"I was a wealthy landowner in EnKarem. I had vineyards, and crops. I had cattle and flocks of sheep and goats. I rented out my winepresses, and made a wine sought after from as far as Egypt. I made beer, and sold it. We traded year-round, my wife and I. We planted and harvested crops year-round as well. We even owned a weaving house here in the city. In fact, I sold it to a man named Lucius years ago when my children were small.

Journey

"On the day our youngest daughter was born, my wife, Rachel, died. I had made plans for seven children. I had built the house between the sycamores, just for her. There was no time to say good-bye. She was ripped from me." He looked at his friends, his eyes filling with tears.

He wiped his nose, and looked into the eyes of his friend. Judah looked at him with compassion. "Go on," he said.

"I stopped wanting to live. I never held the baby. I couldn't. The servants took care of her, and found a nursemaid. I hired a Greek woman, who taught the children to read. I wasn't kind to them. They must hate me." His voice broke. He stopped to wipe his eyes.

"By then I had begun drinking heavily. I spent a lot of time at the races. I gambled with the tax-collectors. I stopped going to synagogue. I broke the feast days. I don't remember much during those days. It's like a dream...."

He looked at the shepherd with recognition. "There was a day when I asked my steward to take a load of new wineskins to King Herod's summer palace in Masada. We had received an order from Chuza, his steward. I had forgotten about that until now."

Eleazar looked at the Bedouin. "You were my steward," he said. "Your name is Baruch."

At the sound of his name, something stirred inside the man called Shakah. Somehow, he knew Eleazar's were true. "Was I married?" he asked.

"No," Eleazar replied. "You were an indentured servant. When you were thirteen, your father was unable to pay his debt to me. He sold you to me for the cost of his debt. I taught you to figure, and to trade. I taught you to keep records. Then, about five years into your term of service to me, both of your parents died. It was then I took you in as part of my family."

Baruch's mind was working, trying to make sense of what he was hearing. Eleazar continued. "When you became older, you asked me to keep you, rather than set you free and put you on the street with no future. So I did. You were always a part of our lives."

He paused. "I always dressed you in the finest of clothes, and paid for your care. I remember the rabbis told me it was my duty to care well for you. You were an orphan."

Pieces of his past, visual scraps of memory were beginning to find their way together; forming a continuous picture in Baruch's heart and mind.

"I think I remember," he said slowly. "You weren't in the warehouse much after Mistress Rachel died. I worked alone a good deal of the time." He paused. "What happened to the children?"

"I have seen my son. He also is named Eleazar. Rachel wanted it that way. Every so often he will come and see me, although it has been more than a year now since I have seen him. I do know he was working with a caravan owner at one point. I don't know much about either of the girls." Eleazar looked at Judah. "Miriam married and moved away. And Mary...." His voice trailed. His friends waited for him to continue. "If it had not been for Master Judah's grandchildren, I would still be begging on the streets in Jerusalem."

For a few moments, silence hung in the room. Judah noticed the shadows were lengthening. Hadassah would be waiting at home with a dinner prepared. He spoke.

Journey

"It's getting late. It's time to stop working for today. Let's go to my home where we can continue this conversation."

Baruch replied. "That would be a good thing. Before we go, I just want to ask one question, Master Eleazar. Why would you be calling me for help in my dreams?"

The old merchant looked at him. "God might be answering my prayers, Baruch. I have recently begun rebuilding my holdings in EnKarem. Today, I was seeking the Lord's blessing on the vineyard, and I brought a first-fruits offering to the Temple. Not long ago, when I began, I asked Adonai to send someone to help me. I cannot do the work alone. It is a huge under-taking, and I discovered today that some days my strength fails. I am getting old. Perhaps the days of drinking took too much from me."

"Are you expecting me to resume my life with you, as your steward?" Baruch asked, his mind racing. What would he tell Abram? What would happen to his future? Inwardly saddened, he realized, his reality was what he had feared.

He had been a slave.

Eleazar looked at him with wise eyes. "I have no expectations," he answered simply. "I just want to do my best with the years I have left."

As Judah walked into the courtyard of his home that night, his friends Joseph of Arimathea and Nicodemus were waiting for him. He greeted them.

"Well, this is a great and unexpected blessing!" he said. "It is good to see you, especially since we have been unable to pray together in the afternoons lately."

"How is the process of chronicling of the School Library going for you?" Joseph wanted to know.

"We are almost finished," Judah answered. He patted Baruch on the back. "This young man brought us a new shipment of scrolls today. Once they are added to the index, the task will be completed." He rubbed his hands together. "Then we can meet together once more."

Nicodemus spoke, his voice serious. "Judah, we are here because Hadassah sent for us. She asked us to come."

Judah noticed that his friend spoke tentatively, as though something was waiting to be shared. He looked from one friend to another.

"Is Hadassah ..?"

"Your wife is well, Judah," Joseph said, "but you might want to have a seat. Get comfortable. Have a cup of water."

Nicodemus had gone into the kitchen courtyard to find Hadassah, who returned with him. She was veiled, and had covered her hands with cloths. What had she been doing? Assessing her appearance, Judah felt a faint sense of apprehension, but remembered his friends' words. He looked to her expectantly.

"Husband," she said. "I'm so glad you're home." She looked at Eleazar. "Thank you for the grapes. It's so good to see you again. Are you well? We are thankful to have you in our home." She looked at Baruch. "Welcome. I will see to your needs as soon as we settle the matter at hand."

Journey

The two surprise guests nodded their agreement to her, and she continued. "Judah, something has happened to Simon. I have been speaking with him out in the courtyard. He is on his way to live in Bethany."

Hearing the name of the village, Judah felt as though arrows had pierced his soul. "Bethany?" he asked hoarsely. "Why? What's happened?"

"The physician sent him there. Apparently, the problem with his arm, and his eyes' sensitivity to light was more serious than just him working too hard. The disease has been in his body for more than a year, now." She paused and took a deep breath. "Abigail was getting him some salve the other night, and discovered a lesion on his back."

"What kind of lesion?" Judah asked, alarmed.

Hadassah looked at Nicodemus, and then at Joseph. There was no easy way to prepare her husband.

"It's leprosy," she said simply.

The word hung in the air. It was a death sentence. Without a word, everyone in the room knew what it meant for Simon's future.

"How? When?" Judah spoke the words before he could stop them.

"He is in the courtyard," Hadassah repeated. "He wants to see you."

Judah stood up and pushed past his wife and Nicodemus. He walked into the courtyard, looking for his son. "Simon?" he called. "Where are you?"

From behind the animal stalls, a voice spoke. "Don't come any nearer, Father," he said. "I am unclean now." His voice broke. "I have been sent to live in the leper settlement near Bethany."

"How did it happen? What...." Judah didn't know what to say.

"The best Abby and I can figure is that it began about a year ago. A leper who thought he was cleansed came to me to have me verify his healing. He wasn't clean. I remember not covering my hands when I touched him. I didn't wear the veil when I looked into his eyes. I must have become infected at that time."

"Are you sure this is the right diagnosis?" Judah asked.

Simon's voice was brittle. "More than sure. I went to two of the other priests as well, and they confirmed the physician's findings. I have become a dead man to all I love."

"I want to help you. Isn't there something I can do?" Judah yearned to hug his son; to touch him. But he could not.

"Nothing can be done. They gave me two choices. The first one was not really an option. They said the family could leave the house in Capernaum, to find another dwelling, perhaps here with you, and I could stay in the house. I would not be allowed to go out, or receive visitors. It would be like living in a prison. I couldn't uproot the children like that, so I chose the second option."

"Bethany?" his father inquired.

"Yes, considering I can no longer serve as a Pharisee, since I am unclean. They will need to send another man to serve Capernaum." Simon paused. "Father, I need to ask you a favor."

"Anything," Judah answered.

"The elders of the city have ordered our house be cleansed according to the Law. Abigail and the children must remove themselves from it for the purification time. After it is inspected they will be allowed to return."

"You want to know if they can come here during the process."

"Yes. It would mean a great deal to me." Judah could not remember a time when his son had spoken so humbly. "When will we see you again, son?" he asked.

"Unless you come to Bethany, I will not see you again."

"How will you live?"

"At the foot of the hill, just outside the cemetery, there is an settlement for lepers. I will have other lepers for company, and I have taken my scrolls with me. I was told the Temple provides meals for them….. for us." Simon's voice trailed off.

"The physician said sometimes there are abandoned houses in the town people can just move into. I might be able to do that, if there is a house available." His voice sounded hopeful.

Suddenly, Judah was struck with an idea. "What about *asking Jesus* to pray for you?" he suggested. "I have heard that he has healed leprosy. He has healed many…"

His son interrupted. As quickly as it had gone, the old edge in his son's voice had returned. "I will not ask an insurgent for a miracle. I don't need him."

Judah sighed. So, the independence had still not broken; conversation had reached an impasse once again. "I will pray for you, Simon. Please never forget that I love you."

"I love you too, Father. I'm so sorry." There was a pause. "Goodbye."

"I cannot say 'goodbye,' my son. I will pray."

Irritated and alone, Simon turned to go. He had to complete his journey to Bethany before nightfall. A message had been sent ahead of him, to prepare him a place. It was difficult, he thought, to have to announce himself whenever he saw someone approaching.

"I am unclean. I am a leper. Come no further." As he trudged away, he kept repeating himself, warning those who might be unseen in the darkness. The physician had given him a small bell to ring if necessary. It alerted those around him to his condition, protecting them.

Judah stood in the courtyard, until he could no longer hear his son's voice, or bell ringing. "Oh God," he prayed, "How will you reach him now?"

Weeping and heavy hearted, he turned to walk back into his home.

His friends greeted him at the door. "Are you all right, Judah?" "What can we do to help you?" The priest thanked them for their kindness, and then quietly asked to be left alone. He went to the bedchamber he shared with his wife, and fell prostrate on the floor.

"I don't understand your ways, Lord," he cried. "Help me understand. Please help me see. Show me what to do." He lay silent on the floor in the darkness, waiting for an answer. None came. He fell asleep.

When Hadassah came to bed, she did not disturb him.

It had been a difficult day for both of them.

Journey

The next morning, Baruch and the older Eleazar were up early, not wishing to remain as intruders in the midst of Judah and Hadassah's crisis. They had stayed up far into the night, talking; sharing; renewing their relationship.

"Master Eleazar," Baruch had begun, "I know I was your slave. Because of what happened, I have concerns. I know the law. I was responsible for the wineskins you lost; for the loss of trade with King Herod's household. I am indebted to you for the loss of your products."

Eleazar smiled. "Baruch, I don't hold you responsible. You were robbed. I think you have suffered enough."

The younger man had more to say. He had paused, and looked at Eleazar directly. "There is a woman back in EnGedi. She has given me her heart. Her name is Leah."

"Are you married?"

"No."

"Would you like to be married?"

Baruch smiled. "Well, that is my question. I would like to go back to the tribe, and ask for her hand in marriage. I don't know how she would feel about marrying a slave and leaving her family, now that I know where I came from."

He paused. "I would like to tie up the loose ends of my life. For example, I was appointed trade overseer for the tribe. I need to hand those records and accounts over to someone else. I know you have the right to demand that I just come with you now…" He paused, looking at Eleazar.

The older man smiled. "What would you choose to do if you were a free man, Baruch?" he asked.

The younger man thought. "I think I would want to go and marry Leah, and still train someone to do my tasks for the tribe. Then, if you were willing, Leah and I would come back to EnKarem and work with you. If I could choose, I think that is what God would want me to do. It is the reason he gave me the dreams."

Eleazar was surprised. "You *want* to come and help me? And you would bring this Leah?"

Baruch laughed. "If she is willing, I would bring her as my wife."

For a short time, the older man said nothing. Baruch could tell he was working through something in his mind. Then he said, "May I come with you to the camp? I have never been to a Bedouin encampment before. I would like to see how it operates. Besides, you need someone to go with you. You don't want to be attacked on the road."

And so it was settled. The two men left Jerusalem that day, headed for the wilderness springs of EnGedi. As they saddled the camels the next morning, Eleazar spoke words he had been holding for some time. "Baruch?"

The younger man stopped, looking at him; this newly-recovered owner and father. "Yes?"

"I don't want…" he paused. "When we leave EnGedi, I want you to go to EnKarem with me."

Journey

"Yes, Master," Baruch answered. "I thought we had settled that."

"We have," the older man responded, looking him in the eye. "I just want to make something clear."

"What is it?"

"You had your freedom long ago. You are not my slave. You are my friend….." his voice halted. "You are a son to me; you and my Eleazar."

Baruch said nothing. There was a long pause. He stopped his tightening of the saddle strap, and turned to stare at Eleazar. The old man saw his response, and found more words in his heart.

"Do you still *want* to come with me?" he asked.

Baruch nodded. "I need to know about my life… before."

"Then we will leave here not as a master and slave, or even as a man and his steward. We will leave here as partners."

Baruch was stunned. "Are you sure, Master Eleazar?"

The old man smiled at him. "It's high time I did something for someone else in my life; and for the right reasons." He attached a saddlebag of foodstuffs from Hadassah's kitchen to the camel. "Besides," he laughed, "I will never be able to patch the plaster in the winepresses by myself. Think of this as your payment. Your work will earn your partnership. You and Leah, and your children, will have a home after I am gone."

Baruch did not know what to say. "Thank you, Master Eleazar," he offered. "I'm not sure what to say."

Eleazar responded kindly. "Just call me Eleazar," he said. "It has been a long time since I have had someone consistently with me to share time and conversation."

Saying goodbye to Judah and Hadassah, they headed out.

Baruch's heart was full of thanks. God had answered his prayers.

Eleazar's heart was full of wonder. God had been working all along.

―――

The rabbis in Jerusalem agreed, "The Lord created seven seas; but the Sea of Galilee is His delight." Looking at the splendor of the Lake's blue water contrasting with the brown and green background of the surrounding mountains, who could disagree?

The Sea of Galilee was known for erupting suddenly, furiously, with sudden storms. The cooler winds descending from the mountains collided with the warmer winders by the Sea. Many a fisherman had lost his boat or even his life over the years. The storm the past evening had been no exception.

"She is an unpredictable woman with a violent temper," Zebedee had commented about the Sea, on more than one occasion.

This morning, as usual, the old fisherman waited for his ships to return. Of special concern were his sons. The day before, after Jesus had finished teaching for the day, his boys had taken a boat across the water to the other side. During their nighttime journey, a fierce storm had come up from nowhere. It had died down as suddenly as it had risen.

Zebedee was concerned by their delay. Had the boat capsized? Were they lost?

Journey

He squinted as he caught sight of a small dot on the other side of the Lake. Was that them? Yes! There they were. The dot would show itself to be his boys, he was sure.

He recognized the sail.

Later that day, James spoke with his father about the storm.

"I've never seen anything like it, Father," he said. "It came up from nowhere. There were eight or more of us in the boat. Jesus asked us to cross to the other side. He was weary, so he went to the back of the ship to lay down to rest. He fell asleep. I don't know how he did. We were about half-way across, when the wind began pounding the sail. I had to take it down."

"So, you were too far out to turn around," his father commented.

"We were too far from land on any side." He looked at Zebedee. "In all my days I have never seen a storm like this one. Have you ever been in the middle of a circular wind? It was a like tempest on the water; so unusual. It began to whip the water into a foam. You know, John and I aren't usually ones to be afraid, but all of us were. The waves were huge swells. They were so high the water began to come in over the side."

"What did you do?" Zebedee asked. A boat larger than Simon Peter's had sunk to the bottom when hit by smaller waves than the ones his son was describing.

"Peter and I were sure we were all dead men. Andrew and Philip were bailing water. John though it would be good to wake Jesus."

"He was still asleep?"

"*Sound* asleep; I thought he might be hunkering down because of the storm. In fact, a couple of us asked him, 'Jesus, don't you care that the water is coming into the boat? We could die here!"

"How did he respond to that?"

"Well, it was a funny thing, Father." James stopped and scratched his head. "He stood up in the back of the boat. He smiled at us. He said, 'The low level of your trust in me has made you fearful.' I have been thinking about that statement since we pulled into shore."

Zebedee nodded, thinking. "Trust in him," he mused. "What does that mean?"

James continued. "Here is the rest of the story. After making that statement, he moved to the center of the boat, and held to the mast. The waves were hammering us. We were sure we would all go down. The wind was howling so loudly, I could hardly hear him.

"Then, Jesus looked out over the water. It was as if he was speaking to a person we couldn't see. He shouted out, "You stop that! Peace, *now!* Be still!" The young man paused, remembering, a look of utter amazement on his face.

"What happened then?" Zebedee wanted to know.

James snapped his fingers. "Just like that, the wind stopped. We were dead in the water. The water went still, too. There were just a few laps against the side."

"Just like that?"

"Yes, just like that. It could only have been a direct result of what he did." The young man looked at his father. "Who is this man? Even the winds and the seas do what he tells them to do! Have you ever seen anything like it?"

"No, I haven't," the old man answered.

Journey

Hearing a noise behind him, Zebedee turned to see Simon Peter. The younger man spoke to James. "Did you tell him about the pigs?"

James laughed. "No I didn't; not yet."

Peter joined them. "It was amazing."

"You tell him, Peter. I'm going to go and greet the rest of the family. I'm going to see what Mother has made that I can eat." James began moving towards the house.

Peter looked at Zebedee. "Have you heard about the two men who were living in the desert area on the other side of the lake; over in Gadara?" When Zebedee nodded, he continued. "Well, after the storm, we were just glad to make it to shore. So we pulled the boat up on the rocky part of that side of the Lake. For my part, I wanted to rest a little. I wasn't looking forward to heading back; because I thought we would have to row. The wind had gone so still.

"We had just begun getting out of the boat, when those two men came running down at us from out of the caves. Neither one of them had a stitch of clothing on. Both were bleeding from cuts on their skin; I assume cuts they had given themselves. They weren't even able to talk to us. They just growled and snarled like animals. I was afraid when I looked into their eyes.

"All of a sudden, one of them did speak. But the sound was low and guttural; it didn't even sound human. It said, 'What do you want with us, Jesus, you Son of God? Did you come here to torment us before the time?'"

"How did they know his name?" Zebedee asked. "Had any of you been calling him? What did they mean; before what time?"

Peter responded. "It wasn't like that. I don't think this voice belonged to either one of them. They were possessed."

"Were?"

"Well, Jesus didn't say a word. The demons just kept talking. They said, 'if you do cast us out of these men, we beg you, don't sent us to the Abyss."

As he listened to Simon Peter's account, Zebedee felt he was gaining deeper understanding regarding Jesus' true identity. Who had *ever* shown that kind of power and authority with God? Yet, as he thought about it, Jesus did not treat any of them like they were in a lower station.

If Jesus was a picture of God, the older man realized, everything he had thought, or believed about his religion would have to change. If explaining God was Jesus' mission, this example was a God of relationship. Believing in him will mean I will have to rethink everything I know. Am I willing to do that, he wondered?

Simon Peter was speaking, "Zebedee, did you hear me?"

Zebedee responded. "I'm sorry, Simon. I drifted off. Go on."

"The people over in Gadara are gentiles. They have herds of swine the same way we herd goats and sheep. Well, there was a herd of close to two hundred swine, not far away from where we were standing. We could see them, *and* smell them! They had been feeding on the grassy knolls just above the caves and shoreline.

Journey

"When the demons spoke, Jesus asked them 'Who are you?' The demons said, 'Our name is Legion, because we are many.' Jesus commanded them to come out of the men. The demons said, 'Please send us into the swine.' So Jesus said, "Go!'

"It all happened so fast. Philip and Andrew moved to help each of the men, so they didn't injure themselves. At first, they couldn't get close to them. Then both men doubled over, and began to scream. One fell to the ground.

"All of a sudden, while we were watching, the entire herd of pigs became violent. First they turned on each other, and began attacking each other. Then the animals in the back of the pack, began pushing, driving those in front towards the cliff's edge." He paused. "You know, every one of them fell into the sea and drowned."

Zebedee looked at him thoughtfully.

"Perhaps that violence was a sign of God's absence," the older man observed. "When the demons went into them, they stopped following, and became driven."

Simon Peter paused. "That's true, Zebedee. I hadn't thought about that." He pondered for a moment. "You know, the pig herders had almost the same response as the pigs, come to think of it."

"What do you mean?"

"Well, the herders ran into the city, and told what Jesus had done. By the time the crowd had gathered where we were, both of the men were bathed, and clothed and telling us their stories." He paused and looked at Zebedee. "Do you know why the people came where we were?"

The older man shook his head. Peter continued. "I thought it would be because they were *thankful* to see the men free and sane; able to return to their families. But it wasn't so. Even after seeing *both of them* sitting calmly, just talking with Jesus; the people of the city asked us to leave. 'Go away,' one man shouted at Jesus. 'We don't want you here!'"

"Didn't they show appreciation at all? Didn't their families come?" Zebedee asked, knowing the usual response to Jesus' miracles was a hunger and request for more miracles.

"Perhaps the families lived too far away. I don't know." Peter shook his head. "That amazed me, too," he said. "Both *men* were thankful. One said, 'I will follow you to the ends of the earth.' Jesus told him to go home to his family and friends; to tell them what God had done for him. He told the man to try to explain the compassion and mercy of God to his family."

Both men considered the statement for a moment. Then Zebedee spoke.

"How would a person begin to explain the compassion and mercy of God?"

~~~

It had been Nicodemus who suggested Jairus BarJacob for the synagogue ruler's position in Capernaum. "He would do well there," the sage offered to Judah. "He comes to our prayer gatherings, and he is about the same age as your son. He is a good man."

"Yes," Joseph agreed, "His children are about the same age as Simon's. Perhaps his wife, Gedalia, would be a good friend to Abigail. Their children could play together."

Journey

Judah stood in the portico behind his home, looking out on the city of Jerusalem. It was true. Jairus had been a solid choice. He felt certain the man would look after his daughter-in-law in Simon's absence.

It was strange though. The Law allowed a wife to choose whether she wanted to follow her husband in cases like these. Abby's choice had surprised him. It had been unexpected, although understandable. She said plainly the move wouldn't be good for the children.

While he did agree with her, the decision had made other situations evident in his mind. Judah had always believed Simon's marriage was in better condition than it was evidencing itself to be. There were too many things coming to light the past few days. Had he been blind, or just oblivious?

As a leader; a ruler; Jairus was kinder than Simon. Was it more approachable? *Touchable?*

Jairus had asked for his counsel several times since the move to Galilee. How could he best reach the fishermen? What did Judah think of a certain approach to a passage in Jeremiah? Where did Judah think would be most effective location to hold the commemorative services for dedicating scrolls? How could he best serve the people? What was permissible in regards to caring for small children and widows?

Judah couldn't remember those questions ever being asked of him before; even by Simon; *especially* by Simon.

Jairus seemed to be a more trusting leader than his son as well; was it more forgiving, or just more secure? He allowed those with poor skills to learn to develop their skills. He encouraged those in the community who did not attend synagogue to take part in events. Of late, he had been seeking counsel from Judah regarding the best way he could spend his time. Did the older man think it was a good idea to visit those who attended the synagogue on days between the Sabbaths? Should he go to their homes? Should he tell stories like the new prophet, Jesus, was doing?

Jesus was another subject, entirely, he mused. His mind took a turn into different territory.

Just this morning, the Great Council had been in session in the Court of Hewn Stones. The young priest, Saul, had interrupted their discussions regarding the division of land. It seemed the cemetery near in the Jabbok valley was in need of more room. Landowners gathered in the council's session to discuss the matter.

"Excuse me," Saul opened the closed door. "Prince Joseph, you asked any news of the prophet Jesus worth knowing be brought to you immediately."

Joseph Caiaphas stopped mid-sentence to answer him. "Yes, Saul?"

"May I come in, sir?" the young priest wanted to know.

Gamaliel, Saul's tutor, answered. "Come sit with me, my boy."

"What do you know?" Caiaphas asked, as Saul made his way across the room.

"Well, we just received word from Jairus in Capernaum. His daughter was ill for some time, and died two days ago."

Journey

The group of men voiced sadness and compassion in regard to the loss of a child. "How did she die?" someone asked.

"They didn't say," Saul answered. "But it seems that when Jairus knew she was ill, he went looking for Jesus. He asked the prophet to come and heal her. While they were on their way to Jairus' house, apparently the people saw him in the street. The crowd became enormous."

"I hear it usually is when he speaks these days," Gamaliel offered.

Joseph Caiaphas had frowned. "What happened?"

"Well, a woman who had been bleeding for twelve years got down on her hands and knees and crawled through to touch him. When she touched the bottom of his robe, she was healed. Jesus stopped and asked, 'Who touched me?'"

"I would think so," said one of the Council. "When he discovered her condition, did he then go away and sequester himself because he was unclean?"

Saul laughed. "Has he ever done such a thing? I don't think so." He paused. "Jesus told her to be comforted, and to go her way in peace."

"What about Jairus?" the high priest looked at Saul impatiently. "What was so important that you interrupted our session?

Saul paused. "Sorry, my lord; it seems that while they were on the way to Jairus' home, the ruler's servants arrived with news of her death. When Jesus heard their message, he touched Jairus arm, and said, 'Don't be afraid. Trust me.'"

"You're sure those were his words?" Caiaphas wanted to know. When Saul nodded, he commanded, "Continue."

"Then they arrived at Jairus' home. The mourners and musicians had already assembled. They were getting her body ready for burial, since it was afternoon. Jesus disrupted the funeral. He told them not to mourn. He said she was only sleeping."

"Had the physicians checked her well?" Judah wanted to know.

Saul looked at him. "I asked the same question, Master Judah. She really was dead." He continued. "Well, as you can imagine, everyone laughed at him. So, he sent them all away. Then, he took Jairus and Gedalia, and his fishermen friends inside to where she was being prepared. Apparently, he emptied *that* room as well."

"Poor Jairus," one sage commented, "to have his daughter's funeral interrupted in such a way."

"Is that it?" Caiaphas looked at Saul.

Saul looked back. "No sir; not quite. Ten minutes later, she walked out of the door of the house and hugged everyone. And she was hungry."

There was silence in the room. Was it true? Had Jesus really raised a little girl from the dead? Did the man have power over death as well as disease? What did it mean?

The high priest had not known what to say or do. He had looked at Saul, "Thank you for letting me know, Saul," he flourished, looking around the room. "Well, we know his power cannot be from God, because he breaks the Law to do what he does."

Judah frowned, pulling on his beard as he thought. What Law? There was nothing in the Torah about such a law. He could only remember a law about specific soiling making a person unclean.

But again, Oral Traditions had added to the original Law. Those added traditions were now being held in the same esteem as the Commandments of God. Was this the reason for the deterioration of passion in those who served in the Temple? Were the traditions of men replacing the Commandments of God?

"Love the Lord your God with all your heart, all your soul, all your mind, and all your strength; and love your neighbor the same way you love yourself. This is the Law and the prophets," Jesus had said. As Judah considered, he could see the God Jesus described was much simpler than the one he had come to believe in.

"Religion is complex," Joseph Caiaphas had told them yesterday.

Is it... Is it really? Judah wondered.

He could see the same attitudes and judgments the high priest carried manifesting themselves in the manner Simon in which approached the priesthood. Thinking about his conversations with Simon over the past several years, each time they had discussed the Capernaum post, his son's communication had usually been laced with phrases separating the Pharisee from those he served: *Us and them; We and they.*

Simon, and those he emulated, viewed everyone who wasn't part of the priesthood as "unholy." No wonder he had been insecure, the older man thought. His son didn't trust anyone. Conversely, Jairus, his replacement, held a more generous viewpoint. Judah remembered a conversation during a recent prayer gathering when Jairus had expressed his conviction that *all* those who called upon ElShaddai should be considered holy.

Perhaps the leprosy was an expression of God's judgment.

Judgment, he reflected; Of what?

The old priest stopped in his reverie.

No, it couldn't be. Judah had been coming to a new understanding of late; something deeper.

ElShaddai was not a god with a dualistic nature, like the gods of other nations. He was consistent and unchanging. He did not play tricks, or play games.

He did not pounce.

Judah's thoughts went to the discussions he had shared with Nicodemus, Joseph, and several others who had been able to hear Jesus speak when he had been near Jerusalem. The God Jesus presented was the original God of Israel; His true nature could not be found the image of the God presented by those holding the Oral Law and Orthodox Traditions.

Jesus' God was the Healer; the Compassionate; the Merciful; the Life-Mender.

Would such a God, use leprosy as a judgment against His creation?

Seeing it now, Judah was sure that Adonai would not violate his nature.

What about Pharaoh being allowed to drown? Wasn't that an expression of judgment? The voice inserted itself like a dart.

The priest paused in his considerations.

Journey

If he followed the concept to its final conclusion, the priest realized he would see God as vindictive; One who played favorites; One who was exclusive.

Another Voice, one Judah recognized, spoke clear and strong.

All of Egypt was given ten chances to obey Me. They had the opportunity for healing and protection. They didn't want it... from Me.

The sage's mind continued in inner dialogue. *Then....... was the condition in Simon's body an indication of the state of his soul?* He shuddered. He remembered Simon's independent refusal to seek prayer for his healing.

"Please heal him, Lord," he prayed; his focus upon the boy he had known; the real and unseen part of his son's being, buried underneath his defensive mechanisms. "Help him. Cover my failings."

When had Simon begun to believe that he could earn his place with God? Surely he and Hadassah had never taught him that view-point, although he knew many of Simon's friends had been raised with such thinking. Where had he failed to teach him? Where had he neglected to pass on his own experiences with the One and Only God?

He has to have his own experiences with Me. He will never become strong living from your experiences. Let go. Let him learn.

The Voice spoke gently, changing the course of his thoughts.

"Yes, Lord," the sage responded. It was simple. It was all he could do.

He would continue to pray.

~~~~

Just north of Caesaria Philippi, where the Jordan River emerged from underground caverns, Jesus stood looking into the water. Nearby, Simon Peter and Andrew sat with James and John. On the other side of the shallow stream, Philip and Nathaniel sat with Judas and Thaddeus. A few feet away, Iscariot and Matthew were grouped with the Zealot and Bartholomew. Sitting close by, were John Mark, Joseph Barsabas and Matthias with James, Jesus' half-brother. It was a quiet moment; a break from the demands; a retreat from the pressures presenting themselves of late.

Many of these followers of Jesus had recently returned from being sent out to serve. It had been a learning exercise. Jesus had brought them here to discuss what they had learned in the process. Many people had been healed, demons had been cast out, and lives had been changed. They had operated in different towns, in teams of two. Now, gathered back together as a group, each man had returned with stories to tell, and questions to ask.

The Master was teaching them how to do what he did, Simon Peter realized.

This particular moment was filled with quiet thoughts and contemplation. Having just completed a question and answer session, each man's mind considered the words Jesus had spoken.

In the midst of the silence, Jesus spoke.

"Who do men say that I am?"

Philip answered him. "Some say you are Elijah, come back from the dead."

The Zealot spoke. "Some say you are John the Baptist."

Journey

There was a moment more silence. Jesus spoke again.

"Who do *you* say that I am?"

It was a contemplative question, designed to help each man discover what he really believed about the Teacher. Simon Peter was the first one to answer.

"You are the Promised Deliverer; the picture of Who God is, come into the world to rescue us."

Jesus looked up from the water, and into Simon Peter's eyes.

"That kind of trust and relationship with me is the foundation of what I want to build on the earth. I am about to build my Church; and the very authority systems of Hell will not be able to stand up against Her."

Journey

Fragments

As she stood in the empty synagogue, Abigail tried to calm her mind. The new ruler had taken the post almost two months prior, but she had yet to meet him. He had sent word for her to come to the synagogue this morning.

She and the children had been staying at a local inn for the past few days, working a little at a time towards moving back into the house. Almost everything they owned was still where they had left it that day. Much had been left out in the weather, and was ruined. Some things had been stolen. She still had not been able to find the children's sleeping mats.

There were so many things she would need to purchase.

With what money, she wondered?

Simon had no income now. She could not work. The savings were almost gone. She was thankful Judah had given her a little coin to pay for the inn.

"Look, mother," her daughter, Elizabeth, said, handing her the message on the clay tablet. "It's from the man who took Daddy's place, Jairus BarJacob."

"I wonder what he wants," she had murmured, taking the tablet.

"Oh mother, don't worry so. He probably just wants to say 'hello.' Maybe he has some of father's belongings and wants to return them."

"Perhaps," she responded.

Now, she stood waiting. Was this where he had asked her to come? It had been difficult to think clearly since Simon's diagnosis. Why had life suddenly become divided into two parts for her and the children? There was life *before* the diagnosis; and there was life *after* the diagnosis.

Had God intended for leprosy to become a defining factor in her life, she wondered?

"You will have to begin again, Abby," Simon had said. "Please live your life. I want you to be happy." He had said it gently; for the first time in their marriage. Then, he had turned and walked away, escorted out of the city by two foot-soldiers.

She frowned. Why was his tenderness so fleeting?

Why had touch-ability begun to emerge when he was untouchable?

It wasn't fair.

She heard a noise behind her. Turning, she saw the new ruler, Jairus, coming through the door, with a group of young students behind him. "Ah, here she is," he spoke, as if to himself. He looked at Abigail, and said nothing.

Not sure what to do or say, Abigail relied upon her training. She would not speak until she was spoken to. She would not step outside of the very narrow boundaries allowed those women in her position. It would not be a good idea to get off to a bad beginning with her husband's replacement.

Had he spoken to her, or to the students, she wondered?

After a few awkward moments, Jairus broke the silence. "Are you Abigail?" he asked.

"Yes, Master Jairus," she replied. "I received your message this morning, and I am here."

"Please," he said. "I don't like titles. Just call me Jairus." He paused. "That is, unless you are one of my students." At this, there was a ripple of humor among the young men behind him. "Now," he continued. "I have heard your home is in disarray. Is that true?"

Abigail was uncomfortable with the question. What a question! Had he called her here to mock her? She shuffled her feet, shifting her weight. She looked down at the floor. Her thoughts began to race once again.

The day of Simon's diagnosis, her husband had returned home from the physician's residence accompanied by three soldiers, a town magistrate and two of the physicians' assistants. Without a word to anyone, the magistrate had begun nailing a notice to the door stating,

"This home is unclean and undergoing medical inspections. Do not enter!"

A diagnosis of leprosy meant their home would undergo the customary Roman inspection and cleansing first. Then, it would be subjected to the Jewish cleansing process as a secondary religious purification.

She and the children had received only one hour's notice. Armed men had removed everything they owned from the house, and placed outside, where it would be inspected for visible signs of the disease. All of keep-able belongings would then be scrubbed, and left out for public viewing while the home was inspected. Anything with signs of the disease, including bedding, dishes, clothing, or utensils, would be burned by Roman law.

The military had escorted her to Judah and Hadassah's home in Jerusalem. She and the children were allowed to stay with only family members, by Roman law; in case the disease ran in family lines and was inherited.

No one knew how it began.

Leprosy was a phantom appearing out of nowhere.

The Roman cleansing involved inspection and fire. The process took two weeks. For that period, they could not enter their home. The Jewish cleansing took another two weeks. During that period, also, they were not even allowed on their property. The empty house was assigned a military guard.

After the Romans had burned the walls they found suspect for leprosy, the Jewish rites of cleansing began. The walls had been thoroughly inspected for signs of the creeping disease. Stones in one wall had needed replacement, new mortar and plastering.

Then the house had been scrubbed. *Scrubbed! By other people!*

It was as though she had become an outcast also;

As though she had not kept a clean house.

"You and your brood will have to find another place to live for the next month or more," the magistrate told her. "Where are your husband's belongings?"

Journey

Numbly, she had indicated the bedchamber she and Simon shared. The man subsequently sent Roman soldiers with Simon, to oversee the packing of his belongings. Then, for a few quick moments after her husband left, she had been allowed to gather a few items and her children for the journey.

At least they had travelled by wagon, and were not expected to walk the entire way, like Simon.

Poor Simon, she thought. She hadn't thought she could feel sorry for him. She hadn't thought she would miss him.

She looked around the synagogue.

Simon had spent many happy hours in this place.

Silence had lengthened, and become awkward, as Jairus waited for Abigail's answer. "Mistress Abigail," he repeated. "Is it true that your house is in disarray?"

Shaking out of her thought pattern, Abigail answered. "I'm sorry. It's still difficult to stay on track. Sometimes my thoughts just run away from me, and I follow them."

"Emotions, too, I would imagine," Jarius spoke kindly. "I was asking, because my students and I have discovered we have a free afternoon. I am not permitted to allow these hoodlums to roam about unattended, so I need to find an activity I can assign them to."

Abigail was amazed. Simon would never have cancelled classes for an afternoon. What was the priest saying?

"What does that have to do with me?" she questioned.

"Well," the ruler looked at his students. "They are strong young men. They need to learn the 'people-side' of the priesthood. I think we should *all* come and help you to put your home back in order. After all, you are a *priest's* wife. We should care for our own."

"They removed Simon's place as priest," Abigail corrected him. "I am a *leper's* wife."

"A man's physical condition does not change who he is. It cannot remove his value; or his calling," Jairus responded. "You have more value than you realize, woman. We all do. Jesus is teaching me that."

Gratefully, Abigail accepted the help. It had been like moving in all over again.

"We will finish this today," Jairus promised.

As they worked, her memories continued.

The days with Judah and Hadassah had been filled with sadness, even though the grandparents had tried to provide light moments for the children. One conversation in particular drifted through her mind.

Sitting the garden outside, sharing late day breezes, grandfather Judah had been telling the children stories from Simon's childhood.

"Why did Daddy have to go away?" Dorcas asked.

"He got sick," Daniel answered.

"Why doesn't he talk to Jesus?" the little girl wanted to know. "Jesus can fix anything."

David had inserted his opinion at that point. "Jesus is an insurgent. That's *worse* than leprosy."

Judah had looked at his grandson, assessing him. "*How* is he an insurgent, David?"

Journey

"That's what Father said about him," David answered defensively. "I'm not even sure what it means."

"An insurgent is a person who has no use for those who have been placed in authority; to serve, to protect, to teach, to nurture. It is a person who teaches others to be rebellious. Those are people, who rob and steal from others; who hurt others for their own gain. Many times, they fill people's minds with lies, causing uprisings and revolution, destroying peace. Many countries have fallen out of power because of an insurgent." He paused.

"Oh," David had responded.

"Is that the kind of man *you* think Jesus is?" Judah queried. When David responded with a stubborn shrug, he continued. "You will have to decide what you really believe."

Working to reconstruct her home, Abigail considered her father-in-law's words. She would have to talk with David, her son, and ask him for a response to the lessons he had learned from his grandfather.

"Hello! Where is Abigail?" Abby heard a woman's voice. Someone was entering through the front door. Stepping into the hallway, she saw a tall, graceful, although somewhat overweight woman, with a jolly face. She was holding a large basket and a wineskin. Beside her, was a little girl, who was also carrying a basket.

"I'm Abigail," she said, not knowing the stranger. "Can I help you?"

"I'm Gedalia, Jairus' wife," the woman introduced herself. "This is Amita, our daughter."

"She is your oldest?" Abigail asked.

"She is my only!" Gedalia answered, laughing. "She becomes more and more precious to me every day."

The little girl shyly put out her hand for Abigail to shake it. "I'm happy to meet you," she said.

At her motion, Abigail suddenly realized it was the first time since Simon's diagnosis that anyone, her children included, had offered to touch her. It was almost as though she silently been declared unclean as well has her husband, she realized.

As she returned Amita's handshake, her attention was drawn over Gedalia's shoulder. Were there other women coming up the walkway? Gedalia followed her glance. "Oh, by the way, my new friends say they know you. We all came to help you get ready to live here again."

Abigail didn't know what to say. At the sight of Salome, Julia, Elsbeth and Mary coming through the door, her eyes filled with tears. How she had missed them! She had forgotten how good it was to have friends.

They had brought food: food for her, food for the rabbinical students, sweets for the children. Had they each cleaned out their store-rooms? Where had it all come from? Later, after the meal, Abigail and Elizabeth found themselves trying to find room as they put away foodstuffs.

The rabbinical students worked to repair the wall plaster; removing soot, whitewashing the walls.

Journey

As the afternoon wore on, Abigail made note of items still needed to complete the refurbishing of their home. The soldiers had burned all of her pillows and bed-linens, along with all of the wooden utensils used for food.

She would need to replace the water-pots. Even the rope had been considered contaminated. How would she ever…..

"Do you know what you need yet?" She had been making a list on a clay tablet when Julia spoke.

"I have a good idea," Abby answered. "There is just so much. I don't know where to begin."

"Why not start with the sleeping areas?" Julia offered. "That way you can let the children sleep in their own home tonight, and not at the Inn."

"Do you know where I can purchase sleeping mats? Cheap?" was the question.

Mary was bringing in a stool she had scrubbed clean, and had overheard the conversation.

"I know just the place! In fact, we could go right now!" she interjected. "Julia, do you think we could use the chariot to run to Migdal?"

Julia responded quickly, anticipating Mary's solution. "I will send for Adelphos to bring it right away." She looked at her friend. "I think it's a great idea."

The women continued to work as they waited for the chariot.

As they waited, Abigail took notice of her son, David, and his communication with a new-found friend, Amita. The two of them were less than a year apart in age. Observing, she found herself eavesdropping on their conversation.

"How did you get sick?" David asked.

"I don't know," she answered. "Mother said I go a chill. I did cough a lot; and then it was hard to breathe."

"What happened?" The boy took a sip of water from the cup in his hand.

She looked at him. "I died," she said simply.

David choked on the water he had taken into his mouth. "You *what?*" he asked.

"I died. But for me, it didn't feel like that. I couldn't feel my body, but I was in a different place all of a sudden. It was peaceful there, and there was lots of music. I remember a lot of light."

"What do you mean, 'it didn't feel like that to you?'" David wanted to know. "You died. You stopped living, right?"

"My body died," Amita explained. "But the inside of me didn't stop living. It was still there."

"Okay," David said slowly, trying to comprehend her words. "Are you making this up?"

"No, it really happened," the girl told him. "Ask my Mother. It happened right after we moved here. You were at your grandfather's house. They were in the middle of the funeral preparations. They even had put salt and ointments on me, since it was afternoon."

"Then how are you here?" he inquired skeptically.

"Daddy went where Jesus was, and Jesus came to our house."

"So?"

"I heard his voice in the place where I was. He said, 'Little girl, arise.' And I got up and had dinner." She shrugged.

David didn't know what to do with what he was hearing. Had the man his own father had declared a dangerous insurgent really raised someone from the dead? Was it wrong to help like that, he wondered?

An hour later, Adelphos arrived with the chariot. Mary sprang into action, planning what items she would bring from the storeroom in Migdal.

Abby, if you could choose any color; any color at all; what colors would you choose for your home?

Abigail considered her. Was *this* the woman Simon had rejected? Why would she even want to help his family? "I like the colors that don't show the dirt," she answered.

"But what about *vibrancy*?" Mary wanted to know. "Think about the flowers. What color?"

The woman paused. She had never seen Mary like this before. "Blue," she said. "I like blue and green."

"All right," Mary responded. "We will be back in a little while."

"Thank you," was all Abigail knew to say, watching her go.

"Where do this bench and table go?" Gedalia asked, coming into the room. "I think the couches and small tables are clean now. We've been working most of the day of them. Where do you want them, Abby?"

Abigail walked with her new friend into the large room where Simon had held the dinner so many weeks prior. "We keep them in here, against the walls. The tables are stored underneath each one."

Working with Gedalia and the students to place clean furniture in the restored and renewed home, Abigal felt a wave of gratefulness for those who were helping her. Many of these were in the group of people Simon had considered "unholy" and "unclean."

But were they?

Perhaps they were just ordinary. Did Simon consider himself to be *extra-ordinary,* she wondered?

They had comforted her, and helped her. Had he? Ever?

She bent over to move a small food table into position under its designated couch. In doing so, she saw a chunk of something on the floor, glistening.

She reached for it. The piece was stuck under the ledge of stone against the wall. Funny it had been missed somehow. She yanked on it to pull it free. She turned it over in her hand.

It was a small, white, stone fragment.

What was it? Then she remembered.

Mary had broken an alabaster jar, just inches from where she was standing. Without thinking, she smelled it. Was there still fragrance?

A slight aroma of the perfumed oil still remained. The memory of the figure of Jesus sitting….. where?… just there….. surfaced in her mind.

Journey

"He who is forgiven much, loves much. He who is forgiven little, loves little."

She could still see the reaction of shock and anger in Simon's eyes to Jesus' words. He had always said he needed no forgiveness; he had never done anything wrong.

Abruptly, she was struck with sudden awareness.

I blamed Simon; but I had the same attitudes he did. I just directed them towards him, instead of everyone else.

"Oh, God," she whispered. "Oh God, please forgive me. I have loved *little*." She brushed a tear from her cheeks. "I have loved myself the most. Teach me to love much. Teach me to love well."

It was evening before everyone had taken their leave. It was nightfall when she tucked her children into their new beds.

She looked around her home. There were new coverings, linens, dishes…. Many of the items had been brought to her by Mary that afternoon. The synagogue had provided her with two beautiful new water-pots, and basins for washing.

Her children were bathed and fed. Brand new lamps burned in each of the alcoves. She was home once more.

"It is Adonai's desire to take care of the widow and the orphan," Jairus told her as he was leaving. "We are your friends, Abby. Send me a message anytime."

Then, standing in the walkway in front of her door, he had turned, speaking over his shoulder as he reached the street. "I have already enrolled your son, David, in classes at the synagogue for the next term. He is a Pharisee's son, and destined for service."

"Are you sure, Master Jarius?" she asked, amazed there would still be a place provided for David's training and development.

"Absolutely! His father's disease has nothing to do with *his* destiny!" the ruler responded. "And don't call me 'Master.' Gedalia and I want to be your friends."

She smiled as she remembered the kindnesses others had shown her. She knew she could never pay it back.

Leaning against the cool, plastered wall, in the deepening shadows, the single mother closed her eyes.

She reached into her pocket, her fingers finding the small, stone fragment. She lifted it out and inhaled its lingering aroma once again.

"Thank you, ElJireh," she whispered.

It was then Abigail realized; her heart was filled once again with the desire to pray.

In the middle of the Negev desert, the younger Eleazar stopped at an oasis to water the camels, and the workers traveling with his caravan. He had paused at this particular oasis in the past, during travels with Ebenezer, his mentor and benefactor.

"Always look for an oasis with a Nabataean tent," the old man had instructed him. "The water and provisions they sell are a little pricey, but you have a guarantee the water is not poisoned or full of disease. And, once they are paid, these people will protect you as though you were their own family."

Eleazar had seen the evidence of those caravan drivers who had not followed Ebenezer's advice.

No man wanted to die a slow death in the desert heat.

He checked the load of goods they were bringing back from Egypt once again. Lucius' plan to trade silks and Israeli herbs had been well thought out. Trade had gone well, he considered. Egyptian oils and spices would be in great demand at home, especially among the Romans.

He sighed. How long had it been since he had sat in the courtyard with Miriam? How long had it been before that, when he had seen his father in EnKarem, in a similar courtyard? Was it six months; a year?

Using the shard of a broken water-pot, the young man dug out a space in the sand for himself. Over the years, he had discovered it was cooler to do so. He would sit here, under one of the oasis' many date palms, while the animals rested.

It would be good to try to doze for a little while.

Drifting off into sleep, the memory of his last departure from Jerusalem became a part of his dream.

"Well, that's it." Lucuis patted the neck of the camel last in line. "I think you're loaded up." He lifted the linen band from around his neck, to wipe the beads of perspiration from his face and neck. He looked up. "It's still early. Why is it so steamy already? Is it hotter today than yesterday?"

Eleazar looked at his friend. "It's all that pita and cucumber sauce my sister keeps sending you," he laughed.

Lucius patted his belly, and chuckled. "Don't forget the date and honey bread. My, that woman can cook. You know, I just hate to see all that good food go to waste."

Then, Miriam was smiling at him, holding out a plate of stuffed dates. "Come home, Eleazar. Sharon and I are making food for you. No more dried fish; no more stale bread. You can take a bath."

He smiled. Such dreams kept his focus looking towards home. It had been a good decision to hire Talmi as a steward and handy-man before he had departed on this journey. Sharon, Talmi's wife, had become an instant friend to Miriam. It was unusual for him to sense trustworthiness in people straightaway, but he had with this couple.

They had come to Bethany, hoping to be able to spend time with Sharon's cousin who was in the last stages of some sort of consuming disease. When they couldn't find a place to live, a friend had sent them to Miriam. Would she be willing to rent out a room?

In the end, Eleazar had struck a bargain with Talmi. The couple would receive housing and food, in exchange for certain tasks. Talmi would help around the house, keeping the grounds and buildings in order and in good repair. Sharon was to be a companion to Miriam, helping her wherever needed; cleaning, cooking, serving, organizing. Three afternoons each week, the duo would be provided time to visit with Sharon's cousin.

"They are the provision of God," Miriam had told him. "I knew you needed to go, but I was concerned about being here alone."

She would be so thrilled with the oils and spices he was bringing home, he anticipated. Perhaps it would spark her to try to reopen the clinic. Perhaps she would discover a new way to season meat. Thinking of food drew his mind once again to Lucius.

He chuckled. He needed to sleep now. It would be good see Lucius again; especially with such a fine profit to show for his labors.

"Thank you, Leah." Baruch finished draining the wineskin his new wife had brought to him and the older Eleazar. He looked at the old man. "How are you doing?"

The landowner rolled his shoulders, and moved his neck from side to side, stretching. "Not bad, considering the years," he answered. "I didn't remember how much work this could be."

"Didn't you hire this to be done the first time?" Baruch reminded him.

"Yes, I did," was the reply. "But even then, I couldn't just watch. How do you think I learned how to do this?"

"I hadn't thought about it until you said something," the younger man said.

Eleazar moved closer to the fire, and stoked it. "I think we need more limestone from the cave," he murmured. "I will get the stone, if you will draw the water."

"I'll be right with you," Baruch responded. "I have just a little more plaster to spread on the wall of this press."

"You're doing a good job, Baruch." Eleazar waited until he was finished. "My knees don't like to get down on the ground like that anymore. They creak and complain."

The young man looked at him and laughed with understanding. "It's all right, really," he said. He scraped the trowel on the grass. "All right, it's finished." He looked around. "How many more presses are left?"

Eleazar counted. "I think three more."

Baruch took the handles of the handcart. "Let's go back to the cave."

For the rest of the afternoon, the two men worked together. First, they chiseled small chunks of limestone from the inside of the cave. Then, moving to the fire they had built next to the winepresses, they heated the chunks in a flat copper pan over hot coals.

When air inside the limestone expanded because of the heat, the porous stone crumbled into particles. Eleazar then added small amounts of sand and water, stirring until the plaster had a smooth and spreadable consistency. The work was tedious and time consuming; also somewhat stressful. As soon as the plaster was usable, it had to be spread quickly, before it hardened again. Baruch had become frustrated in the learning process several times, discovering that once-hardened plaster was more difficult to re-heat and spread than the fresh product.

As they worked, Eleazar and his new partner discussed, assessed and made plans.

It was good to have someone to share the time with, the older man realized. He would never take the gift of having someone's company for granted again.

Journey

For his part, Baruch had found himself awash in a somewhat new world. It had been several months since the day he had met Eleazar in the School Library. How had life become so accelerated, he wondered? How had he come to this place?

It had taken more than a week to teach his record-keeping skills to the replacement Abram had chosen. Then, Abram had insisted upon a full Bedouin wedding, complete with seven days of negotiations. The negotiations were followed by wedding traditions: days of feasting, music, folk dances and stories.

"There will be no simple ceremony, Shakah," Abram's eyes had twinkled as he had called him by his Bedouin name. "Where is your family? Who will speak for you?"

Baruch was thankful Eleazar had decided to come. "This man has been my father since I was a boy," he explained, as he told Abram what he had learned about his past.

Abram had entered into semi-serious negotiations immediately, drawing Eleazar and Baruch in with him. "She is worth more than you can pay," he said to Baruch. "You cannot afford her."

Baruch had laughed. "No one can afford a woman!" he answered.

Abram had slapped him on the back. "Wise man, wise man," he chuckled. "Yes, you will do well."

Leah's father had insisted she be given the traditional money headdress. The women of the tribe filled the encampment with bright colors. He still wondered where all the food had come from.

His bride was beautiful that day; the image etched into his memory. "She still *is* beautiful," he told himself.

He was married; *a husband.*

They had forced him to do the "dance of war" in company with the older, married men. It was a wedding ritual intended to show his prowess and ability in protecting his future bride. Baruch was not sure he had shown anyone anything but his insecurity.

He had followed the steps of the older men in the dance; and not too well at that.

Afterwards, one of the shepherds had comforted him. "*Every* groom dances that way. No one knows what to do at first. That is why they have you do it."

They departed the encampment with gifts; so many Abram had made them the gift of two camels. Arriving in EnKarem, Eleazar's cupboards were subsequently stocked with rice, grain, and other foodstuffs.

The journey had taken longer than they planned, as the tribe had given them a rather large compilation of sheep and goats as well. "You cannot drive them faster than they are willing to walk," Abram advised them. "Had you not made an agreement with Eleazar, there was been a black goat's hair tent prepared for your beginning with Leah. We will find another use for it."

Abram was a generous man, Baruch considered. He would miss him.

"If you do not like your new life, Shakah, please come back to us." The old man's eyes had misted as the threesome had embarked on their journey. He had hugged his daughter. "Don't leave an old man alone," he told her. "I want to see you again before I die."

Baruch had spoken for them, as was customary. "We will not be strangers, father." At the sound of the term coming from his own lips, he choked. Abram had put his hands on the younger man's shoulders and looked him in the eye. "You are a good man, Baruch. We will not forget you."

Remembering even now, Baruch felt emotions rising. His thoughts went to Eleazar. Did *he* still battle with being left alone? Did *he* miss *his* son?

The older Eleazar's son had stopped at EnKarem on his way through with a caravan several months prior. Where had he been headed? Egypt?

"Father! Look at this place!" The younger man had been amazed to see his father upright standing in a field, harvesting barley. "What has happened to you?"

His father dropped the scythe and had run to his son, embracing him. "I am so glad to see you! I have wondered when you would come again. I couldn't remember where you said you were living."

The caravan driver was taken aback by his father's forthright disclosure. "You look great!" he said. "What happened?"

The older man had pulled away, looking into his son's eyes. His own eyes were full of tears. "I was begging, full of drink and bitterness, on the streets of Jerusalem. Two children found me, and took me to a priest's house. They fed me, clothed me and put me to work. When I became strong again, I came here."

The young merchant looked around, appreciating his father's efforts. "You repaired the vineyard. You planted crops. Are you sure you aren't working too hard?"

"It's good for me." The older Eleazar dabbed the sweat from his face. "I want to rebuild; at least, something of what I squandered away."

Struck by his father's word usage, the younger Eleazar looked at the older man, assessing him. "And the drink?"

"I don't need it anymore." The landowner spoke simply, honestly. "I should say, 'I won't *use it* anymore. I have been reading the scrolls again. Baruch and Leah, and I have been discovering Truth. We even took a trip together to hear the Healer, Jesus, speak." He looked at his son. "I am becoming a changed man."

"I am so glad," Eleazar responded. "I know Jesus. He is a friend of mine. Mary and I used to trade for fish and baskets with one the families who now are his closest followers."

At the mention of his daughter's name, Eleazar brightened. "Where is Mary, son?" he asked.

Eleazar paused, not sure he should disclose the answer. "She is living in Galilee, with some friends. She was in Migdal for a time, but she became a follower of Jesus as well." The younger man said nothing of Mary's struggle, or the years of her emotional struggles because of her father's abuse. Was their father even aware of the effects of his actions? Did he know she had almost lost her life? The younger Eleazar didn't think so.

"I would like to see her," the father stated. "In fact, I would like to see both her *and* Miriam."

Journey

Eleazar had responded with noticeable reserve, but kindly. "I will be glad to pass that on the next time I see them both. But it might be some time before I see either of them." He nodded towards the camels. "This is Lucius' caravan. We are headed out to Egypt."

"I want to make things right, Eleazar." The words had hung in the air, creating tension and conflict.

Listening, Baruch had wondered. How could Eleazar possibly make everything right? Weren't some things better just left alone? He had been able to tell by the look in the young caravan driver's eyes, Eleazar was thinking the very same thoughts.

"Are you sure you want to go to the feast in Jerusalem?" Julia Flavius was leaning against the door frame of Mary's room in Capernaum. "If you want to see your sister, Justus would be glad to send Adelphos with you. You wouldn't have to worry about the crowds."

"No," Mary replied. "It is a perfect opportunity to learn. Jesus is taking the seventy who just came back from their assignment. He will be teaching them every day. I have so many questions to ask." She looked at her friend. "Besides, there are other women traveling as well. It would be nice to have a change."

For a moment, Julia was tempted to go with her, but decided against it. Victoria and Helena wouldn't do well on a journey that long, or that far away from home. "Take what you need, and leave anything you choose to," she said. "This will always be your room, until you tell us otherwise."

Mary looked at her. "You have taught me so much, Julia. This is the first real home I have ever known; the first real family I have ever known. Thank you."

"I don't know what *we* did," she responded. "You've become a part of our family." At the sound of Helena's call, she moved to go outside.

"That's what I mean," Mary murmured, watching her go.

Looking around the room for her satchel, she began to choose the items she would pack for her journey. After a few moments, she came to the side of the room where her dressing table stood. Displayed in its center were the larger pieces of what had been a sealed jar, filled with perfumed oil.

It was amazing, she considered. When the jar was perfect, she had displayed it in her room, as some kind of unreasonable goal to be attained. When she had hidden herself away, and looked to medicate her pain with experiences and pleasures, she had hidden the jar away as well; afraid to admit she had no answers. Now, as her soul was healing, her perspective clearing, it was the broken pieces of the jar which were on display once again. Now, they served as a reminder of what Jesus was teaching her.

Everyone is broken in some way; even when it is disguised by an image, she thought.
But when the image is broken, and poured at His feet,
Healing begins.
Quietly, she noticed.
Awed, she drew a breath, remembering the night of her Freedom.
There still was a slight fragrance emanating from the cracked edges of the alabaster.

Journey

The Mistress Dido, respected citizen and confidante to the masses, was becoming angry. "I don't give refunds!" she repeated, this time raising her voice. It was obvious to her she was being ignored.

She would not be played; no matter whom the celebrity might be.

On the other side of the salon, Syrene was restocking pastries on a tray, midday. Several clients and their attending slaves had halted therapies mid-treatment. Everyone had been drawn into the drama taking place near the front doorway of Dido's salon.

"I'm not asking for a refund," the Syrian governor's daughter said calmly, yet again. "I am returning these crystals; the oils; *and* the potions. They don't work."

The woman's lack of discretion embarrassed Dido. Of course they didn't work, she thought to herself. No one expected them to. But you didn't *say* so where people could *hear* you. What about the gods?

Dido looked around, and realized her loss of decorum had created a public spectacle. The daughter of Iullus Antonius, governor of Syria, Phoenicia, Israel and Samaria, was standing in front of her. She had just waltzed in, expecting to see the owner. Didn't she realize the salon ran on a schedule?

Dido looked at the woman, somewhat peeved. It would do no good to say anything, she reasoned. Her father was confidante to the wife of the emperor. He was the son of Mark Antony, and a close friend of Tiberius Caesar. This woman could kill her on a whim.

What was she doing? She tried to re-direct the conversation.

"Mistress..." she began.

"Mistress Dido," Iulla Antonia interrupted. She had had enough. "I want an exchange of free services, and I want it now. If I don't receive what I want, I will call my guards to help you see my point of view. Do you understand me?"

"I do understand, Mistress," Dido replied, "completely." She had no intention of giving ground. "Do *you* understand that I cannot take back merchandise after it has been purchased? I am very willing to give you free services, however." She called a tall, physically flawless, young man to her before the aristocrat could answer her. "Give Mistress Iulla every courtesy, and any treatment she desires," she commanded.

"Yes, Mistress," the young man replied. He eyed Iulla with interest.

The governor's daughter was not to be appeased quite so easily. "Dido," she reiterated, "I don't *want* these items. I am going to leave them here. Destroy them for all I care." She looked at the young man disparagingly, up and down. "On second thought, I do *not* require any services today."

Dido was at a loss to understand the woman's reasoning. "Why don't you want them?"

"I told you. *They don't work.*"

"Mistress Iulla, these things take time."

Iulla Antonia looked at her with a long, hard glance, born from years of seeing the people beneath her as disposable. After long moments, she decided she would explain to this.... this....*salon* owner.

Journey

"My daughter was ill, as you know. She had visions; she was possessed. You have tried to help me with her for years. You know this."

Dido nodded. At least the woman was speaking to her. She took a breath. Iulla continued.

"We tried the potions. We hung the crystals. The apothecary put her on a special diet. We bathed her in milk. We tried everything; all of your therapies, to no avail. We made sacrifices to Zeus, we offered her to the temple priests for the purging of her soul; still nothing.

"One day, a slave in our household told my husband there was a Healer from Israel who was speaking near the coast, by Tyre and Sidon. He had healed many. We had nothing left to lose, so I had our chariot driver take me to hear him. His words were amazing. He didn't speak to convince or persuade. He was certain. He had answers to questions I had not even asked yet. I knew what he was saying was true." She paused and looked at Dido. "I made a fool of myself calling after him and his followers. But they didn't seem to hear me.

"Then, afterwards, I went to him and commanded him to heal our daughter. He said 'no.'"

"He said what?" Dido asked.

"He told me 'no.' He said he had been sent to heal the children of Israel." She looked at Dido. "I had always looked down on the Jews. At that moment, I wanted to become Jewish, so my daughter would be healed."

"What happened?"

"Well, I went back and fell down on my knees in front of him. I tried to convince him to heal her. He said, 'I can't take meat that belongs to the children, and give it away to the dogs; to the gentiles.'"

The entire salon gasped. The man had actually called a Roman ruler's wife a dog?

Enjoying her audience's responses, Iulla put up her hand. "No, it wasn't like that. I realized at that moment He was addressing my attitude. I had come to him, seeing myself as a ruler; someone set above everyone else; thinking I deserved more attention; wanting my own way. That was the "gentile" he was referring to. In that moment, I saw that when I came to Him, I wasn't really entitled to receive anything."

Dido responded. Iulla's account had sparked a question in her heart. "Didn't that offend you? Weren't you angry?"

Iulla looked at her and laughed. "Of course I was offended! What do you think? I'm some sort of monk or something?" She continued. "But I felt something in my heart change. Something shifted inside me. Suddenly, I didn't care so much about how I looked or whether my feelings were hurt. I said, 'Lord, help me, please.'"

Dido asked, "*You* called *him* 'lord?'"

Iulla nodded. "I did. I knew *I* didn't have the power to heal my daughter. He *did.* That put me in a position of being weaker than him. I told him, 'Everything you are saying is true, Lord; but even the dogs get the fragments when they fall from the master's table.' I realized that to this Healer, this Jesus, healing her would be like getting few fragments, nothing more."

Dido was amazed at her candid account. "What did he do?"

"He told me that when my heart changed, it had made the difference. I realized I had begun to trust him. Imagine," she said, "*me; trusting someone.*"

"Your daughter," Dido commented. "How is she?"

"She was up and playing with her friends the next morning. She has been well ever since."

"How do you know the crystals didn't just finally come through?" Dido asked.

Iulla Antonia straightened to add dignity to her stature. She looked at Dido and said nothing.

Dido stuttered. "Is that *all*?"

Iulla looked around the room and decided she would complete her story. It was important these people understood, she concluded.

"No," she said, "there is a little more. One night our family was here in Caesarea Philippi to see a play; you know a family excursion. We were on our way into town, and I had an urge, and needed to find a facility for personal relief. Our servant pulled the wagon over. My guard and I went looking for a private spot where I could relieve myself. I don't like to do that sort of thing out in public, you know.

"Well, we had pulled over to the side of the road in the mountains. Now, listen; there were no clouds in the sky, and it was early afternoon. Just behind the mountain where we stopped, we saw a bright light, like lightning, begin and grow brighter and brighter. I was fascinated. My guard went with me, and we investigated.

"Just over the top of the ledge where we were, we saw a man on top of the next mountain. Then, suddenly, he wasn't alone. Two other men joined him. The light centered on the three of them, but was emanating from the first man. Their clothing became like the sun. I will remember it for the rest of my life.

"Did anyone else see this?" Dido asked.

"My guard," Iulla repeated. "Oh, and there were three other men at the foot of the next mountain, watching. Then, after a time, the light lifted. The second two men just disappeared. The first man was left alone, and he came down the hill. He talked with the three men, and then we heard thunder. But it was thunder that spoke words. It said, "This is the Son I love. I am very happy with Him. Listen to Him.""

"You heard the voice of a god?" Dido asked. She looked at the listeners around them in the salon. "You heard the voice of a god," she stated again; this time more emphatically.

"No," Iulla spoke clearly. "Not *a* god, Dido. No *other* god ever healed anyone, or helped anyone, or made anyone's life unexplainably better. This is the *only* God. I am now fully convinced."

"So," Dido inquired, not seeing a connection, "What does one thing have to do with the other?"

"Oh." Iulla paused, and then spoke slowly. "The man who emerged from the light was the very same man who healed my daughter."

"The same man? Are you sure?" Dido wanted to know.

Journey

"The very same," Iulla repeated. She dropped the crystals, the vials of oils, and the small bag full of potion mixture on the counter. "So now you understand. I don't want these things anymore. They aren't really helpful." She turned to go, and then looked over her shoulder. "Have a nice day."

Satisfied she had concluded the purpose for which she had come, the Roman governor's walked out the door.

Conscious of observing eyes, the salon owner bristled. *How dare she treat me this way,* she thought! Dido looked around the room at her slaves, most of whom were staring. "Well? What are you looking at?" she thundered with thinly veiled rage. "Get back to work!"

~~~~

"*I* was called by the Master first." The voice was Simon Peter's.

His brother hit his arm. "You only went to hear him, because I told you about John the Baptist," Andrew muttered.

"But the Master changed my name to Peter. It means "Rock."

James and John began laughing. "You're an idiot. It means you have rocks in your head. Or, maybe you *are* a rock. You sank when you tried to walk on water."

"Hey," Simon retorted, "at least *I* got out of the boat."

Judas jibed. "Listen, none of you are as important as me. If I didn't manage the money for our group, you would all go hungry."

"Oh, please," James snapped, "you don't think we see you take money out and buy yourself "a little snack" when we walk through the marketplace? And yet, when I came to you and asked for money to buy fish, you said 'it's not in the budget right now." He looked at everyone in the group. "Who do you think you are? You act like a money-lender! Some of the money in that pouch is mine, anyway!" He paused. "When John and I are on our thrones in Jesus' kingdom, we'll see where *you are.*"

Peter rejoined the conversation. "Hey guys," he interjected. "'Sons of Thunder' doesn't really describe you anymore. I mean, let's talk about your Mama fixing your place for you." His voice took on a higher pitch, to imitate Salome. "Jesus, would you please make it so my sons get the best seats in your kingdom? I have it all worked out for you. You could put one over here on this side, and the other over there on that side." He went back to his normal tone. "You both are still a couple of Mama's boys."

"Hey!" John spoke up. "I didn't have anything to do with that!"

"At least we don't live with our *mother-in-law*! What's up with that, Simon?" James jabbed. "At least you have someone to tell you what to do!"

"Yeah, *Peter,*" John answered, "How come your mouth is like a bad archery student: ready, fire, aim?! If someone's going to say the wrong thing, everyone knows it's going to be you. The Master is always pulling you back into line! You *need* live with *someone's* mother!"

"Hey James! John! Neither one of *you* could *get* a woman!" a voice yelled from the back.

"John, just own up to it." It was Thomas this time. "I get so tired of all of you vying for position, and trying to curry favor. You're such little boys."

233

John doubled up his fist. "Oh yeah? Mister, 'I'm not sure that will work' and 'Well, actually'? You drive me crazy. You're always correcting everybody. Stop it. Just stop it."

"Yeah, well," Philip added. "Thomas, leave them alone. It can be irritating to be around *you*, too; analyzing all the time. Who made you an authority? Since when have you had 'all wisdom'?"

Mary and the other Mary moved away, into the larger group of seventy who were also traveling on the road. "I hate it when they argue like this," the Magdalene told the older woman.

"I know what you mean," Jesus' mother answered. "But brothers do argue, sometimes. Didn't you ever argue with your siblings growing up?"

"Sometimes, I guess," Mary replied, thinking about Miriam and Eleazar. "We never really fought like this, though. We were the only friends each other had."

There was a short silence as they walked together.

"So tell me," her friend asked, "what have you been learning since we last talked?"

The younger woman brightened. "Oh my," she answered. "How do I choose just one thing?"

"Just tell me," the older Mary encouraged. "Start with whatever comes to mind first."

"Well," she answered, "there was the time when he fed everyone in the wilderness. Were you there that day?"

"No, but I heard about it."

"He had been serving people, healing them all day long. Then he began to teach. We were all transfixed, unable to get enough of what he was saying to us. No one wanted to leave. At one point during the day, I noticed the sun was beginning to descend. I think it was Peter who said something about it first, but we all knew the people were hungry. I know I was hungry.

"I did still have some water, though. The food I had brought in my satchel was long gone."

"What happened?"

"About mid-afternoon, Andrew asked Jesus to send the crowds away. He explained it was getting late, and they would need to let families go into the towns and buy food. It was like he didn't think Jesus had thought about that."

"What did Jesus say?"

"He looked at Andrew and said, 'No. You feed them.'" She laughed. "You should have seen the look on Andrew's face. It was priceless.

"Apparently, Philip had been asking people if they had food, thinking that we could somehow get people to share with each other. But, everyone else was just like me; they had eaten what they had brought with them. Philip told Jesus that he had figured it would take more than six months in wages just to give everyone a small bite, there were so many people."

"How many?"

"It was about five thousand men, without the women and children; if we counted them all, it was close to fifteen thousand people."

Mary smiled, remembering. "Then, a little boy came up to Jesus. He was only about six or seven, or about the age of Abigail's Daniel. He had a lunch he wanted to give away. Philip hadn't wanted to hurt his feelings, but it was the only food for miles."

"What was it?"

"His mother had packed him five little barley loaves, and two small fish. Apparently, he had eaten whatever sweetmeats or fruit she had sent. It was good for us that he hadn't eaten the rest of it, although when I think about it now, I'm sure Jesus would have done something just as wonderful. When Philip told Jesus what was in the basket, the Master smiled and said, 'Can I have it?'

"Then what did he do?" the older woman wanted to know.

"He lifted up the basket, and prayed, 'Blessed are you, O Lord, King of the universe, who brings forth bread from the earth!' Then he lowered the basket and began taking pieces of fish out and giving them to the twelve. I hadn't thought there was that much fish, but there was. When he finished breaking the fish, and giving it out, he broke the bread as well.

"When he put the basket down, I looked into it. There were still fish and loaves in it! As though the Source would always have a supply.... Then, as the twelve began to break the bread and fish Jesus had *given them* into pieces to share, *their* bread and fish continued to be given out.

"They never ran out of food; and everyone ate and was full. In fact, there were twelve baskets left over, full of fish and bread, one for each of the men who served. No one could have eaten another bite."

The older Mary pondered for a moment. "Someone told me that they thought it was a miracle because everyone shared what they had with them. Is that what you saw?"

The Magdalene looked at her and shook her head. "There was so much food; each person would have had to carry a full satchel with them, and then share it. But when Philip was asking for food to share, people's hands were empty; even the women. In fact, there was more food left over than someone could have carried away from the place where we were."

"The food just multiplied?"

"It did. In fact, when I ate the bread, it tasted fresh; as though it had just come from the oven in the marketplace. It didn't taste like it had been in a boy's lunch basket in the heat all day. The fish was the same way. It even felt cool to my fingers; not dried out at all! I found myself wanting to eat more and more of it." She paused. "I've thought about it many times since then. It's made me want to give Him everything I have. If he could multiply a *lunch* like that, what could he do with my *life*?"

"I wish I had been there."

The Magdalene continued. "I remember him making a statement later about how he was the bread of life, sent down from heaven. He said he was God's provision for humanity, like the manna in Moses' day. Do you know what he meant by that?"

Journey

The older woman responded. "I have listened to him as he has taught that very thing." She looked at her companion. "Did you know that he says his purpose in coming is to be the final sacrifice for sin? In fact, John the Baptist called him the 'Lamb of God.'"

The Magdalene looked across the field to the horizon. "I would like a better understanding of the things he says. Sometimes I feel as though I get it, and then other times….."

The older Mary put her arm around the younger woman's shoulders. "I think we all feel like that, child. No matter how far down the road we each get, I think we each should always feel as though we are just beginning."

There was silence for a moment, as they walked. Then, the younger Mary spoke once again. "It wasn't long after that he fed another group, this time of four thousand men, plus women and children. I wasn't able to be there for that."

She paused. "Do you think we could sit and talk with Jesus later? I have a couple of questions I've wanted to ask him."

"I'm sure you could ask him, anytime," the older woman responded. "Why don't you just go over there?"

"I would feel better if we could go together," the Magdalene responded. "Maybe the opportunity will present itself…. Later."

―――

The toddler was only around three or four years of age, Simon Peter thought; not much younger than his own son. As Jesus was speaking, Simon had been watching the little boy. The little boy was watching Jesus intently; listening. What was it about Jesus that drew the children to him, Peter wondered?

"Did you have a good discussion on the road?" Jesus asked the twelve. "I'm sorry I missed it."

Within the circle, the men looked at him, and then at each other; silently choosing to withdraw from communication as soon as possible.

How does he go right to the heard of matter, Simon wondered? Did he know they had been arguing about their personal status and importance as His followers once again?

Sitting down, Jesus motioned for each of them to join him. The fire had been built not long ago; soon it would be time to cook. For now, it seemed, the Master just wanted to speak with them.

"Anyone who *wants* to be first," he said, "this is the one who will be the last and servant of all. When someone wants to be the boss in this realm, they push themselves, they dominate and control; they intimidate. It isn't going to be this way among you." He looked at each of them clearly and evenly.

"The Kingdom works this way: When you want to receive, you give. When you want to lead, you choose to follow. When you want to be first, you take the last place. The Kingdom is a reflection of the glory of God."

Then He picked up the little boy Simon Peter had been watching. He set the child in the middle of their gathering. "If someone receives even a little child in my name, they are receiving me. When you receive me, you receive the one who sent me." He looked around the circle to each of them.

"And anyone, *anyone* who is not willing to open their heart completely and become trusting of me like a little child, will not enter the Kingdom of Heaven at all."

"There is a difference between child-*likeness* and child-*ishness*." Jesus let the words hang in the room. "What will you allow your heart to yield to? That is who you will become."

~~~~

Miriam sat on the window ledge in the upper level of her home. Her back was outside her house; her feet inside on a stool. The shutters needed scrubbing.

Talmi came around the side of the house, pushing the handcart. He had been cutting and stacking firewood most of the morning. Now, he was headed to groom the grounds. Looking up, he stopped to stare. "Mistress Miriam," he admonished, concerned, "What do you think you are doing?"

"Cleaning," came the reply. "I haven't had a chance to clean these shutters since Abiel died. "I wouldn't want anyone to see the dust!"

"You should let Sharon do that," he suggested. "Why don't you go inside?"

Miriam turned her head to look at him. "I will not allow someone else to do this," she said. "By the way, where is she?"

"I don't know," Sharon's husband answered. "I thought she was with you. I have been cutting firewood all morning." He paused, thinking. "Did she go to the marketplace? I think I remember her telling me we were out of some things."

"Oh, that's right," Miriam remembered. "I gave her a list. She didn't tell you? I received a message this morning from Galilee, from my sister. It seems she is coming home to visit us."

"So that's why you want all of this done," Talmi spoke with discovery. "You want things to be perfect for her visit. Didn't she live here for awhile?"

"For more than eight years," Miriam grunted the words, as she worked to scour away a particularly stubborn patch of soil. "I haven't seen her in more than twelve years."

"When will she arrive?" he asked.

"I don't know. From the message it seems it will be tomorrow, or the next day." She paused. "What if I miscalculated? What if the message meant today?"

"Is she travelling alone?" Talmi wanted to know.

"No, she is bringing Jesus, the Healer, with her. Have you heard how many people travel with him now? I don't even know how she met the man, except that he is friend of Eleazar's. Apparently they are all coming to this house; *my* house! Oh, I wish Lucius hadn't sent him with that caravan." She looked at him; "One more window to go."

For a moment, she disappeared into the house; then reappeared at the next window. When she saw him still standing there, she spoke, "Talmi, if you don't have anything more to do than to watch me work, I have a list in here. I would be more than willing to share it with you."

Journey

"I'd hate to get in your way, Mistress," he replied with a chuckle. "You do everything so....so... completely."

In response, Miriam balled up her rag and threw it at him. It hit him squarely, soaking the middle of his chest. "Good aim, too!" he laughed.

"Oh!" she uttered. "I want those dishes we use to feed the birds filled as well! Make sure you take care of that while you are out there!"

"Yes, Mistress," Talmi responded. "Although you know, no one will care about that."

At that Miriam stopped speaking to him. "I have to do it myself if I want it done at all," she muttered to herself. There! She pulled back to inspect her work. The shutters were clean. No time to rest; there were still too many other things to take care of.

When Sharon returned from the market, Miriam put her to work washing down the plaster walls, the first item on a long list of expectations.

Long after nightfall, the exhausted couple fell into bed. "Do you know what she had me do today?" Sharon asked her husband. "After all the walls were cleaned, she wanted to make sure no mice had gotten into the grain bins. She made me dump each one out completely, and scour it out. Then, we had to grind enough grain to make fifty loaves of bread. Fifty!"

Talmi pulled his wife to him. "I have never seen her like this. Hopefully, this wasn't her nature before Abiel died. Is this the woman Eleazar keeps praying will return from grieving?"

Sharon giggled, and snuggled in next to him. "Perhaps she will relax after Mary gets here."

Her husband smiled. "I hope so. We will need sleep if she is bringing as many people with her as Miriam is anticipating."

It was midmorning the next day when Jesus arrived in Bethany. Miriam heard a crowd coming down the street, as she was sweeping the terraced waiting area outside the former clinic. At first, she was surprised, and then she realized the throng she was observing had to be the one she was been expecting. She stood, leaning on the broom, intently watching the faces coming into view. Which one was her sister? It had been so long, she wasn't sure she would recognize her.

Who were the other women in the group? Did Jesus travel with women too? Somehow, she had thought it would be only men. Then, she saw Mary, walking with two other women, one older and one about the same age as her sister. She took her cleaning utensils inside and put them away. She washed her hands. She smoothed her hair and pinched her cheeks for color.

She took a deep breath and went out the door to meet her sister.

After all of her preparations, she wasn't sure she was really ready.

Later that day, the two Mary's, Salome, and Elsbeth sat together in the central courtyard of Miriam's home.

"I love the painted designs on the walls in here!" Elsbeth exclaimed, as she gazed at the myriad of colors. "It feels as though I am outside! And what a wonderful idea to have the well on the inside of the house! It's almost like having your own aqueduct!"

Salome agreed. "What a beautiful courtyard, this is." She looked at Magdalene. "You say your brother-in-law copied the design from the house you grew up in?"

Mary nodded. "Yes," she said. "This was my favorite retreat when I was younger."

"I can see why," Salome told her. "Why is the house so large?"

"Abiel was a physician. He felt God wanted him to help those who were sick. His parents helped him build the house, and supported his practice here."

"Is Miriam a physician as well?" the older Mary wanted to know.

Magdalene paused. She hadn't thought about Miriam in that light. "I know she helped Abiel, and treated people sometimes." She looked at her mentor. "I'm not sure how to answer. I don't know."

"It's been a long time since you were here," Mary comforted her. "A lot can happen over the years."

Elsbeth changed the subject. "Mary," she began.

Both women answered her. "Yes?"

They all laughed. It was something that happened all the time.

Elsbeth spoke again. "Magdalene," she said. "You're sure you don't mind if I call you that?"

The younger Mary responded. "I don't mind; anything to help us avoid confusion."

Simon Peter's wife seemed at a loss for words. "Can I ask you something?"

Mary nodded.

"I don't know how to make friends with your sister, Miriam. I have tried several times to talk to her, but she is too busy for me. I know there must be so much to do, with seventy or so of us descending unannounced, but she won't let me help."

Salome lowered her voice to speak. "It happened to me too. I'm so used to all of us working together. She seems to want to work alone. Are we in the way?"

The older Mary spoke up. "I don't think we're in the way. Maybe she just doesn't know how to ask."

"No," Elsbeth replied. "I thought that too. But when I offered to draw water for cooking, she told me to come in here."

Magdalene listened. It was somehow comforting to hear these women speak the emotions she had struggled with in regard to her sister in years past. It was also a little uncomfortable to realize she was going to stay here with Miriam after all of her friends had moved on to the next location where Jesus would be teaching.

Miriam had not changed.

"It is just her way," was all she could find to say.

"Well!" Elsbeth stood to her feet quickly as she said the word. "I am not going to just sit here and let her do everything alone."

"She does have Talmi and Sharon to help her," offered Salome, although she was also standing to her feet.

"They looked a little weary to me," Elsbeth commented. "Does anyone else want to go with me? I think if we all flood in at once, and refuse to take 'no' for an answer, she will have to allow us to help."

The older Mary stood and moved to Elsbeth. "I think it's a great idea," she said, looking at Salome. "Let's try it." They looked at Magdalene.

"I'll come with you in a minute," Mary said. "I just want to sit in this courtyard for a moment or two."

As the threesome was moving through the doorway, they bumped into Jesus coming into the courtyard. He was alone.

"Hello, ladies," he said. He spoke to the older Mary. "Have you seen Mary Magdalene? I had a moment or two, and I remembered you had said she had a couple of questions for me."

His mother motioned with her hand, indicating that Mary was seated in the courtyard. Magdalene's back was to the door, and she was unaware of the happenings behind her. "Thank you," Jesus said, as he stepped aside to let the women pass.

As he stepped through the doorway, Mary turned her head, suddenly noticing him. Startled, she jumped up. It was a reaction she had not experienced since her childhood, when she had been in a very similar courtyard with her father, the older Eleazar. Immediately, she felt self-conscious of her responses; afraid she had somehow divulged a fault or defect that would render her without value.

She had never felt this way around Jesus before? Why now?

If Jesus had noticed her discomfort, he said nothing. Instead she heard, "Mary? I've been looking for you. I heard you had a couple of questions to ask me."

"Y-yes," she stammered, looking down at the floor, quickly trying to regain her composure. "I'm sorry. The courtyard in the house where I grew up was just like this one. That was where ….. everything…."

Feeling Jesus' eyes on her, she looked up. "I know," he said. "It's all right."

He moved over to the stone bench where she and Miriam had folded laundry so many years ago. He sat down and patted the stone. "Let's talk."

Wanting to be able to look at the expressions on his face, Mary took the position of a student. She sat on the floor, giving Jesus the bench. "What did you want to ask me?" he inquired.

"Well, there are several things I have wondered about. First, I want to understand the meaning behind the parable you told about the man who planted his ground. John told me that there was a meaning to each thing in the story, and I wanted to make sure I grasped the whole picture of what you were saying."

"Which parable?" Jesus laughed. "I've told several parables about farming."

She laughed with him. "The one about the sower who spread the seed, and there were different kinds of soil. You said that some fell on the road and the birds ate the seed; some fell where there were rocks and stony patches, and there was no depth; some fell where the thorns and weeds were already growing, so the seed was choked out…"

"And some fell on good soil," Jesus finished, "giving a crop of thirty, sixty and a hundred percent return."

"That's the one," she replied, relieved that he remembered. "What does it mean?"

Jesus smiled. "Well, it's one of my favorites."

"Mine too," Mary replied. "But I don't understand it. Does it have a deeper meaning?"

"That's why I like it," he told her. "The seed is the Word; the truth of God's purpose and nature. The soil by the side of the road is the man whose heart and mind are hardened. Whenever Truth is presented, it cannot find a place to put down roots in the soul, because it is argued with, or resisted. The enemy comes and steals it away.

"The stony soil represents the heart of a person who hears Truth and receives it gladly. As soon as the seed hits the soil, it begins to put down roots, and the person begins to grow. But then, when things become tough, or difficult, perhaps the result of persecution or misunderstanding; the person becomes offended, or chooses to remain comfortable instead of choosing to grow. Truth withers where it is prevented from growing.

"The third soil is the heart that is filled with distractions; perhaps it is money, or success, or fame; perhaps the distractions are relationships and reputation. Whatever the diversions, those are the weeds and thorns that choke out Truth.

"I see," said Mary, discovering. "The seed has life in itself. It has to be given room in the heart. Is that right?"

"Yes, absolutely," Jesus replied. "The problem is that in each type of soil, no changes were made to accommodate the seed."

"When I work in the garden, I have to pull the weeds," Mary said. "I also take the stones away." She thought for a moment. "We sometimes have ground that has been walked on; we have to break it up."

"That is how good soil is made," said Jesus. "And, we sometimes add fertilizer, don't we? And, some weeds have to be dug out by the roots."

"If we are talking about learning hard lessons through Pain, then yes, I have added more fertilizer than my share," Mary agreed. She thought for a moment. "Are you saying as well, that there are differing qualities of good soil?"

"Yes," Jesus replied. "But the reason I used soil in the story is because soil can be changed. No one needs to settle for the soil they have when they first hear the Truth. It takes a lot of work to turn a roadside into a watered garden. Remember, 'you will be like a watered garden, and a spring of water, whose waters fail not.' Abba Father is always at work in the heart."

She paused. "So, the night of my deliverance, what kind of soil did my heart have?"

Jesus looked at her. "Your will was bruised, and it was weak, but it was good soil."

Mary felt her eyes beginning to fill with tears again. "You pulled roots out of my life that night."

"Yes," said Jesus, "and infection." He paused, seeing Miriam walk through the door of the courtyard.

"I know. I felt my life change," Mary replied.

Journey

"Jesus!" Miriam stood, hands on her hips, in the courtyard. "I need to speak with Mary."

Jesus looked at her and smiled. "We are talking, Miriam."

"Can't you do that later? There is a lot of work to be done!" Mary's sister demanded.

Again, Jesus looked at her. "We will be right with you."

"Lord!" Miriam plopped down on the bench next to Jesus. "You don't care, do you?"

Mary began to feel uncomfortable with Miriam's insistence. She could feel her old emotions rising. She should just shut down what she was feeling, and do whatever it was Miriam required. Couldn't her sister just get along with people, without making demands, she wondered?

Had she really been ready to come home?

"What is it I supposedly don't care about?" Jesus chuckled.

"You don't care that Mary has abandoned me, and I have been left to do all the work alone!"

"Oh my, Miriam," Jesus answered, knowing she had *not* been left alone. In unanswered tension, silence hung in the courtyard.

Jesus turned his head to look at her. "Miriam, you are distracted and overloaded with so many demands. You are driven to do everything; *everything*….. Stop: in *this* moment. Listen. Look at me. Only *one thing* really matters. *Only one thing.*"

He paused, watching her. Miriam was looking into Jesus' eyes. Silently observing, Mary noticed a small change in her sister's facial expression. Then she saw it. Tears began to fall; first one, then more, then many.

For many moments, no one spoke. The Spirit of God was hovering in the room, ready to give another kind of deliverance; this time to Mary's sister. Mary found herself wondering. Would this confrontation end like all the others; with Miriam receiving comfort and understanding, without change happening in her to benefit her and those she lived with?

Would she really yield?

Suddenly, Mary saw a connection between herself and Miriam she had never seen before. She had run away and tried to medicate herself with physical comforts and luxury. Miriam had quietly taken control.

Whatever Miriam felt she controlled was not allowed to hurt her. So, as a result, she controlled *everything*.

Jesus was speaking. "Mary has learned to choose the *one thing;* that good part. The understanding has come to her at great cost." He looked at Mary and smiled.

"I will not take that away from her."

Miriam nodded, weeping. Jesus put his arm around her and hugged her. "Give it to *me*, Miriam. Trust *me*. I will heal you. Be yourself. It will be all right."

At that moment, Miriam's walls began to crumble.

Her heart was becoming good soil.

For the next several hours the three of them sat together in the courtyard, sharing Truth and laughing. Miriam discovered a long lost joy; a love for her little sister she had forgotten. Mary regained a relationship she had come to believe would never be possible.

Journey

Jesus had made everything new again.

No one cared about the bird feeding dishes being filled, or the shutters being scrubbed. Nor, had anyone inspected the grain storage bins.

No one was critiquing or evaluating. Miriam felt Fear lift from her life as she had looked into the eyes of Jesus. Her heart began to breathe.

As she went to bed that night, she found she was actually thankful for new friends. Salome, Elsbeth and Mary of Nazareth, had finished making dinner, and she had chosen the *one thing*.

~~~~~

Four days later, Jesus and his companions departed Miriam's home to visit another city called Bethany beyond the Jordan, on the northern shores of the Dead Sea. Many of those who lived in Miriam's, and now Mary's, village had heard Jesus was staying at Miriam's house. During the last two days of his visit, the poor and afflicted stood in line in the clinic terrace, seeking a touch from the Healer.

So many lives were transformed. So many hearts changed.

As they left the village, people lined the edges of the road to express gratitude, or to give gifts for their journey.

In Jerusalem, the evening of Jesus' departure, Lucius was getting ready to blow out the lamps in the weaving house. He had finished business for the day, and sent the workers home. It was time to eat and go to sleep. He looked at the angle of the sun. Perhaps he could still make it to the marketplace….

Moving articles around on his desk, he was looking for his missing keys, when the courier arrived. Where were those keys? The courier would have to wait until he found them. Probably another order; Why couldn't people wait until morning?

Looking up, he recognized one of his own men, hired for his ability to speak Domotic, the language of the Egyptians. Had the caravan arrived early, he wondered?

"Hello, Seth," he greeted the man. "Are you back so soon?"

He hadn't noticed until now. The man was panting. Apparently, he had run a long way.

"Master….. Lucius," he began. He bent over and put one finger up to indicate he needed to get his breath.

His tone let Lucius know something was wrong. He moved to get the man some water. "What it is? Has something happened?"

Seth took the water with gratitude. He nodded, still trying to get his breath. "You have to come; *now*. We will need a wagon."

Lucius sprang into action, without learning the reason for Seth's urgent insistence. Ten minutes later, the two men were pulling out of Jerusalem.

"Where are we going, and why?" Lucius wanted to know, as they stopped at the marketplace for bread and full wineskins.

"It's not far," Seth told him. "We are just a little past the Israel border in Philisita. We had just turned off the Coastal Road to come towards Jerusalem."

"What is wrong?" Lucius was becoming impatient with Seth's evasive manner. "Why did you need a wagon?"

"For Master Eleazar," Seth's concerned eyes met Lucius' surprised gaze. "As I said, we turned off the Coastal Road. Master Eleazar was checking the load. He wanted to get into the city before nightfall." He paused. "Livna, the old female camel, has been in a bad humor for the past week. I think she is sick, or just tired of crossing the desert. She has been spitting, and resisting us all the way home. Two days ago, she threw up in the desert heat.

"Anyway, Master Eleazar was checking the tightness of her saddle strap, and she turned her head and bit him. It happened so fast. None of us were ready."

"Didn't he use the whip?" Lucius wanted to know. "Was anyone helping him?"

"We took all the precautions. You know how camels are. He sent me to get you."

"How bad is it?" Lucius asked. A camel's bite was more feared among caravan drivers than bandits, if the truth were told.

"It isn't good," Seth replied. "All of the meat has been torn from the bone just below his shoulder on his right arm. It took me an hour to stop the bleeding. The camel spit on the wound after she bit him, so I am concerned for infection. We will have to watch him."

"Did you bind up the wound?"

Seth answered. "Yes, but not very well. We traded all of the silk in Egypt. We did very well, by the way. The load is all spices and oils coming back. When I bound the wound, all I had on hand was an extra toga in someone's saddlebag. I'm sorry to say it wasn't very clean either. I ripped it into strips to bind it."

"Did you have anything to cleanse the wound?" his employer wanted to know.

"I used the rest of the water in the wineskin to cleanse it. I put the meat together as best I could, but he was in such pain. You know he doesn't complain; but he was screaming. He finally passed out. For a little while, I thought he was dead, but then he began to groan."

Lucius sped the horses to a run. This had become urgent. They had to get to Eleazar before nightfall.

The jackals always began hunting for blood at sunset.

Journey

Emergence

It was midnight before Lucius returned to the city with Eleazar in his wagon. He would have to rouse a physician from sleep, he told the city watchman at the gate. Who was the best? Receiving directions, he reined the horses for the south part of the city.

"It is a miracle this man is still breathing," the physician told him. Elyada had been binding wounds and delivering babies for some thirty years or more. "I have never seen anything like it." Shaking his head, he looked at Lucius. "The camel tore the muscle, it is true, but the pathways for blood flow to his heart are still intact. He owes his life to whoever bound up the wound in the desert."

Lucius was relieved. "Will he survive?"

The old man had smiled. "It's too early to tell; but I think so. Just watch him for fever and infection. Tell whoever takes care of him to give him olive leaf tea every hour to build him up."

Elyada refused to take Lucius' money for treating Eleazar. "Go with God!" he had said, locking his door. Treatment had taken two hours, and it was still before daylight. "If you know your way from here," the old man told him, "I am going back to bed.

Lucius decided to take his friend directly to Miriam's house in Bethany. Eleazar would receive better care there, he reasoned, than in the weaving house. As he entered the village, he noticed streaks of light beginning to peek through the clouds on the horizon.

It might rain today.

Eleazar was in a semi-conscious state when the wagon pulled up in front of his sister's home. With his focus totally set on his friend, Lucius began calling for Miriam even before he got out of the wagon. "Miriam! Wake up! Miriam? It's Lucius. I have brought Eleazar."

When no lamps were lit immediately, Lucius called again, this time pounding heavily on the door. "Miriam! Miriam! It's Lucius. Wake…"

He was mid sentence when a sleepy Miriam opened the door. "Goodness, Lucius! What is it?" she yawned. "Why are you here in the middle of the night?"

"I brought Eleazar home. He was bitten by a camel. We almost lost him," his voice broke, as the stress of the night caught up with him.

As the meaning of his words dawned upon Miriam, she moved into emergency mode. "I'll be right back," she said. "Let me make sure I have a place for him. I will get his bed ready."

She sped up outside the stairs to the roof, as Lucius prepared to carry Eleazar inside. Going back to the wagon, he noted that his friend's eyes were open.

"Where am I?" the younger man asked weakly.

Journey

"We are at your home in Bethany," Lucius responded.

Eleazar looked at his arm. "Where is Seth? The caravan?"

"Everything is fine. The caravan is heading into the city as we speak. You did well, Eleazar. Do you remember what happened?"

The younger man closed his eyes. His head was reeling, and pounding at the same time. "I was bit by a camel," he stated. He noticed Lucius climbing into the wagon.

"Yes, you were," Lucius said. "And you have lost a lot of blood. You need sleep; lots and lots of it." He slid one arm under Eleazar's head, and the other under the man's knees. "I'm going to lift you now," he said. "I'm taking you to your room."

It's good I'm such a strong man, Lucius thought. At least "bulky" counts for something!

Slowly he maneuvered out of the wagon, carrying his friend, making his way up to the sheltered arbor on the roof.

"I'm not as young as I used to be," he grunted to Eleazar.

"The oasis Bedouin has my sandals," Eleazar replied, delirious. "Make sure he doesn't fall in."

"Oh, I see how you are," Lucius said, chuckling.

Arriving on the roof, he noted Miriam had lit a lamp inside the arbor, putting out a sleeping mat and cushions to make her brother more comfortable. "He will be cooler up here than in the house," she said. "I love the breeze that blows up here, even in the daytime."

Lucius looked up and realized the accuracy of her words. Abiel had constructed the house under shade trees. "It's a wonderful place to put him, Miriam," he replied. "He will rest well here."

She glanced at him. "You look tired, Lucius. Why don't you go downstairs and get some rest? I'll sit here with him."

"I really can't stay," he replied. "Seth and the other workers will be arriving at the weaving house with the caravan any time now. I must get back to Jerusalem."

Miriam was visibly disappointed.

"I will come back and check on him as soon as I can," he offered.

"Thank you for bringing him home."

"Please keep me posted on how he is recovering."

"I will."

As she settled down to rest once again, across from her brother, Miriam listened to the sounds of Lucius' wagon making its way out of the village.

"Thank you, God, for bringing him home to me," she breathed as she dozed off to sleep a little longer.

The next morning, the two sisters watched, as Eleazar's forehead became even warmer than before. Miriam used compresses and herbs to try to lower his temperature. She looked at Mary. "I can't get him to drink the teas if he isn't awake to do it. What do you think we should do?"

"I don't know. You have always been the one to know these things," Mary answered. "Why don't we send a message to Jesus? He loves Eleazar. He would come and heal him."

246

Journey

Quickly, Mary wrote a message on a clay tablet, and called for Talmi. "Talmi, I need to send you on an errand."

"Yes, Mistress. What do you need me to do?"

"Find Jesus," she instructed. "Tell him 'Eleazar, the friend you love dearly, is sick.' Ask him to come and heal him. Hurry."

Talmi kissed his wife good-bye and headed towards the last known destination of Jesus, the Healer. As he travelled, he prayed he would arrive before Eleazar turned for the worse.

~~~

At the other end of the road, near the village of Bethany, a woman carried a basket to the edge of a hill and waited. The walk from Jerusalem had taken her several hours. Below her, was a settlement of individuals, no longer recognized by the outside world. Considering themselves to be 'walking dead,' many had ceased contact with those they had known ... *before*.

Seeing her approach, a veiled and hooded figure began to trek from the valley, laboring with each step; stopping some six feet from her.

"Yes, Mistress?" The voice was scratchy and hoarse. The woman was unable to distinguish whether the figure was male or female.

"Can you help me? I am looking for my son."

"There are many sons here," came the reply.

"He is new to your settlement. He came a few months ago," she said, her voice giving her emotion away.

"He would be one of the ones in the caves, Mistress."

"His name is Simon. He is still young."

"I don't know him, Mistress, but I can look for him, and pass a message along."

"Oh, yes," she said, "please. And would you give him this basket of food and necessities?"

"We are *all* hungry here," was the reply.

"I thought the Temple provided for your meals," she said without thinking.

The leper looked at her carefully. "They told me that when they sent me here as well, but it isn't really true. They never send enough for everyone."

"Please take a loaf for yourself then, as well," she offered, placing the basket on the ground.

"Thank you, Mistress. I will do my best to find him."

Hadassah turned to leave. She had no guarantee the person who had taken her basket would actually deliver it, she realized.

But she had to try.

It had taken her too long to summon the courage just to do what she had done today.

In the valley below, Simon the leper sat alone in a cave. The lamp he had brought with him from Capernaum was almost out of oil. He opened his mouth and took a deep breath. Of late, he had been unable to breathe through his nose. Another leper had told him it was a symptom of the disease.

Journey

The conditions in the Bethany settlement were not what he had anticipated at all. He had expected to be given a house to live in; not deposited into a cave! It seemed there was a waiting list for houses, as well as a waiting list for tents!

Levels of status existed here as well, he thought.

No one cared that he had been a Pharisee. No one asked him for his opinion, or his advice. He had to draw his own water, and cook his own food. There were no guarantees of safety. No guards defended his possessions, or his sleeping blanket.

He leaned back against the rock wall, and closed his eyes.

"Abby, I miss you," he said hoarsely, feeling sorry for himself. Lately, it had hurt him to talk. Would he lose his voice as well? Abruptly, a mental picture of his wife materialized in his mind. He saw her on her hands and knees, cleaning up a spill *he* had made near scrolls -- in the room he had set apart for study. Supposedly too tired to bend over, he had called her to come from the other side of the house.

"Wife! Come and clean this mess up!"

She had come so quickly. She always had when he called. "I will have to get a basin and a rag, Simon," she had said. "What did you do?"

"Just clean it up," he had bossed. "And be quick about it." And later it had been, "Can't you work faster, Abigail? I'm trying to get something done here."

He winced. He hadn't thanked her, or even touched her. Come to think of it, he hadn't even felt gratitude. Why had he been unable to appreciate the things she had done for him?

Come to think of it; Why had he never been able to rest and celebrate when a task had been accomplished? There had always been just a drive to complete the next task.

Why had he treated her as if she were in his way?

Then there had been the time he had grabbed her arm, and snarled a threat into her ear in the marketplace. He had forgotten about it until just this moment. Had he bruised her arm? Had he bruised her heart? She had just remained silent...

The picture changed. He was eating alone in the large, front room of the house. Abigail and the children had crowded on a rug outside. He had insisted in following the cultural custom of the day; men first, women and children following. He had sat in comfort on his couch inside, while they had waited for his scraps outside.

Had he really done that? Yes, it was true. He remembered. It had been raining slightly. Abigail had stuck her head in the door.

"Simon, it's raining. Are you finished eating yet? Can we come in?"

"Get out, woman! I'll let you know when I'm finished here." Silently, she had closed the door, and waited for his summons.

Little Dorcas had gotten the sniffles from being cold and wet, he remembered.

Had he told her he was sorry?

<u>Was</u> he sorry?

He should have given her real apologies, he realized. Not the "I'm sorry you're upset," or "I'm sorry you don't get it," statements. He should have been genuinely sorry, "I was wrong to be selfish. Would you forgive me?"

Journey

But no, he had never said those words. Not to Abigail.

Not to anyone.

Day after day he had been haunted by his words and deeds; and he had discovered there was time to remember.

One-by-one they came before him; memories of his life... *before*. One-by-one, they marched into his silence; unannounced, trumpeting to his sense of Entitlement and Selfishness. Daily, he was confronted with his thoughts... his self-absorption .... his anger.

Had he really treated her like a slave? Had he really allowed her to carry the heavy things, and care for his children, while he walked in front of them all --- carrying *nothing*?

Had he really told her she was stupid and unnecessary?

How could he have been so egotistical, he wondered?

A familiar, nagging voice inserted itself into his thoughts. *She is a woman. She should expect such treatment. You are a priest. You are better than other people.*

No, he thought miserably. I am a leper. I am unclean.

Unclean!! Unholy!!

There was no one to blame here in the valley...

Besides, here in this place? No one here cared about who was to blame.

Life had become what it was.

Each leper had become consumed by their own Pain.

Each leper knew there was no escape in the valley; no escape but Death.

Simon shook his head. He had been so blind. He had been pre-occupied with attaining and ambition; his focus had been set on self-advancement.

He had missed the most precious elements of living.

He remembered his arrival in the village. He had gone to the house designated as the village official's home.

"Which house can I move into?" Simon had demanded of the man. "I was a Pharisee. I should have some considerations, I would think."

The man had laughed at him. *"There is no status here. Your life is about to change. All lepers are the same. If there is room in the caves, you may stay there. Otherwise, you will be out in the field.*

"Several years ago, the Bedouins donated goat's hair tents, but those are only obtainable on a next-in-line basis. There is a long waiting line for those. Houses are only given to those lepers whose families have moved here with them, and even then, you cannot share rooms. You can come and go, but you have to keep your distance."

"But I was told I could have a house," Simon had protested.

"I don't care," the man had replied callously. "You can't have one."

"Who takes care of us?" the former Pharisee had inquired; "Of the lepers?"

The man had looked at him, surprised. *"Takes care of you? You* have *lived a pampered life, haven't you? What do you think? We have servants here? We have people volunteering*

Journey

to serve..... LEPERS? Your disease is a death sentence. So go to the valley, and wait for it to come."

It had been a rude awakening for Simon. Suddenly, he found himself on the receiving end of the very rules and traditions which formerly had given him privilege. In fact, he remembered days when he had debated over those rules and traditions, holding they weren't stern enough to express the strict and stringent mindset of his God.

He had loved the rules!

Now….. it was an uncomfortable position to be in; detested, disgusting to others, forgotten, nameless. He had ceased to matter to other people, he reasoned.

Did he still have value in God's eyes?

He had been *sure* his value was determined by how much he could do, and how well he could do it. But now he was banished… for something over which he had no control!

There had been nothing to do in the cave. He had been so angry.

"It's not fair! I don't deserve this, God! I have done nothing wrong! Send your judgment to someone else!" He had shouted to the walls… and to God. There had been no response; only Silence.

Then, as the reality of his situation took ownership in his soul, he began to read the scrolls he had brought with him. In the pits of desperation, he started with Moses' books.

It had been during that season -- Isolation turned into Solitude.

One day, a phrase from his reading became stuck in his mind. He kept coming back to it, over and over again. It was as though Someone was speaking to him.

Noah found Grace in the eyes of the Lord.

Grace. As a boy, his father had told him, "Grace is getting something *good* that we *don't* deserve. No other god or belief system teaches it. Elohim is the only God of Grace."

Simon had spent hours in the cave, contemplating his father's words.

Noah had been part of a violent culture. He and his people *all* deserved to die… but Noah found *grace.*

God had looked at him with Grace.

What did a man have to do to have God look at them with Grace, he wondered?

Simon had read the accounts of God making covenant with Abram; the beginning of the nation; the beginning of the priesthood. God had performed the rituals of covenant making while Abram was asleep!

Sleeping men can't keep covenants, he realized. God had taken the responsibility for both sides of the agreement. Why, he speculated? Why hadn't he forced Abram to stay awake and complete his part of the agreement?

Because I knew Abram's weaknesses and tendencies to fail. My covenants never fail.

The Voice had spoken to him in his dreams, as *he* was sleeping…. Had it been a dream, a vision or his imagination?

What did a man have to do in order for God to make a covenant with him, he wondered?

Journey

He had read about Lot, Abram's nephew. Had anyone been there to hear it, Simon would have gladly admitted he saw himself in the man. Selfish; self-willed; full of conflict….So many bad choices; and yet, God rescued him.

By the time he reached the giving of the Law on Sinai, Simon was beginning to see a completely different picture of the God he had always thought he knew.

He made a secondary discovery as he studied. Perhaps he had seen God through eyes of superiority, because he had never allowed himself to admit weakness.

He had always avoided vulnerability.

He had mistakenly thought that was what it meant to be a man.

It hadn't been *confidence;* or *warranted godliness*; or even a *righteous judgment……*

It had been pride; just Pride; plain and simple.

How could a man be a man, without Pride? What example could he follow?

His mortification had become so deep one morning he had pulled out the scroll of King Solomon's proverbs. He had wanted something more casual to read. Within the first or second turn of the scroll, his eyes had lit upon a phrase that had returned to his heart for days.

"*A high look and a proud heart is sin….*"

He hadn't considered that concept before.

Sin was something that needed to be turned from; something that required sacrifice. It was the missing of the bulls-eye. His arrow had fallen short of God's mark –

He had thought working harder would assure him of perfection.

But there it was, right in front of his eyes.

A proud heart…. Is sin…

Simon knew his heart had been filled with high looks. He had looked down on others…. He had let his judgments define him.

"Oh God," he murmured, his heart heavy with discovery, "I am a sinner. I didn't see it until now."

He had thought he understood the Law …. *and* the prophets! But these concepts were completely new to him. Before, God had always been seen as a King of Demands, the Enforcer of His Own Authority. Simon had even defined God's nature to others: exacting a price for rewards, punishing bad behavior, judging and rejecting parts of creation that didn't please Him.

Now?

He recalled the morning his inner grasp of God's nature had begun to change. He had been reading the accounts of his nation's deliverance from the Egyptian Pharaoh. He had always viewed the Ten Laws of Moses as ten threats or demands.

Thinking about it now, he wasn't sure where his concept had come from…. It certainly hadn't come from *his own* investigations of the Scriptures….

Today, he was studying the building of the Moses' tabernacle. It was strange. Until today, he had always skipped over the passage, thinking he knew what it said. He had not caught God's title for the Ark of the Covenant.

Mercy Seat.

Mercy, he thought….. *Mercy?* Somehow it didn't make sense.

His mother's words from years prior flashed; "Mercy is *not* getting something *bad* that we *do* deserve."

Was *that* the meaning of God's covenant, he thought quietly?

Grace…. *and Mercy?*

This was a new view of God for Simon. Was it possible he had misconstrued the character and nature of his God?

What about Strength? Power? Authority?

The Voice had spoken again. *Grace and Mercy define these elements; they are the illustrations of my Identity.*

If this was so, Simon considered, his entire life had been based upon a misunderstanding. Was that even possible?

Yes, it's possible.

The Pharisee had served a different god. Simon's god had demanded reputation; image; perfection…. Simon had reacted accordingly, as had most of his peers.

To achieve that false perfection, the priest had created his own rules for living; rules that were stringent and vindictive; rules expressing disapproval for failings; rules based in suspicion and accusation.

Intimidation; Fear; Politics…

He had worked hard at keeping the rules… His works had been his sacrifices to the image of False Perfection.

It had all been about Doing; and how well he could do it.

Now, he could do no works. He could not earn his place.

Slowly, he realized. His knowledge, his works, his reputation; all had been an effort to build up his own sense of self.

"How could you allow me to become so hard-hearted?" He cried. "God, you could have prevented this…. *If* you cared."

Even as he said the words, Simon felt the hardness rising once again inside his chest. Had that been his downfall? He didn't want his heart to go to that place again.

No. He couldn't blame God for his choices.

"I'm sorry, God," he murmured.

As a Pharisee, Simon now realized he had put God's name on the image he himself had created. He had then represented his own creation as though it were God Himself.

"I have misrepresented you," he spoke to the walls. "Is that why you had me removed? Is this judgment?"

The Voice came once again, this time gently.

Don't blame me for the results of sin. The serpent is still destroying; still deceiving.

"Forgive me, Lord, please," he said, weeping now. "I didn't know what I was doing. I want to know you now. It doesn't matter what it looks like. Please teach me. I'm ready to learn now."

Journey

As the light from his lamp diminished, Simon drifted off into the first peaceful sleep he had experienced in weeks.

Several hours later, a raspy voice spoke into the darkness. "Is there anyone in this cave?"

He stirred. Was it a dream, he wondered?

The question was repeated. "Is there anyone in this cave? Answer if you are there."

"I am in here," the former priest answered. "Who is asking? Do you need shelter?"

"No," came the response. "I am looking for a man named Simon. A woman was at the overlook this morning."

Suddenly alert, Simon stood, and moved towards the person speaking. "Who was it?" he asked. "Did she leave her name?"

"No, no name." The person paused. "She left you this basket. She gave me bread."

Simon came outside the cave. He was surprised to see a hooded, veiled figure, standing, waiting for him. "Thank you for bringing it to me," he said humbly. "What is your name?"

"My name is Chaziel. I am from Samaria. Where are you from, Simon?"

Simon was so glad to have someone to talk to he forgot he didn't like Samaritans. "I am from Capernaum. How long have you been here?"

Chaziel coughed. "Too long. I am about to go on a journey."

Simon assumed the man was referring to the prospect of dying. "Me too," he said quietly.

Chaziel's deep, raw voice rose a little in intensity. "You are going with us? I didn't know the message had travelled this far. Do you know how many others have decided to come?"

"Where are we going?" Simon wanted to know. He hadn't received a message, nor was he about to admit that fact to his new friend.

It was so good to have someone to talk to. He was weary of being alone.

"We are leaving in the morning," Chaziel told him. "A group of us, who are tired of just waiting here to die, are going to make a journey to find Jesus, the one they call 'the Healer.'"

Simon bristled a little, at first, and then caught himself. "Do you really think he *can* heal you?" he asked guardedly.

"Did you know he was in the village last week? He stayed at the home where there used to be a clinic. I didn't go to him then, but several others did. He healed them. They have gone home."

Silence hung between them, as each man contemplated the word.

Home.

"Simon, I have nothing left to lose," Chaziel replied. "I have lost my family, my children, my home, my life. If he cannot heal me, I will just prepare to die."

The former priest understood the man's feelings. Still, he felt a little reserved about trying to find Jesus. Whether it was his own emotions, or a warning from God, he couldn't tell. What if he had been wrong about Jesus, he wondered? "I will go with you," he heard himself say.

"Here is the basket the woman brought for you. She didn't tell me her name." Chaziel handed it to him. "Meet us at the overlook tomorrow morning, just after sunrise. You will have to bring all of your belongings with you. Nothing left behind here remains, I'm afraid."

Journey

Simon nodded. "I will be ready. Thank you for allowing me to go with you."

Chaviel nodded and turned to walk away.

Simon opened the gift basket his mother had brought him. He smelled it. The aroma of his parents' home filled the basket. His eyes filled with tears, as he realized how much he missed those he loved.

I wish I could have seen her; even from a distance, he thought.

Why had he not appreciated them properly?

Discovering oil and a fresh wick in the basket, he once again lit his lamp. What else had she brought? He rummaged through the contents; bread, dates, cheese. There was enough for more than one meal! And fresh grapes!

He had not realized how hungry he had become.

He ate until he was full for the first time in days.

Unexpectedly, he was looking forward to the morning.

―――

"You should see his living conditions," Hadassah told Judah that evening. "It's deplorable." She paused. "They are worse than beggars…and the smell!"

Judah looked at her. "You went to Bethany today?"

She lifted her chin, a little defensively. "I left before sunrise, while you were sleeping."

"I wondered where you went," he murmured to himself. "No one would answer my questions."

"He is our son, Judah. Besides, I was careful. One of the servants went with me."

"I was not finding fault with you, wife. I was simply asking a question."

Hadassah relaxed. "Yes, I went to Bethany today. There is an overlook at the end of the road at the top of the hill. I could go no further. In the valley below, they keep the lepers."

"I thought Simon said they were putting him in a house?" his father recalled.

"I went to the magistrate's office. He directed me to the valley. The newer ones to the settlement are forced to live in caves. At least he found a cave… I saw many who were living in the open field; out in the weather. The cave is better than that. To get out of the cave, he has to wait until a Bedouin tent is available."

The old priest could not believe his ears. His son was living in a cave?

Hadassah continued. "I couldn't believe what I was seeing." Her eyes filled with tears. "People living like animals…. and there is no food. They only live off what people give them… " She looked at her husband. "I waited too long to go."

Judah looked at her alarmed. "Why? Is Simon sick? Did you see him? Did you talk to him?"

She sighed. "No, I didn't see him. The man I saw didn't even know *who* he was, or *where* he was."

"'They are the walking dead,'" Judah quoted.

"It is worse than that," the grieving mother replied. "Just from being in that atmosphere, I can tell you. Simon has no hope. The way they deal with this disease has stripped him of his

Journey

sense of value. He is a number; he has no name. It is a horrible place." Her lament wove into weeping.

Judah drew his wife to him, and held her, comforting her. "I'm not sure it was such a good idea for you to go," he said quietly. "You must settle it, Hadassah. We have lost our son. To be a leper means he is waiting to die."

Leaning against him, in his embrace, Judah felt his wife stiffen, even as she continued to hold him. Although her voice was muffled by his robes, he could hear her determination rise. "I will not allow my son to die in such a place. He needs a house, Judah."

"What do you want *me* to do, woman? I am not a magistrate!"

She pulled away to look him in the eyes. "*Do* something for him. You are a member of the High Council. You are a man with power. Use it. Use it for our son."

The idea had not occurred to Judah before. What could he do? His mind began working.

The next afternoon, taking two Temple guards with him, Judah went to visit the magistrate in Bethany. After an hour of negotiating, the man went with him to find an empty house for his son.

When the contract was signed, the magistrate went with Judah to the overlook at the end of the road. Observing the settlement below, the old sage found truth in his wife's words. "Why do you let them live this way?" he asked the magistrate.

The officer had shrugged. "They came here to die. We let them."

Judah looked at the man, his sudden anger simmering just below the surface. "They should die with *dignity*," he reprimanded. "Find a way."

Since no one among the lepers at the overlook knew Simon, or where he was living, Judah left the contract for the house in the hands of the magistrate. No one ventured into the valley.

"I will be back to check on the progress of this man," he warned. "Make sure he gets word of this provision. Do not fail me."

He had turned on his heel to leave, shaking. He had never spoken to anyone like that before. As he walked away, the old priest considered. He could see how Caiaphas and other men like him had become drunk with their own power.

It was a fearful temptation. "Help me to be careful, Lord," he prayed. "I never want to misuse the power you have given me. Help me to only serve, and serve well."

The Voice spoke, taking him by surprise.

You did well, Judah.

~~~

In Qumran, a little girl ran into the Scriptorium.

"Master Eli! Master Eli! I was told to give this to you *right now!*"

Across the room, a ripple of "shh!" was heard, reprimanding the child for her exuberance. In the middle of the aisle, between the rows of copyists, Eli turned and put his finger to his lips, smiling.

"What is it, Hannah?" he whispered.

Journey

Her response was also a whisper, but one which was heard in the far corners of the room. "My Daddy says to give you this message. He says it's from Jerusalem, and you should come see him, *right now!*"

The Overseer looked at her, his eyes twinkling. "Thank you very much!" he whispered in a volume similar to hers. "Tell him I will be *right there!*"

Hannah nodded, and ran out of the room. When she was gone, Eli spoke to those working with him.

"This is the message I have been waiting for. My daughter, in Jerusalem, is about to have a baby, and I have been asked to come and attend the birth. I will leave the Scriptorium in the capable hands of Issachar until I return. Please honor what he says. Treat him as you would me. If you need me, I will be staying in the Essene Quarter."

"We will miss you, Master Eli," one of the men spoke. The sentiment was echoed through the room. "Come back to us soon."

"I will. I will." Eli replied, as he selected a couple of scrolls to take with him from the storeroom. "It isn't every day that a man gets to greet a grandchild."

~~~

In the middle of the nation, near the Jordan River, near a small town called Aenon, a large crowd had gathered on the grass.

Not far from the river's edge, the older Eleazar spread a blanket for Baruch and Leah. The threesome were taking a break from the rebuilding tasks at EnKarem for a few days.

"I need to hear him again," the older man told them. "His words feed my soul."

"Mine too," Leah agreed. She grasped his hand. "You are a good man, Eleazar."

His eyes misted. "I'm not sure how true that is, child," he answered. "I have a long way to go."

About fifteen feet away, a mother and her children were also seated on a blanket, straining to hear instructions being given to the crowd about water usage, and where to find food.

"Shh!" a boy whispered to his sister. "I want to hear the story!"

"Give me back my blanket!" she protested.

"Benjamin!" his mother admonished. "Give it back to her now; quickly. I don't want to miss the story either."

"Shh!" the boy whispered again. "He's standing up!"

Seeing her brother was distracted, the little girl saw her chance. She gave the blanket a yank, retrieving it.

"Hey!" he yelled. "That hurt my hand!"

"Shh!" his sister replied. "Jesus is talking now." She stuck her tongue out at him.

"A rich man; a noble man had two sons," Jesus began. "The younger one said to his Father, 'I want my inheritance before you die. I want you to give me my portion.'"

A murmur went through the crowd. Had the boy wanted his father dead? What about the years the man had left?

"So," Jesus continued, "the man divided everything he owned, and gave it to his sons. A few days later, the young man gathered everything his father had given him together. He left his home. He left his father, and went to a far country.

"Now, when he arrived in this land, it was obvious to everyone he was a man with money. People thronged to him; at first, he had many friends; they influenced him. He bought big houses. He bought expensive gifts and threw large parties, trying to gain their approval.

"But, he was a *young* man with money. You and I know, looking at him now, that the boy trusted the wrong people. He bought things he didn't need. He made no investments. He didn't save. He didn't work.

"As his money and goods began to lessen, he began to drink, and waste the remnants of the substance his father had worked so hard to provide for him. Even when his purse was empty, he continued to try to keep up the false image he had created for himself.

"Finally, he was left alone. His houses were gone; his friends; his money; everything."

"Ever-ting?" A little girl in the crowd asked. Jesus looked down at her and laughed. He picked her up, and looked at the crowd. "Everything," he answered.

"What happened then, Jesus?" someone asked.

"Yes, what then?" another man called.

Jesus looked around, continuing the story, still holding the little girl. "Well, He had wasted everything he had been given on disorderly living. There was nothing left.

"Finally, one day, he decided to look for work. But he had no skills. He had always resisted learning from his father, thinking he knew it all already. The only job he could find was with a pig herder."

The crowd responded. Jews were not supposed to even touch a pig. How low would this boy go? He had already violated the Law on so many levels.

"He should be stoned," someone shouted out.

Jesus smiled. "There's more. Listen." He looked at the little girl. "The pig herder hired him to feed the pigs. Since the boy had no money, he was allowed to eat whatever the pigs left behind."

"Ee -yooh!" She curled up her nose. "That's bad."

"Yes," Jesus told her, in front of the crowd, "Very bad indeed."

He looked at the girl's parents, who were seated at his feet. He went on. "Well, that year, the rains didn't come. The heat was unbearable. Because of the drought, the crops failed. As a result, a famine swept through the country where he was. The young man was hungry and had no money for food. One day, because of the famine, the pig herder discovered he had no money for feed for his pigs. So, he stopped feeding them his left-over vegetables. Instead, he gave the pigs carob husks to eat."

Farmers in the crowd looked at each other. The famine in Jesus' story had been a terrible famine indeed. Carob husks, the empty shells after sweet seeds were removed, were usually burned for fuel. For his animals to be given husks to eat, the pig herder was trying just to keep them alive as long as possible!

Journey

"Did the man eat the husks?" the little girl asked Jesus.

Serious, Jesus looked at her. "The pigs didn't leave him anything to eat, little one. He was *so hungry!*"

"Serves him right," someone said. Others agreed with him.

"One day," Jesus said, "the boy woke up. He said to himself, 'Hey, when I was at home, even my father's servants had so much to eat, they would leave some behind. What is wrong with me? I could home and get something to eat!'

"So, he began to work out a plan in his mind. He would go home to his father. But he couldn't just show up, he figured. He would have to say the right things, and at least show *some* kind of attitude change, even if it wasn't real. He thought his father would only respond if he did things perfectly.

"So, he stood up, and climbed over the fence of the pig pen. He started towards home. He knew it was a long walk. While he was walking, he worked out a speech he could say; a speech he thought would cause his father to give him the response he wanted."

"Did he smell bad?" the little girl asked.

"Yes," Jesus replied, chuckling, and wrinkling his nose at her. "Horrible."

"That's nasty," another little girl said. She had worked her way up from the back of the crowd. She sat down at Jesus' feet. Looking down, Jesus saw an entire group of children who had also worked their way from other locations in the crowd. All of them were sitting en masse around his feet.

They could get no closer.

Jesus put the little girl he had been holding on the ground, where she joined the group. She sat down, close to her parents. He continued.

"The boy talked to himself. He said, 'I will say the perfect things. I will tell him that I know I have sinned against heaven. I have sinned against *him*. I will tell him that I realize now that I've lost the chance to be called his son. I will tell him... no, I will *ask* him to make me a servant in the house.

"He said, 'He will feed me then.'"

"This boy is trouble," one of the older men interjected. "He hasn't learned a thing."

Jesus smiled at him. "Perhaps, my friend."

"Didn't his father know he was being tricked? Didn't he realize what kind of nature this boy had?"

Jesus smiled again. "Perhaps."

"What happened, Jesus?" Benjamin was now sitting at the Teacher's feet.

"Well," he responded, looking at Benjamin, "his father was a wise man; a good man. Every day, he went to the top of the house to look down the road for his son's return."

"Is he nuts? He's better off without that loser," another man spoke up.

Jesus chuckled. "Every day the father watched. For years, he waited. Then, one day, a figure appeared on the road, just at the top of the hill. Who was it? Could it be? It was!

"The father recognized his son's walk. He had been waiting. He saw him coming, even before the boy realized how close to home he really was. The father got so excited, his heart began to pound. Then, as his son came closer and closer, he saw the state the boy was in. His heart filled with compassion, and he ran towards him.

"He ran?" a little girl asked. "Rich men don't run."

Jesus laughed. "This rich man did. He didn't care what it looked like. He just loved his son."

He paused. "He ran," he repeated. "Not only did he run to his son, but when he reached him, he wrapped him up in his arms and hugged him.

"The boy took a deep breath and started the speech he had prepared. 'Father, I have sinned....' But his father interrupted him. He hugged him again, and kissed his neck!"

"But he smelled bad!" one of the crowd protested. "He was filthy like a pig!"

Jesus shrugged. "The father didn't care about that. He called the servants. He alerted the house. He said, 'Go get my best robe! Put the family ring on his finger! Get shoes for him! Kill the calf we have been raising for a feast day!!

"The father shouted 'My boy was dead; but he is alive again! He was lost; but I have found him again!'

"The entire house began to prepare for a party. All the neighbors and friends were invited. There was so much food, it was like a wedding!"

The crowd had fallen silent. Who had ever heard of a father who responded like this? Who was the father in the story, they wondered? Surely it was no one they knew.

All of Jesus' stories had to do with Elohim. Was Jesus painting a picture of God for them? But the Storyteller had not finished yet. He continued.

"Now, the *elder* brother was out in the field, working. He had been there since before sunrise. He did the same thing every day, without fail.

"He had plowed; he had planted. He had worked all day long. Seeing the sun was going down, he decided it would be all right to stop for the day, even though there was still so much to be done.

"As he came near the house, he was amazed to hear music playing! People were dancing in the yard! When he asked someone what was happening, they told him his father was throwing a party because his brother had come home.

"Well, the older brother was instantly angry. He felt forgotten and neglected. He went looking for his father. He said, 'Are you telling me that I *he* gets a party? I have worked, and toiled for you. I never broke a rule. I never asked for a thing. But now, this idiot, who has squandered his life away, comes back, with his tail between his legs. And you .... You kill the feast calf? For him? He *never earned it*. Are you going to let him get away with his behavior? You're *blessing* him? That doesn't teach him *anything!*'

"His father put his arm around him; but the older brother pulled away. He still had more to say. 'Do you love him more than you love me? You never even once offered to give *me* so much as a baby *goat* to kill, so that I could have a party with my friends.

"'I don't get it,' he said to his father. 'He burned up his best years with prostitutes and drunkards. Why does he get the celebration? *It's not fair!*'"

People in the crowd nodded. Almost everyone had compared their life with someone else's, and experienced feelings of anger over injustice at one point or another. They identified with the older brother.

Jesus looked around from face to face. "The father hugged his older boy. He said, 'Son, don't misunderstand. You have *never* left me; you have been a *faithful* son. All that I have is yours. But don't you see? We have something *huge* to celebrate today. Your brother has come back to me from the dead. We had lost him; but now he is found again.

"There is hope for him to learn once more."

People in the crowd began to ask the Teacher questions. Those who travelled with Jesus knew those discussions would lead to miracles.

In the middle of the story, Talmi arrived with Mary's message. It had taken him five days to find them.

John noticed his arrival and went to greet him.

"Talmi!" he cried. "What are you doing here?"

"I have a message from Mistress Mary for Jesus," he answered, panting.

"Is everything all right?" John wanted to know.

"No," was the simple answer. "Master Eleazar is ill. She says for Jesus to come quickly…. Please."

"I will tell him as soon as he is done with the story," John promised. "Are you hungry?"

"Yes, very. Thanks for asking." Talmi followed John to where Jesus' followers were standing in the crowd. The older Mary was sitting with another woman, named Joanna, who had been traveling with them for some time now.

Looking up, the older Mary saw the two men approaching. She stood up. "Talmi! What are you doing here?"

"He brought us a message from Magdalene," John told her. "Eleazar is sick."

Mary looked at John. "Jesus will want to know," she said. She looked at Talmi. "When did you eat last? Are you thirsty?"

"It has been a while," he answered.

For the rest of the afternoon, the servant rested under a shade tree, regaining his energies. It was nightfall before he was able to speak with Jesus.

"Mistress Mary sent me," he said simply, sitting by the fire after supper. "She says to tell you 'the one you love dearly is sick.'"

Jesus looked at him. Talmi had gazed back. "Thank you for the message, Talmi," he looked at Simon Peter and John. "We will go back to Bethany."

"Now, Master?" Peter asked.

"No, but soon," was the reply.

~~~

Atticus and Titus stood in the Battalion Commander's office in Capernaum. When orders had arrived from the governor's office in Syria for the next six months, Justus had summoned the two foot soldiers to his office. They stood waiting, as the centurion looked through the lists.

Journey

"It seems we have been ordered to supplement the ranks in Jerusalem during the Jewish feasts this year, beginning with Passover. Governor Antonius is concerned about crowd control. It seems he is afraid Jesus might be a threat."

"The Healer?" Titus asked. "Is that possible?"

Justus shook his head. "Someone who doesn't understand his message has been spreading rumors, I'm afraid. It just makes more work for us."

"Who will you assign?" Atticus wanted to know.

"Let's look together," the Commander responded. "Both of you are more aware of how the men relate to each other when away from the garrison. We cannot afford any internal skirmishes, especially when our superiors are anticipating revolt. Take a seat. We will work on it together."

~~~

The next day, Talmi returned to Bethany from Aenon. Upon hearing he had arrived, Mary went to find him.

"Did you find Jesus?" she asked. "What did he say?"

"He told his followers they would be coming back here," Talmi responded. He had begun digging weeds from the garden.

"We had best prepare for his arrival then." Mary turned to see Miriam coming up behind her. Apparently her sister had overheard the conversation. Miriam looked up to see both Talmi and Mary looking at her.

"What?" she asked. "We will need to get the house ready."

Mary was the one to respond to her. "Why don't you let me be the one to work on that, Miriam? You've been so busy taking care of Eleazar."

The older sister put her hands up in defense. "It's not like before, honest," she reassured them. "I just want to have clean linens available for everyone, and make sure we have enough food to share. That's all." She paused, and looked at Talmi, assessing him. Then she spoke again. "Talmi, would you forgive me for pushing you so hard?"

Surprised, the man looked up, and saw the genuine concern on Miriam's face. "Why, yes, Mistress," he responded kindly. "I was just doing my job."

"I know," she said. "I've just been realizing lately, since Jesus was last here, how many times I listen to Fear. Most of the time, I'm afraid someone will disapprove of me, or will reject me, if things aren't done 'just so.' As a result, I tend to push and control." She paused. "I just want you both to know that I see it now, and I'm trying to change. I'm sorry."

Mary's heart filled with compassion for her older sister. "I understand," she said, "more than you know."

"Miriam! Mistress Miriam!" the voice was that of Talmi's wife, Sharon, calling from the rooftop. "I need your help! It's Eleazar! I think he's stopped breathing!"

Startled, all three of them dropped what they were doing, and ran to the stairway leading to the roof. Sharon met them coming down.

"How do you know?" Miriam asked, pushing by her to get to the roof.

Journey

"I took the blade of the knife and held it under his nose like you showed me to do. There was no vapor," Sharon answered.

Miriam had reached the covered arbor. Falling to her knees beside her brother, she lifted his hand and put it to her cheek. She felt his head and his neck for signs of a pulse-beat. She put her ear to his chest. She double-checked Sharon's findings. Finally, she sat back on her heels, and looked at Mary.

Mary stood under the arbor, watching her sister move into action. She observed her brother. His skin was almost white. The wounds to his arm and shoulder had soaked the bandages once more. Slowly, she knelt next to him, on the opposite side as her sister. With a thumb, she lifted one of his eyelids to check for movement or response to the light.

Nothing.

"He is gone." Miriam looked at Talmi and then at Mary. Her eyes were hollow.

"I thought he would come," Mary said numbly. "I thought he would be here."

"Who?" Miriam asked.

"Jesus," the younger sister replied sadly. "But it's too late now."

Talmi left to make preparations for Eleazar's burial. There were only a few hours left in the day, and the man would have to be buried before nightfall.

As they cleansed his body, Miriam and Mary were weeping. They applied myrrh and aloes to his skin. With Sharon's help, they lifted his body onto a long strip of linen, some fourteen feet or more long. Eleazar's body was laid on top of the strip, with one edge just above his head. As Miriam placed his hands at his sides, and covered his face with a small handkerchief, called a *souderion,* she was overwhelmed with emotion. She had wiped his nose and face many times during his illness, with just such a cloth.

The reality she would never do so again, suddenly hit her with a fury. She began to sob. "I can't do this, Mary. Can you help me?"

Disheartened and angry, Mary looked at her. "I can, and I will." She covered her brother's face, and pulled the other end of the linen coverlet up over him

"Sharon," she called. "We are ready for the wrapping strips now."

The three women worked for the next hour in silence.

～～～

At the top of the hill, at the agreed gathering place, a group of lepers waited to know their next step.

"How many were going with us?" Joram, one of the older lepers, wanted to know.

"We don't know yet," said Avishar. "Chaviel is coming. I think he had an exact count."

"I don't think we should allow ourselves to be led by a Samaritan," Joram argued. "If anyone leads us, it should an older man, say, someone else."

"You, perhaps?" The voice belonged to Ethan; well respected among them.

"I just say we should leave now. We have been waiting long enough," Joram contended. Just then, he caught sight of Chaviel coming up from the valley, accompanied by another man.

"It's about time you showed up," he muttered.

Journey

"Honestly, Joram!" Chaviel greeted him. "What else did you have to do today? Some pressing engagement, perhaps?" He smiled and looked at Avishar. "The final count is ten. There will be ten of us going on the journey."

The man who came with Chaviel was silent, observing the chemistry between the group; assessing where he should try to fit in.

"What is your name?" Avishar asked him. "You're new to the settlement, aren't you?"

"My name is Simon," the former Pharisee answered. "I haven't been here long."

Joram spoke again, this time with disdain. "He's a *cave dweller*."

"That's true," answered Simon. "And I am a leper."

As his statement hung in the air, the former priest could feel himself being appraised. Would they *allow* him into their company, he wondered? He remembered days when his own heart had been less than inviting to those he didn't know, or was suspicious of.

After a short pause, Ethan chuckled. His chuckle became a laugh. Avishar looked at him strangely, and asked, "What?"

"He is a leper," Ethan repeated, chuckling again.

"So are you," Avishar said, not understanding Ethan's humor.

Ethan nodded, laughing harder. "So are we all!" At that, Avishar, Chaviel and the rest of the lepers began to laugh in varying degrees; all except Joram.

Avishar slapped Simon on the back. "I *like* this man, Chaviel! *He* can walk with *me*!"

Simon sighed with relief. He realized he had never had a friend before. This would be a new experience.

―――

Mary sat in her room in Miriam's home. In her hands, she held a piece of alabaster stone. Turning it in her hands, she continued in thought. It had been four days since Eleazar's death. Since then, their home had been continually filled with people.

The priests from the Temple had come and gone; praying blessing and comfort over them. Physicians had come, who had been friends of Miriam Abiel. It seemed the entire village had shown up at their door at one time or another.

Several of the merchants from the marketplace in Jerusalem had come.

Lucius had also travelled from Jerusalem, bearing gifts. He had stayed for a short while, mourning the loss of his friend. He somehow felt responsible. Miriam had sent him home with food.

Mary looked at the shelves, and the tables; they had been given so much! Each time a neighbor came to the door, it seemed they came with food. Why was it that when people didn't know what to do, they brought food, she wondered? Although she knew they meant well, she had to admit she hadn't even felt hungry since the afternoon they had wrapped her brother's body.

Sighing, the woman stood to stretch. She had been inside too much the past few days. Perhaps if she went up to the roof, into the sunlight, or even under the arbor, she thought.

No. Eleazar had died there. She would not go there again – not for a long time.

Her eyes filled with tears once again. Angrily, she brushed them away.

What would they do now; she and Miriam? Old thought patterns had been surfacing this morning.

Did Miriam really want her here?

She heard a noise. She paused to listen.

Someone was coming through the front door. Going to look, she discovered it was Sharon. "Mistress, Miriam says I should come and find you. She says Jesus is coming up the road, although he is a ways away yet. She sent me to begin preparing for their arrival."

"Oh," Mary said. "I wonder what he thinks he can do *now*." She looked at Sharon. "Have we had any other guests this afternoon?"

Sharon smiled. "A few of the priests from Jerusalem returned about an hour ago, along with one or two of the villagers. Oh, and Master Lucius has returned with a few of the women from the weaving house who we know. They are right behind me. We are all going to work to prepare food together."

Just then, the door opened again. Several women entered. "Hello, Mary," one of them said. "How are you doing?"

"I don't know; I think I'm recovering," she replied. "It's hard to tell. The grief seems to come in waves."

"I understand. Let us know if we can get you anything."

Mary nodded, and retreated to the quiet sanctuary of her room. She picked up the alabaster fragment once again and sniffed its fragrance. Unexpectedly, she realized she was angry; angry at Jesus.

Why didn't he come when we called him, she wondered?

Why hadn't Eleazar been healed?

Could she trust him again? Would she be able to?

Without warning, images of Jesus speaking in Galilee presented themselves in her mind.

"Fear not, little flock. It is the Father's desire to give you the Kingdom. He wants you to have it. He won't withhold from you."

"I am the door to the sheepfold. Anyone who enters in through me will find food for their soul, and they will be rescued from destruction. Anyone who tries to tell you there is another door is a thief and a robber.

"You want to know about the thief? You can recognize him because he only comes to steal, to kill, and to destroy. My purpose, on the other hand, is to give Life; real Life; brimming and overflowing; abundant Life.

"I am the Good Shepherd. I lay down my life for my sheep. No one is forcing me.... I do it because I want to."

He has come to give life, she thought. How was that possible for Eleazar.... now?

Come to think of it, what was the idea of "living forever" Jesus kept speaking about? How was eternal life possible? Was it a metaphor?

She knew Jesus was truly who He said he was. He had proven that the night of her deliverance, and many times since then.

Now, she just wanted to understand.... Why hadn't he come when she sent for him?

Hadn't he received her message?

No. Talmi had delivered it. So, why had Jesus delayed?

Outside, Miriam was beginning to walk towards Jesus, to greet him, and walk with him to the house.

"Miriam!" Jesus called. "It's good to see you!"

She looked at him with a little reserve. "It's good to see you too." She paused. Should she say what she was thinking? "I wish you had been here sooner. Eleazar is dead."

"I heard that," he responded.

"You know, if you had been here he wouldn't have died," she said factually. She looked at him, and quickly added, "but I know, that even right now, whatever you ask, God will do. He will give it to you."

Jesus looked at her and smiled. "Your brother is going to rise again," he said.

"I remember you taught us about the last day, and how the dead will rise. I know he will rise again on *that* day," she said. Was he mentioning that now to give her hope, she wondered? Was he telling her to put her mind on the eternal nature of Life, and not think about her brother's death?

Jesus stopped walking, and stood still in the road. Miriam took a few steps, and then realized he was not next to her. She turned, looking to him.

"Miriam," he said, "I am the Resurrection and the Life. When a person puts their trust in me, believing and accepting that I am who I say I am; even when they die, they will live; and live forever. Do you understand this? Do you believe it?"

Her answer would have been different a year ago, she realized. But now? Seeing the miracles, the healings, the changes in her sister, even the changes in her own heart, she had come to a firm decision about his identity.

She looked him in the eye. "Yes, Lord, I believe it," she answered. "In fact, I believe you are the Promised Deliverer; God come as a man into the world."

"You are certain?" he asked her.

"Absolutely," she answered.

At that moment, Talmi stepped into the conversation. "Mistress," he whispered, "Sharon wants me to ask you which dishes you want served for the meal. There seem to be too many to pick from, she says."

Miriam looked at Jesus. "Excuse me, please," she said, and went into the house. After answering Sharon's questions, she noted Mary was not anywhere to be seen. "Where is she?" she asked her friends, who were preparing the food.

"She went into her room when she heard Jesus was coming," Sharon said. "She seems upset."

Miriam went to Mary's door and opened it. She stuck her head into the room. "Mary? Are you all right?"

"I'm fine," came the answer. "I just wish I could understand."

"Jesus is here. He wants to see you. Why don't you go out and greet him?" Miriam prodded.

Journey

Grudgingly, Mary stood up, to make her way where her sister was standing. "Why didn't he come sooner?" she asked.

Miriam looked at her with compassion. "I don't know," she replied quietly. "I'm sure he would have been here sooner if he could have been. He has always been a good friend to us.... and to Eleazar."

Mary shrugged. "I know," she said. "I'm just sad."

Taking her outer wrap with her, Mary walked out of her room, across the front room, and through the door of the house, without speaking. She could feel her emotions rising to the surface. She didn't trust herself.

Then, just as she stepped over the threshold, she saw Jesus, surrounded by his followers. A few of the priests from Jerusalem had assembled as well.

Inwardly, a memory of her shattering the jar, and weeping at his feet in Capernaum came rushing up like a tidal wave. She had been struggling, battling for remnants of her will. She did not want to acquiesce to attitudes; attitudes threatening to endanger her soul once again.

Without thinking of what she was doing, she began to run. As soon as she got to Jesus, she fell to her knees in front of him. Grabbing his feet, she began to wail uncontrollably.

"If you had been here, he would not have died! Where were you? I don't understand! Help me understand, Lord! If only you had been here!" The torrent of her words trailed off into sobbing. "I sent for you! I asked! I don't understand!"

Mary's emotional outburst had stirred the sensitivity of Eleazar's friends in the crowd. They also began to weep. Behind her, the women who had been serving in the kitchen were wiping their eyes and sniffing.

What would these two sisters do without Eleazar, they wondered?

What would happen now?

Jesus looked down at Mary. How fragile this little one was!

He bent down. Putting his finger under her chin, he lifted her head to look at him. He wiped the tears from her face. He smiled at her, his own eyes brimming over onto his cheeks.

He looked at the crowd. When his eyes fell on Miriam, he stopped. "Where did you bury my friend?" he asked, his voice breaking.

"Let me show you," Miriam said, wiping her eyes, and moving forward.

They walked with Jesus, his arms around them.

Not far behind the house was a cave in the side of a hill. Abiel had chosen it as a family burial location long ago, when he had built the house. A large stone was rolled in front of the cave's opening, to seal in decomposition odors from the bodies buried there.

"He is in there," Miriam pointed to the cave. "He is buried with my husband."

For a long moment, the only noises anyone could hear were quiet whimpers, and soft sniffles. No one said a word.

Finally, Jesus spoke. "Miriam, I want you to remove the stone."

Miriam's immediate reaction was based in her practicality. "He's been dead four days now, Master. Are you sure we want that smell to come out here?"

Journey

Stepping forward, alone, Jesus spoke again; this time to his followers. "Move the stone away from the cave," he instructed. James and John moved to do what he had requested.

Miriam frowned. "Jesus, I'm not sure...."

He turned his head towards her. His clear and steady gaze stopped her words. He spoke. "Didn't I tell you that when you trust me with all of your heart, you will see the glory of God?"

He looked up. "Abba Father," he said. "Thank you that you listen when I talk to you. I want the people standing here to know that you listen as well. Please help them to believe that You sent me."

He lowered his chin, and looked at the cave opening. He shouted, his voice deep and strong, filling the atmosphere. To Mary, it felt like thunder. "ELEAZAR!! COME OUT OF THE TOMB!!"

Most of those standing in the crowd had their eyes on Jesus. No one had ever ordered a man to come to life like this before. They were amazed, and surprised; most wanted to see what the Teacher would do next.

But Mary's eyes were fixed on the doorway of the tomb. Suddenly, a wrapped figure appeared, rising up from the darkness into the doorway. Was she imagining it? If it *was* Eleazar, he would have had to have floated through the air. His feet had been bound tightly. She knew. She and Miriam had wrapped him. How was it possible?

Mary's feet broke into a run for a second time. Then, she was standing next to him. Was he really moving, struggling to get free from the wrappings?

"Get those things off of him," Jesus said. "Let him walk freely."

Mary looked up. Miriam was on the other side of their brother with barbering scissors. Laughing together, they cut through the burial clothes.

"Eleazar, stand still!" Miriam admonished. "Talmi, can you help me?"

But Talmi had gone inside to find Eleazar a toga. His employer would want something to wear once he was able to breathe.

"I'll help you, Miriam," Mary said.

"Sorry," her sister answered. "I *want* your help." She glanced at Jesus, as she handed Mary the scissors. "Here, Mary; why don't *you* do a little of the cutting?"

It was a happy moment. Jesus had raised Eleazar from the dead! He had raised others from the dead... but no one who had been dead for four days before! People in the crowd who had wondered about Jesus were now convinced.

Everyone wanted to hear him speak.

Everyone wanted to hear Eleazar as well. What had he seen? What new understanding could he give them?

After the supper was served, discussion went on for hours.

They were all so caught up in the celebrations no one noticed the plain, short, man, in servant's clothing. He quietly ate and left the party early. No one thought anything of it.

They didn't know him or recognize him.

Journey

"I want you to go with these rabble rousers, these rebels," the man's employer had instructed, over two weeks prior. "Join yourself to them; interview people. I want witnesses."

Malchus, the servant of the high priest, had quite a story to tell his employer, Joseph Caiaphas. His master would want to know what had happened today.

On the road towards Jerusalem, ten lepers had stopped in their journey to find the Healer.

"I can't get it open!" Avishar was frustrated. A fruit vendor had passed by the group of men close to an hour ago, and had thrown food to them. Avishar was trying to peel a pomegranate, without much success.

Ethan spoke up. "Why don't you just ask for help? You know you can't do it."

Avishar looked at his friend in sudden anger. "I can too!" he cried. "I don't want anyone's help."

Ethan looked at Simon, confiding. "Last winter, the leprosy reached his hands, and they began going numb," he explained. "That's why he only has two fingers on his right hand. He burned them off in the fire, trying to get warm."

Joram spoke. "Avishar, give me the pomegranate. I'll peel it for you."

Avishar sighed, handing his friend the fruit. "I just get so weary of having to depend on someone else. Sometimes I dream of what it would be like to have a thumb again!"

"Just think," Chaviel interjected, "your wife won't be able to ask you to do anything requiring thumbs when you go home. Come to think of it, Avishar, how did you get the wineskin open this morning?"

Avishar laughed. "Well it was difficult. I didn't want to wake anyone. The last time I took a drink by myself, I put the thing between what's left of my teeth, and pulled it open. I pulled out a molar as well." He paused. "I wasn't going to do that again…"

"So what did you do?" his friend repeated.

Sheepishly, the leper looked at his friends. "I put the stopper between my toes, and pulled."

The response of the group was a combination of "Yuck!" and "Disgusting!"

Joram spoke. "Did you wash your feet first? I saw what we walked through yesterday."

Avishar laughed. "Where would I find a leper's bath? You know we aren't allowed to even *stand* in a river! I was thirsty!"

Amos, another in the ten, spoke up. "Does it matter? Avishar, don't be so independent. Listen, I can't even see out of one of my eyes. If it were me, I wouldn't have known if the wineskin was dirty or not. At least you can see! You just can't get it open! " He looked with his working eye at Joram. "How many times have you said to me, 'You can't see, so I will be your eyes'? We all need each other."

Joram spoke up once again. "Listen, at least I have both of my eyes, and all of my fingers."

"…and half of your brain!" Ethan interrupted.

Journey

As the crowd around him erupted into laughter, Simon smiled. His thoughts began. How had these men come to such a place of honesty? There were no pretensions here. There could be no hiding behind an expert reputation.

He felt a thud on his back. The hand belonged to Chaviel.

"You're too quiet, my friend," he admonished. "Does our humor offend you?"

"No, nothing like that," Simon responded. "I was just thinking that God allowed me to come here. I think it was the only way I would discover how thick the Pride on my soul had become."

"What were you… before?" Amos wanted to know.

Simon looked at his new friends, suddenly fearful to tell them he had been a Pharisee. Over the past few months, he had discovered a prevalent attitude among those in the settlement regarding his sect.

"Uh, I lived in Capernaum," he replied.

"Yes, but what did you *do*? Were you a fisherman?" Amos asked again.

Simon paused. To these men, those who wore robes of office, and served the Temple, had come to represent a higher social order; an exclusive faction. In his reading in the cave, he had discovered Elohim's original purpose for their office; to serve those in need, to be *inclusive* and *inviting*. Standing with the lepers now, he realized, he had become like the other Pharisees around him; finding more and more things to ascertain fault with; creating finer and finer filters of purification. As an end result, there was nothing that really completely pleased God in their eyes.

It had been a hurtful discovery.

"I…" he paused. "I was a Pharisee." There it was out.

He expected them to shun him; to move away, rejecting him, as he had rejected others during his days in Capernaum.

"Oh," Chaviel commented. "Is that why you are always inside, reading?"

Simon hadn't thought about it before. "I suppose I wasn't sure anyone would want to know me. So I hid away."

Avishar chuckled, his deep voice still strong. "You'll have to be careful about that, Simon. If you don't come out in the sunlight, your skin could develop a condition."

Simon joined him in laughing. "I don't know what to say to that," he admitted.

"It's high time you learned, boy," Joram thudded him once again. "You need to learn how to develop relationships. We will have to come up with a new name for you, one fitting your office."

Now there was a word he had been considering of late, Simon thought; *relationship*. Sitting in his cave, he realized he had never really had a relationship with God. He had worked to serve him, yes. He had memorized the facts and the lessons, yes.

He had tried to keep the Law.

In reading, he had learned that Judah, his father, had been right. *Perhaps we have added too much to the Ten, and the health laws*, his father had said, not once, but many times.

Journey

How would a person live without the oral traditions? The entire nation now believed the oral traditions had the same depth and power as the original Words of God. Such had been the prideful mistake of his fellows.

It had always been Elohim's desire to have a relationship with His creation, he realized. But now? Religion had undermined Relationship.

He could see now he had substituted his own sense of personal purity; his ability to keep the rules in his own strength; for a relationship with God.

He had made himself aloof, to hide his weaknesses.

How had people strayed so far from relating to their God, he wondered? Had it been the result of constant rote and repetition, without the explanation of meaning? Had it been the lack of personal encounters with the Living God? Had it been the hounding to remember duties and responsibilities? He had done it in his office in Capernaum.

When had divine energy become replaced by human effort?

"Simon, did you hear me?" Chaviel was speaking.

Simon looked at him, and realized he had been lost in thought. "I'm sorry," he said. "My mind drifted off."

"We will wait for you to find it. That's something you cannot afford to be without." This time the humor was Ethan's. "Lord knows what this disease does to a man."

Chaviel repeated the question Simon had not heard. "I asked you what you have been learning from your scrolls," he said.

"It would be good to hear from the prophets, or the psalms again," Joram spoke. "If there is one thing I really miss, it is being with my friends in the Presence of God."

"Yes, talk to us about ElShaddai, and His heart to comfort us," one said.

"Or, the lessons from Samuel's books; how He rescues His people," another suggested.

Chaviel looked at Simon. "I'd like to hear about Naaman again." He was referring to a Syrian soldier, a leper who had been healed by Elohim's instructions through Elisha, the prophet.

"It was his account that encouraged me to leave the settlement and find Jesus," he said. "I don't want to have the battle with Pride that Naaman did. I have decided that I will do whatever Jesus asks to become clean again."

"Me too;" "Yes;" "I agree." Comments were murmured around the former Pharisee's ears.

"Go ahead, Simon. What can you teach us?"

Simon looked at them, a new awareness in his heart. "I don't know," he replied. "I have learned so much from each of you, just being a part of this group."

"What is God saying?" a voice inquired from the back of the group.

After a short pause to gather his thoughts, Simon spoke.

"Well, I am no prophet," he said slowly. "I can just tell you what I have been discovering about Him for my own life."

"Go ahead!" prodded Chaviel. "That's what we want to hear about. That is when God becomes real."

Journey

Simon looked at his friend. *That is when God becomes real*, he considered.

"Well," he said, "when I came to the settlement, I was angry. I didn't realize how angry I really was, until the magistrate refused to give me a house. I thought because of my status and position, I would be given special consideration, but I wasn't. The Law didn't care where I had come from. And, because I was now unclean, it had decreed that I didn't have a future either.

"I sat alone in the cave, mostly feeling sorry for myself. I had never had to wash a dish, or make my own bed, or even cook a meal before; so all of this was new to me. I can see now I was living my life based in a picture of God I myself had concocted, rather than the God Who really is."

"I began to think God had forgotten me; that I had lost my value. After all, I couldn't do the work of the priesthood anymore. Then, one afternoon I decided to try to sleep, since my eyes hurt in the bright light. I read one or two of the Psalms before lying down. I'm not even sure I wasn't still doing it out of duty at that point.

"Well, there was a phrase that seemed to rise off the scroll to me. It said, "The God of Jacob." I had always thought of myself as a leader in Israel. That difference struck me. Jacob was the man who wrestled with God and won. He was the trickster, the usurper, the deceiver. He had stolen his brother's inheritance.

"As I lay down that afternoon, for the first time, I saw that the father of our nation had been in need of a Redeemer; a God who could change his nature. When he was willing to wrestle with God until the light broke through, that is when he became a Prince and founder of a nation.

"When I awoke from that sleep, I saw I had been on a journey downward for a long time. I saw myself like Jacob, and realized I was in need of a Redeemer.

"I have been wrestling with God ever since."

"Why?" asked Joram. "Why don't you just yield?"

"I don't know," replied Simon. "I think it's because I want to understand what will happen, or I just want to be able to have input into what God does with my life."

Chaviel laughed. "Yielding means: choosing to trust. I thought that would be easier for a Pharisee."

Simon looked at him, seriously. "In truth, I think it has been harder. I have had too many layers, each one with its own place of learning and commitment."

"What do you mean by 'layers'?" Amos wanted to know.

"Well, looking from the outside, I always thought that a life of relationship with God would be an event; a one-time thing; based on His rules of behavior. I see it. I do it. Things change.

"But I am discovering it is not like that. My relationship with God has become a journey. It is not as much about His rules, as it is about the *condition of my heart towards Him*. God is peeling the layers off of my soul; the things I have protected myself with; my defense mechanisms; my methods of survival. Each stop along the way has presented me with a new lesson. And, at the end of each lesson, I am more able to trust; more willing to be vulnerable.

"When I first came to the settlement, I hid away because I could not reconcile my image and reputation of who I *thought* I was, and what I *thought* I deserved, with the *reality* of being a leper. I was used to being the center of my world; I felt entitled to certain attitudes from others; I had demanded to be treated a certain way. I defended myself, saying that because I was a man, or a Pharisee, or a father – whatever title; I deserved to be given special privileges. I thought I should be allowed to get away with poor behaviors. That was the first lesson I had to learn."

"I had to learn that as well," Chaviel spoke, encouraging his friend. "I was a wealthy businessman in Samaria. When I came to the settlement, it didn't matter. Not only did my status not matter, but I was put at the bottom of the ladder because of my skin color and nationality."

Simon nodded. "I used to be part of the ones who would *do* such things to Samaritans," he commented. "As I sat in the cave, I thought about the choices and steps I had taken to become ensnared in the Trap of Entitlement. I saw a progression throughout my youth. It began with *insecurity*, which everyone deals with. I was afraid of others --- what they might think. When I closed off my heart, not bringing it to my father, or mother, or even to God, asking for healing, I became *self-conscious*.

"As I held on to that, I allowed myself to think independently, receiving no instruction for rescue, not asking questions to grow, I became *self-centered*. The only place I felt secure was when I placed myself in the center; my feelings, my preferences. I really believed my opinions were the only correct view on situations, on people. I became argumentative, and would debate over the tiniest of details. I was full of Pride.

"Then, as time wore on, I became consumed with my own desires, my own goals, my achievements. Ambition began to drive me. I became filled with Self; *a selfish man*.

"One day, I was reading the very account you described, Chaviel; the story of Naaman, and his cleansing from leprosy. The prophet told him to go to the Jordan River, take seven baths, and he would be clean. I found myself identifying with Naaman's response. 'I can do *that* at home. He should have at least come out of his house to see me, since I came this far.'

"It was Naaman's servants who convinced him to at least try what Elisha had told him to do; they had more trust in the Word of God to the prophet, than Naaman did. I wondered as I read whether he was tempted to stop bathing on the fifth and sixth bath; whether there was any change at all.

"I found myself thinking, 'would I have followed through, and finished the seventh cleansing?' Then I felt a challenge on the inside of my soul. It wasn't a Voice yet, just an impression. How deep was I willing to go? How deep would I allow God to go in me; just one cleansing, or two, or seven?"

There was silence on the road for a few moments. Then Ethan spoke up. "It's true, Simon. ElShaddai *is* a God of relationship, isn't He? He related to Adam, to Noah, to Moses, to Abram, to Isaac. He met each man where he needed to in order to touch their lives. I was a tax collector; and skeptical. To me, the religious leaders have always made God feel so out of

Journey

touch. For me, relationship with God has meant that I must look at what I don't know. It means becoming weak in my own strength, and admitting I don't know; asking questions."

"Look!" the voice was Avishar's. He pointed to a large group of people walking toward them. In response, each leper covered his head and hands, and looked down at the ground. Each one pulled out a small bell, and began ringing. "We are unclean!" Avishar cried out. "We are lepers! Stay away from us!" The rest of the lepers began to echo his words, in varying degrees of hoarseness and volume.

As the crowd approached, it was Simon who first recognized Jesus. The young Carpenter was walking in the center of the road, surrounded by followers. He noted James and John, the sons of Zebedee. He also saw the woman who had invaded the dinner in his home in Capernaum.

Had that been the night before his diagnosis?

It seemed so long ago.

For a few moments, it seemed the crowd would pass by them, avoiding them. So, Chaviel,, the leader among them, began to cry out, rasping and hoarse,

"Jesus! Master! Please have mercy on us!" The other lepers joined him. Simon listened. Could he really call *Jesus* his *Master*?

The passing crowd had stopped. Simon saw Jesus move towards them. He put his head down, and pulled the hood of his cloak over his head. He did not want to be recognized. He did not want to be embarrassed; being seen by those he used to know.

An inner prodding reminded him of his latest battle inside the cave; inside his soul. He would not give Entitlement a place. This might be his only opportunity to find healing. Was he willing to take it? What was his Pride worth to him? Coming to decision, Simon lifted his voice with the others, who were continuing their pleas. "Jesus! Son of David! Master! Have mercy on *me*!"

Jesus looked at them. Chaviel told Simon later that he felt something change when he looked into the Healer's eyes. "Something in me jumped up and came to life!" He said, describing the moment.

For Simon, there was no sensation, no awareness of change.

Raising his voice to be heard, Jesus said, "Go now, friends. Show yourselves to the priests."

Was that it, Simon wondered? Wasn't he going to touch them? Wasn't he going to make some great demonstration? There were ten of them! Didn't he know how far they had walked to find him?

Naaman felt the same way, the prodding within him reminded.

Simon, standing next to Joram, turned to walk away. For some time, they walked, a deep sense of disappointment looming. It was Amos who spoke first. "I thought he would come over to us. It wasn't like I thought it would be."

Chaviel looked at his friend. "It is all right. We can go back to the settlement, now, knowing we tried." He paused, looking at his blind friend's face. He stopped. "Amos," he said, looking more carefully, "which of your cheeks held the lesion that shriveled your nose?"

Amos removed the hood from his head. "My left," he answered, lifting his hand to feel his nose. He looked at Chaviel. "See?" He pointed to his nose.

Chaviel looked where his friend had indicated. Joram did as well. Both men spoke at the same time. "It's gone!"

Hurriedly each man of the ten began to check his own hands, then his feet, and arms and face. Amos put his hand over his good eye, and began to shout, laughing with relief at the same time. "I can see! I can see with both eyes! Look at me! I can see!"

Simon unwrapped his hands, removing his hood and head wrap. Oh, this felt good! He could feel the breeze. He didn't need to squint or cover his eyes. It felt so good just to feel good again. He took a deep breath.

Where had his Pain gone?

Beside him, Joram, his limp departed, was already moving towards Jerusalem. "He said we should show ourselves to the priests. Let's go." He pulled on Simon's arm. "Come on! Let's go!" He pulled on Ethan and Avishar.

The nine were some distance down the road together, before they realized Chaviel was not with them.

Running in the opposite direction, the former Samaritan merchant had followed the crowd of Jesus and his followers. He found them eating a meal at a roadside food stand on the road. He did not stop or slow his pace until he had fallen down in front of Jesus, kneeling at his feet.

"Master! I was a leper, and you healed me!" he panted. "I just want to thank you!" He was weeping now. "Thank you, Jesus! It is so good to walk without pain again."

Jesus squatted down to share an eye-level communication with Chaviel. Reaching to touch his shoulder, the Healer spoke. "Friend, you are welcome." He looked around at his followers. "How many did we count in their group? Ten?" He looked at the former leper. "And you are the only one who returned? Where are you from?"

Chaviel looked into his Healer's eyes. "I'm a Samaritan," he answered. "I just wanted to thank you."

"Your trust and belief in me has made your life healthy now. Go on from here with Peace in your heart," Jesus said to him.

"Thank you," Chaviel said again. "You have given me my life." He turned and ran back down the road to find his traveling companions.

Headed towards Jerusalem, Simon was remembering Jesus' words. *Go and show yourself to the priests.*

Which priests, he wondered? Surely not Joseph Caiaphas, or any of the men in the high priest's Circle of the Friends of God.

Remembering his former allegiances, he shuddered.

Whom would he seek?

The face of his father flashed in his mind.

Journey

Yes. He would start with the afternoon prayer gathering of priests and leaders in his father's home.

It was time for real reconciliation.

It was time to build relationship.

Journey

Fresh Bread

It was mid-afternoon when Chaviel, Avishar, Ethan, and the others, arrived with Simon at Judah and Hadassah's home. During their travel that day, the group had removed bandages and wrappings from their limbs; where wounds and deformities had been hidden. On their way, they had found a place on the side of the road to burn the now unnecessary bindings.

From some unknown place in his satchel, Chaviel had produced a comb. Each man had taken a turn grooming his beard and his hair. By the time they reached Simon's parents' home, each of them had the appearance of very poor common folk; dressed in rags, every one carrying all their earthly possessions.

And so it was, when they arrived; Judah was standing in the center of the prayer gathering, answering a question, when the group walked in unannounced. Simon had asked the others to enter in front of him. The first face the old man saw was Avishar's.

"Yes?" Judah questioned the man, as the group walked into his home, like impoverished wanderers up to no good. "Can I help you? If you need food, please go around to the kitchen in the back outside. The servants will give you something to eat. Mistress Hadassah is not here today."

Avishar smiled. "He told us to show ourselves to the priests. Isn't this a priest's home?"

Judah was a little taken back. "Yes, we are priests," he said. "*Who* told you?"

"Jesus," he said, matter-of-factly, "the Healer." He paused. "We were lepers."

Joseph of Arimathea, Nicodemus, and several others stepped forward from the group.

"You say you were healed of leprosy?" Joseph asked.

"Yes, sir; it's a fact," answered Joram. He rolled up his sleeve. "Now, which one of you wants to check out my skin for me?"

Nicodemus and Joseph looked at each other. "I will," they both said together. A sort of assembly line began, impromptu in the entryway, with former lepers standing in line, waiting to be declared clean. Each one knew that declaration was the first of two steps between them and their homes and families. After this process, a specific sacrifice would be offered at the Temple.

Simon pulled the hood from his cloak back up over his head, and kept his head down. He was purposely silent during his friends' examination process. He was waiting for his father. He wanted to see the initial look on Judah's face.

Finally, it was his turn. He was the last in line.

Judah looked up at the hooded figure in front of him. "Let me see your arms, son," he said. He inspected both arms well. "And your trunk and back," he requested. Simon complied.

Journey

"Those areas are clean," the sage said. "Your legs are next, and your feet."

By this time, the other lepers had whispered to those priests examining them, informing them of Simon's presence. The entire room had stopped and was watching Judah's inspection of this last leper.

Judah spoke distractedly to the man in front of him, trying to ease any uncomfortability. "Where did you come from?" Chaviel answered the question for Simon. His voice had been returning to its healthy tone and vitality all afternoon. His voice was smooth as he spoke.

"The disease can destroy the voice, Master. I will speak for him. We have come from the settlement in Bethany," he replied.

Judah stopped midway through the process. He looked at Chaviel. "My son is there. *He* is a leper. Do you know him?"

Chaviel looked at the priest. "What is his name, Master?"

Judah took a deep breath, and let it out slowly. "His name is Simon," he sighed. "But he would not have gone with you to see Jesus."

He directed his attention back to the subject in front of him. "I need to see the top of your head, and inspect your scalp and neck now," he instructed.

Chaviel spoke to Judah. "Do you miss your son, Master?"

Judah looked at Chaviel. "So much it pains my chest. I don't know how his mother and I will continue. I think about him every day. I remember our days together when he was small. There are times….."

Judah had stopped speaking mid-sentence. His mouth hung open. His eyes were filled with tears. He was finding it difficult to breathe.

Simon had pulled back his hood, and was removing his cloak. His eyes were also full of tears. With exposed brokenness, he smiled at his father.

"Is it true?" Judah whispered, stunned.

"Jesus healed me on the road."

"Jesus – You went to him?"

Simon nodded. "We went to him as ten. He looked at us and said, 'Go and show yourselves to the priests.' And so we are here. Where else would we go? You are the best priest I know."

"Oh, my son!" Judah half-cried, half sobbed, opening his arms to envelope his son. He looked over Simon's shoulder to his friends. "God has given me back my son!"

Hugging his father, Simon cried into the man's sleeve. "I love you, father!" He paused. "I am so sorry. I was arrogant. I was wrong."

For a long moment, Judah held on. Then, pulling away, he looked deep into his eyes, assessing him.

"You are not the man I knew months ago. You have changed. I can sense it."

"Yes," came the reply. "We need to talk. I have so much to tell you."

"I can't wait to hear it," Judah answered, his eyes brimming again. "We will have time. Now we will have time."

Journey

He motioned to the other men had come with Simon. "Come and sit. We gather together to pray each day. Pray with us." He paused, looking at his friend, Joseph. "Although today might be a day Adonai has set aside for rejoicing. He has answered an old man's prayers."

Much later that day, Hadassah returned from helping a widow. Unable to sew, the woman had asked for her help in finishing new clothing for her constantly growing children. It was Nicodemus who saw her coming up the street. He went back inside to prepare the others.

In excited anticipation, Simon put his cloak and hood back on, covering his face. He stepped back into a corner, while everyone else re-enacted the inspection ritual from earlier that day.

Coming through the door, Judah greet her. "Good afternoon, wife. I invited Joseph and Nicodemus to stay for dinner."

She looked at him. His face was brighter than usual. Was he feeling all right? She decided to say nothing in front of his friends. "Do the servants know?" She asked.

"Yes, I think so," he replied. She walked by, intent on going to the outside kitchen. He paused. "Hadassah,...."

She turned, and came back into the room where he was.

"Yes?"

"I wanted to ask you something. These ten men have come to us. They were sent by Jesus, the Healer. He healed them, and they have asked us to inspect their skin for lesions."

Hadassah's heart skipped a beat. Looking around the room, her eyes fell on Chaviel. Where had she seen his rags before? She couldn't remember.

She looked at her husband. "Yes?"

"Can you help us?"

Hadassah was not sure what to say. "I am not a priest, Judah. I wouldn't know where to begin."

A voice she had known since his infancy spoke from the corner. "No, but you *are* a godly woman, Mistress Hadassah."

She sank to the floor. It *sounded* like Simon's voice. But no, it couldn't be. Her hand went to her throat. Simon would never have looked for Jesus.

In spite of her thoughts, she looked around to find him. Suddenly, he was there, wrapping her up in his arms. "I wanted to come home and tell you 'thank you' for the oil for my lamp," he said. "You know, in the basket."

"How? When?" She looked at her husband. "Why didn't you tell me?"

"I am telling you!" he replied, laughing with everyone else in the room.

Her eyes went back to Chaviel. "You were the one I gave bread to, weren't you?" she asked.

"Yes, Mistress," he smiled, "and it was the best bread ever."

"I want to know how this happened," she said. And so they sat together for the next several hours, renewing their relationships.

It was good to be alive.

Journey

Simon's friends were amazed to learn of his relationship to a member of the High Council.

"*You* are a member of the Court of the Hewn Stones? Really?" Joram asked Judah. He looked at Simon. "I thought disease and trouble weren't supposed to hit families like yours, because you are more holy; set apart from all of us. I thought you lived above all of the garbage the rest of us deal with every day."

"Many people think that," Judah told him. "But we are just like everyone else. Pain has no boundaries when it comes to the human condition."

"I thought I *deserved* to be kept from it," Simon interjected. "That kind of thinking almost destroyed me."

The room was silent for a moment. Then Judah spoke.

"Simon, I bought you a house," he said.

"You what?" his son asked.

"I bought you a house in Bethany. I think you had already left to find Jesus when I did so. The magistrate has the contracts. I don't know what we will do with it, now that you are going home."

Simon was silent for a few moments. "I don't think I will be going home," he said quietly.

Hadassah was surprised. "Why not?" She asked. "Abigail will want to know...."

"I have hurt her. I abused her. I am sure she doesn't want me," he said.

"But the children need their father!" Judah spoke assertively.

"Abigail is very capable. In some ways she reminds me of you, mother. She will be fine."

Judah looked at his son. "Are you sure you aren't being selfish in this decision? Are you resisting the responsibilities? Are you choosing wisely?"

Simon looked at his father with a blank stare.

A little frustrated, Hadassah spoke once again. "Simon, we didn't raise you to be a man who leaves his family. Your wife and children need you to step into the place of leadership. Your boys need a good example of manhood. I cannot believe you would be so irresponsible as to walk away. What are you thinking?"

There was an uncomfortable pause in the room. Those who had come to the house for the prayer gathering were sure this was a conversation that should be taking place behind closed doors. Joseph reached over and tapped Nicodemus on the knee. Should they leave quietly?

Avishar and Ethan looked at each other. Joram spoke up.

"Simon, we don't want to intrude."

Simon looked around the room, aware of the company he was in. "No, it's all right," he said. He looked at the older men. "You all knew me from the time I was a small boy." He looked at his new friends from the settlement. "Perhaps the lessons I have learned will help you."

He spoke carefully, gently. He looked at his parents. "My family; especially Abby; they don't *need* me like I was. I was raising them to become just like me. I was a terrible example." He looked at his father. "I think I will stay at the house in Bethany – for a time, anyway, until I am sure the changes in my soul are permanent."

He looked towards the window. "I don't ever want to see that look in her eyes again. I want to build her up, not tear her down. I want to nurture her, protect her, take care of her; rather than expecting her to take care of *me...*"

He looked at his mother. "Did you know I expected her to just continue the process of mothering; not the children, but – *me?* I demanded she rotate her attentions around me, fulfilling my every whim. Somehow, I thought it was my right; like she was less important as a person than I.

"When the children were born, I somehow saw them as additions to my own personal status. It made me more important to have a child; I didn't see their need to be known, or to be heard. And worse, I became angry at them for stealing her attention away – from *me.* I whined, I pouted. I badgered and criticized all because I wasn't willing to be a man. I expected her to just do more and more, without any help from me. I thought my position elevated me to a place of master – I expected to be served – continually." He paused. "Would *you* want to live with that kind of a man, mother?"

Hadassah shook her head.

"Not only that," Simon continued, "but I was never the example I should have been as a synagogue ruler. I was distant; aloof. I never involved myself in the lives of the people I was supposed to be serving. Didn't you tell me once 'a synagogue ruler is an example of Elohim to the people he serves'?"

Judah nodded. "Yes, I did say that."

"I see things differently now. Back then, I thought I was supposed to be a different image; stricter, harsher. I was my own god, in the name of serving ElShaddai."

His parents were silent. Judah realized his son was grappling with a larger issue than his leprosy had ever been. Had their constant attentions to him as a boy produced his attitudes, he wondered? With a pang, he remembered telling a friend that Simon was the center of his world.

Simon continued. "What would it look like if I became the man I am called by Adonai to become? How would Abby respond? Would it be better? I don't know.

"I do know that our lives could never go back to what they were. I don't *want* to go back there. I want to be stronger; better, somehow. I still don't know what that would look like." He paused. "I have to think. There are areas I am still afraid."

He looked at his father. "How long will it take me to grow out of this?"

Judah and Hadassah looked at each other across the room.

This was a new man indeed.

~~~~

"So, what was it like to be with Moses and Elijah on the mountain?" John asked. It was a rare moment, when he had the ability to be alone with Jesus. The question had been burning in his mind for a little over a month now.

"What do you mean, John?" Jesus responded.

Journey

"Well, you were with them on the mountain for quite a while. I watched your robes turn a bright white, and then the Voice like thunder spoke. It was obvious who they were." The young man paused. "I just wondered what it was like."

Jesus smiled at him. "It was a taste of Home for me. They are my friends."

"How are they your 'friends'? They lived so long ago, didn't they?"

"There is no time in the spiritual realm. It is eternal. It is co-existent all around us. In fact, when my creation worships, the Throne of Heaven comes wherever that worship is taking place. Abba's Presence and His Spirit are the same thing. He has no beginning, and no end. He has no limit."

"I think I understand," John said. "And you are somehow the physical representation of that Presence."

"I am," Jesus said.

"How does that relate to *me?*" John wanted to know. "How do I become a part of that realm with you?"

"When you opened your heart to my Spirit," Jesus explained, "the unseen part of you that was dead became alive. It is what I said to Nicodemus when we sat together at the Inn. That part of you went dormant, or dead, as a result of Adam's choice to disobey in Eden. Now, because you have chosen to be led by my Spirit, becoming my follower, everything changes. There is a relationship then, which begins between the newly re-born human spirit, and the Creator's Holy Spirit."

"It is the Spirit of God who speaks, teaching and reminding of those things Abba Father has said. He is the One who holds everything together."

John looked at Jesus. "What about you?" he asked. "I want to understand who You are."

Jesus smiled as he answered. "There was a time when I was equal with God. But, in that place of unity, as one; we all three knew a sacrifice would have to be made. Someone would have to serve as a Guide for the sons of man. A Pathway would have to be re-opened to the Paradise Adam was tricked into giving away.

"So, when it was time, I emptied myself of everything that made me equal with God. I wanted those I created to know that I understand what they feel; that I don't reject or judge anyone because they are weak, or less than perfect. In fact, I want to cover their weaknesses with my Strength; their pain with my Healing; their weariness with my Rest.

"I want those who invest their lives in me to be assured that I can identify completely with their yearnings and their pain."

He paused, looking at John.

"I wanted to walk with my creation in the cool of the day once again."

"So, how does this work?" John asked. "Are you *part* of God, and other parts of God are running things while you are with all of us, doing miracles, and teaching?"

Jesus laughed. "Not in the way you think. We are One, and yet we are Three; distinct, but the same. We have unity. Do you understand?"

"I'm not sure," John replied. "When you said you 'emptied yourself,' what does that mean?"

"Do you remember the night Mary broke the alabaster jar at Simon's house?" Jesus asked him. "Do you remember how the broken shell of the jar caused a fragrance to fill the room? Do you remember how the ointment poured out and ran everywhere?"

When John nodded, Jesus continued. "It is the same with my life. I have come to be poured out. The breaking of my body, and the pouring out of my life; this is the only Pathway for my Creation to come Home to me. The fragrance will fill eternity."

"So this is a rescue." John stated, making the connection.

"Yes," Jesus replied. "This is a rescue."

～～～

Moments after Judah left for the Temple the next morning, Mistress Hadassah called the house steward to the courtyard.

"Who would you send on an errand if you needed speed and trustworthiness?" she asked.

He thought for a moment. "I would send Abel," he answered. "He's young, but he's quick; and he's street-smart. He won't be delayed."

"Good. Please ready him to deliver a message for me to Mistress Abigail in Galilee. See if there is a wagon going that way we can pay. Better yet, outfit our own wagon, and send him with it." She paused. "Is he good with the animals?"

"Not yet, Mistress."

"Find someone to accompany him. Their entire purpose will be to take care of the animals. I would like them to leave within the hour. The message is 'Come to our house for the Feast. It is urgent.'"

Knowing the story of Simon's homecoming the steward smiled.

"Yes, Mistress. They will be ready to go within the hour."

～～～

In Bethany, Chaviel and Simon were working to repair the plaster on the outside of Simon's new house.

"I want as many of you to live here as want to," Simon said to his friend. "I will be living here for a time. I'm not sure when I will go home to Capernaum." He paused. "I'm not sure there is anything there for me."

"Well, it's always good to get your feet under you before you begin some new venture, I always say. This is as good a project as any to fill the time," Chaviel answered.

The particular area of the village they were standing in was new to Simon; so far removed from the settlement. It was just across the road from an extremely large home with an outdoor courtyard, as well as an indoor courtyard. Who had built such a mansion, he wondered?

On his second morning, he had been organizing his scrolls by the central window, when he had seen a familiar face walking out of the door to the huge home.

He yelled through the open window to catch the man's attention. "Tradesman! Eleazar! Good morning!"

Eleazar startled, and looked around, his eyes finally coming to light on Simon. "I know you!" he exclaimed. "Did *you* buy this house?"

Journey

"Well, it's a long story," Simon said. "I was a Pharisee; then I became a leper. Now, I am a healed leper, and not ready to go back to Capernaum yet. But, before I was healed, my father used his influence to help me obtain this house. So, here we are. It will be a home for my friends and me." He looked at Eleazar. "I didn't know you lived here. I thought your home was in Galilee."

"The fabric-trade business Mary and I began years ago is still based in Migdal. Our friend, Joseph, is our steward, and he does quite well there, living with his family. We have been traveling with Jesus off and on for the past couple of years." He indicated the large home. "This is my other sister's home. Her name is Miriam. She is a widow. Mary and I have come to stay here now; although Mary is somewhere in Jericho with Jesus at the moment."

"I thought this was a clinic at one time. Does your sister run a clinic?" Simon wanted to know.

"Not anymore. She hasn't wanted to have a practice since Abiel, her husband, died almost two years ago. Abiel was a physician," Eleazar explained. He changed the subject. "How did you become a healed leper?" he asked.

Simon looked at him. "Jesus healed me," he said. "It's hard to explain what happens in your heart when His Life touches you. It changes you forever."

"I know what you mean," Eleazar agreed. "I was bitten by a camel several months ago. I developed an infection and fever. My sisters sent for Jesus, and he was late getting here. I was in the grave for four days. Jesus called me out, and brought me back to life."

Simon looked at his friend. Two years ago he would have laughed at Eleazar's words and called him a fool.

Now?

He believed the man.

"I wonder if you could come for dinner one night this week," he said. "I would like to learn more about what happened to you," he said. "I know Chaviel, Avishar, and the rest of my friends would also like to hear your story."

"I would like that, Simon. In fact, Jesus and just a few of his followers are coming to the house today or tomorrow. They will be staying through the feast. Could they join us for dinner as well?"

Simon was overjoyed. "I would love it. It would be a chance to renew friendships." He paused. "I just have one problem."

"What is it, friend?" Eleazar asked.

"I don't have anyone to serve the meal. And I am a terrible cook."

Eleazar laughed. "I know a woman who loves to get her hands dirty. I'll ask Miriam to come over and set up the meal plans with you. Does that sound like a good idea?"

～

On the edge of Jerusalem, Justus Flavius sat on his horse, as he and another centurion reviewed the troops standing at attention. Next to him, also on horseback, was Antonius Longinus, the centurion commander for the city of Jerusalem.

"In two days," Longinus shouted, "this city will be filled with people from all over the empire. The opportunities for criminal behavior will be innumerable. You are the only protection the people have. You must be ready to do whatever is needed to maintain order. There will be a few special details chosen; worthy men who have proven themselves in the heat of battle; I will post the lists.

"It is the Prefect's tradition at this time to release one man from prison, in honor of the Jewish feast of Passover. The traditions of these people are different from our own. The religious practices of these people are different from our own. Remember that Rome is kind. The emperor allows a man to think for himself. Do not use undue force. We do not want another revolt, like the one several months ago. It took our men three days to execute all of the criminals."

Listening, Justus shuddered. He had seen the crucified corpses lining the road. It was rumored the Prefect had even gone so far as to cause one of the men to be sacrificed, alive, on the Jewish brazen altar. It had been a topic of discussion among Jesus' followers for days.

Antonius Longinus continued. "Any man who violates my orders, or the orders of Commander Flavius, will be scourged and discharged. Does everyone understand and agree to comply with these orders?"

En masse, some 300 foot-soldiers, and those who served in leadership over them, drew their right hands into a fist, and pulled them over their hearts in salute. "Hail Caesar! Hail Longinus! Hail Flavius!" they shouted in unison.

"Then you are dismissed," Longinus commanded. "Details will be posted before sunset!"

As they retreated to his quarters, Longinus invited Justus to share a meal. "Each year, I grow more and more weary of this assignment," he confided to Justus. "Each year, the execution list grows. Our ability to keep a tight grip on the people lessens."

Justus popped a grape into his mouth. "Why do you think that is?" he asked.

Antonius looked at him. "I think it is because Pilate has no understanding of what it means to govern. His solution to everything is death; death by hanging, death by crucifixion, death by sword….."

"But the people fear him?"

"Fear? Yes, they fear him," Antonius responded. "But they do not respect him. He will not serve as governor long without respect."

"It's true," Justus agreed. "My grandfather served with Julius Caesar on the battlefields. He earned the respect of his men by letting him know his life, and listening to them."

"He earned the respect of his people as well," rejoined Antonius. He paused. "Well," he said, picking up the stylus, "let's get to work on these duty rosters, shall we?"

Through the afternoon, the two Commanders worked together to place the many details of peace-keeping soldiers throughout the city of Jerusalem, and its environs during the upcoming civilian celebrations.

"There is always a crucifixion or two in the middle of these things," Longinus told him. "It is a messy detail, so I won't burden you with it. I will make sure you and your men have street duties, and lighter fare. That way, your men can still see the city; and enjoy a little of the

Journey

festival. It's really quite an experience, if it is your first time." He looked at Justus. "Do try the food from the street vendors. It's really quite unusual…. and good too."

Justus looked at the man with gratitude. He had been in battle, and had executed criminals. He was no stranger to the uglier aspects of soldiering.

But he had never crucified a man. Standing next to Longinus he had discovered something about himself.

He never wanted to.

~~~

On the road between Jericho and Jerusalem, some four miles or so from Miriam's home, Jesus and his followers had found a secluded, shady spot to eat a meal together. There were less traveling with them now than in days prior.

Jesus had told them he was going to Jerusalem. He had also been making disturbing statements lately. "The chief priests and scribes will arrest me," and "I will die, but I will rise again."

His stories had become more serious as well.

It was as though he was preparing them for something, Mary realized.

As the crowd number had lessened, she found herself walking among the people, introducing herself, getting to know different individuals. It was good, she considered, to expand your understanding; getting to know how people thought; learning from others. Somehow it made her world larger; it expanded her own heart as well.

As she walked through the crowd, now seated in various places, eating their afternoon meal, a man approached her.

"Are you Mary?" he asked. "The one they call Magdalene?"

Something about the man's manner bothered her, she realized. Cautiously, she answered, "Yes, Mary is my name. My friends call me Magdalene to avoid confusing me with another Mary in our group."

"Can I speak with you?" the man asked.

"We are speaking now," she responded.

Taking her words as a cue to begin, he spoke. "You have not seen me for a long time."

Slowly, she came to awareness. She knew this man. She appraised him. He was thin, his hair was white. The years had taken a toll on him. His skin and hands were wrinkled, and he stooped when he stood.

She looked into his eyes. He returned her gaze.

"I have been following Jesus since before Aenon," he said. "I have waited for the right time to speak with you."

Unexpected anger raged toward the surface in her. Where had it come from? She backed away from him, in recognition.

"I'm sorry," she said coldly. "I can't speak with you now." Shaken, she quickly retreated to safety; to the circle of followers, where Jesus was. She sat down quickly, trying to melt into the group. Suddenly, she wanted to become invisible.

Seeing the look on her face, Nathaniel, now seated next to her, was concerned. "Are you all right, Magdalene? Did something happen?"

She looked down at the ground. "I'm not ready. I can't face him," she muttered.

"Who?" Philip asked, drawn in to the situation by Nathaniel's attention.

"Him." Like a small child, Magdalene pointed to the man who had come up to her. "He wanted to speak with me, and I can't do it." Her eyes began to fill with tears. "I can't talk to him. I'm not ready."

"Who is he?" Philip asked her.

"What's wrong with me?" she asked. "I shouldn't feel this way….. I was so rude to him."

"Who is he?" Philip repeated.

She paused, looking at him. "He is my... my *father*." The words came out simply, honestly.

Her response had been icy. As she turned to walk away, Eleazar chided himself for his poor timing. For weeks, he had contemplated how to approach her; a small, private setting might scare her; a large, public setting might scare her.

He had come to the conclusion there was no right way to do this.

His heart yearned for connection with the days he had lost.

How could he find the right place and time to start again with her?

Or should he just give up?

Did he even have a right to ask?

He stood, watching, from the outside of her circle. As he did so, emotions long shut away; those which only emerged at EnKarem in private moments; did so once again.

Inside the circle, Mary looked up and realized that across from her, Jesus was also watching.

He spoke.

"Mary," he said. "There is a difference between forgiveness and healing."

"But Master, you know what he did to me!" she protested. "I can't go *back* there. I hadn't thought you would ask me to."

"What will you do with that relationship?" Jesus asked.

"I don't know, yet. Can't I just ignore him, and go on with my life now?" she objected. "He frightens me."

"You don't have to revisit those days *alone*," he said. "I am with you now." He looked around the circle. "We all are with you now."

"I know, but…" she stammered. "I don't know how to …"

"Don't close your heart to survive," Jesus told her. "Just guard the entryway. If you are to continue to grow, you must keep your heart open."

"Letting go is difficult," Elsbeth offered, coming to put her arm around her friend. "Ask Simon what we have had to deal with in living with my mother these days."

Mary looked at Elsbeth, not comprehending a connection. She looked at Jesus, her eyes filled with confusion. "But he's standing right there!"

Journey

"Mary." Jesus spoke her name gently; kindly, quietly. "This is no different than the room you saw yourself in the night of your deliverance. The battle you are fighting *now* is a battle with your *own* desire to get even; to be independent; to judge; to exclude." He stood and moved to the center of the circle. He lifted his arm to her in invitation.

She looked at him.

He was smiling at her. He was encouraging her.

He was teaching her; telling her to choose.

Just choose.

It wouldn't all go away, she realized. What was it he had said; *Forgiveness is different than healing.*

She considered. From what Jesus was saying; at this point, she wouldn't be able to experience personal growth if she shut her heart. This was hard; how could she even look at her father, knowing what he had done to her!

No, she speculated. She *did* want to grow; but she felt *weak*. What if the battle was not about forgiving, but about a willingness to *try* to forgive?

Jesus spoke into her thoughts. "Just begin the process, Mary. You won't be able to do it all at once. It will take time."

At that very moment, she remembered one of the stories Jesus had told almost a year prior.

There once was a wealthy king whose servant owed him a debt

of millions. It was so vast, there was no conceivable way the man could repay him. So he forgave the debt. Then, the forgiven servant had left the palace, and run into another man, also a servant, who owed him a few coins, easily repaid on payday. When the second slave had refused to pay, the forgiven slave had grabbed him by the throat, and had him arrested.

When the friends of both men told the king what had happened, the king asked the forgiven servant, "You received so much mercy from me, and yet you could not give a little to someone who had wronged you?"

The king's question had stuck in Mary's mind since that time. Each occasion she had remembered her father, or a memory of her abuse had presented itself, she had struggled with feelings of anger and injustice; and hatred.

Was Jesus saying her pain didn't matter anymore? No.

What he was offering to *her* was an even deeper Freedom.

Freedom: from the anger, the sense of injustice, the hatred; the right to be victimized. She understood. She could not move forward from this place until that inner battle was resolved.

"I can't do it all at once," she said to Jesus, rising to her feet.

"No one expects you to," he replied. "Just keep your heart open." He asked Elsbeth and Joanna to stand and go with Mary to a quiet spot where they could pray, and talk, out of the view of the rest of those who were travelling with the group.

From the other side of the field, Baruch and Leah had observed the older Eleazar's encounter with Mary. Leah had guessed her identity. Over the past year, the couple had come

Journey

to know their employer's life well. They were working with him to rebuild it. Baruch had come to stand by the older man.

"Did you get a chance to tell her?" he asked Eleazar.

"No, she said she didn't have time, and just walked away," he replied, disappointed.

"Are you sure you want to do this today?" said the younger man.

"I feel this is a good time. I prayed. I have sought God. If I give up now, I know I will go home and just give up completely." As he spoke, his shoulders sagged and his voice welled up with emotion. The memories raced forward; building the business, losing the business, Rachel's death, little Miriam and Eleazar, his losses, the unexplainable ache in his soul. He saw himself coming after Mary, telling her she was his property, telling her she looked like Rachel….. using her. Was he an animal? Why had he given in to such actions?

He was never sure if it was guilt, fear, or determination which drove him to do what he did. Abruptly, he broke away from conversation with Baruch, and moved toward the circle where Mary was now standing next to Jesus, and two other women.

His feet broke into a run. When he reached his daughter, his words overtook him.

"I didn't know," he began. "All I could see was my own pain. I don't know how to make it right. I wish I could go back and fix it. I was blind for so long." He paused to take a breath. He looked at Jesus.

"I don't care who hears me, anymore," he cried. He was weeping now. "I should never have touched you that way. I hurt you. I know I did. I didn't know then, but I know now."

He reached for her, and she involuntarily stepped back. He fell to his hands and knees.

"Mary, I'm sorry! Please forgive me! Please! I can't go on from here without that."

Stunned, his daughter watched him. It was as if she were watching what was happening from another place. Why was he doing this? Why now? Without warning, her father grasped her feet. As he did so, his tears began to wet them.

It was unusual sensation for Mary. She had never felt strong emotion towards her father before. She wasn't sure what to do. As though waking up, her heart stirred. She had always felt numb before. What was this?

She felt compassion, unexplainable and undeserved, for this man.

She looked at Jesus and remembered his words.

Forgiveness and healing are not the same thing.

I can give him that, she reasoned. It isn't nullifying the results of what he did. I don't have to trust him, or allow his opinions to rule my life again.... I just need to forgive him..... God, help me, please. I just don't want to be controlled by my Pain, or my Offense any longer. I would like to treat him without Fear, or even Judgment.

I want to move on. I need to move on.

She knelt down, and touched his back. "I do forgive you," she said, haltingly.

He lifted his head. "I'm so sorry, Mary. What can I do to make it right?"

"You can't," she said simply. "You can't make it right. We can never go back. All we can do is go from this point on. I'm not able to trust you; I don't know you. I still have to heal. We will have to learn as we grow."

Journey

"I would like that," he said. "Could we be friends, at least? Would you come and see me, in our old house at EnKarem?"

Not feeling safe enough to accept the invitation, she offered to welcome him in a place where she would have those she trusted around her. "Why don't you come with us to Bethany?" she offered. "Miriam has a lot of room, and I know they would like to see you as well. Perhaps we could go with you to EnKarem after the feast."

"I would ….. *we* … would like that," he answered, speaking for Baruch and Leah also.

―――

In Bethany, three men were having a discussion.

"Mercy can only be activated by a heart in desperation for it," Joram stated again, sitting next to Avishar. "It doesn't work unless someone realizes what it is."

"I disagree," Simon said. "Mercy is mercy whether it is recognized or not. Think about Chaviel, for instance. None of us realized *we* needed to thank the Healer until we were halfway to Jerusalem! Chaviel went back and gave thanks right away. Are you telling me that we received less mercy than he did?"

Joram grunted. "But we were *all* desperate! I can't think of one instance when mercy was just indiscriminately given."

"But, Joram," Simon contended. "Wouldn't that mean that God develops favorites?"

"I don't think so. I think God is waiting for response. That is the lesson I am coming to." He snorted. "I hate arguing with scholars."

Simon laughed. "You might be right, Joram. If it is the lesson you are seeing, I don't want to argue. I'm sorry. It's really nothing to argue over."

"It might be me," the older man replied. "Even my mother said I carry conflict within me."

"What do you want to do about that?" Simon asked him.

"I don't know," the Joram replied, now frustrated. "Enough of this! I'm going outside!"

"He is changing," Avishar noted, as they watched Joram leaving.

"Yes, he is," Simon agreed. "A little at a time…. He reminds me so much of myself… before. Always having to be right, always looking to get the last word, defending my positions; I was always working. The things I thought were God's lists of demands were the lines I allowed to define me. In the end, I avoided anything of beauty, or design. I became a very small person."

"What do you mean?" Avishar asked.

"My soul became small. And yet, as I think about what Jesus says, I am realizing God wants to have a relationship with me; a relationship that enlarges, rather than confines."

Avishar responded. "I always thought just being religious would guarantee me a happy life; but it never did. When that first lesion of leprosy was found on my body, I blamed God, thinking I had earned a better life somehow. I never even *thought* about relationship," he admitted. "Until I met Jesus."

Two days later, in the evening, Simon the Leper opened his home to serve a meal. The guests in attendance were very different from those who had been invited in Capernaum.

Journey

Chaviel, Joram, Avishar and Ethan were in attendance. The rest of the lepers who had been with them on the road had returned to their homes. Jesus, and the twelve who were now traveling with him full-time were also in attendance. Simon had also invited his father, and his father's two closest friends to come; Nicodemus and Joseph of Arimathea.

He fully expected his mother to come as well. He knew that Jesus' mother would be visiting with the women in the kitchen. He hoped they would become friends.

Lastly, the younger Eleazar had discovered that his father had been traveling with Jesus from Jericho. He stopped to visit on the way to his home in EnKarem, with a married couple in his company. So, those two men would be attending as well.

Simon had made sure to invite the man's wife to come, to spend time with Miriam and his mother.

All afternoon, Miriam and Joanna prepared the meal with Elsbeth, Leah and Mary, in Miriam's outdoor kitchen. After preparation, the food would be brought across the street to Simon's house, and served on one low table in the middle of the room. There were no individual couches, so Miriam had loaned Simon some cushions from her living space. The women arranged these around the table, allowing for the men to eat in either a reclining or seated position.

As he surveyed the room, Simon found himself comparing the space with his home he in Capernaum. How bare and sparse these preparations were, he thought! Abigail had always brought a touch of beauty to their life together.

I miss her company, he realized. *I wish I was a stronger man; she needs someone stronger than me.*

When guests began arriving, Chaviel and Avishar served as greeters, inviting them into their small abode. It was dusk before everyone arrived, and were settled. Miriam and Elsbeth began bringing in the food.

"It was good of you to invite us all to eat with you, Simon," Nicodemus said. "I am honored to be allowed to be part of such a gathering."

Judah agreed. "Thank you for including us, too, son," he said.

"I just wanted to have the opportunity to get all of the people I care about together for a meal," Simon told them. "The last time I had such a meal, the next day didn't turn out exactly the way I had planned."

"I am amazed both of our fathers know each other," the younger Eleazar spoke. "Who would have thought such a thing could happen?"

"The common thread between us all is this man," Joram spoke, pointing to Jesus.

"It's true, Master," Simon Peter commented. "You are the reason we are all together tonight."

Jesus smiled. "I think we are all here to hear Eleazar's story, aren't we?" he asked. "This little village has become extremely busy of late; especially since he has come back to us."

"It's true," Simon spoke. "Just this afternoon, Ethan counted… how many?" He looked at Ethan.

Journey

"I counted no less than twenty just today alone. People are coming into town and finding a reason to walk by Mistress Miriam's house. It's getting so that neither Eleazar nor Miriam can walk outside without being approached by someone," he said.

Nicodemus looked at Eleazar. "Are you aware that Caiaphas has given instructions regarding your life?" he asked.

Eleazar was surprised. "Why?"

Judah spoke. "I was in the High Court yesterday morning, after the session, and I heard them talking. The chief priests are trying to find a way to arrest Jesus. They are afraid his following has become too large. It is even attracting attention from Rome. Caiaphas said it would be wise to kill Jesus and save the nation from Roman invasion."

Joseph nodded. "That's what I heard as well. They are afraid of a repeated revolt against Rome."

"But why are they including *me* in their judgment?" Eleazar wanted to know.

"Everyone in Jerusalem knew you had died; from the merchants and traders in the marketplace, to the linen weavers in the north at Mt. Arbel. Jesus raising you to life after four days has drawn attention to His power and popularity. If they do away with Jesus, *and* with you, then, in their minds, the threat will be shattered as well," Nicodemus explained.

"When are they saying they might do this?"

"The word yesterday in the Court was sometime during the feast week," Joseph said.

"Then we must do something to save your life," the older Eleazar spoke quickly. "I will not lose my children now that I have found them again."

"What are you suggesting, Eleazar?" Jesus asked.

Eleazar looked at Baruch. "They could come home with us to EnKarem," he said. "No one knows me. I left the marketplace years ago." He looked at Jesus. "As far as anyone knows, I'm just an old man who used to beg on the streets of Jerusalem."

"You would have to do more than just move away," Joseph said. "Caiaphas has connections in every part of the nation. He would find you. You would have to change your names as well."

"What would we change them to?" Eleazar asked, still trying to get his mind around the concept that someone involved in God's service would want to see him dead.

"Something that doesn't sound Jewish," Nicodemus suggested. "And it would have to be something you would answer to in the marketplace; a name that wouldn't confuse those you already do business with outside of our nation."

"Eleazar," his father said, "do you remember going to the marketplace with Mary's nursemaid as a boy?"

"Yes," his son answered slowly.

"Do you remember the name the tradesmen would call me when they spoke in Aramaic, in order to trade with us?"

"I'm not sure," the young man answered.

"Well, there were two or three merchants who we dealt with in EnKarem, from other nations. In order to trade with us, none of us spoke each other's language, but we did speak Aramaic."

"I remember Clio teaching us to speak Aramaic, and Greek," Eleazar said. "We all learned, when she taught her son."

"These men translated my name into Aramaic, and each time I dealt with them, they called me by that name. Why couldn't you just translate your name to Aramaic?" his father suggested.

"That would work!" Judah exclaimed. "You would need to leave town and begin to speak Aramaic. No one would recognize you, then. At least until this threat blows over."

There were parts of the conversation Miriam did not hear. She had gone across the street with Elsbeth to bring back meat and bread for the rest of the meal. Coming in the door to her home, she saw Mary seated on a stool.

"Mary," she said, "don't you want to come over and join us?"

"Yes, I do." Mary looked at her. "The last time Simon had a dinner party, I broke my alabaster jar at Jesus' feet."

"Why?" Elsbeth wanted to know.

"It had come to represent everything I had failed at becoming," Mary told her. "I wanted to pour all of it out at Jesus' feet, and begin something new."

Miriam looked at Elsbeth. "Our father told us it represented our mother, and how perfect she was. He told us the alabaster was the color of her skin. He wanted us to remember we had something to live up to." She looked away and stood, remembering.

"You remember too?" Mary asked.

"It troubles my thoughts more than you know," her sister answered. "I would like to get rid of the guilt and torment I feel. Every time I look at that jar, I want to scream; *'I will never be as perfect as her. I'm not good enough!'*"

Mary was amazed to hear the thoughts she herself had battled with, coming out of her sister's mouth. "But you always have everything so under control," she objected.

"It's not real, Mary. In truth, I feel driven to achieve and prove myself all of the time," she admitted. "You are the strong one."

" No, not me," Mary replied. "I wish you could see what I feel like on the inside."

Miriam looked at Elsbeth, who had returned with the meat tray. "Go on ahead of me, Elsbeth," she instructed. "We'll be right there."

Before going to the kitchen to take hold of the bread, Miriam went to her room. She returned with a small gray bag, tied with a silken thread. She handed it to Mary.

"Here," she said. "I want you to do with this what I cannot. I heard how you washed his feet that night. Eleazar told me. I am not brave enough to invade that room of men. I could never do what you did. Would you pour this out for me?"

Mary didn't know what to say. "I can never worship *for* you, Miriam."

"I'm not asking you to," her sister replied. "I will be worshipping as I watch what you do. Help me with this, please. Please."

Arm in arm, the sisters walked silently across the street to the home of Simon the Leper. As they walked in the back door, Miriam picked up the meat tray, and moved into the room. Mary walked into the central room, holding her sister's alabaster jar of spikenard.

Once again, she stood behind Jesus at his feet. This time, she dropped to her knees before she began. This time, the seal to the jar broke easily.

So orderly, she thought, *just like Miriam.*

Looking up, she saw Miriam watching her, standing with a serving tray on the other side of the room, tears streaming down her cheeks.

Jesus turned around to face Mary. She poured the perfume into her hands and began to rub it into his feet. As she did, the fragrance of the spikenard oil began to rise and fill the room.

"I thought she did this once already," Thomas spoke quietly to John.

"It is the way she worships Him," John responded. "I have not seen anyone else do this. It is Mary's style."

"But it is so extravagant a gift," Thomas replied. "That little jar held at least a year's wage."

Eleazar, the younger, was mouthing something to Miriam. "Whose jar is it?" he asked.

Pointing to her chest, she mouthed. "Mine." Then, "Can we talk later?"

He nodded.

Mary had finished rubbing the oil into Jesus' feet. She stood now, as he remained seated, and poured more of the oil out, this time over His head. It ran down, mingling with his hair and beard, ending on his neck and shoulders.

As Simon the leper watched, he realized he was being given a second chance to understand vital Truth.

There could be no real worship without a breaking open.

To really worship was to begin life anew.

The picture of Mary lifting up the jar and bringing it down hard to shatter it open flashed in front of his mind.

He remembered Jesus' words in his home at Mary's first expression of worship. "He who is forgiven much, loves much."

Silently he prayed. "Oh God, help me to love much. Please forgive my condition. As you forgive me, fill me; heal me. Help me understand your ways."

Judas, the Iscariot, thinking he would find agreement in the room, raised his voice. "Why would you let a woman waste such an expensive ointment like this, Master?" He looked around. "It would have been better if she had sold it and used the money to feed the poor."

There was silence in the room for a moment, as the contrast between Judas' words, and Mary's broken expression spoke for itself.

Mary had knelt back down now. She was pouring what was left of the oil on Jesus' feet. The excess, she began wiping away with her hair.

Jesus looked at him, and spoke in an even tone. "Judas, leave her alone. The poor will always be with you. Someone will always have a need. But this… This is Mary's expression of worship."

He looked at her, and then at Miriam. He continued.

"She has anointed my body beforehand …. for burial."

Two nights later, Joseph Caiaphas paced the living area inside his palace. Sitting at a table nearby were several members of his Circle of the Friends of God, including his father-in-law, Annas. His servant, Malchus, was standing in the center of the room, waiting for instructions. Caiaphas was muttering to himself.

"We have the means now," he was saying. "But I don't want to arrest him until we have everything in line." He looked at his father-in-law. "We can't afford any slip ups."

"I know," Annas agreed. "Did you see the support he had from the crowd yesterday? It was unbelievable! They treat him like he is some sort of King or something."

Caiaphas sneered. "That will be his crime: 'King of the Jews.' His actions today tied it for me."

"What did he do?" Malchus asked carefully.

"That's right, you weren't back yet," his employer responded. "Do you remember when he first came to the Temple? Do you remember how he overturned the money-changing tables? We had animals running everywhere. It took me over a year to convince the merchants they would be safe doing business with the Temple in the Gentile Court once again.

"Well, today, he did it again! He pushed over the tables. He chased the merchants and the animals out of the court again. He said we had made the Temple into a den of thieves. He totally undermined my authority, and I will not be treated this way.

"You remember how we had worked to make it easier for the merchants to bring their goods in, by coming in through the back entrance? Well, today, he would not allow anyone to carry anything through the other Courts."

Malchus was baffled. Why would anyone want to arouse such anger in Joseph Caiaphas? Wasn't Jesus aware of what a dangerous man the high priest could be?

Joseph continued his pacing, using a mocking tone. "'My house shall be called a house of prayer for all nations,' indeed," he fumed, quoting Jesus' words. "I pulled the Circle of Friends in here, so that we could find a way to arrest him, but when we went back to enforce our plan, the Court was full of people, there was nothing we could do. They were all listening to him teach.

"It seems the blind and the lame, and every other misfit in the city had decided to rush up to the Court of the Gentiles to see Him. 'He teaches with such authority, Caiaphas;' 'He has to be the Promised One, Caiaphas;' 'Don't you just love him, Caiaphas;'" He groaned. "I am so sick of this man getting all the attention! He had the nerve to actually heal people today; *without following the Ritual Laws!!*"

Journey

He stopped pacing and looked at his servant. He had been struck with an unanticipated thought. "Did you find any witnesses?" he asked.

Malchus looked down at the ground, shuffling his feet. He felt the breath of his employer close to his face. He looked up and saw the raging heat in Joseph's eyes.

"Well?" Caiaphas threatened.

"Uh, I have been following their group, Master," he began. "You said I should go to the places where he broke the Laws. So, I went to the leper's house. They are very willing to admit that Jesus touched a leper."

"So what's the problem?" the high priest demanded. "Bring the witness back here!"

"I have to produce a *leper* in order to make the story viable," Malchus told him. "There is no leper he touched who is still a leper."

"What about the dead girl? The one in Capernaum?"

"She isn't dead anymore. He raised her... *and* the young man in Nain."

"What about that woman, the one bleeding for twelve years?" Caiaphas insisted.

"She is strong, and healthy, and working; and no longer bleeding." Malchus paused, assessing the safety of continuing his explanation. "Master, this is a great problem."

"You think so?" Caiaphas asked, sarcasm dripping.

"Well," his servant went on, "I have traveled everywhere Jesus has been in the past three years. I have been unable to find any person whom he has *made* sick, or caused *to become* blind. In fact, everyone seems better off just to have known the man. Are you sure he's a criminal?"

Caiaphas turned swiftly. Malchus did not see the shadow before it hit his head this time. After the first blow, he covered his head with his arms, and bowed down as far as he could go to the ground to protect himself.

Caiaphas was shouting now. "He *will* be arrested. He *will* be stopped. I will have his blood before the end of the week!!" He stepped back from Malchus, panting, and raised his finger to the man's face. "You had better be careful which side you choose, Malchus," he warned, intimidating. "It might just decide whether you live or die."

He shoved his servant towards the door. "Now get out of my sight!"

―――

Under the cover of darkness, Joram, Avishar and Ethan labored with Simon and Eleazar to load a wagon full of goods. As the house began to empty of personal effects, Miriam and Chaviel worked to transfer foodstuffs from the larger home into Simon's house.

"Would you like the cooking pots as well?" she whispered to Simon on her way across the street.

"I have nothing, Miriam. I would be grateful for anything you want to give me."

"Keep the cushions and the lamps, then," she said. "I am leaving the food and the dishes as well. Oh, here are some teas for treating illness. They are still marked with Abiel's writing. You will use them more than I will."

"Are you sure, Mistress?" Simon asked.

"I am sure. Thank you for saving our lives."

Journey

"You're welcome. Thank you for serving at my dinner," the man responded. "Can I ask you a favor? My parents have summoned me to come to their home tonight. Do you think you and Eleazar could give me a ride for a part of the way?"

Eleazar joined them. "Well, we're loaded. Do you have everything, Miriam?"

"Let me take one more walk through the house to be sure," she answered. She looked at Simon. "I found a pair of Mary's sandals. Would you see she gets them?"

"Certainly," Simon replied. "I don't know when I will see her. Peter said she was staying with them for the time being, while you both got away."

"That reminds me, as soon as we get into the wagon, Joseph says we must begin using our new names," her brother told her.

She looked at him, trying to remember.

"Our Aramaic names," he reminded her. "What was yours?"

She paused momentarily. "Martha," she said. "And you're Lazarus."

Two hours later, Chaviel was awakened by the angry sounds of men pounding on the locked doors of the home across the street. Fiery torches lit the midnight sky. Receiving no answer, threatening visitors pounded began on his own door.

Joram opened the entry. "Yes? Can I help you?" he asked.

"We are looking for the man and the woman who live in the house across the street."

Chaviel stepped to the doorway next to Joram. "This is Simon the leper's house, sir," he said.

"A leper's house?" the man echoed. "You live with a leper?" he asked, looking at Chaviel.

"Everyone who lives in this house used to live in the settlement, my lord." Chaviel answered truthfully. "Now we live in this house. As for the man and the woman, I think they moved away."

"Where are they now?" one of the soldiers asked, as the group moved away from the two men, assuming they were still full of leprosy.

Joram shrugged. Chaviel again answered. "I don't exactly know," he said.

Frustrated and angry, Caiaphas' guards returned to the Temple.

Chaviel and Joram breathed a sigh of relief.

That had been a close call.

~~~

Judah and Hadassah sat on the rooftop of their home in Jerusalem, looking at the stars and discussing the day's events. They had been sitting in silence for a few moments.

"He has been teaching in the Temple courtyard every day this week," Judah said.

"What happened today?" she asked.

"A crowd has gathered every day to hear him. He had a lot to say this afternoon about the condition of the ruling class in the Temple."

Hadassah was interested. "What did he say?"

"Beware of the leaven of the Pharisees."

"Just like that? So plain?"

Journey

"Exactly like that," Judah responded.

Hadassah considered. "It's a good illustration, really," she said. "That attitude puffs a person up, and fills them full of air. Not only that, but it grows, and makes the loaf bigger than it was at the beginning." She stopped. "How would you get leaven out of bread?"

Judah shrugged. "I don't know, wife. You are the baker."

She smiled. "Was there more?"

Judah sat forward and lowered his voice. "He spoke to the rulers, who were standing around listening. He said, 'Beware, scribes and Pharisees! You keep all the outward laws and you don't care about the condition of the inside of your hearts. You are blind guides, leading the blind. You have left the most important parts of the Law behind, in your ambition to be seen. On the outside you look good, and everyone thinks you are holy; but on the inside you are full of rottenness and dead men's bones. You are full of extortion and excess. You are hypocrites.'

"He said, 'You have killed the true prophets. You are a generation of poisonous snakes!' Then he told the crowd, 'Be careful about trusting the scribes and Pharisees. They like to walk in long robes, and be given special treatment. They like receiving honors for doing nothing. But they make a show of praying to God for long periods of time, when they really deceive themselves. They don't really know God. They steal from the widows and orphans, and make it look like it was the right thing to do.'"

Hadassah was stunned. "Does he realize he is saying these things in the very center of Joseph Caiaphas' center of operations? Did Joseph hear him?"

"Oh, yes," Judah nodded, looking out over the city. "He heard him, and then called another meeting of his Circle of Friends. And as soon as Joseph left the Court, Jesus went to observe those who were donating money in the treasury."

"Why?"

"I think he wanted us to get another lesson about the heart. There were all these people there, each one in line. As each turn came, different people put in different amounts. You know how it works. A priest walked up with a really large purse, and emptied it. You could see there were gold and silver coins in the bag as he dumped it. A rich landowner stepped up behind him and gave another large purse. Then, an old widow hobbled up to the bin. Very slowly, she pulled out two coins; together they didn't even equal a half shekel.

"Do you know what Jesus said? 'This woman gave more than anyone.'

"More than anyone?" Hadassah repeated.

"The he explained. He said, 'She gave all she had.'"

A call came from downstairs. "Hadassah?"

Hadassah stood and went to the side of the house. "Abby, come on up!" she called.

As Abigail made her way up the outside stairs to the roof, Hadassah went back to her seat next to her husband. He looked at her incredulous.

"Abby?" Judah asked. "*Abby?* You sent for her, didn't you?"

"Yes, I did," she looked him in the eye. "David will be a man next year, and he needed to be here for the feast, at least that's what I'm going to tell his father."

"Hadassah," he began, "you know how I feel about parents who meddle with their children's lives."

"I'm not meddling, Judah," she answered. "I'm just creating an opportunity, that's all. If God brings something good to pass, it will be because we gave Him an opportunity."

"God can do things all by Himself," Judah told her. "He doesn't need a woman to help him."

"So you say," she replied, smiling. She directed her attention to Abigail. "Come and sit with us Abby. Did you bring the children?"

"You told…. Uh…" Abigail looked at Judah. "No. I didn't bring them."

Judah looked at his wife. "Hadassah! Now, you're lying to me?! This is not how I wanted to see this happen... I'm not sure it is a good idea to press Simon. What has happened in his heart is real, and lasting. We must give God time."

"Well, God will have to work a little faster now," Hadassah answered nervously. She wrung her hands and looked at Judah. "I'm sorry, I was trying to help. I have been so excited about the changes in him. I couldn't wait."

Judah nodded. "Knowing you, he will be showing up at the door any moment." He looked at Abigail. "She is notorious for this kind of thing, Abby. Don't let yourself be pushed or prodded."

Hadassah looked at her husband in mock hurt. "Why, Judah, you know that I would never…"

She was cut off by the sound of Simon's voice on the ground floor. "Mother? Father? Where are you?"

Judah answered, frowning at his wife. "We are up on the roof, son. Come on up."

They listened to the sound of Simon coming through the house, out the back door and up the stairs. In the shadows created by the night, he didn't notice the third figure sitting with his parents, just behind the arbor wall. He went to his mother first.

"Hello, mother. I got your message. I'm sorry I'm a little late. I was helping some friends move."

Judah spoke. "The friends we ate with the other night?"

"The very ones."

"Did things go well?"

"Better than we planned."

"That's wonderful. I'm proud of you, son."

For a few moments, Silence hung in the air between them. Finally, Simon spoke.

"I'm here. What was the urgent situation that needed my attention?" Simon looked at his father. Judah shrugged. He then looked at his mother. Hadassah looked back at Judah. She answered.

"I'm really sorry, Simon," she began. "Your father says that I have too much to say sometimes. I think this is one of those times."

Judah looked at the shadowy figure of Abigail on the seat behind Simon's standing figure. "What do you think, Abby?" he asked.

"Abby! Did you bring Abigail here?" Simon turned around, looking for his wife.

Abigail stood, looking at him, not knowing what to say. "Hello, Simon," she said shyly.

At a loss for words, Simon gazed at her. "Hello, Abigail," he answered.

She is still so beautiful, he thought, even after five children.

"Well, now that introductions are completed, I think I need to go downstairs and cook something," Hadassah announced, as she stood to her feet. She looked at her husband. "Would you like some tea, Judah?"

Grumbling, Judah stood. "I think you manipulated this whole thing, Hadassah, and I want you to stop doing things like this. God can work on his own. He doesn't need us to get in the way. Besides that, you lied to me. You told me my grandchildren were coming."

Hadassah smiled. "I said I was sorry. I'll try not to do it again. And I didn't lie! All I said was….." Judah interrupted her.

"I know what that means," he groused, going down the stairs. "You'll just be more *careful* the next time. I told you Simon wasn't ready. *He* told you he wasn't ready. Did you listen? No, not to me…."

"I know, Judah," she answered. "Can we just let them see if they even *like* each other anymore? I'll make you something to eat. Come on. I said I was sorry…."

Simon and Abigail could hear his parents' voices continuing, as they moved farther and farther away, into the house. They looked at each other and laughed.

"You came for the feast without the children?"

"I came because your mother sent me an 'urgent' message."

"What did she say?"

"She said, 'come to our house for the feast; it is urgent.'"

"Oh."

There was silence for a moment or two.

"How are the children?" he asked

"Good. They miss you."

"How are things at the house?"

"Good. Things are good."

More silence. This time it lasted long enough for the quiet to deepen the awkwardness between them.

"Abby," Simon started, and then paused.

"Yes?" she answered.

"Nothing," he said.

More silence followed.

He looked down at the ground.

She found the stray threads on her tunic, and bit at her cuticles.

"What were you going to say before?" she asked.

He sighed. "I have all these things in my heart and mind I want to say to you. My heart is so full, but then the words become lost somewhere before they reach my tongue."

"I know what you mean," she said. "I have so many questions, but I'm afraid to ask them."

"Why?" he asked.

She paused. "Do you really want me to tell you?"

He pulled back. "I think so," he said slowly."Go ahead."

"I'm afraid of you" The words hung in the air. There, she had said them; finally.

"You are?" he asked, surprised, although he inwardly knew he shouldn't be. "Why?"

"I'm afraid of your anger, your sarcasm; your judgment. I never can do anything right. You fix my words. You correct me like I'm a child. You never listen to me, and worst of all…." Her voice trailed off.

"Worst of all, what?" he asked.

"No, it will make you angry," she answered.

"Abby, look at me," he said. He moved next to her, and took her hand. He lifted it to his lips and kissed her palm, and then the back of her hand. He spoke, his voice husky with emotion.

"I've been so wrong, Abigail. I have treated you poorly. I have injured you, and abused you. God gave you to me as a precious gift, and I only thought about how I could use you for myself."

She started to speak. He lifted his finger and put it on her lips to quiet her. "I'm not done. I know we have a long way to go. I was waiting to come home because I wanted to be sure that my heart had really changed; that I wasn't in some sort of temporary dream phase because the leprosy was gone. I didn't want to come home the same man I was….before."

As he was speaking, her eyes had filled with tears. Hearing the words she had been desperate to hear him say, had released a wave of emotion from her heart.

Seeing her tears, he put his arms around her and held her. At his touch, she collapsed into tears, sobbing hard; releasing years of pent up anger and emotion. Perceiving the depth of her pain caused the wells of his eyes to fill also, spilling onto his cheeks.

After long moments, she pulled away. "I got your sleeve all wet," she said, trying to straighten the fabric.

"I don't care," he answered. "It will dry."

"Now," he said, continuing the conversation, "worst of all, what?"

She giggled, blowing her nose. "I was going to say 'you never hold me, or touch me, or pursue me.'"

"Well," he said, "apparently *that's* changed. I was afraid what I was experiencing was temporary. I wanted to make sure I had really learned something from all this."

"We could find out together, couldn't we?" she asked. "I have been learning lessons also."

"Do you think you could put up with me again?" he said.

Her eyes filled with tears again. "Oh, Simon, I've missed you so much. I was so selfish. I had shut my heart away.

Journey

"When I was cleaning, I found this little piece of stone from Mary's alabaster jar. You know the one she broke at our house that night. Jesus words kept coming back to me, "He who is forgiven little, loves little." I needed to open my heart to God's love; not just for you, but for everyone."

She pulled the stone fragment out of her pocket and showed it to him.

She continued. "I was so closed off and angry. But then, Jairus, and Gedalia, and even Julia Flavius showed up at our door. You should see our house, Simon. I am amazed at God's provision."

"I want to love much; I want to live my life bigger than I have." She flung her arms open, and almost knocked him over. "Oh, I'm sorry," she said, pulling back, instinctively expecting a reprimand or reprisal.

Instead, her husband laughed.

"You are so excited! I love seeing you this way; alive and animated! He pulled her to him and kissed her. "Let's talk awhile," he said.

"Talk?" she repeated. "I would love to!"

They spent the next several hours, beginning a new adventure; learning what it meant to spend quality time together, experiencing deeper relationship than they had ever known in their marriage before.

Knowing and being known.

New Wine

The sun was just peeking through the shutters in Eli's room in the Essene Quarter. The old man opened his eyes sleepily and stretched, waking up.

It was quieter here than in the rest of the city. Only the monks and their families lived here. There were no horses, no merchants, no hawkers. It was a peaceful place.

Eli had enjoyed his stay over the past few months. In the beginning, he intended to stay for his grandson's birth, and return immediately to Qumran, but Ezra, the overseer for the Essene Quarter, had asked him to stay. Would Eli help to organize areas, training and instructing younger men in the ways of their sect? Would he keep his old friend company for a while?

"So many of these younger men have new ideas," Ezra had confided in his friend. "Sometimes I would like to have someone closer to my own age to talk to, even if it is just for a short time."

After checking with his superiors in Qumran, Eli had been given permission to stay. Today marked seven days before the time was completed. He would leave just after Passover.

His tasks had lessened as of yesterday. The young men he had been training in interpretation and communication skills had finished their course of study. For the rest of his time in the Quarter, his time was relatively his own.

He went through his morning rituals a little slower this morning. It was good to be able to take his time, he thought. He should probably look for Ezra, to see what help he could be in the preparations for the feast day. Had the meat been purchased, he wondered?

Walking across the compound, Eli looked up and saw his old friend coming toward him. "Good morning!" he said.

"Good morning, Eli," Ezra responded. "Did you sleep well?"

"Yes. I don't know if I will be able to settle back into desert life, after getting used to the wonderful breezes up here."

Ezra nodded. "Where are you headed now?"

"I was coming to find you, actually, to see if there was anything I could do to help with preparations for the feast," Eli explained.

"I can't think of anything," the older man said. "Most of the families will be eating in their own homes this year. Has anyone invited you?"

Eli shook his head. "No, but that's all right. I might see if my daughter could take me in." In the Jewish culture, the upcoming feast was a holiday! This month was the first month of the New Year. The feast marked a family day; the beginning of a new season!

Journey

Eli smiled as he considered. ElJireh had commanded Moses that each family would feast, and then stay in their homes, waiting for the Angel of Death to pass over their house; leaving each one alive. It had been the beginning of sacrifice as a nation as well. Judgment had not come near them, because their homes were marked with the Blood of a Lamb.

The next morning, they were free men, and a nation had been born.

Over the centuries, it had become yearly tradition after the feast for families to draw together, telling stories, laughing and talking; celebrating the goodness of their God.

Eli considered. He would enjoy holding his grandson tonight.

"I will go by her home later today, and see if they have room for me," he said. The Jerusalem overseer nodded. "That would be a good idea." He paused. "I am working on cleaning the Great Room for our next meal and gathering together. Would you like to help me?"

"Surely," Eli responded. "What do you need?"

"Can you draw water to wash the floor?"

―――

In his normal administrative manner, Philip was working through the details for the feeding of those who would be in their group that evening. "I'm not sure where we will be able to find a place large enough for all of us tonight, Master," he told Jesus privately. "I have checked all over. The city is packed."

Jesus smiled. "Abba knows what we need, Philip. He brings people into our pathway at the right moments." He looked around the group. "Peter? John? Can I see you a moment?"

When the two men came where he was, Jesus gave instructions. "I want you to go and get the room ready for all of us to eat the Passover feast together."

Simon Peter and John looked at each other. "Where are we going, Master?" John asked.

"When you go into Jerusalem, you will see a man coming towards you. He will be on his way back to his home from drawing water. Follow him to his house. Go into his house after him.

"When you are in the house, ask to speak to the overseer of the house. When he asks you what you need, tell him: 'The Master asks to use your Great Room, to eat the Passover with his followers.'"

"Does he know you?" Simon Peter asked.

Jesus didn't answer. He continued. "They will show you a large room in the Upper part of the city. It is already furnished. Make preparations for the meal there."

"We will leave right away," John answered.

Less than an hour later, two men followed Eli home from the well. Arriving at the gate to the Essene Quarter, he turned to look at them. "I can see you are following me," he said. "Was there something you wanted?"

"The Master said we would find a *man* with a water-pot, and he would lead us to an overseer," John told him.

Eli looked at them strangely. Something inside of him was stirred at the words, "The Master."

"Who is your Master?" he asked.

"Jesus," Peter answered, "the Healer. We have been traveling with him for the past three years."

Eli looked at them, and turned back towards the house. "Come with me," he invited. Arriving inside the Great Room, he called to Ezra.

"Ezra! There are visitors here to see you."

From the back room, Ezra entered. "What is it, Eli? Did you call me?"

"I said," Eli raised his voice, "'there are visitors here to see you!'"

Coming into the room, Ezra saw Peter and John. "How can I help you?" he asked.

"The Master asks to use your Great Room, to eat the Passover with his followers."

Eli watched as his mentor responded. "You are standing in the Great Room." He paused. "Who is your Master?"

"Jesus, the Healer," they replied.

Ezra smiled. "I prayed he would come here." He looked at Eli. "I think Jesus is the One we have been waiting for."

Eli's heart skipped. His mouth dropped open. "The Promised Deliverer? Here? I have prayed every day to not miss Him when he comes."

"I think he is the One," Ezra repeated. "All the prophecies point to him." He looked at Jesus' two followers. "What do you need? How many of you are there?"

~~~~~

That evening, Judah and Hadassah opened their home for those who had been traveling with Jesus, and weren't one of His twelve leaders. Mary, Zebedee and Salome, Elsbeth, and Jesus' mother, Mary, found themselves welcomed into the priest's home, along Simon's friends from Bethany.

There was no need to invite Simon. He hadn't left his parents' home since the night he had reunited with his wife, Abigail.

~~~~~

As the twelve entered the Great Room for the feast, they were greeted with a surprise. Jesus was standing just inside the door. He lifted his arms to them in greeting.

"Welcome to the Feast!" he greeted them, smiling. "Come and eat!"

~~~~~

In the Jerusalem garrison, Justus Flavius and Antonius Longinus reviewed the duty rosters for the next day.

"The day of the feast, there is always some sort of trouble," Longinus warned. "Make sure you get a good night's sleep tonight."

"What type of thing happens?" Justus wanted to know.

"This religious feast is a celebration of some sort of victory for these people. It has something to do with Egypt," Longinus told him. "It is supposed to be their birthday as a nation; so all their patriots and rebels come out of the woodwork. I guarantee you there will be a hanging or a crucifixion before tomorrow is over."

~~~~~

Journey

It was just a piece of bread; flat and round; not raised. It held no leaven. Jesus had picked it up moments after the door had slammed.

Every eye had turned to the Master. Judas Iscariot had just stormed angrily out the door. Jesus dipped bread into a bowl of sauce with Judas, and told them Judas would betray him. Then, the Master had apparently sent the man on an errand, saying, "What you have to do, do quickly."

It was just a piece of bread. Jesus raised it over his head and prayed the traditional prayer of the Passover celebration. "Blessed are you, O Lord, King of the Universe, who brings forth bread from the earth!"

"Amen," the chorus rang around the room.

Jesus took the bread and tore it apart, handing a piece to each of them. As he did, he spoke. "This is what my body will look like. It will be broken – torn; bruised for you. I want you to have a part in it. Eat."

When they had each eaten their portion, he picked up a cup of new wine. Celebrating the Passover, he lifted it up over his head as well, and said, "Blessed are you, O Lord, King of the Universe, who brings forth fruit from the ground!"

"Amen," the chorus again rang around the room.

The Healer took a drink from the cup and passed it to each of them. As he did, he said, "Drink all of this; it represents my Blood. It will be poured out – for you. It will reverse the power of sin."

"Later when you look back on this night, take bread and wine like this. Let it represent my body and my blood. Remember me."

Peter and John looked at each other. Jesus had been saying a lot of things like this lately, telling them he was preparing for his death. He had explained the visions of the prophets of old to them, and explained the end of days. He had given them specific instructions for living their lives. He had told them he would be going away, but would send a Comforter to replace himself.

It was James who broke the silence. "Jesus, if you are going away soon, who will you be leaving in charge?"

The question was not intended to begin a war between the men, but it did. Old fights resumed. Who was the greatest? Who had changed the most? Who deserved more recognition?

As debate became disagreement; disagreement became argument; argument became dissension and division; no one noticed Jesus rise from the table. Accusation, Anger, and volume overpowered the atmosphere of the room.

Eli and Ezra, who had stayed to serve the meal, watched and listened in bewilderment.

"Boys!" Jesus shouted over the dim. He placed a wooden stool on the floor in front of the table, in the center of the room. Looking, the twelve men were shocked at his appearance. He had removed his tunic, or over garment, and stood in a simple toga, looking like a servant. In one hand he held a basin full of water. In the other, he held a rag. Tucked into his belt was a rather large towel.

Journey

"What is he going to do?" Thomas whispered to his neighbor.

"James, would you take off your sandals and come and sit on the stool, please?" Jesus asked. He looked around the room. "Would each of you take off your sandals?"

Sheepishly, James removed his sandals, and moved towards the stool. As he did so, Jesus began to share. "When people who refuse to serve God want to show who has more power, and who is first, they use intimidation and Fear. They hold things over people's heads. They make people pay. They like to be called 'boss' and given authority."

The Master knelt down in front of James, and began to wash first one foot and then the other. He continued speaking.

"It is not to be this way with you. The one who is the greatest among you will be the one who takes the lowest place and is willing to serve."

"Thomas, would you come?"

As James rose from the stool, Jesus embraced him, and prayed. James was visibly shaken when he returned to his seat.

Jesus continued sharing as he bathed Thomas' feet. "Who is the most important or the most necessary?" He continued. "Is it the one who sits down to eat, or is it the one who serves the meal?" He looked at Eli and Ezra.

"I was considered the most important tonight, but I am doing the work of the lowest house slave."

After praying with Thomas he said, "Andrew, would you come?"

"You are the ones who have stayed closed to me through everything. The Kingdom has been given to me, and I am giving it to you. I want you to eat and drink with me at my table from this point onward."

And so it went, until there was only one man left in the room with dirty feet. Jesus said, "Simon Peter, would you come?"

Simon Peter reacted. His hands went up in front of him. "Why would you want to wash *my* feet?" he said.

"You won't understand it fully right now," Jesus said. "But you will later."

Peter responded. "I don't want you to wash my feet. It is not your job to do this. I can't let you serve me like that."

"Peter," Jesus spoke. "Do you realize that if I don't cleanse you, wash you; remove from you the dust that tries to keep you from unhindered relationship, you will have no part with me? You won't come to a full awareness of who I am, or what I am doing."

Slowly, the reality of the potential consequences for his resistance dawned on him. He would be counting himself out, throwing away his relationship with Jesus, just because of Embarrassment and Pride.

"Master!" he cried. "I want to be part of everything you do." He was getting up, and moving to the stool. "Please. I understand now. You are talking about my life; my heart. Don't just wash my feet. Wash all of me!"

Laughing, Jesus said, "Just sit down, Simon."

Journey

Then, as Jesus was finishing his task, Simon Peter spoke. "Lord I would follow you anywhere. I would do anything for you."

Jesus stopped what he was doing, and looked his friend in the eyes. "Simon," he spoke evenly, "before the rooster crows on the third watch, you are going to deny that you even *know* me; not just once, but three times."

Close to an hour later, in the Court of the Gentiles, Joseph Caiaphas was making a speech. For the past hour, a mob had been gathering, in response to his summons. Runners had been sent runners through the streets of Jerusalem, just after the Passover meal had ended in most homes. The messengers knocked on the doors of everyone and anyone who owed the high priest a favor, or had a petition pending. It was time to call in the debts of those who had borrowed his kindness.

As they reached each house, the runners were instructed to knock. When the door was answered, the runner said, "The high priest has an emergency, and wants to see you."

Within an hour, a group of a hundred or more had gathered. Within two hours, the number was more than could be counted. At the appointed time, dressed in his full regalia, Prince Joseph Caiaphas stood on top of a bench to address the crowd.

"Brothers!" he began. The crowd began to still and turn towards him. "Brothers! I have something of great concern that affects the welfare of not only your home and your family. It threatens to destroy the very fabric of our nation. If we do not act quickly, and tonight, we each could lose everything."

A murmur swelled through the crowd. What was his concern? This must be a real danger indeed. He was continuing.

"There is a faction which has been growing in our midst. It began small and harmless enough, but now it has concerned even the courts of our Roman overlords. Have you not noticed the extra troops moving through our city this week? Those are men who have been assigned to quell this faction, should they try to bring a revolt against our conquerors.

"We know that from the days of Judas Macabbee, our God has allowed us to continue as a nation. He has protected us. He has placed men in our Temple Court to serve as benefactors, and guides, to keep us from losing our ability to live. They have given us wise counsel, and helped us to avoid the temptation of destroying our nation with revolution. We have maintained."

"You are the one who has ruled us well, Caiaphas!" someone in the crowd shouted. Caiaphas smiled and motioned with his hands for the comments to be held down.

"Thank you," he said. "I appreciate your trust. Having said all of this, I must warn you the leaders of this faction are at this very moment *here*." He paused. "They are here in Jerusalem."

"Let's do away with them!" a response was shouted.

"Help us!" another shout was heard. "What do we do, Caiaphas?"

The high priest had more to say. "I do not want *all* of their leaders; not yet. I will be happy if we could just apprehend their instigator. Once we pull that peg, the entire tower will

Journey

fall. Please understand. I don't want you to think I am a bloodthirsty man. I am just concerned for the wellbeing and safety of our nation."

"Where are these rebels?" one of the merchants shouted. "Let's go get them now!"

"I have one of their group right here," Joseph pulled Judas Iscariot forward, stationing him in front as he continued speaking. "He has agreed to help us. He has seen the error of his ways, and has made an agreement with the High Council for thirty pieces of silver. He will lead you.

"I cannot go. I wouldn't want this arrest to be misunderstood as a political move. It needs to be seen as an action taken by citizens who are loyal to our Roman overlords.

"Once you have the insurgent in hand, bring him back here to the Temple for questioning. Keep him under guard. Then you can go back to your homes."

Temple guards began to hand out unlit torches, which were then lit by those who held them, from wall torches on the Temple wall. With swords drawn, the stirred-up mob left the Court of the Gentiles, to find the nameless rabble rouser who would bring destruction to their lives.

In Gethsemane, Jesus knew they were coming. He had gathered his followers around him. He had said good-bye. He had prepared his friends for what was approaching.

He was in prayer.

~~~~

On the rooftop at Judah and Hadassah's home, the women sat in conversation.

"Where are Miriam and Eleazar, Mary?" Jesus' mother asked. "I was sure we would see them here."

Magdalene smiled at her. "Nicodemus and Joseph of Arimathea saved their lives. Apparently the high priest wanted both of them dead because of Eleazar's resurrection. They have gone back to our childhood home with our father."

Mary was surprised. "The home we've talked so much about since we met?" she asked. "Did you say *your father*?"

"That's what I said," Magdalene responded. "It is taking time, but healing is coming. You know, I wasn't even aware of my need for it. I would have lived like that forever."

"We all would have," Mary agreed. "I am making a journey of discoveries of my own."

"Like what?" the younger woman asked.

"Like what it really means to really let go of control," Mary answered; "Like choosing to trust when I don't understand, or when I have less than all the facts."

Magdalene laughed. "It must be the same journey I'm making. There is a part of me that is developing each day. I am finding out no matter how old my body might be I am still a child on the inside. When I bring that child to Adonai, to Jesus, that is when growth happens in my heart."

"Those are pretty deep thoughts for such a young mind," Mary replied.

"Jesus has been the answer to my pain," Magdalene said, smiling. "As I... we.. have travelled with him, I have realized. Each time something would happen I didn't like; each

Journey

time I would experience rejection, the temptation to become self-centered and full of pity would be there.

"Before my deliverance, I didn't choose. I just let my feelings run wild, tearing me apart. In fact, I had hidden the child-like part of myself. I covered it for years with other things; clothing, business, reputation, money, sex, success." She looked at Jesus' mother. "I thought that child got in the way of an image I was supposed to become."

Mary nodded. "But that was who you really were?"

Magdalene smiled, and agreed. "Exactly."

It was the third watch of the night before the servants in the high priest's palace were allowed to retreat to their own rooms that night. Malchus had been unable to change his clothes since the incident during the arrest. His entire shoulder and neck had been covered in blood. Now it was caked to his arm.

Caiaphas had not allowed him to change.

"People need to see that," he told his servant. "Let them know what kind of people we are dealing with here."

"But, I'm fine now," Malchus had protested.

"That doesn't matter," Joseph countered. "Besides, I need you to attend to this man. Make sure he doesn't try to escape."

Standing in front of a basin of water, Malchus worked to scrub off his own dried blood.

What was the name of the Galilean who had cut off his ear? It was Simon; Simon Peter. That man had been ready for a fight.

It was a good thing Jesus stopped him. He would have been dead for sure, Malchus thought.

He couldn't remember much of the arrest. Iscariot had stepped up to greet Jesus, and kissed him on the cheek. "Who do you seek, friend?" Jesus had said to the mob.

"We want Jesus of Nazareth," one of the mob declared.

Jesus smiled. "I am – he." Malchus remembered a shockwave of power coming out from Jesus as the words were spoken. He had felt as though he was punched. Others had been knocked to the ground also.

Jesus had repeated the question. "Who did you say you are wanting?"

"You heard me," the same man yelled. "We want Jesus of Nazareth!"

"I am the man you are looking for," Jesus said. "If it's me you are wanting, let these others go."

The servant of the high priest didn't remember much after that. He had seen Simon Peter's upraised arm, and something glittering against the torchlight. A searing pain had raged through his head. He screamed in shock and anguish.

"My ear! You idiot! You cut off my ear!"

Before anyone had time to do anything, Jesus dropped down to the ground, and picked up the ear. As he placed his hand on the side of Malchus' head, healing his wound, he turned his head and spoke to Simon Peter.

Journey

"Put the sword away! This is the not what we are here to do! Once you begin using a sword to make a way for yourself, you will have to keep it up until the day you die!"

He looked at the Temple guards. "Why didn't you arrest me in the daylight?" he asked, as they bound his hands. "I have been there teaching every day. But then, this shows who you really are. You would only come in the power of darkness."

Malchus watched Jesus the rest of the night. He listened to Annas' interrogations. He watched the officers strike him, drawing blood, causing the man's eyes to swell up.

Annas had sent Jesus, still bound, from the Temple to Caiaphas' palace. As they stood outside, waiting to be summoned by the high priest, the servant had observed a conversation taking place nearby, at the fire-pit.

"You have a Galilean accent!" a kitchen maid was saying. "You are one of Jesus' followers!"

Amazed, Malchus saw the face of the man who had cut off his ear. "No," he said. "You have me mixed up with someone else," the man contended.

Seeing the girl standing by the fire, two Temple guards joined them. Hearing Simon speak, one of them said, "I think he was with Jesus in Gethsemane."

Again, the man denied it. "I don't know what you're talking about," he said.

The second soldier spoke up, getting closer to Simon Peter. "No," he said, gazing intently at the fisherman. "I think you're lying to us. You *were* with him."

Looking from the girl's face, into the eyes of the soldiers, Simon Peter felt the beads of sweat forming on his forehead and neck. Terror seized his heart. He did not want to be arrested; or die. He began to curse. He yelled at the soldiers.

"Damn it! I told you I don't know the man! Who the hell are you to tell me who I know and don't know, you bastard! Leave me alone!! I've had enough of this….."

In the middle of his tirade, a bird's trumpet call was heard, announcing the end of the night season. A lone rooster was crowing.

Simon looked around him. Had anyone else heard the sound? Had it been real?

Looking for an exit plan, his eyes fell on Malchus.

Then he stopped. Next to Malchus, Jesus stood. Their eyes met.

What was it he saw in the man's eyes, Malchus wondered? Whatever it was, it had disturbed him.

The man who had healed his mother-in-law, had mended nets with him, had walked on water with him, had stopped the storm, had healed him…

This man had known what he was capable of doing.

Judas had betrayed Jesus to be arrested, Malchus thought. That had been an open act of treachery. But, to Judas' credit, what *he* had done was transparent; a visible act, plain and simple. His motivations were easy to see; money and self-preservation.

But this man, he considered? *His* treachery was hidden; secretive; subversive; silent. Malchus had seen that type of treachery many times within the Temple walls. No matter his personality or appeal as a man, the servant considered, Simon Peter had less consistency or

Journey

dependability as a friend than Judas. With a man like this, you wouldn't see the betrayal coming until the heat was on.

Simon had denied any involvement; any knowledge; he had betrayed his own identity. He had lied to save himself.

Looking into the eyes of His Master was apparently more than the fisherman could do. Filled with remorse and self-pity, Simon Peter ran to find another place within the city where he could be alone.

~~~

It was a good four or five hours later when Malchus saw Jesus again. Sometime close to daybreak, Joseph Caiaphas met with his Circle of the Friends of God, in the central courtyard of his palace.

The men who gathered for prayer at Judah's house were not invited.

"There are enough of us to pass judgment," Caiaphas declared.

Jesus was led before the Council, to be questioned. This would be the first of many such inquisitions that day.

"Are you the Promised Deliverer?" Caiaphas demanded. "Tell us!"

Jesus looked him in the eye and answered. "If I tell you I am, you won't believe, will you? If I ask you a question, you will not answer me; nor will you let me go."

Caiaphas laughed, sneering at him. "Are you the Promised Deliverer?"

"After this, I will be seated in the place of power at Abba's right hand."

"Then you are saying you are the Son of God?"

"You say that I am," he replied.

"We don't even need witnesses, now," Caiaphas looked at his Circle. "He is condemned by the words coming out his own mouth."

Caiaphas passed sentence that very moment.

The high priest's temple guards blindfolded him. They began to play a game. As they hit him with a stick, they would say, "Who hit you? Can you prophesy? Come on and tell us, Jesus. Who hit you?"

Malchus watched those he worked with as they spat and beat Jesus until he was black and blue. Some grabbed his beard, pulling chunks out by the roots. His face was bleeding and swollen.

When the "trial" was over, Caiaphas summoned Malchus from the corner, and instructed him to put Jesus in the lower dungeon; the torture chamber he had paid to have constructed many months prior.

By that time, the servant had decided he no longer wanted to work in the Temple. This wasn't how he had seen himself serving his God. After securing Jesus in the dungeon cell, he went to the well to draw fresh water. He carried it down the stairs.

"Jesus?" he said quietly. He could see the man lying on the stone bench protruding from the wall.

"Yes?" came the reply. How could he still speak, with no trace of anger, or discouragement? Malchus wondered.

Journey

"Would you like some water?" he offered.

"Thank you."

Malchus entered the room. He shuddered as he looked above his head, and saw the observation gallery, and the round hole for hanging in the ceiling. What would happen to this man?

"I wanted to say…." He paused, and looked to make sure no one could hear him. "I wanted to tell you 'thank you' for healing my ear."

"I'm glad I could help you," came the reply.

By six in the morning, just after dawn, Jesus stood before Pontius Pilate, the Roman Prefect. He was again awaiting judgment. Finding no reason for sentencing in the man, realizing his popularity, the Pilate wanted to delay a decision as long as possible.

He sent the man across town to be questioned by King Herod.

However, by the half of eight in the morning, Jesus was brought back to Pilate for sentencing. Malchus had waited for him at Herod's court. What was it about this man, he wondered? Why were they all so angry? What had he done?

Herod had given his officials one of his many splendid robes to use in some sort of mock ceremony. As Herodias and her daughter watched, Jesus was punched and kicked by the king's soldiers. Malchus heard Herod tell his wife that it was a good way to become friends with the Roman Prefect.

She laughed. After all, wasn't this man a cousin to the prophet who had condemned their marriage several years prior?

Now, standing in Pilate's court once again, Malchus was weary. He couldn't imagine what the condemned man must be experiencing. He looked around. He had never seen such a crowd. How many were here? Two thousand? Three?

Caiaphas' mob from the night before had moved through the throng, stirring them up, instigating a demand for execution.

Afterward, Malchus was cleaning out the cell in the lower dungeon, when he came upon a discovery. He noticed the stains of Jesus' blood on the stone bench, and began working as usual to scrub the stone clean. For the first time in his experience, he was unable to remove the blood stains from the stone.

Oh well, he thought, and stepped away.

He never knew what drew his attention to look at the wall again. But suddenly, he was stopped in his steps. There, in the stone, etched in bloodstains, was an image, almost like an artist's rendering.

It was the face of Jesus, the Man who had been lying there.

What was it he had heard the man tell Caiaphas?

"Even the stones will cry out…"

He had to get away from this place, he decided.

Journey

At daybreak, close to the half of five, Judah and Hadassah were awakened by a pounding on their front door.

Judah sat up from his sleep. "Did you hear that?"

"What?" Hadassah turned over, and covered her head.

The pounding came again; this time accompanied by Nicodemus' voice. Judah moved quickly to get to the door and unlock it. Nicodemus pressed his way in.

"What is it, Nicodemus? We are not due at the Court for a couple of hours?"

Breathless, Nicodemus entered, and leaned against the inside of the door, shutting it. He looked at Judah.

"They arrested him."

"Who?" Judah asked, alarmed.

"Jesus." Nicodemus followed Judah as he moved back towards his bedchamber.

"Caiaphas did?"

"And his mob. You know how persuasive he can be."

"When?"

"Just after the feast last night."

"What?" Judah couldn't believe his ears. He paused to think. "So the Death Angel has passed," he said.

They stopped at the door to his bedchamber. "Hadassah is still sleeping," Judah told his friend. "Wait here. I'll be right back." Hurriedly, he dressed. This morning's Court would be a difficult session if Jesus were on trial. He put on his headdress.

Hadassah sat up when she heard him come in. "What is it, Judah? Why are you up so early?"

"Caiaphas has arrested Jesus," he told her.

"What?" Hadassah was amazed. "How?"

"I don't know yet. Nicodemus is here, and we are heading to the Court early to see what can be done. I'll send you a message." He moved to kiss the top of her head. "I love you."

Absently, she kissed him back. "Love you too. I'll see you tonight…" She moved to get up. "The women will want to know. Simon will want to know."

The two friends moved out of the gate and into the street. As they walked towards the Temple, Nicodemus spoke. "The streets are empty. Have you noticed? And it's silent as well."

Judah shivered, although it was not cold. They were crossing the marketplace. Usually the vendors began their sales before daybreak. Today, the streets were bare. "Something isn't right," he said.

"Judah," Nicodemus began, "what did you mean before; 'the Death Angel has passed'?"

"I was reading last night, after the feast. The women were on the roof, talking. We had read the story of the Exodus as part of our meal celebration, you know. Well, before I went to bed, I felt drawn to read some of the passages regarding the Promised Deliverer in Isaias' scroll."

Nicodemus looked at his friend. "What did you learn?"

313

Judah began to quote what he had read.

"Who has believed our message? To whom has the Lord revealed his powerful arm? My servant grew up in the Lord's presence like a tender green shoot, like a root in dry ground. There was nothing beautiful or majestic about his appearance, nothing to attract us to him. He was despised and rejected— a man of sorrows, acquainted with deepest grief. We turned our backs on him and looked the other way. He was despised, and we did not care.

"Yet it was our weaknesses he carried; It was our sorrows that weighed him down. And we thought his troubles were a punishment from God, a punishment for his own sins! But he was pierced for our rebellion, crushed for our sins. He was beaten so we could be whole. He was whipped so we could be healed.

All of us, like sheep, have strayed away. We have left God's paths to follow our own. Yet the LORD *laid on him the sins of us all.*

"He was oppressed and treated harshly, yet he never said a word. He was led like a lamb to the slaughter. And as a sheep is silent before the shearers, he did not open his mouth. Unjustly condemned, he was led away. No one cared that he died without descendants, that his life was cut short in midstream. But he was struck down for the rebellion of my people. He had done no wrong and had never deceived anyone. But he was buried like a criminal; he was put in a rich man's grave.

"But it was the LORD's *good plan to crush him and cause him grief. Yet when his life is made an offering for sin, he will have many descendants"*

There was silence between the two priests as they walked the rest of the way to the Temple grounds.

Finally, Nicodemus broke the silence. "Our Friend is going to die today," he said.

"Yes, I think so," Judah replied.

Arriving at the Entry gate, they took note no one was on duty. Nicodemus looked up and saw the young priest, Saul, walking across the courtyard.

"Saul!" he called. "Where is everyone? Do you know what time Caiaphas will convene the Court?"

The young Pharisee crossed the distance between them quickly. Apparently he was on a mission of some importance. "They met just before daybreak, at Master Joseph's palace," he told them. "I thought you knew. Weren't you here?"

Judah and Nicodemus looked at each other. "No, we didn't know."

Saul looked at them, surprised. "Annas and Caiaphas held an early Council. Prince Joseph's entire Circle was there. They arrested that carpenter from the Galilee area."

"Where is he now?" Judah asked.

Saul shrugged. "They left here awhile ago, to take him to the Prefect. The last I heard, Pilate was having him scourged."

"So he will be released, then," Judah spoke up.

Saul shook his head. "No, I don't think so. Prince Joseph is intent on getting rid of him." He walked away, intent on his task.

Walking through the courts on the Temple Mount, they came across a man, huddled in a corner, silent and afraid. Looking a second time at him, Nicodemus recognized Malchus, Joseph's servant and assistant.

"Malchus," he said. "What's wrong? Why are you here…. Like this?"

The man looked up at him with red rimmed eyes. "I am responsible for this. It was me."

"Responsible for what?" Judah wanted to know.

"He is innocent. I know he is; and the Master is going to have him executed."

"Caiaphas has worked to get rid of innocent men before," Nicodemus said. "Why it is different this time?"

"This man," Malchus whimpered. "His blood left an image on the dungeon wall; an image of his face!"

The two priests looked at each other. They would have to see such a thing.

Malchus continued. "He healed my ear! He picked it up like it was nothing, and plastered it back onto my head! And look!" He pulled back the hair on the right side of his head to show them. "It's completely healthy! And he did it while he was being arrested! Who does that?" His hands went to his head.

"I've been sitting here thinking. Where did I go wrong? When did I become so concerned about men like Caiaphas? When did I become so deceived that I feared man more than God?"

Silence hung between them for a moment. Malchus looked at them. "Who is he? Do you know?"

Judah sat down next to Malchus. Nicodemus pulled up a stool from a gate nearby to sit down on.

"What do you know?" Judah asked. "That would give us a beginning place."

"I was sent to spy on him for Master Joseph. I have spent weeks on end following him over the past two years. I saw him heal people. I have heard his stories, and his teachings." The servant looked at Judah, distraught. "I liked him."

Judah observed Malchus' attitudes, and felt the sincerity of the man's words. "He healed my son from leprosy," he said quietly.

"Who is he?" Malchus repeated the question.

"We believe he is the Promised Deliverer," Nicodemus said.

"The One sent to free us from our oppressors?" Malchus asked. "Does Caiaphas *want* us to stay under Rome's rule? Why does he want Jesus dead?"

"I don't think Joseph believes Jesus is anything other than a threat to his own position and authority," Judah answered. "But don't miss the point here. The Promised Deliverer was prophesied, not just as the Deliverer for our people, but for *all* peoples; *all* nations; *all* colors. He was promised for all of mankind."

"What about Rome?" Malchus asked. "The Romans have no oppressors. They *are* the oppressors."

"It's not that kind of oppression, Malchus. That is where my misunderstanding was as well. The oppression is on the inside of man, not the outside. The oppressor is the Deceiver; the Tempter; the source of Evil."

"Can I see this oppressor?" Malchus wanted to know.

"Only in the actions and attitudes of others," Judah replied. "Jesus taught that. We can see what is in the ruling place in a person's life, by looking at how they live their life."

"So, by keeping the Law; going to synagogue; feeding the poor? Is that what you mean?" the servant inquired.

"It's not as much about what we do," Nicodemus said, "as it is about who we are." He looked at Judah. "It is possible to be under oppression inside, and still try to do all the right things."

"What does it feel like?" Malchus asked. "When you have oppression?"

"I never felt like I was good enough," Judah answered. "I was afraid of God. I found myself doing everything based on that fear. I was afraid of disapproval. I was afraid of people's responses. I was afraid of failing. I thought God expected perfection from me; and I was discouraged because I could not give it."

"I feel like that all the time," Malchus said.

"So do most of us," Judah replied.

"Jesus came to show us how to have relationship with God." Nicodemus said. "He told me once that he would be lifted up to die. He said that no one would be able to take his life; that he was going to lay it down willingly." He paused. "I didn't understand, but I'm beginning to now."

The three men were silent for a short time, each one deep in thought. It was Judah who spoke first.

"If Jesus *is* the Passover Lamb, and I believe He is; then he would have had to be thrown into Caiaphas' hands first. The betrayal would have had to come from that corner."

"Why do you say that, Judah?" Nicodemus asked.

"Well," the sage answered slowly, "over time, we have come to depend upon ourselves more than upon the Spirit of God. We have developed patterns that describe God, without His Presence actually needing to be there. We have depended more on our rituals and traditions than we have on experiencing fresh mercies every morning. We have added to the Law by creating oral traditions and requirements. It has become a substitute for what God originally intended for us. It is a religious spirit."

"A *religious* spirit," Malchus repeated.

Judah continued. "Elohim is the Only Living God. We are his people; and we have allowed the religious spirit to deceive us into substituting our own ideas for his. As a result, we have become as lost from relationship with Him as the pagan nations around us."

"How do I get rid of it: this religious spirit?" the distraught man questioned. "I can sense that what you're saying is true."

Journey

Nicodemus reached down to help him up. "Open your heart; as deeply as you can. Be honest with yourself and with God. If you are full of pride, admit it. Ask him to help you. Listen for His Spirit to teach you. He will."

"Something else," Judah added, rising to his feet; "For me, it is helpful when I am willing to admit the struggles I have inside myself to another person as well." He looked at Nicodemus. "We have a group who meet to pray in my home most afternoons."

"I would like to pray," Malchus said. "I've been afraid to even try to talk to God … until now." He paused. "Where were you going when you stopped to talk to me?"

Judah and Nicodemus looked at each other. "We were coming to the Court for the day, but now….."

"Would you go with me to see what has been happening to Jesus? I feel so guilty. If I hadn't informed, or looked for the witnesses…." His voice trailed off.

Nicodemus put his arm around their new friend. "What is happening to Jesus is bigger than you, Malchus. Besides, you didn't know. You thought you were doing the right things. You were driven to gain Caiaphas' approval. That Fear is a terrifying master to serve. It drives a person to do things they would never do otherwise."

"We are *all* equally guilty," Judah told him. "You know this. Without a sacrifice, no one is good enough."

A small group clung together just inside the Fortress of Antonia, Pilate's judgment hall. They had come into the city together in the early morning hours, and had followed the crowd from the Temple to the Fortress.

The groans of the tortured man coincided with the strikes of the lashing being inflicted upon his body. The Roman Lector was well trained; skilled in the art of torture. He could scourge, whip, stretch or flay a man to the edge of death, without actually allowing him to die.

When scourging was ordered, the tool the torturer utilized was called a *flagellum*. It was a larger tool than most he carried. From its wooden handle, three or four leather straps emerged. Glass beads and bits of iron were threaded onto each of the straps, creating lumps along the surface.

As a man was beaten, not only did the straps inflict stripes, cutting into flesh; but the added implements bruised the tissue layers below the surface, many times softening it so much that it fell apart like chopped meat in the marketplace.

The small group huddled as one. There were shockwaves created when each groan was heard. These were taking their toll. Without realizing it, all those who had come to observe, were shaken. They could no longer compose themselves.

When would it be enough?

No one could live through another tearing; another ripping; another bruising. How was the man still standing, they wondered?

He was now standing in a pool of his own blood.

Journey

Many had left the scene, too disturbed to remain. Some had returned to Pilate's Court to wait. Surely the man would be released after such a beating.

In the corner, John, Simon the leper, Magdalene, Mary, and several others were the only ones remaining of the man's huge following.

They looked at each other in shock.

It had to be over soon. Then what would they do?

~~~~

In a pompous flourish, Joseph Caiaphas entered the Court of Hewn Stones, with a few of his lesser priests.

"Malchus!" he called. "Come here, I need you!"

He looked at those in his Circle. "We did it! That insignificant detail is now dealt with… we can get on to the business at hand. What cases were we to discuss today?"

Two of the priests went to fetch the records. He dispatched another to fetch food. He rubbed his hands together. "I'm so hungry, I could eat an entire loaf of bread!" he exclaimed. "Go and get us something!"

The high priest looked down at his shoes. "Oh, look," he said, "I have blood on my sandals! I will have to get Malchus to clean them again."

Abruptly, there was an eerie movement in the room. Were the walls shifting, he wondered? Then a low rumble issued from just below his feet. Was it an earthquake?

The lamp in the room seemed to grow lighter. Was the room getting dark? Was it a sudden storm?

Caiaphas moved to the window. The wind was blowing in a stronger manner than he had ever seen before. The trees were bending! Some had broken in two. Debris was flying through the streets. Where had such a destructive tempest come from?

Looking at the sky, he realized the sky was getting darker. But wasn't this the middle of the day?

"Master Joseph, come quickly! Come quickly!" One of the priests he had sent on an errand was yelling.

Joseph Caiaphas followed the sound of the voice. Just as he would have passed by the entrance to the Second Court, the Holy Place, he stopped. The sound of ripping fabric could be heard. What was it? He moved inside to see.

There, sitting in the middle of the floor, was his father-in-law, Annas. Next to him were Gamaliel and Joseph of Arimathea. They all watched as the 3-inch thick, many-layered, embroidered Curtain, called "the Veil," began to tear apart.

Joseph of Arimathea would say later it was as though two unseen hands were pulling it apart.

As it shredded, a Light with no source emanated from the Most Holy Place. In Moses' day, the source for that Light had been the Ark of the Covenant; the Mercy Seat of God. In Caiaphas' day, the Mercy Seat had been absent for some time. Rituals had continued, without the Power; without the Presence of God; without fire or cloud.

Where was the Light coming from, Caiaphas wondered?

Journey

His peers looked at him, questioning in their glances; although no words were spoken.

Suddenly, Joseph Caiaphas found it difficult to breathe.

He stormed out of the room. Some things just couldn't be explained; that was all.

On the hill, just outside Jerusalem, several thousand people stood watching a man die between two criminals. As the ground began to tremble, and the sky turned dark, many ran to their homes in terror.

"It is God's judgment on us!" one woman cried, as she bundled up her children.

Mary Magdalene looked behind her, hearing the woman gather her children. Who would bring such small children to a crucifixion, she thought?

She looked back toward the crosses.

Jesus had spoken only a few words. She kept hoping he knew they were there. It was said that some men became delirious when hanging on a cross. He seemed to be having trouble getting his breath.

"Father, forgive them," he moaned. "They don't know what they are doing."

How could he even get words *out*, she wondered?

The spikes had been driven into his wrists. There was also one long nail pinning his feet down. She had watched as the Roman soldiers had worked to dislocate a few bones in order to force his feet stay in place.

It was an ancient Persian form of execution.

It was horrible, she decided.

She looked around her.

Dazed and weary, the small band remained.

Jesus had been hanging there so long.

They only crucified the lower class of people, she thought. And yet, Pilate had ordered a sign up over his head; King of the Jews.

The wind was picking up again. She pulled her overwrap around her.

"He's dying," Zebedee said. He and Salome had found them in the crowd this morning, and had stayed with them. "Did they give him something for the pain?"

John looked at his father. "They tried. He wouldn't drink it."

"What was it?"

"A vinegar and wormwood mixture; there might have been some myrrh in it as well. They put it to his lips, and he turned his head away." The son paused. "He told us he wouldn't drink anything from the vine, until he drank it with us again."

"Was he meaning in the after-life?"

"I don't know, father."

Numbly, they watched. Dully, they prayed; hoping for a miracle.

But none came.

"He helped others!" one of the ever-present skeptics heckled, laughing. "Look at him! He can't even help himself!"

Journey

"Yeah," a woman laughed, "Why don't you just come down here and made everything all right – *if* you're who you *say* you are!"

~~~

It was sunset before Antonio Longinus returned to his quarters in the Fortress. Justus Flavius had been off-duty for several hours.

Taking off his sword, and his shoes, Antonius sat down across from him. "It was quite a day today," he said.

Justus did not look up. "Yes, quite a day," he answered quietly.

"Your man Atticus was a real help today, Flavius. I appreciated him getting that foreigner to carry the Galilean's cross. Your men did well. I am going to include a commendation in my report to Rome."

"Thank you," Justus answered, still quiet.

Longinus sat down by him. "What's wrong, man? Have you not eaten? Did you get bad news?"

Justus lifted his head. "One of my best friends died today," he said.

Longinus nodded. "I understand. I'm sorry. Did he die here in Jerusalem or back home?"

"Here," Justus answered, looking down again at the floor.

"Oh," Longinus walked across the room and took two wooden goblets. He filled them with wine. Looking through the provisions on his table, he pulled out loaf of bread. He tore the loaf in two, and began preparing two plates of food. "Come and sit with me, at least. You'll feel better if you eat something."

Unfeeling, Justus rose and came to the table. He sat down across from Longinus, who began to speak.

"In all my years, I've never seen an execution quite like the one we saw today. I've never seen that many people, or that much blood. And, until today, I thought it was against the law to scourge *and* crucify a man. I thought the rulers were supposed to choose."

Justus looked at him. "It still *is* against the law."

Longinus took a drink of his wine. "You know, that one man; the one in the middle; what was his name?

"Jesus." As Justus spoke, his voice broke.

"Oh," said Longinus, tearing a piece of bread. "Was *he* your friend?"

The Capernaum commander nodded. "He was a Healer. He healed my servant. He raised my friend's daughter from the dead. He healed several lepers that I know. He...."

Longinus interrupted him. "He raised someone from the dead?"

Justus nodded.

"I knew there was something about him. You should have heard the things he said from the cross. He gave out forgiveness. He asked a man to take care of his mother. It was like he was looking out for people." He paused. There was one thing he said I didn't understand; garbled, you know....Then he said, 'it is finished,' like he had completed some sort of job or something." The centurion paused to take bite of his food.

Journey

"Anyway, usually I have to break a man's legs so the lungs collapse. That way they die before sunset, and the birds don't get to them. Some of the men don't do it that way, but I hate going back the next day and seeing places where the vultures have had their fill."

Justus shuddered. Longinus continued, his mouth full of food. "This man was already dead when I went to check him. Just before, he had said, "I'm giving my spirit into your hands." I thought he was talking to one of his group that stood there all day. But just after he said it, he let out a long yell."

"I wanted to be certain he was dead, so I took my spear, and opened up his side. It's important to be sure the lungs have really stopped working, you know. It's more merciful, really. I wouldn't want to be buried alive, would you?"

He swallowed his mouthful.

"Anyway, I told my captain 'this man must be the son of God!' When the spear hit the lungs, a fountain of blood and water came rushing out of him. It went everywhere."

"Is that unusual?" Justus asked

"It's never happened before; at least not to me." He paused. "I left my men there to finish the burial detail."

A knock sounded on the door. Justus rose to answer it. "Go ahead and eat, Antonio," he said. "I'll get it."

When he opened the door, Justus was greeted by a young messenger, dressed in the regalia of Pilate's court. "Commander?" the messenger said.

"Yes," Justus answered, not remembering the message would be for Longinus. He took out his hand and took the sealed scroll.

The young man put his fist to his chest and saluted, then walked away. Closing the door, Justus looked at Antonio. "It's a message from Pilate, I think," he said.

"Go ahead and read it," came the reply. "Are you going to eat your meat?"

"No, I'm not really hungry."

Longinus moved Justus' plate in front of himself, and continued eating. Justus opened the message and read.

"We have both been summoned to come to Pilate's palace."

"Why?"

"It doesn't say."

"Let's go then. Let me just clean up a little."

When they arrived in Pilate's court, the two officers were ushered immediately to the throne room. Pilate looked up from the scroll he was reading. He rolled it up and gave it to the scribe who stood by him.

"Yes, that is what I wanted to say. Make sure you include the extra details I told you."

"Yes, sire," the scribe responded.

Pontius Pilate looked at the men before him. "So, Longinus, I'm sorry to call for you. I know you've had a long day." He looked at Justus. "Who is this?"

"My name is Justus Flavius, sire. I serve Rome in Capernaum. My men and I were summoned as support for the Passover detail."

Journey

"This has been a nasty business," Pilate commented. "At least it will be over tomorrow." He looked around the room, and raised his hand to indicate a man in priest's robes standing just to the left side of the *bema*, or judgment seat where he sat.

"Longinus, this is Joseph of Arimathea. He is a wealthy man; well respected in the city. He has asked for the body of Jesus, the Nazarene. He wants to take care of the burial requirements for us. He will need help getting the body down."

Longinus and Flavius looked at Joseph. "We will see to it, my lord," Antonio answered.

"There's more," Pilate said. "I also called you here because we have a small complication. Caiaphas has yet again managed to put a fly in my ointment. He has 'requested' that we set a watch on the tomb for three days. It seems this man said he was going to rise from the dead or some such nonsense. I want you to seal the tomb and set a watch. Rotate the men if you have to. I know they are all tired after the week." He paused, thinking.

"That's all," the Prefect finished. "You can go."

As Justus and Antonio turned to go, they heard him speak to his assistant. "I asked you for water and a towel."

"I brought them to you, sire," the assistant responded.

"I know. I used those. They are soiled now. I need *another* basin of water," Pilate commanded. "I need to scrub my hands again."

"Yes, sire. I will do whatever you say. But if you keep washing your hands, you will rub them even rawer than they already are."

"Don't presume to tell me what to do, man!" the Prefect angrily replied. "Who are you to tell me if my hands are clean or unclean? I have to get this blood off of them!"

Outside the palace, the three were met by another priest. He was waiting in a wagon. "What did he say, Joseph?" Nicodemus asked.

"He gave me the body," Joseph answered. "But these gentlemen have been asked to seal the tomb and guard it."

"I have myrrh and aloes to anoint his wounds and prepare him for burial, here in the wagon," Nicodemus told him.

"It will take a huge amount," Joseph said, with a sad sigh. "How much did you bring?"

"About a hundred pounds," came the reply.

"That might be enough," Joseph answered. "We had better hurry. Nightfall is coming."

~~~

Three days later, just before sunrise, Mary Magdalene and Mary, the mother of Jesus, made their way to Joseph's garden tomb. "Surely they will let us anoint his body," they told each other. "What should we do if no one is there? Who will break the seal and move the stone?"

As they neared the path leading to Joseph's garden, both women were unexpectedly knocked to their feet. The ground was shaking again, this time with more force and power than either of them had ever seen. Below them, the earth roared, thundering.

Was the world coming to an end?

Journey

Just beyond where they were on the path, a flash of lightning lit up the sky.

"Did you see that?" Mary asked Magdalene.

"Yes." She answered. "Where did it come from?"

"I wondered that too. It didn't come from the sky."

Both women broke into a run. As they entered the clearing in front of Joseph's tomb, they stopped in astonishment.

The great flat stone, some six feet in diameter, had been rolled away from the door. Who had broken the mortar seal?

Around them, on the ground, looking as though they were dead, were five Roman soldiers.

However unusual, these were not the things that drew their attention.

Sitting on top of the stone, to the right of the open doorway, was a young man. He was clothed in a blazing, white garment. He shone with a piercingly bright light. It emanated from him and enveloped him. It moved as he moved.

And yet, they observed, he was real.

The young man looked at them, as though they had been expected. He smiled. "He is not here," he announced. "He is risen -- just like he said."

"What did you say?" the older Mary asked him.

"Come and see." The young man indicated the open doorway to the tomb. "Go in, and see the place where he was laid."

Not exactly sure what they should do next, the two women looked at each other. They would have to pass this glowing figure in order to go through the door.

The older Mary took the lead. Taking Magdalene's hand she led them through the doorway. Was it authentic? Magdalene watched the young man, to see what he would do.

He seemed to be enjoying himself.

He watched them as they passed. He smiled at them.

Entering the grave, the two women were greeted by two more young men in glowing white garments. Both were sitting on the bench where Jesus' body had been placed the day after the feast.

Was it brighter in here, the older Mary wondered? Where was the Light coming from?

Who were these men, Magdalene questioned? They carried the same Light and Substance with them she had encountered the night of her deliverance.

Were these *angels*, then?

She couldn't stand up in this atmosphere, she realized. She fell to her knees. So did the other Mary.

The angel sitting on the head-plate spoke, looking directly at Magdalene. "He is not here," he said clearly. "He has risen. Look here. This is the place where he was."

The second angel, sitting at the foot-plate, looked at the older Mary and smiled. "Go and tell the learners -- and Peter --- He is going before you to Galilee," he said.

Journey

What? The women looked at each other, and walked out of the tomb. Upon their exit, they were greeted by Salome, Elsbeth, Joanna, Abigail and Hadassah. Each woman was carrying a bag of myrrh and spices.

"Good morning!" Hadassah said.

"What are you doing here?" Magdalene asked.

"We came to anoint the body. We've decided we will unwrap him if we have to," Salome spoke.

"It's not here." The older Mary spoke with a new conviction.

"What's not here?" Salome asked.

"The body; it's not here." Mary looked at them as she repeated her words.

"Did you see the angel?" Magdalene asked. "He was sitting right here."

"No, we didn't see an angel." Joanna looked at her strangely. "But we did see the soldiers running down the road as we were coming. One of them said something about going to make a report."

"To Pilate?"

"I don't think so. They said something about giving account to Caiaphas." Abigail answered.

"I think one of them was in Commander Flavius' regiment," Elsbeth offered. "I remembered seeing him before."

The older Mary looked at Salome. "The angel said we should tell the disciples the Master is alive, and will be waiting for us in Galilee."

Salome's face broke into a smile. "Are you sure?" she asked.

Mary glanced back toward the open door. "Pretty sure!" she answered.

The group of women left together, talking and sharing. It would be wonderful to share the news with John, and James, and Andrew…. They couldn't wait to see their faces.

But Mary Magdalene couldn't find the strength to leave the garden area. Old emotions began to surface.

If he wasn't here, where was he?

She looked back through the tomb door.

Yes, the two angels were still sitting there. She just wanted to be sure.

Her thoughts began to race. Her eyes filled with tears. The pent up fears of the past few days began to rise in a torrent of emotion.

She began to weep; the sense of abandonment overwhelming her once again. What would she do – *without Him?*

"Why are you weeping?" The angel at the head plate asked, his voice coming through the open doorway.

"Because they have taken my Master away; I don't know where he is," she answered. How would she learn to live her life, she wondered? Who would teach her the things she was still missing? Who could she ask?

Would anyone else understand her heart?

Journey

Perhaps she just needed to find a place to have a good cry, she thought. Looking down, she turned, and almost ran into someone.

Oh, she thought. *The gardeners are here to tend the grounds. I will have to go somewhere else to be alone.*

"Why are you weeping?" the gardener asked.

There it was; the same question. Magdalene decided to get some answers. There *had* to be an answer. She would find strength somewhere inside herself to handle this. She took a deep breath

"Sir," she said. "You are the gardener. If you have taken his body somewhere, please tell me where it is...." Her voice broke, and she began to weep harder. Sobs were beginning now. She had to get the words out. "I .... will...come and take... his... body... away."

There was a short stretch of silence. She didn't know what else to say.

Where could they have laid the body?

The Gardener spoke, gently; kindly, quietly.

"Mary!"

From the deep caverns of her soul, her being resonated with response. This was the Voice that shattered her chains in the storeroom. This was the Voice that called her brother back from beyond the grave. This was the Voice that had shaped her identity since the night of her deliverance.

This was the Voice of her God.

She fell to her knees, and took hold of his feet in worship, weeping. "Oh, Master!" she cried with relief. "Jesus!"

He knelt down and lifted her to her feet. "I haven't ascended to the Mercy Seat, Mary. Don't cling to me yet." He paused. "Go and tell my friends that I am ascending -- to my Father; and your Father -- to my God; and your God."

She stood up. Looking at him she realized he was shining. It was the same light she had seen surrounding the angels; but it was brighter, stronger, somehow. She took a deep breath, and smiled at him.

"I will, Master," she replied, her heart suddenly light. She turned to go, and then excitedly took a step to return to him. Thinking better of it, she turned again to go the other direction, returning to her task, remembering his words. For a moment, she looked back at him. He was watching her and chuckling. Yes, it was Jesus.

She ran from the tomb. Was this a song she was humming? She didn't know. She had never been so full of joy. He had kept his promise.

I will not leave you alone. I will come to you.

Perhaps she could still catch up with the others.

A few moments passed.

The older Mary, Salome, and the others, were still moving towards the city. In actuality, they were not too far ahead of her. Coming off the pathway which led to Joseph's family home, the group turned onto the main road. Suddenly, a man stood six feet in front of them.

"Good morning, friends!" he called in greeting.

Stunned, the women looked up. No one had seen him walking down the road.... Where had he come from?

"It – it's *Jesus!*"

The older Mary stood in shock for a moment. Then, all at once, she ran to him, and dropped to her knees, grasping his feet. Was he real? Was it really true?

The other women gathered around him as well; Salome and Joanna, Hadassah and Abigail. Elsbeth just stood weeping. Each one found themselves wanting to confirm what their eyes told them. They too, touched him, hugged him.

As the discovery of reality became clear, a sense of fear emerged. The desire to be separated from such power; somehow given a "safe distance," whispered to them.

"Don't be afraid!" Jesus looked clearly at Salome and those standing back, beginning to just observe.

"It's all right! Come closer!" he said. "Go and tell my friends I will meet them in Galilee."

The women had run elatedly to deliver the message.

At first, it had not been well received.

At first, the men had not believed them. "Silly women!" a few said. "Magdalene has always been too emotional!"

But then, Simon Peter and John decided to confirm the story. John had gone into the tomb first. He was convinced, and had told them all so.

Poor Simon, Mary considered. He had been sure it couldn't be true: even when his wife told him her experience!

Then, he had looked into the tomb's doorway and seen the wrappings neatly folded. The handkerchief Nicodemus had placed over Jesus' face that night was over to the side, as though he had wiped his face before getting up. In disbelief, Simon Peter had gathered the linen wrappings to his chest.

He had wept, full of remorse, for hours.

He *still* wept easily, and *often*.

No one knew when, or where, but the Master found Simon Peter at some point during that first day. She could only envision the conversation which had taken place between them.

Peter didn't talk much about what Jesus had said to him, but just the mention of it in conversation always brought him to tears.

The fisherman had been different since then too, she considered.

He was gentler, less impulsive; certainly less forceful in his opinions.

Elsbeth had confided that changes had taken place at home as well.

In Jerusalem, on the day of his Resurrection, others who had been buried in graves around the city were seen also alive again. Many of these people spoke to strangers on the street, telling them about Jesus, and explaining who He was.

After that, Jesus had appeared to so many.

Journey

His half-brother, James, had seen him that first day as well.

Then, the Master had suddenly appeared on the Emmaus Road. The two men traveling hadn't known who he was. He had explained everything; teaching them about the Law and the prophets. At the end of the day, they had invited him to stay with them, to share a meal and continue talking.

"It wasn't until we sat down to eat together, that we knew who he was," Cleophas told everyone. "No one breaks bread like Jesus." He paused "Then, he just disappeared."

One night, they were all gathered together for a meal. Several of the group had not yet seen him. Thomas refused to believe unless he could touch Jesus, like the women had done. Suddenly, the Master appeared in the room. "Here, Thomas," he said, "touch the wounds in my side, and in my hands."

Thomas didn't know what to say. His stubbornness and intellectual debating melted away in that moment. He began to really believe.

Justus and Julia Flavius were convinced by the account of the resurrection morning told to them by Titus, the foot-soldier from Capernaum. He had been part of the guard assignment at the tomb, knocked to the ground by the earthquake, blinded by the Light coming from the tomb; convinced when he had seen the angel.

Titus had confided in his Commander regarding a pay-off attempted by the high priest. "He handed us each a bag of money, and told us we were 'under orders from the prince' to keep what we had experienced a secret. He expected us to tell everyone that we had failed in our duties; that we had allowed someone to come and steal the body."

"I know you did your job, son," Justus had told him. "You are only expected to obey the orders of Rome."

Titus had sighed with relief. "Thank you, Commander."

The high priests did not know what to do; Caiaphas had no solution. Many of the priests turned to choose the Living God; and joined Judah and Nicodemus in prayer.

Then, one morning in Galilee, Jesus cooked breakfast, and ate with them.

The night before, Simon Peter had been experiencing his normal inability to sit still. He looked at the other six men who were with him at the time. "I'm going fishing tonight," he said. "I need to feed my family."

"We'll go with you," his friends told him.

And so they all piled into Simon's boat. They cast the nets all night long, without catching even one fish. At one point, Simon Peter was so frustrated; he told the men he had determined he was just not destined to catch fish. At daybreak, as they were coming in off the water, Thomas noticed a man standing on the shoreline.

"Did you catch anything?" he called across the water.

"Nothing." James responded.

"Put the net on the other side of the boat," the man called. "There are fish there."

Thomas and James chuckled. Why not?

Journey

So, they cast the nets one more time. Pulling them back in, James and Thomas began to call for help. The net was overflowing with fish!

John looked at Simon Peter. "That's got to be Jesus," he whispered to his friend.

On the shore, other friends and workers friends ran towards the boat, to help bring in the catch. James and John decided to just row for shore, dragging the net behind through the water behind them. No one wanted a sinking boat that morning.

Simon Peter jumped into the water and swam to shore. He didn't want to miss this opportunity, like he had others. He greeted the man, and moved to help pull in the nets.

Peter told them all later he was reminded of the first instance Jesus had told them where to fish. The second time it happened, he made a discovery.

This time, his net didn't break.

As soon as the catch of fish was on the shore, the man called to them, "Come and dine with me! Bring some of the fish you have caught."

Following him, to a place not far from shore, they encountered a fire of coals. It was here Jesus cooked their breakfast; roasted fish and fresh bread.

After the meal, Jesus invited Simon Peter to walk with him.

"Simon, son of Jonas, do you love me more than anything else?" he asked.

Simon was surprised by the question. "Yes, Master," he answered. "You know we're friends. Yes, I love you."

Jesus was silent for a moment. Then he said, "Feed and look after my little ones."

As they sat by the fire, Jesus repeated the question. "Simon, son of Jonas, do you love me more than anything else?"

Puzzled, Simon looked at Jesus. "Yes, Master," he answered again. "You know we're friends. You know I care about you, and think highly of you. I want your approval."

Jesus waited for a moment, and then said, "Cherish and nurture my older ones."

A little later, Simon Peter and John were walking along the shoreline with Jesus.

Jesus said, "Simon, son of Jonas, are we really friends? Do you really love me?"

Simon's eyes filled with tears. Why was his Friend asking the same question three times? Was it to remind him of his betrayal? Grief filled his heart for a moment.

He looked at Jesus. The Master was smiling at him, waiting for a response. Suddenly, he remembered the lesson of the nets. The first one had broken, the second one had not.

Don't be afraid, Simon! You will catch people!

As he considered, Simon Peter had later disclosed that each time the Master asked his question, it had dug deeper into his soul.

Through tears he had answered.

"Master, you know everything. You know everything about me. Please; please know that I love you."

Jesus responded a third time, "Feed and take care of my older ones."

He had paused, and looked Simon in the eye. "When you were younger, you could go where you wanted to… when you are old it will not be like that."

Simon Peter took stock in the words. Was Jesus warning him of something?

Journey

For forty days after his Resurrection, Jesus walked and talked with his followers in Galilee. He taught about the Kingdom, and prepared them for the days ahead.

Towards the end of the forty days, Jesus led them back to Jerusalem. One morning, he walked with them to a place just outside the village of Bethany.

There were a little over five hundred of them. They sat down on the grass, to listen to him teach.

It was like the days …. Before.

At the end of the teaching, Jesus gave them instructions. "I want you to go back to the city. I will be sending Abba's Promise to you. He will fill you with power to speak up for me; and to live the life I have called you to live.

"Wait for the Promise. He will come with power. You will receive this power. You will be able to express what has happened so that people will understand; first in Jerusalem, and Judea, and Samaria, and then the entire world."

They stood, watching, as Jesus rose up. He was still speaking to them, saying good-bye, as his figure began to rise off the ground. He disappeared into the clouds above them. For long moments, everyone stood, looking up, waiting for something else to happen.

"Why are you standing here looking up into the sky?"

The voice took them by surprise.

Two young men in brilliant, blazing white stood where Jesus had been standing. What had the one said?

He continued. "This same Jesus; the one you just saw being taken up into heaven, will come back; *in the very same way He left.*"

He had ascended; like he had said he would.

And He would come back again.

Eagerly, they all returned to Jerusalem. Some returned to the Temple, and some to the Essene Quarter. Jesus had asked them to wait.

Journey

Epilogue

Upper Room – Jerusalem
29 CE
Day Fifty

Today was a Feast Day.
It had been fifty days since Caiaphas had arrested the Master.
It had been forty seven days since Jesus had appeared to Magdalene.
It had been seven days since they had seen Him rise into the heavens.

~~~

So much had happened.
Today, they would celebrate the provision of the Law from Sinai. The entire nation would remember the day ElJireh brought water from the rock in the desert.
It was a day to connect with the Living God.
It was a day to remember Jesus.

~~~

John looked out the lattice window of the Great Room in the Essene Quarter. What was it Jesus had said about speaking with Moses?
"It was like a taste of Home for me," the Master had said.
John had been thinking about Jesus since the sunrise this morning.
What would Jesus' home taste like? What would the atmosphere be like, he wondered?
In remembering, he saw something he had not noticed before. The closer Jesus had come to his time of crucifixion, the more determined he had become in his behaviors. And yet, when he spoke to them during those days, His words were more and more focused on his anticipation of reunited with the Father.
"I am going away to prepare a place for you."
"I am the Father are one."
"I will send you another Comforter, and He will teach you all things."
"The Spirit of Truth."

~~~

Across the room, Judah and Hadassah were talking with Zebedee and Salome. Simon and Abigail, were spending time with Magdalene, and Justus and Julia. The Essene monks and their students were already deep in discussion with Nicodemus, Joseph and a few of the other priests from Jerusalem. Malchus was sitting with Philip and Nathaniel, asking questions.
That was a mark of a disciple, John observed: the willingness to ask questions.
Around the room, small clusters of Jesus' followers were sharing, talking. John smiled.

They had needed this time; these days of waiting.

It was the only way to mark an end of one season, and the beginning of another, he realized.

~~~

"I would like to call us all together, John. What do you think?" Simon Peter was standing behind him. "I think we should do something as a group to celebrate the Feast."

"I think it's a great idea," John answered, turning.

Simon Peter needed no further encouragement. He turned around from speaking to John and raised his voice.

"Friends," he waited for voices and room noise to settle. "Friends, today is a Feast Day. It is a day for celebrating our identity as people who believe in and serve the One Living God. It is a day for remembering God's provision and protection in giving us boundaries to define our lives."

He looked at Elsbeth. He smiled at his wife, and continued. "I'm not sure exactly how we should go about doing this, but I think it would be good to pray together, and share together about the goodness of God."

A murmur of agreement rose in the room.

~~~

Suddenly, the shutters of the Great Room blew open. A strong east wind began to blow into the windows. Accompanying the wind was a rushing sound. Was it wind, John wondered? Was it water? Thunder?

Looking around the room, he saw the clusters of people he had been observing. Within each circle, every person was praying, or speaking; some were singing. In some circles, eyes were closed. In some circles, eyes were open. Here and there, hands were raised, as people were giving praise and glory to God. Some groups were more expressive. Some groups were not.

The wind grew stronger. Over the heads of those in the room, Light began to glimmer. Tiny sparks of Light hung in middle space, growing and intensifying as the worship continued. Finally, over each person's head, a flickering, iridescent flame hovered just above each person's head.

Even the children were experiencing this amazing phenomenon.

~~~

John had been expressing his thoughts to God all morning. Now, he was experiencing a reciprocal communication. He was more aware, more open. With the wind had come a brand new sense of intimacy and relationship.

It was like Jesus was actually with him again. He could sense His Presence.

~~~

Nicodemus found himself remembering Jesus' words, and receiving unsullied understanding: "The Spirit of God is like the wind. You can see what He is doing, but you cannot contain Him, or see Him."

~~~

Journey

As the Wind penetrated their space, each person was breathing in; receiving fresh Life from the supernatural manifestation of their Master's pledge.

As each person breathed in of the Wind of the Spirit; their breathing out was filled with new language. Everyone was suddenly speaking a language they had not known before.

One by one, people stood, unexpectedly desiring to experience movement outside of the Great Room.

In the street outside, the wind had been localized to just the Essene Quarter.

People stopped to discover what was making the sound they were hearing. All through Jerusalem, dedicated believers in the Living God had gathered for the feast from every corner of the empire. Now each one was hearing the story of Jesus in their own language.

For a long time, those from the Great Upper Room moved about the city, continuing to speak in this new Expression of God's Grace.

"Aren't the people who are speaking to us, mostly from Galilee?" someone asked. "How did they learn my language?"

"How is this happening?" someone else questioned. "This man has never been to my country!"

Someone else said, "These people are just drunk on new wine!"

In the middle of the incident, Simon Peter stood up. He drew the rest of the twelve around him, and began to address the crowd.

"Brothers and sisters!" he shouted. "These people are not drunk! It's only six in the morning!! No one has been awake that long!"

The crowd laughed with him. He continued.

"This is the promise that was spoken by the prophet, Joel: 'I will pour out my Spirit on all flesh; and your sons and your daughters shall prophesy. Your young men will see visions; and your old me shall dream dreams. On my servants and my handmaidens, I will pour out My Spirit.'"

~~~~

As Simon Peter shared, anointed and filled with the Promised Comforter, the Holy Spirit, more than three thousand people decided to believe in Jesus, and who He said he was.

In one day!

~~~~

Looking back, John realized the Holy Spirit had been poured out like Living Water; to satisfy the hunger and thirst of everyone who would believe in Jesus.

It was a spiritual explanation of the picture of the Moses' miracle; just as water had come from the Rock when it was struck, so the Living Water had poured out from the Spiritual Rock, Jesus.

On the day when the Law had been given to seal the Old Covenant, Jesus had sent his Holy Spirit to seal the New Covenant.

~~~~

As those there that day began to grow in understanding, this new organism, this Body, discovered there is a Nature and Personality to the Person of the Holy Spirit.

Journey

As the days progressed, miracles took place at the hands of those who had walked with Jesus, and the Holy Spirit led believers learned to listen to His voice.

Relationship and Community were established for the people of God.

A fresh journey had begun.

~~~~

After his conversion some years later, the young Pharisee named Saul, turned Paul, would write:

"There is no disapproval or religious judgment to those who are in Christ Jesus; for those who walk after the Holy Spirit, and not after the flesh; for the Law of the Spirit of Life in Christ Jesus has set me free from the Law of sin and death. What the Law could not do for me, because it carried the weaknesses of the flesh, God did. He sent his own Son, who came in the form of a man. This man condemned sin that ruled in the flesh. He did this so that right standing with God could happen in each of us; who walk, not following the flesh, but following the Holy Spirit."

This was what Jesus promised to all of us; Empowerment; the Comforter...The Holy Spirit.

Jesus continues to change water into wine in people's life every day. He is still the Healer; still the Teacher; still the Deliverer, still the Miracle worker.

He invites you, dear reader to join Him. Where will your journey with Jesus take you?

A Note to the Reader

There is always a risk involved when an author tries to deal with Scriptural persons, or addresses theological approaches. In so doing, I have certainly taken a risk; a risk that I might offend someone, or create controversy.

This has not been my intention, or my purpose.

The historical information included in the book is as accurate as I was able to support, through close to five years of research on various topics.

For the first 1900 years of her existence, the church at-large accepted historical documents regarding Mary of Bethany and Mary Magdalene. Due to the apostle John's comment in chapter 12 of his account, it was commonly accepted the first anointing of Jesus by a woman who was a sinner, was descriptive of Mary's unique style of worship. In the last 100 years, some more skeptical scholars have questioned this, however. Personally, I believe she followed a journey similar to the one presented here.

The second journey described in the book, however, is open to conjecture. There are no documents or evidence to support Simon the Pharisee taking the journey described here. However, again, for my own life's journey, I would rather choose to find a way to bring to congruency those parts of Scripture commonly debated and picked apart by skeptics.

It is reasonable to believe that Jesus Christ came to touch a concentrated number of lives in a dynamic and irrefutable manner, affecting greater effect, and deeper change. So, for that reason, and for the purpose of presenting the relational theology presented here, Simon's journey has thus been offered.

In ancient times, citizens of Israel were known to name their children with names that echoed their personal relationships with their God. They were also fiercely opposed to using Gentile, or pagan names. For this reason, Miriam and Eleazar are the names I chose for the supporting characters. Also, since sons inherited and daughters did not, it was reasonable to believe the jar given to Mary was one of three, rather than one which stood alone.

I leave the conclusions as to actual facts regarding Simon's true identity up to you.

In ancient Israel, and in Israel today as well, those who are devoutly Jewish in their beliefs do not feel permitted to say the name of God. In the Christian Bible, we commonly refer to God as "Jehovah." In the Old Testament, God refers to himself by various names, such as the ones I have utilized in this manuscript. In order to provide authenticity to the Jewish culture of the people presented here, I changed the name "Jehovah-Jireh" to "ElJireh" – El meaning "God," Jireh meaning" provides." The persons living in that time in history certainly must have had a way to communicate regarding these descriptive names of God; this is my feeble attempt to provide a way for that to occur.

Journey

The image of Jesus on the wall in the dungeon cell of Caiaphas' palace does exist. I witnessed it with my own eyes on a trip to Israel not long ago.

The EnKarem winepresses do exist. They were discovered by archaeologists at Kibbutz Tzuba, a 15 minute drive from Jerusalem. The kibbutz is located close to the ancient village of Ein Karem; so you see why it has been named so.

Should you desire to do further study, I have included a partial bibliography of my research materials following this letter.

I thank you, dear reader, for taking time to read this book, and this letter. I hope both have blessed you, and opened a door for the Spirit of God to breathe fresh upon your relationship with Jesus.

I pray His richest blessings upon your life,

Debbye Graafsma
2009

Bibliography

1. **Furniture: a concise history** by E. Lucie-Smith, ©1979 New York: Oxford University Press.

2. **Gems in Israel**. Published by Yael (Zisling) Adar. Copyright © 1999-2002 Yael (Zisling) Adar

3. **World Encyclopedia of Archaeology: The World's Most Significant Sites and Cultural Treasures** by Dr. Aedeen Cremin **(Editor); © 2007 Firefly Books**

4. Books by Alfred Edersheim: **Sketches of Jewish Social Life, Life and Times of Jesus the Messiah, The Temple; Its Ministry and Its Services**; various copyright dates, Hendrickson Publishers.

5. **The Hayford Bible Handook**, Jack W. Hayford, editor, © 1999 Thomas Nelson Publishers.

6. *Who was Mary Magdalene?* by James Carroll, Smithsonian Magazine, June 2006

7. **The New Catholic Encyclopedia, 2nd Edition,** Catholic University of America © 2002

8. **The New Complete Works of Josephus** by Flavius Josephus, William Whiston, and Paul L. Maier ©1999 Kregel Publications, Grand Rapids, MI

9. **Best Exotic Baby Names: New, Historical, Ancient, Mystical** by Allison Jones and G. Kirscheimer, © (Paperback - Feb 14, 2008)

10. **The Reese Chronological Bible,** edited by Edward Reese (dating system by Frank R. Klassen), © 1980 Bethany House Publishers

11. **Greek Religion,** Walter Burkert. © 1985 Harvard University Press

12. **The Search for the Twelve Apostles,** by William Stuart McBirnie, © 2008 Tyndale House Publishers.

13. **The Chemical Muse: Drug Use and the Roots of Western Civilazation** by D.C.A. Hillman, PhD. © D. Hillman 2008, St. Martin's Press, New York.

14. **Twelve Ordinary Men,** by John MacArthur, © 2002 Thomas Nelson Publishers.

15. *Jerusalem's Essene Gateway* by Bargil Pixner, Biblical Archaeology Review, May/June 1997 issue. (article can be read online at www.centuryone.org)

16. *Online Resources* –
www.blueletterbible.com
www.biblehistory.com
www.gemsinisrael.com
www.wrongdiagnosis.com/leprosy
www.sciencedaily.com/releases/2008/01/080123114601.htm
www.wikipedia.com
www.greekmythology.com
www.religioustolerance.org
www.children-of-israel.org
www.chabad.org
www.maps.google.com
www.sciencecodex.com
www.keyway.ca (Church of God daily Bible study)
www.pansplace.com
www.wcg.org (Laws and Festivals, Agricultural practices)

Debbye Graafsma is available for speaking engagements and personal appearances. For more information contact:

Debbye Graafsma
C/O Advantage Books
PO Box 160847
Altamonte Springs, FL 32779

info@advbooks.com

To purchase additional copies of this book or other books published by Advantage Books call our toll free order number at:
1-888-383-3110 (Book Orders Only)

or visit our bookstore website at:
www.advbookstore.com

Longwood, Florida, USA
"we bring dreams to life"™
www.advbooks.com